The Shaken Realist

ESSAYS IN MODERN LITERATURE

FREDERICK J. HOFFMAN

The
Shaken Realist

ESSAYS IN MODERN LITERATURE
IN HONOR OF
FREDERICK J. HOFFMAN

EDITED BY
MELVIN J. FRIEDMAN
AND
JOHN B. VICKERY

LOUISIANA STATE UNIVERSITY PRESS
BATON ROUGE

Acknowledgments

Parts of Mr. Friedman's introduction appeared in earlier form in *The Massachusetts Review* and *Commonweal*. This material is being used here with the permission of the editors of these two periodicals. The relevant material is reprinted from *The Massachusetts Review,* © 1965, The Massachusetts Review, Inc., and from *Commonweal,* © 1967, Commonweal Publishing Company, Inc.

Library of Congress Catalog Number: 77–108199
SBN Number: 8071–0933–9
Manufactured in the United States of America by
Kingsport Press, Inc., Kingsport, Tennessee
Designed by Barney McKee

How cold the vacancy
When the phantoms are gone and the shaken realist
First sees reality. The mortal no
Has its emptiness and tragic expirations.
The tragedy, however, may have begun,
Again, in the imagination's new beginning,
In the yes of the realist spoken because he must
Say yes, spoken because under every no
Lay a passion for yes that had never been broken.

—WALLACE STEVENS
"Esthétique du Mal," Section 8

Preface

JOHN B. VICKERY

Originally this volume was planned not as a memorial but as a testimonial to the permanent place Frederick J. Hoffman holds in the growth and quality of modern literary studies in America. Then came the news of his death on Christmas Eve, 1967, and the carefully guarded surprise of a *festschrift* for his sixtieth birthday year was no longer realizable. Yet even during those days immediately following, when the numbness of shock and grief was all but total, there was never a moment's doubt but what the plans for this book should and would continue. In conversations, letters, and telephone calls, stunned friends—many of them not able to be contributors—urged the fulfillment of the initial plan and generously offered aid and counsel of varied kinds. To all of them we are deeply grateful.

A person who could inspire such a volume might be expected to have uncommon vigor, intellect, and commitment. Throughout his life Fred Hoffman had all of these. He was born in 1909 in the small Wisconsin town of Port Washington where together with his brothers and sisters he received his early education. At an age far earlier than most of us he was aware of the world in which he wished to live and of the need for independence in achieving it. Hence he set

vii

out on his own journey to Byzantium the first phase of which took him to Stanford and the subject to which he was to devote his life. Graduating from Stanford in 1934 after a brilliant undergraduate career, he went on to the University of Minnesota where he received an M.A. in Philosophy in 1936. In 1942, after graduate work at the University of Chicago where he also taught part-time, he received the Ph.D. in English from Ohio State University.

His teaching career began at Ohio State where he served as instructor and later assistant professor in the English department, service that was interrupted by his appointment as a Fellow of the Rockefeller Foundation in 1945. Though the years were difficult ones for higher education, his advancement was swift. After a brief stay at the University of Oklahoma, in 1948 he joined the faculty of the University of Wisconsin where he was to spend the next twelve years. In the course of this time, most of it spent as a full professor, he also served as a Fulbright lecturer at the Universities of Rennes and Grenoble and as a visiting professor at Harvard University, the University of Aix-en-Provence, the University of Washington, and Duke University. He was also in considerable demand to lecture on specific literary subjects, to participate in symposia and colloquia, and to deliver series of lectures both to undergraduate and graduate audiences. Schools honoring him and being honored in this fashion include the Sorbonne, Texas, Michigan, Minnesota, Duke, Ohio State, UCLA, and Notre Dame. The last named institution signally honored him by appointing him to deliver the first annual Ward-Phillips Lectures in English Language and Literature.

A prolific scholar and a painstaking teacher, Fred was also dedicated to strengthening and furthering the aims of his profession. To this end he eagerly and with a deep sense of obligation assumed the burdens of various professional activities. For a number of years preceding his death he was a consultant editor and a member of the editorial board of *Publications of the Modern Language Association.* He also served as a consultant and editorial advisor to *American Literature* and *College English* as well as faculty advisor to

Wisconsin Studies in Contemporary Literature, a journal which he was largely instrumental in inaugurating. For most of his scholarly career Fred Hoffman served diligently and wisely as a manuscript advisor to a number of university presses including those of the University of Wisconsin and Princeton University.

Substantial though his contributions were in professional activities, it was in his own writing that Fred wrought his greatest shaping influence on his profession. Articulating knowledge and sharing discoveries were for him the supreme acts of scholarly responsibility. He assumed this responsibility at the very outset of his career when his doctoral dissertation was published as *Freudianism and the Literary Mind,* and he continued it until his death. In the course of twenty-odd years he wrote or edited some twenty books while also contributing several hundred articles and reviews to professional journals. Of many of these Professor Friedman speaks clearly and with illumination in his Introduction. Suffice it to say here, that despite problems in later years so agonizing and diverse as to overwhelm a lesser human being, Fred Hoffman never once flagged in his devotion to and regard for his profession and the humanities generally. Such a record testifies to his energy, discipline, and commitment. But nowhere is the depth of his love of books, the life of the mind, and the pleasures of the imagination better conveyed than through his personal library. From his earliest student days he bought books joyously and enthusiastically. He was fond of observing that there was no town in the United States in which he had stayed overnight that he had not bought at least one book. The result was that he amassed what in all likelihood is the most distinguished and complete working library for scholars in modern literature in America. Fortunately the collection will not suffer the dismemberment which is often the fate of scholars' libraries, for it has been purchased in its entirety by Rice University.

The recital of work accomplished and books purchased does not, however, begin to capture the full picture of Fred Hoffman's nature and being. Commitment to literature and the values of scholarship he had in absolutely uncompromising measure. But he was never one to admit that disjunction between research and teaching which the facile and the lazy erect year after year. Teaching based upon meticulous preparation was a given for Fred, a condition to be met without equivocation or evasion. At the University of Wisconsin he invariably rose at 5 A.M.—during the terms he taught it—to review his 8 o'clock sophomore literature survey lectures. And later in California all his colleagues and friends knew that the day of his graduate seminar was a time of deep seclusion for him. On this one day they had to grapple with their problems alone without calling on him for his usual generous advice and sympathy. Yet they knew without question, too, that his dedication to them was fully as great as to his teaching and writing. Reading their manuscripts, counseling them in times of personal and professional crisis, defending them from unwarranted charges and pressures in the University community were only a few of the things Fred's friendship meant. It also meant after class coffee, Saturday excursions to bookstores (preferably in some other town), baseball games, long and exuberant lunches, and regular late afternoon gatherings for drinks, news, jokes, and speculations about the passing scene including quizzical compassion for those who admitted to being White Sox or Bills fans. But personal memories are best kept as such, and each of us has his own special ones where Fred is concerned.

Doubtless all who knew him can agree on his absolute integrity and his complete willingness to pay whatever price it exacted of him. Perhaps some sense of this is best conveyed by the words of one whose position during critical days gave him both familiarity and objectivity. Shortly after Fred's death, he remarked:

> To me his most distinctive characteristic, and the one I most admired, respected and remembered him for, was his courage—his moral courage as a scholar and his physical courage as a man. He had standards and he was willing to state them. He had the courage to say this work of scholarship is excellent and that is trash, this is wrong, or vulgar, or fraudulent, or just mediocre. And he had the courage to resume a full,

active career as a scholar and teacher following a heart attack that would have forced less courageous men into retirement.

It is this quality of courage, perhaps, that this collection seeks to honor above all. The courage to assert the importance of scholarly study of modern literature, the courage to insist on standards of professional excellence, the courage to continue breaking new intellectual ground and extending imaginative frontiers, the courage to attend to these even in the face of grave physical illness and appalling emotional desolation, these are the legacy to which both his life and his works testify.

The plan for this volume was to bring together a number of essays on modern literature by former students of Fred's and by his peers in the study of modern literature. No particular effort was made to restrict the contributor in his choice of subject on the grounds that this would most accurately reflect Fred's own wide-ranging interests and diversity of critical strategies. Nevertheless, an illuminating spectrum has emerged, which catches many of Fred's own concerns. Just as he himself felt a prime obligation to major figures and texts so, for instance, Professors Hassan, Krieger, and Miller in their essays on Hemingway, *Murder in the Cathedral,* and *Mrs. Dalloway* probe some modern classics. Similarly, what Fred essayed in *The Twenties* and *The Mortal No,* Haskell Block and Nathan Scott mirror in their essays—the large-scale generalization delineating a historical and thematic facet of twentieth-century literature. And finally, there are essays like those by Professors Casper and Hoffmann that admirably catch Fred's own restless curiosity about the contemporary writer and his achievement. As a coda of particular appropriateness in a volume honoring Fred Hoffman, there is Mr. Yannella's detailed bibliography of Fred's own work. To a scholar such as Fred the starting point was always the determination of what had been said on the subject by others. And there can be no better way of honoring him and learning from him than to know where he said what on which subject.

When this volume was first projected, it seemed both appropriate and inevitable that it should be discussed with Mr. Richard L. Wentworth, the Director of Louisiana State University Press. Nearly twenty-five years ago the Press published *Freudianism and the Literary Mind,* the first of Fred's many books. So there was a special sense in which it would share in honoring Fred's career and now his memory. In addition, the Press has also had close and pleasant relations with a number of Fred's students who have contributed significantly to its publishing achievements. Happily Mr. Wentworth and the Press were in complete accord with the proposals of myself and Mr. Friedman; throughout they have been helpful, cooperative and highly knowledgeable in making the plan a reality.

And speaking of reality, a word is in order, perhaps, concerning the title of the collection. The phrase "the shaken realist" comes, as the epigraph indicates, from the eighth section of Wallace Stevens' "Esthétique du Mal," a work for which Fred had an especial regard. He went to it for the title of his major study of death and the modern imagination, *The Mortal No.* Three years later he returned to the same work and passage to title his next book *The Imagination's New Beginning.* The continuity of theme and concern in the two books was underscored by their titles. No more fitting title could be found for a collection honoring the man and his work than one from this poem by Stevens. Like the poet's realist, Fred had been shaken by the reality he saw even as he had felt the coldness of "the vacancy/ When the phantoms are gone." Yet for him too, "under every no," under every violation and betrayal (even the posthumous ones), there still "lay a passion for yes that had never been broken." And to grapple with the mortal no with the aid of a passion for yes is what, in their individual ways, the essayists here have done. In doing so, they have honored Fred Hoffman implicitly as well as explicitly. To them, Mr. Friedman and I are deeply indebted. Those who, for one reason or another, were unable to contribute, we know will join in treasuring the memories of a rare friend and a surpassing professional example.

Introduction
The Achievement of Frederick Hoffman

MELVIN J. FRIEDMAN

Frederick Hoffman revealingly began one of his early essays: "This is an age of criticism and research." His own career profited immensely from this fact. For him literary criticism was the most serious of obligations and the surest way of communicating with one's peers. It carried with it, as he suggested on several occasions, both responsibilities and privileges. Hoffman understood the perils of impressionistic criticism and avoided its easy formulas by basing his discoveries about the literary text on solid and respectable grounds; he was among the first to insist on the interpenetration of criticism and research.

He was also among the first to assert the respectability of modern (and even contemporary) literature as a scholarly discipline and as a legitimate subject for serious discussion in the classroom. Courses in the literature curriculum which are prefixed with the words "modern" and "contemporary" are now commonplace in every university catalogue, but they were not when Frederick Hoffman started his career, fresh from his Ph.D. at Ohio State, during the 1940's, or even when he left Wisconsin for Riverside in 1960—just after starting a new journal, *Wisconsin Studies in Contemporary Literature.* As late as November, 1965, writing in *The Nation,* Hoffman was still eloquently asserting the position he held from his earliest years: "I am, of course, also a teacher of modern literature, and I happen to believe that it can and should be taught. . . . It is quite possible to teach *Naked Lunch* and *Corydon* and *Death in Venice*—that is, to communicate with students with respect to them, beyond the merely 'new critical' technicalities, without being 'tainted' by whatever infections they may contain." In 1965 Hoffman's was no longer the lonely voice it had been, say, in 1945, when he published his first major work, *Freudianism and the Literary Mind*. A new breed of professor-critic was beginning to applaud such ways of reading modern literature as Hoffman demonstrated in his books and articles, and such ways of teaching it as he demonstrated in his research-oriented seminars and in his large lecture classes.

There is more to be said about the debt all teachers of modern literature owe Frederick Hoffman for his inspiration and for his long-time courageous stand. But it seems more important at the moment to evaluate in some detail his critical performance. His approach does not noticeably resemble that of the Kenyon Critics, the Chicago Aristotelians, the archetypal or myth critics; neither does it retreat into the safety of literary history nurtured on a decorum bred by the New Humanism. Hoffman has the unusual and delightful habit of changing method to suit his literary needs. This flexibility, together with a fondness for literature and the accompanying urgency about elucidating it, characterizes his many books from *Freudianism and the Literary Mind* through *The Imagination's New Beginning* and *The Art of Southern Fiction* (both published only a few months before his death on Christmas Eve, 1967).

Walter Sutton's *Modern American Criticism* (1963) devoted several astute and sympathetic pages to *Freudianism and the Literary Mind*—which now in its second edition and its second paperbacking is universally regarded as a classic of its kind, as it skillfully negotiates the uncertain tightrope stretched between literature and psychology. Sutton's book, however, fails to mention Hoffman's second pioneering study, *The Twenties* (1955). We should say something about it here because what he calls (in the preface to the second edition) his "strategy of presentation" has considerable bearing on all of his work. In *The Twenties* Hoffman moves from the "raw material" of the historical or social document, with at most a journalistic value, to the end-product, the literary "text." The method seems to depend on the intelligent union of the German notion of *Geistesgeschichte* with the French notion of *explication de texte*. We might compare its "movement" to another work of complex critical design, Erich Auerbach's *Mimesis*. The difference is that Auerbach starts with the text and derives the literary period from certain stylistic and historical attitudes expressed in it. Hoffman ends with the text because he feels that it is the age which should illuminate the text for the broadest kind of literary experience. Thus we read with much the same enthusiasm as we follow Hoffman through the "temper of the 1920's" on the way to a close study of *Hugh Selwyn Mauberley* as we do when Erich Auerbach reverses the process and leads us gradually towards the difference between the Old Testament and the Homeric styles by starting out with a microscopic examination of a passage from the nineteenth book of *The Odyssey*.

Hoffman makes a statement in his preface to the first edition of *The Twenties* which makes clear his view of literature: "Literature is not valuable simply because it 'uses' the matter of the time, nor merely because it has degrees of formal excellence, but because it helps us to see the reality of any idea in a full, clear, and meaningful form; the form *is* the matter, the matter is *in* the form, and the reality which is thus formally given is a moral and aesthetic anecdote of one or another aspect of the time." This credo is comprehensive enough to allow for Hoffman's various critical stances and for his immense flexibility as a critic. Hoffman has been assuring us all along that literature offers the best response to a culture that we have; he has made this point more consistently and tellingly than any critic I know of.

With the publication of *The Mortal No* in 1964 we discover an interesting pattern in Frederick Hoffman's work. At ten-year intervals he gave us three major critical books, each of which has supplied us with a separate set of literary metaphors. In between he gave us a series of shorter studies, usually of individual writers, which offer applications of the procedures devised in *Freudianism and the Literary Mind*, *The Twenties*, and *The Mortal No*. He somewhat reversed the order of things with his *Samuel Beckett: The Language of Self* (1962) which anticipated the longer and more ambitious *The Mortal No* and announced its arrival: "The idea of this book grew out of an extended study . . . of the variants of death imagery and symbolism in modern literature." With the publication of *The Imagination's New Beginning* in 1967, however, it became clear that Hoffman was sufficiently preoccupied with his latest "strategy of presentation" that he would allow it to linger on into the third decade of his life as a critic. Hoffman doubtless intended this short book, with its origins as the Ward-Phillips Lectures at Notre Dame, as a lengthy appendix to *The Mortal No*.

This very serious career as a critic reaches a kind of apogee, I think, with *The Mortal No*. It is probably the most original literary study—in design, approach, and content—we have had since *The Anatomy of Criticism*. The frequent references made to *The Mortal No* by the critics who have contributed to this *festschrift* offer agreeable witness to its suggestiveness and to its intriguing variousness.

The Mortal No has a worthy and admirable purpose: it attempts a redefinition of modern literature in terms of a new set of metaphors, concerned with the intruding presence of the secular in the midst of the religious, of the spatial in the midst of the temporal, of the decorous in the midst of the violent. Such paradoxes are set up as "secular grace," the spatialization of time, the merging of the "assailant" and "victim." Literature since *The Red and the Black* (1831), Hoffman tells us, shows a gradual breaking down of boundaries and distinctions, a gradual closing in for the hero. (Hoffman would agree with Sean O'Faolain in *The Vanishing Hero* who also dates "modern" literature from *The Red and the Black* with its "disintegration of the social Hero.") Martyrs are possible outside of the church as in Malraux and Silone; a sense of time is obscured by the presence of distracting objects as in Beckett; the victim wills his own assailant and seems to conspire with him as in Kafka. Everything in modern literature seems to prepare for violence. Hoffman says this better than I can: "In fact, the major theme of this book may be described as the history of man's attempts to account for violence, to anticipate it, and to adjust to its dislocations."

The literary historian is always active: Hoffman begins the first section, which he calls "Grace," with a discussion of the nineteenth and early twentieth-century backgrounds of his subject. He offers full-scale and fresh analyses of *The Red and the Black, The Princess Casamassima, The Secret Agent, Nostromo,* and *Howards End.* In each case he finds a mannered, decorous society falling apart and forcing violence on a "hero *manqué.*"

Under the intriguing category of "secular grace" Hoffman turns to a twentieth-century version of the ideological novel which is clearly removed from the nineteenth-century social amenities. Violence is now linked with martyrdom, and "heroes" like Ch'en (*Man's Fate*), Pietro Spina (*Bread and Wine*), and Rubashov (*Darkness at Noon*) emerge in an "atmosphere suffused with a secular haze." (In an influential study published in 1958 R. W. B. Lewis had already christened this literary species "picaresque saint.")

Part Two of *The Mortal No,* which is called "Violence," traces the relationship between assailant and victim. Hoffman demonstrates the gradual depersonalization of the assailant from person, to ideological instrument, to mob, to machine, to landscape. The last is the most devastating because of its complete dehumanization. The "assailant as landscape" assumes its most characteristic form in the literature concerned with concentration camps and army prisons; it "suggests either a narrow constriction of space or an immense expansion of waste." Sartre's *No Exit* and Eliot's *The Waste Land* are both relevant and would supply the metaphors for the extremes of constriction and unlimited space. In another category are the numerous war novels and discussions of concentration camps which Hoffman catalogues in appropriate groups.

In the chapters on war literature Hoffman returns to a method which he used with such success in *The Twenties*. He brings together documentary material with works of considerable literary importance. His perceptive analysis of Hemingway's war stories and novels offers a fond reminder of the pages on *The Sun Also Rises* in the second part of *The Twenties*.

The most completely realized of the chapters in this second part of *The Mortal No* are probably the two in which he concentrates on selected works of genuine interest to readers of the modern novel: one offers a brilliant parallel study of *Crime and Punishment* and *An American Tragedy;* the other illuminates *The Trial* as the final stage of "assailant as landscape." Frederick Hoffman begins in the first of the two chapters by distinguishing between the types of authorial omniscience expressed by Dostoevsky and Dreiser; he finds them to be at opposite poles. Then he proceeds to locate the "landscapes of violence" in the two novels which he plans to study. If the victimization of Clyde Griffiths is more complete than Raskolnikov's it is because Dostoevsky's character "participates actively in both crime and punishment," thus reducing the distance between assailant and victim. The implication is clear that Raskolnikov is well on the way to Kafka's view in *The Trial* of "the victim conniving with the assailant in his own destruction." Kafka marks for Hoffman an extreme case of the fading out of a human, personalized assailant in favor of an ambiguously realized landscape which can cause "serious dislocations in the moral balance."

The third part of *The Mortal No* completes the triadic metaphor of grace, violence, and self. Hoffman begins with the notion, which he already expressed in his Beckett study, that modern literature moves from metaphysics to epistemology; it is clear that he is trying to do something in this third part which he promised in the earlier book—to write "the history of the self in modern literature." He comes remarkably close to realizing what seems to be an impossibly ambitious undertaking. First he sets his limits: "The principal literary concerns of our century have been the definition of an isolated self, its precise location in both space and time, its relationship to objects and to process." Hoffman moves with systematic caution through the nineteenth-century New England background, exploring Emerson, Thoreau, and Emily Dickinson on his way to Henry and William James. He lingers for some time over William James's notion of self, expressed in his famous metaphor, "stream of consciousness." Almost all of this first chapter of the third part is concerned with American literature: this is one of the rare occasions in *The Mortal No* when Hoffman restricts his commentary to a single literature; his habit is to range widely across various western traditions in the most accomplished "comparatist" manner.

His next category is "the self in time." Hoffman considers the changes in the notion of time as the mechanical gives way to the Bergsonian *durée*. By quoting Rimbaud's "Car Je est un autre" and linking Emerson's view of self to the notion expressed in Rimbaud's *lettre du voyant*, Hoffman builds up a nineteenth-century version of the "isolated self" which prepares for the psychological imbalances of the twentieth century. Hoffman traces the uneasy relationship between time and space—which will eventually lead to a spatialization of time in Alain Robbe-Grillet and his French contemporaries. There are already signposts along the way as in Gertrude Stein (earlier the subject of a Hoffman pamphlet in the Minnesota series) and Virginia Woolf, where objects are arranged artistically in space, often with a superposed "vision," notoriously in *To the Lighthouse*. Hoffman offers one of his characteristically fine *rapprochements* at this point which I can't resist quoting: "Miss Briscoe's painting is to Mrs. Ramsay's scene what *A la Recherche* is to Marcel's illumination: the form to give the seal of permanence to an experience that is vivid and profound, but still exists in time and is subject to death."

Next is a chapter on Joyce and Lawrence (two novelists Hoffman has concentrated on since the days of *Freudianism and the Literary Mind*) which critically parallels the earlier chapter on Dreiser and Dostoevsky. We have here another splendid example of literary confrontation. Hoffman identifies Joyce with Lawrence by suggesting a common revolt against the "Christian myth," which ends up in "metaphoric substitution and revision." Hoffman cleverly calls this chapter "The Book of Himself," thus forcing the autobiographical notion but also sustaining the importance of the French Symbolist reference for modern literature: Hoffman's chapter title is a revision of part of Mallarmé's "il se promène, lisant au livre de lui-même" (which Joyce, incidentally, quoted in the library section of *Ulysses*). Hoffman finds abundant examples of secular grace in Joyce and Lawrence; he is especially successful with Leopold Bloom who "represents the extreme of its tendency to detach Christ's humanity from the context of his divinity."

The Mortal No ends with a discussion of existentialism and its various forms; Sartre and Camus, as might have been expected, are the pivotal figures. Hoffman discovers in existentialist literature the crucial relationship between the self and objects in space (or "otherness" as Sartre has expressed it). Sartre represents for Hoffman an extreme example of the spatialization of time: "Sartre, for whom time is largely a manipulation or a projection into 'moments of consecutive space.'"

Hoffman briefly treats the *nouveau roman* in his conclusion. Almost all of the metaphors which Hoffman has so convincingly and elaborately set up apply, it seems to me, to novelists like Robbe-Grillet, Michel Butor, Nathalie Sarraute, and Samuel Beckett. (He already applied certain of these to Beckett in his *Samuel Beckett: The Language of Self*.) When Hoffman says, "Modern literature is much concerned with the economy of violence and with the spatial figurations it causes," or, "The most effectively shocking of modern scenes is that in which the disorder of the soul is imaged in a disarray of objects scattered in space," or, "The primary emphasis in the literature of a secular world is spatial," I keep wishing that he would relate these remarks to the *nouveau roman;* they apply so well. They cut quite as deeply into the new literary ambience as the manifestoes of Robbe-Grillet, the collections of essays of Nathalie Sarraute, Michel Butor, and Claude Mauriac, the book-length metaphysical probings of Roland Barthes and Maurice Blanchot.

The Mortal No, it is not too early to say, has helped refashion our critical apparatus; it has given us subtle new optics for viewing modern literature. It is an interdisciplinary study which demands not only a knowledge of western literature since 1830 but also more than a passing acquaintance with psychology (of both the Freudian and Jungian persuasion), anthropology, theology, and painting (Hoffman is fond of introducing the *Guernica* to explain a literary mood). If one requires more background, Hoffman's amazingly detailed footnotes will offer comfort; the longer footnotes are reference libraries in miniature, thoroughly and intelligently combed. Hoffman's kind of criticism makes large demands on the reader but he offers all the bibliographical and critical tools to make the experience profitable. Careful attention to *The Mortal No* yields more handsome returns than one is likely to get elsewhere. It is a study which, like the best modern poetry, should not only be read but re-read. The pejorative "secondary source" has been attached to criticism for so long that it is hard for us to appreciate in what way a book like *The Mortal No* is an art form in its own right.

The Imagination's New Beginning is a more hopeful title than *The Mortal No.* Both titles are taken from the eighth part of Wallace Stevens' *Esthétique du Mal*—which in turn is probably a composite of two Baudelaire titles, *Curiosités esthétiques* and *Les Fleurs du Mal.* Hoffman has been preoccupied for some time with the uses of the Symbolist aesthetic from Baudelaire through Wallace Stevens, and it has offered him, in *The Imagination's New Beginning,* a series of striking metaphors, such as Baudelaire's image of the abyss and Yeats's and Eliot's views of the Incarnation, which have helped him explain the theological tensions and disproportions of modern literature.

Hoffman tells us in his preface to this 1967 book that it is intended to follow his *Samuel Beckett: The Language of Self* and *The Mortal No*. And indeed they seem almost composed to resemble a triptych, with the slender side panels (*Samuel Beckett* and *The Imagination's New Beginning*) flanking the imposing center panel (*The Mortal No*). The subject matter also goes well with our notion of a triptych—traditionally used as an altarpiece in a church. For Frederick Hoffman's work of the last five years of his life was connected with the literary side of the new ambience discussed in such works as Ved Mehta's *The New Theologian;* he joined Nathan Scott, Hillis Miller, Maurice Friedman, Gabriel Vahanian, and others in suggesting a new kind of secularization of the religious experience in literature.

In *The Mortal No* Hoffman chronicled a literary "inferno" of vast proportions. In *The Imagination's New Beginning,* with its more optimistic title, the concern is with a more "purgatorial" literary condition. Hoffman quotes to great advantage Beckett's view of Joyce's world as being purgatorial, with its "absolute absence of the Absolute." This expression has come back to haunt a decisive segment of modern literature. Many of the writers faced with this dilemma have tried to find a rhetoric suited to their literary needs, one, according to Hoffman, "that will stand satisfactorily in the place of reality."

The four sections which compose *The Imagination's New Beginning* look at different responses to the purgatorial. The first offers a series of definitions, and glances briefly at images of the Incarnation in modern poetry from Baudelaire through Stevens, passing by Eliot and Yeats. The second concentrates on Joyce's Stephen Dedalus and his search for a rhetoric. We are told, for example, that "the principal importance of Joyce's artist as a young man is stylistic." The third chapter is mainly concerned with two "friends of God,"

Dostoevsky and Kazantzakis, and their wrestling with the Christian myth. *The Idiot* and *The Last Temptation of Christ* are the touchstones used to illustrate the types of Christ figures in modern literature. The fourth section makes certain judgments about the American scene and examines two rather unlikely bedfellows, Henry Adams' *Mont-Saint-Michel and Chartres* and Faulkner's *A Fable*—which belong together in the way that they offer "a nostalgic view of a religious past."

The "texts" Hoffman chooses to illustrate the types of religious imbalance are remarkably varied. He dwells on Holbein's painting of Christ in the tomb when discussing *The Idiot:* "Ultimately the meaning of *The Idiot* comes down to the Holbein painting." He brings together Henry Adams' nostalgic itineraries into the twelfth and thirteenth centuries with a Faulkner novel set during the First World War. Just as Hoffman uses Picasso's *Guernica* to explain certain literary moods in *The Mortal No,* so he turns in *The Imagination's New Beginning* to works of painting and architecture to illumine novels of the nineteenth and twentieth centuries.

Hoffman's criticism is a splendid working out of an aspect of Malraux's famous theory of the museum without walls. By bringing together works of disparate origins and styles, new truths about the artistic and cultural process are uncovered. But the juxtaposition is never determined by chronology or genre; it is a matter of sensibility and taste.

The Imagination's New Beginning abounds in sober judgments and tasteful responses to the artistic experience. Hoffman has a talent for defining the special quality of a work: *"The Idiot* is one of the great works in the modern history of religious doubt." "The *Portrait* is the record of a succession of experiences and the search for appropriate rhetorics." And so on.

We can borrow a phrase from this last critical statement and apply it to Frederick Hoffman's career: his was always a "search for appropriate rhetorics." This was why he was unable to fall back on easy formulas and why he refused to settle for a single approach. As

Hoffman said of Stephen Dedalus so we can say of Hoffman, "He desperately needs *a* rhetoric at each stage of his growth." This would explain also the restless quality he had of returning to earlier, "unfinished" phases of his *oeuvre,* rethinking, rewriting, and even starting over again. The Twayne book on William Faulkner (now in a revised second edition) took only a summer to write, but the "felt life" in it is a matter of twenty years of reading, notetaking, teaching, and editing two volumes of Faulkner criticism (with Olga Vickery). Although he insists in his introduction to *The Art of Southern Fiction* that "the main purpose of this book is to put William Faulkner aside for a while and to give readers a chance to look at a few of his distinguished contemporaries or near-contemporaries," the ambience is still in certain ways Faulknerian.

Hoffman's next major project was to be the updating of *The Little Magazine: A History and a Bibliography* originally published in 1946. He was anxious, in his usual restless way, to rethink and revaluate a subject which preoccupied him in the middle 1940's. In fact, his first published essay was "The Little Magazines: Portrait of an Age," which appeared in the December 25, 1943, issue of the *Saturday Review of Literature.* The final sentence of this article contains a statement which Frederick Hoffman was to make again and again in different contexts: "We will no doubt notice that the scholars of the forties will find themselves more and more interested in their own century as a fascinating and complex period and will turn frequently to the little magazine for information." As a "scholar of the sixties" Hoffman had rediscovered this urgency about the little magazine—only to leave this final project unfinished.

Contents

XXV

The Shaken Realist

ESSAYS IN MODERN LITERATURE

Part I

THE MODERN TRADITION:
FIGURES AND TEXTS

The Silence of Ernest Hemingway

IHAB HASSAN

Hail nothing full of nothing, nothing is with thee.
—Hemingway, "A Clean, Well-Lighted Place"

I

Hemingway is dead. His work now begins the perverse journey in literary history that the work of great authors undertakes. His work may prove, above Faulkner's, Eliot's, or O'Neill's, above the work of any other American writer of our century, closest to our insanity and hope. Generations come and go, each carrying the banner of a shabby or brilliant despair. Hemingway understood the constancy of death better. With the phrase of Gertrude Stein humming in his youthful ears, and the statue of Marshal Ney rising against the Paris sky, he realized "that all generations were lost by something and always had been and always would be."[1]

Classic as it may now seem, the work of Hemingway engages the forms of modernism on the deepest level; its experience remains central to the time and space we inhabit. The work also reveals its affinities with a tradition that extends from Sade, through Kafka and Beckett, to the inverted literary consciousness of our own day. Hemingway's work shares the silence of anti-literature; his style,

[1] Hemingway, *A Moveable Feast* (New York, 1964), 30.

5

morality, and vision, derive from silence and enlarge its definition.

Like the Symbolist poets, Hemingway wants to purify the language of the tribe; like the Surrealists, he disdains "literature." He values the rigor of art; his contempt is for untruth. Hemingway suspects the power of literature to falsify experience, its readiness to mediate vitality and concreteness. "I used to wish . . . ," he writes, "that I lived in the old days before all the books had been written and all the stories told for the first time. In those days it was no disgrace to drink and fight and be a writer too."[2] Superficially, Hemingway objects to gentility. On another level, he distrusts the accretions of language.

Hemingway's distrust of language has many guises. His vocabulary is perhaps the smallest of any major novelist. To speak is to lie, Burroughs avers. This is fanatic. Hemingway is merely taciturn; he advises curtness in feeling, in action. The few words he imports from foreign languages tend to be simple, even obscene; the essential task is to confront *nada* with *cojones*. For Hemingway, true obscenity is something else; it can be described as "unsoundness in abstract conversation or, indeed, any other metaphysical tendency in speech."[3] Knowing that the currency of words has been inflated by fustian or mendacity, that the connotations of words have been counterfeited, he seeks new values for language in slang, in fact, in understatement.

Slang is a colorful form of reticence. It is metaphor in the process of becoming cliché. Alive, it refers to concrete situations; dead, it serves as impersonal response. Moreover, slang shuns sophistication as it shuns loquacity. It is not only metaphor or cliché but also protest. It issues from the underground of culture. Fact, on the other hand, speaks on behalf of reality, and challenges the imagination to a keener effort. In his interview with George Plimpton, Heming-

---

[2] Quoted by Carlos Baker, "Introduction," *Hemingway and His Critics,* ed. Carlos Baker (New York, 1961), 7.

[3] Hemingway, *Death in the Afternoon* (New York, 1960), 95.

way states that the *Racing Form* represents "the true Art of Fiction."[4] This statement, which may suggest the current technique of the "non-fiction" novel, actually pleads for constructionism. Hemingway makes his point clear: "From things that have happened and from things as they exist and from all things that you know and those you cannot know, you make something through your invention that is not a representation but a whole new thing truer than anything true and alive, and you make it alive, and if you make it well enough, you give it immortality."[5] On fact, the house of fiction stands; without it, the house collapses in a rubble of sentiment. Understatement, by refusing to exceed the authority of language to interpret fact, helps to keep the edifice spare. Hemingway's understatement stems from a private conviction that good things deserve to remain unexpressed; it ends by serving an artistic purpose. Understatement requires omission, and the art of omission is one that he may have learned from the great Impressionist painters, Cézanne particularly. Referring to his early years in Paris, Hemingway speaks of his "new theory that you could omit anything if you knew that you omitted and the omitted part would strengthen the story and make people feel something more than they understood."[6] Omission compels participation. The house of fiction, with its empty spaces, is finally inhabited.

Slang, fact, and understatement, as verbal modes, are equivocal. They appear to harden the surface of language; at first, they seem techniques of semantic restraint or even absence. They produce a stillness. Yet their end is to create meaning; they finally function as techniques of semantic presence. The stillness is haunted by many voices. Such is the duplicity of silence in Hemingway's fiction. Literature creates itself in self-opposition, and style evolves into a pure anti-style.

The mannerisms of Hemingway's anti-style are only too memorable. Repetitions of word and phrase, suggested by the rhythmic

[4] "An Interview With Ernest Hemingway," *Hemingway and His Critics*, 19.
[5] *Ibid.*, 37. [6] *A Moveable Feast*, 75.

experiments of Gertrude Stein, insinuate their significance precisely because they avoid expansion and customary elaboration. Substantives carry the burden of his statements, and make all analysis superfluous. The conjunctive "and," strung on end, gives equal weight to different parts of a period that moves without syntactic modulation. The little that stands before us stands sharply, brilliantly present; the rest is ruthlessly banished. Often, action replaces speech; thought and feeling remain implicit. As Harry Levin put it, "The act, no sooner done than said, becomes simultaneous with the word, no sooner said than felt."[7] We are in the huge and abrupt present, given to us without connectives or transitions. If judgments must be made, they can be made ironically, and Hemingway's irony can be cruel and bitter.

These celebrated traits are seldom viewed in the perspective of anti-literature. The clue comes from Sartre who saw in the chopped-up discontinuous style of Camus' *The Stranger* the form of an absurd vision. The same may be said of Sartre's own *Nausea* as of Hemingway's *In Our Time*. The simple accretion of invariable units, the succession of discrete events, defy synthesis. We are indeed close, as Roger Shattuck discerns in his study of the French avant-garde, to the assumptions of nonsense.[8] For nonsense depends on verbal distinctness and precision. As a mental game, it stands at the other end from disorder or nightmare, Elizabeth Sewell argues in *The Field of Nonsense*. "Nonsense . . . ," she says, "will have to concentrate on the divisibility of its material into ones, units from which a universe can be built. This universe, however, must never be more than the sum of its parts, and must never fuse into some all-embracing whole which cannot be broken down again into the original ones."[9] Fastidious and disjunctive, nonsense devises its own structures, abolishing reference, approaching number. Toward these structures, the anti-style of Hemingway often moves without for-

[7] Levin, "Observations on the Style of Ernest Hemingway," *Hemingway and His Critics*, 110.   [8] Shattuck, *The Banquet Years* (New York, 1961), 339ff.
[9] Sewell, *The Field of Nonsense* (London, 1952), 53ff.

feiting its tragic reference. Its rigor, terseness, and repetitions, its intractable concreteness and vast omissions, resist rhetoric, resist even statement, and discourage the mind from habitual closures. The style emerges from silence and tends toward it again by a process of exclusion; in between, it defies insanity.

Style engages human conduct, and conduct engages fate. Hemingway, we know, abhors the cant of ideology; his ethic is elementary. If you "feel good" after an action, you have acted morally. Morality, then, is a subjective response; but it is the response of one who accepts a code of skill and courage, and knows that death exposes the shabbiness of human behavior. The code is difficult; it offers few comforts and relies on fewer presuppositions. It leaves out much of what history has bequeathed to us of philosophy and religion. The radical skepticism of Hemingway is backed only by what a man truly possesses, his flesh, the home of his mortality. As a result of this reductive ethic, the characters of Hemingway are forced to be tough; they avoid all unnecessary responses to the world around them. But they also exact from themselves the extreme response when circumstances warrant it: speechless violence. In the moment of violence, Frederick J. Hoffman has shown in *The Mortal No,* men function neither as rational nor as historical creatures; they put themselves beyond humanity.

This is why the ethic of Hemingway's characters is not only reductive but also solitary. What they endure, they can never share with others. Existentially, they remain alone; they find momentary communion only in a dangerous ritual. Always, they disengage themselves from the complexities of human relations, and simplify their social existence to the primary functions of the body. "The only thing that could spoil a day was people . . . ," Hemingway once wrote. "People were always the limiters of happiness except for the very few that were as good as spring itself."[10] In eating and drinking, in love-making, in combat, his heroes silence the shrill demands of civilization, and elude the mind's perversity and the

[10] *A Moveable Feast,* 49.

heart's deceit. Their epicureanism is a search for truth, and truth in their day has a withering touch. Truth finds itself by exclusion, though in Rabelais' lustier day, it offered to devour the world whole.

When we exclude enough, we are left with nothing, *nada*. This, and not physical death, is the destiny of Hemingway's heroes. As a symbol of non-being, of the void, of life's ineluctable emptiness, death chills the spine of the bravest: there is no answer to it but suicide. The old fisherman, Santiago, thinks that "man can be destroyed but not defeated."[11] Yet man can indeed be defeated, as the earlier work of Hemingway repeatedly shows. The defeated are not merely tough; they are embodiments of oblivion. Still, even the defeated may possess dignity. The old man in "A Clean, Well-Lighted Place" has failed in his attempt at suicide, but remains a "clean old man." The old waiter who parodies the Lord's Prayer by reciting "Our nada who art in nada, nada be thy name . . . ," understands his client; for he too has excluded all but light and cleanliness from his life.[12] Exclusion is a principle of negation, and as Freud has taught us, the very words "No" and "Not" serve the powers of Thanatos in subtle ways. Exclusion finally leads to death-in-life, the fate of Hemingway's unredeemed. Theirs is the stillness we hear beneath the finicky language, the style of simple truth.

Yet it is perverse to see only the emptiness of Hemingway's world. In its lucid spaces, a vision of archetypal unity reigns. Opposite forces obey a common destiny; enemies discover their deeper identity; the hunter and the hunted merge. The matador plunges his sword, and for an instant in eternity, man and beast are the same. This is the moment of truth, and it serves Hemingway as symbol of the unity which underlies both love and death. His fatalism, his tolerance of bloodshed, his stoical reserve before the malice of creation, betray a sacramental attitude that transcends any personal fate. Though man is doomed to stand and struggle alone,

[11] Hemingway, *The Old Man and the Sea* (New York, 1952), 114.
[12] Hemingway, *The Short Stories of Ernest Hemingway* (New York, 1932), 481.

he may carry his initiative, "push his luck" too far; he may transgress by ignoring the tacit harmonies of the universe. The process of nature continues, heedless of human effort, like the Gulf Stream: "the palm fronds of our victories, the worn light bulbs of our discoveries and the empty condoms of our great loves float with no significance against one single, lasting thing—the stream."[13] Suddenly, we understand those innumerable, small ceremonies of magical penance and propitiation that Hemingway's heroes constantly perform: they are secret invocations of Being at its source. His redeemed characters know that the universe is not Naught but One. And they all cast, like one man, a single shadow across death, the unifier of all our tales. Hemingway himself said: "All stories, if continued far enough, end in death, and he is no true storyteller who would keep that from you."[14] The story rests in silence.

II

Silence serves as a metaphor of Hemingway's fiction though his fiction is unsilent. In 1926, Hemingway said to Samuel Putnam that he wanted to "strip language clean, to lay it bare down to the bone."[15] A year earlier, he realized that aim in *In Our Time*.

The collection begins with a scream: "The strange thing was, he said, how they screamed every night at midnight. I do not know why they screamed at that time. We were in the harbor and they were all on the pier and at midnight they started screaming. We used to turn the searchlight on them to quiet them."[16] The same sketch ends with the image of mules, their forelegs broken, dumped in the shallow bay. The author remarks, "It was all a pleasant business. My word yes a most pleasant business." Then comes the story "Indian Camp." Young Nick Adams watches his father per-

---

[13] Hemingway, *The Green Hills of Africa* (New York, 1954), 102.
[14] *Death in the Afternoon*, 122.
[15] Quoted, Carlos Baker, *Hemingway: The Writer as Artist* (Princeton, 1956), 71.
[16] Hemingway, *In Our Time* (New York, 1958), 9.

form a caesarian operation on an Indian woman, and sees the body of her husband in the upper bunk, razor still in hand, his throat cut from ear to ear. The story resolves itself in an incantation of repeated sounds in distinct images.

> They were seated in the boat, Nick in the stern, his father rowing. The sun was coming up over the hills. A bass jumped, making a circle in the water. Nick trailed his hand in the water. It felt warm in the sharp chill of the morning.
> In the early morning on the lake sitting in the stern of the boat with his father rowing, he felt quite sure that he would never die.[17]

The initiation to birth and death, the vitality of nature, the reliance on the father, the deceptions of the self, remain purely implicit in discrete sensations, and in the magic reiteration of certain words, "boat," "father," "morning," "water." This is the Hemingway scene.

The pointillism of the scene can be more obvious. In "Cat in the Rain," for instance, Hemingway writes:

> Italians came from a long way off to look at the war monument. It was made of bronze and glistened in the rain. It was raining. The rain dripped from the palm trees. Water stood in pools on the gravel paths. The sea broke in a long line in the rain and slipped back down the beach to come up and break again in a long line in the rain. The motor cars were gone from the square by the war monument. Across the square in the doorway of the cafe a waiter stood looking out at the empty square.[18]

This is a scene painted by an Impressionist. The eye provides the frame; the mind provides the transitions; the beholder interprets the pattern. Hemingway controls our perceptions by a careful disposition of lacunae. Each event seems to occur independently, each seems coeval with all other events. The effect is abrupt because it is pristine; a great blankness lies behind it.

Brusqueness also conveys the rush of action. "The Battler" begins

[17] *Ibid.*, 21.   [18] *Ibid.*, 117.

with a brakeman throwing Nick Adams off a moving freight train. Nick walks up to a solitary figure huddled by a camp fire:

> "Hello!" Nick said.
> The man looked up.
> "Where did you get the shiner?" he said.[19]

This is how people meet in a world where violence seldom has antecedents. The slang term is apt; the speaker is a crazy prize fighter whose life may be read in his face: "It was like putty in color. Dead looking in the firelight."[20] Ravaged by publicity more than by blows, the battler roams no-man's land, loathing everyone. His sole attendant is a mannerly Negro who slugs him with a blackjack whenever he turns dangerous. This emptiness, common to so many characters of Hemingway, affects another battler, Krebs, the veteran in "Soldier's Home." "Krebs acquired the nausea in regard to experience that is the result of untruth," the author succinctly explains.[21] Krebs loves no one, not even his mother; his single passion is to avoid complications. Both battlers are anomic creatures, their lives delimited at one end by violence and at the other by the void.

Even in that perfect idyl, "Big Two-Hearted River," the hero constantly senses the contingencies of the void. Nick feels happy in the ritual simplifications of his fishing trip, and he is alone. "He felt he had left everything behind, the need for thinking, the need to write, other needs. It was all back of him."[22] He makes camp: "Now things were done. There had been this to do. Now it was done. It had been a hard trip. He was very tired. That was done. He had made his camp. He was settled. Nothing could touch him. It was a good place to camp. He was there, in the good place."[23] These rhythms suggest a ceremony of exorcism, as Malcolm Cowley has noted; they are the feelings of a happy man hanging on to happiness by the skin of his teeth.[24] But the nature of the specific threat is

---

[19] *Ibid.,* 67. [20] *Ibid.,* 68. [21] *Ibid.,* 90. [22] *Ibid.,* 179. [23] *Ibid.,* 186.
[24] Malcolm Cowley (ed.), *The Portable Hemingway* (New York, 1944), xff.

deleted from the story; the powers of darkness emerge only in a symbol of the greatest reticence, the swamp. "In the swamp the banks were bare, the big cedars came together overhead, the sun did not come through, except in patches; in the fast deep water, in the half light, the fishing would be tragic. In the swamp fishing was a tragic adventure. Nick did not want it. He did not want to go down the stream any further today."[25]

The cold swamp encircles *In Our Time*. Yet the stories have the ring of a bell heard over the frozen air. Between their pure sound, the vignettes flash across the eye once and are never forgotten. The garden at Mons where the Germans get potted as they climb over the wall, the absolutely perfect barricade jammed across an enemy bridge, the six cabinet ministers shot at half past six, Maera lying still, face in the sand, while the bull's horn gores him repeatedly, and Nick, hit in the spine, propped against a church, represent the same awful moment. Story and vignette, sound and sight, blend perfectly, enclosed by the same deep stillness. It is the stillness of terrible truth, and it helps to make the collection the best written by an American in our century.

III

Hemingway saw life as he saw art: a process of laying bare to the bone. Men strip their illusions as they must shed their flesh. The boy who learns of the death and the dishonesty of his father, in "My Old Man," concludes: "Seems like when they get started they don't leave a guy nothing."[26] "They" are agents of the withering truth, and their influence prevails in Hemingway's two best novels, *The Sun Also Rises*, 1926, and *A Farewell to Arms*, 1929.

The Sun Also Rises persists as our paradigm of radical loss. The sun rises on characters, like Jake Barnes, who need to sleep with electric lights switched on six months of the year, rises and sets and rises again without dispelling the dark. In this wasteland, the Fisher

[25] *In Our Time*, 211.   [26] *Ibid.*, 173.

King is fated. Were his physical wound to heal miraculously, nothing would really change. "Oh, Jake . . . we could have had such a damned good time together," Brett says at the end, and Jake, who knows better, replies, "Yes. . . . Isn't it pretty to think so?"[27] Hemingway compresses the terror of his novel into that ironic question. The terror has no reason and no name; it is simply the presence of an absence; and the only recourse of the characters is to discover a rhythm, a style, of endurance. For the best among them, like Romero, there is grace under pressure, which may be the only grace man will ever know.

The novel is predictably circular in structure; we end to begin again. The characters also form themselves in a circle about the hollow center, Lady Brett Ashley, her slouched hat hiding an exquisite despair. The contrast is between Robert Cohn, shabby romantic in a purple land (W. H. Hudson's), and Jake Barnes, maimed stoic and ironist of the night. In this parable of modern love, whores dance with homosexuals, and the impotence of the hero matches the heroine's nymphomania. The quality of Book One is the quality of a nightmare barely kept in abeyance. "It is awfully easy to be hard-boiled about everything in the day time, but at night is another thing," Barnes says in a cold sweat.[28]

In Book Two, fishing and bull-fighting deflect the dread. Brett goes off to San Sebastian with Cohn; Barnes and Bill Gorton go off fishing in the Burguete. The intricacies of love are hushed, the urgencies of worship muted. Barnes tries to pray in a Spanish Church: "And as all the time I was kneeling with my forehead on the wood in front of me . . . I was a little ashamed, and regretted that I was such a rotten Catholic, but realized there was nothing I could do about it."[29] The cold high country near Roncevaux, where Roland once gave his life for God and Emperor and the Twelve Peers, beckons; there the trout swim in clear streams. "I shut my eyes," Jake says. "It felt good lying on the ground."[30]

[27] Hemingway, *The Sun Also Rises* (New York, 1954), 199.   [28] *Ibid.*, 26.
[29] *Ibid.*, 75.   [30] *Ibid.*, 97.

Down on the lower ground, at Pamplona, the society of spiritual cripples waits to receive life from the Feria of San Fermin. The passion they lack, they hope to find as *aficionados* (*afición* also means passion) of the ring. By the time the *feria* is over, Brett has robbed all the men around her of their manhood. Romero stands alone. Can she redeem herself in him? Will she only bring his ruin? Romero has innocence, courage, and grace. His knowledge is from another time, another place. He understands that the bull is his equal, perhaps his other self: "His left shoulder went forward between the horns as the sword went in, and for just an instant he and the bull were one. . . . Then the figure was broken."[31] He can pay homage to Brett, in the ring, without diminishing himself. But when he offers her the bull's ear, she forgets it in the drawer of a bed-table. There can be no true meeting of Brett and Romero, as there can be none between Brett and Barnes. The *feria* turns into a bad dream; the characters disperse.

The reducing cycle nears completion. In Book Three, Brett decides "not to be a bitch," and releases Romero. "It's sort of what we have instead of God," she explains to Jake who has hurried to her side in Madrid.[32] In his view, Brett's sacrifice is genuine because she has paid. "You paid some way for everything that was any good. . . . Either you paid by learning about them, or by experience, or by taking chances, or by money," Jake believes.[33] Everyone pays. Some, like old Count Mippipopolous, pay gallantly; others pay badly. But payment is always reduction, divestment; at the end, the skin shrinks tighter on the skeleton. The best lay down their lives against death, and no one can offer to pay more. Such is Romero who functions in the novel more as a symbol than as a character. His existence incarnates the crucial insight of *The Sun Also Rises:* only in a confrontation with death does life acquire meaning and lose its terror. In this stark paradox, terror is transcended.

The keynote of *A Farewell to Arms* is not terror but doom. The world breaks everyone impartially, and death falls on the earth like

[31] *Ibid.,* 176.   [32] *Ibid.,* 198.   [33] *Ibid.,* 117.

a steady rain. Death comes in war, "suddenly and unreasonably"; and it comes in peace to those who would give birth: "Poor, poor dear Cat. And this was the price you paid for sleeping together. . . . This is what people got for loving each other."[34] Nature finds its final unity in decay.

But there is also the unity of love. Within the great circle of decay, two lovers strive to keep intact: "There's only us two and in the world there's all the rest of them. If anything comes between us we're gone and then they have us," Catherine says to Frederick Henry.[35] There are not two; there is only one. For as Catherine goes on to say: "There isn't any me any more. Just what you want."[36] The circle of decay tightens. There is no place really "to drop the war," as Catherine reminds Frederick; their "separate peace" in Switzerland is only part of a greater biological war. "You'll fight before you'll marry," Nurse Ferguson tells the lovers. "You'll die then. Fight or die. That's what people do. They don't marry."[37] Catherine, of course, dies. Love also finds its unity in doom.

In the Italian mountains, "the picturesque front," the war seems to mark an end to history. "Perhaps wars weren't won any more," Henry wonders. "Maybe they went on forever."[38] It is more certain that the war confutes the collective experience of mankind. In a famous passage, Henry says:

> I was always embarrassed by the words sacred, glorious, and sacrifice and the expression in vain. . . . There were many words that you could not stand to hear and finally only the names of places had dignity. Certain numbers were the same way and certain dates and these with the names of places were all you could say and have them mean anything. Abstract words such as glory, honor, courage, or hallow were obscene beside the concrete names of villages, the numbers of roads, the names of rivers, the numbers of regiments and the dates.[39]

Universal violence compels language to be mute; the public and the private fates of characters converge. The novel ends fittingly with

[34] Hemingway, *A Farewell to Arms* (New York, 1929), 330. [35] *Ibid.*, 146.
[36] *Ibid.*, 110. [37] *Ibid.*, 112. [38] *Ibid.*, 123. [39] *Ibid.*, 191.

an apocalyptic image. Frederick Henry recalls a log crawling with ants that he had thrown into a camp fire. "I remember thinking at the time," he says, "that it was the end of the world and a splendid chance to be a messiah and lift the log off the fire and throw it out where the ants could get off on to the ground."[40] But the messiah only steams the ants with whiskey and they perish.

Yet *A Farewell to Arms* is richer than its macabre insistencies. Rinaldi, Ferguson, the army priest, the barman at Stresa, all move with an independent life. Catherine Barkley, who appears stilted, oddly unreal, finally forces her hidden hysteria upon our consciousness, and in death acquires dignity. Henry remains the Hemingway hero, laconic and inevitable as tragedy. But the novel reminds us that for Hemingway, country is more ample than people. The novel breathes the seasons; it gives the firm touch of places. We feel the pebbles white in the sun, and the blue water moving swiftly in the channels. We shiver when the weather turns cold at night and the rain commences to fall the next day. Still, the narrowness of death ends by pinching our response. Like Frederick Henry, lying wounded in an ambulance, we feel the blood of a dead soldier drip as "from an icicle after the sun has gone." It drips always on the same spot of our skin.

The great phase of Hemingway's art closes with *A Farewell to Arms,* 1929. The stories of *Men Without Women,* unlike some earlier pieces, cannot be charged with "the kinetographic fallacy" which Carlos Baker defines as "the supposition that we can get the best art by an absolutely true description of what takes place in observed action."[41] But their depth is sometimes attained at a price: Hemingway loses the rigor of omission and exposes his sentimentality. The collection, nevertheless, contains such classic fictions as "The Undefeated." Hemingway still knows that words belong to the public domain; the hidden world requires a subliminal language. This is the language that conveys evil in "The Killers." It is also the language of the death of love in "Hills Like White Elephants":

---

[40] *Ibid.,* 338ff.   [41] *Hemingway: The Writer as Artist,* 63.

"They look like white elephants," she said.
"I've never seen one," the man drank his beer.
"No, you wouldn't have."[42]

Here it is again, in the incredible opening sentence of "In Another Country": "In the fall the war was always there, but we did not go to it any more."[43] The threat of oblivion presses syntax into ineluctable shape. The narrator of "Now I Lay Me" lies in the dark, listening to silk-worms chewing; he dare not close his eyes lest his soul depart. The predicament of Hemingway is much the same: he can no more ignore the dark than he can articulate it. The tension of the void bestills his art.

IV

Silence is not only a metaphor of Hemingway's work; it is also the source of its formal excellence, its integrity. We know the tragic tale: Hemingway begins to lose his virtue, his *arete,* in the thirties and never recovers it completely. When he returns to his true form, in "A Clean, Well-Lighted Place" or "A Way You'll Never Be," both collected in *Winner Take Nothing,* 1933, the style contracts again, and sings madly. The last story shows Nick Adams in shock; he "can't sleep without a light of some sort." "That's all I have now," he explains to a fellow officer.[44] The next moment, Nick rants about locusts, and silently babbles: "And there was Gaby Delys, oddly enough, with feathers on; you called me baby doll a year ago tadada you said that I was rather nice to know tadada with feathers on, with feathers off."[45] This is Hemingway still inward with his terror, a terror he could still overcome artistically in the unflawed "The Short Happy Life of Francis Macomber." But the embarrassing evidence against their author stands: *To Have and Have Not,* 1937, *The Fifth Column,* 1938, *Across the River and Into the Trees,* 1950. Even *For Whom the Bell Tolls,* 1940, and *The Old Man and the Sea,* 1952, in subtle ways betray his vision. The black

[42] *The Short Stories of Ernest Hemingway,* 371.   [43] *Ibid.,* 365.   [44] *Ibid.,* 505.
[45] *Ibid.,* 506.

paradox of Hemingway remains the same: he can never stray far from the reticence of death, madness, and the void, without betraying that vision. Critics have speculated about the "fourth" and "fifth" dimensions that Hemingway said, in *Green Hills of Africa,* could be given to prose fiction; they have suggested death, transcendence, and the mystic present. Silence, which bears some relation to these topics, could be conceived as an added dimension to his prose. In that dimension, the reader encounters what is essential of Hemingway.

Yet there is some hidden infirmity in that silence, and it must be acknowledged. It expresses a deliberate restriction of feelings, the tightness of holding tight. Philip Young relates this attitude to the trauma of Hemingway's early wounds at Fossalta, and to a consequent neurosis, identified by Fenichel as "primitivation."[46] "I tried to breathe," Frederick Henry says, after he is hit by a big trench mortar, "but my breath would not come and I felt myself rush bodily out of myself and out and out and out and all the time bodily in the wind. I went out swiftly, all of myself, and I knew I was dead and that it had all been a mistake to think you just died. Then I floated, and instead of going on I felt myself slide back."[47] The fright of nothingness constricts the spirit of the living. Everything *must* be simplified. Everything *must* be simplified and repeated. Freud's theory of the "repetition compulsion" may be glibly applied to Hemingway's career, as he doubles up on his tracks across three continents to confront violence. But if there is some infirmity in Hemingway's silence, it remains personal; it finds its way past the shock therapy, to the insanity of his last years. Whatever ravaged his life, he managed to create a unique literary style, and managed, more significantly perhaps, to create a style of survival that compelled envy and emulation the world over. He chose the final silence when he sensed the irrevocable loss of both his styles. "I did nothing that had not been done to me," he once wrote, and kept his promise to the end.[48]

[46] Philip Young, *Ernest Hemingway* (New York, 1952), 139ff.
[47] *A Farewell to Arms,* 57.   [48] *Green Hills of Africa,* 101.

A Sketchbook of the Artist in His Thirty-Fourth Year: William Carlos Williams' Kora in Hell: Improvisations

SHERMAN PAUL

Perhaps he is modern. He addresses himself to the imagination.
—Marianne Moore on Williams (1927)

This book . . . is probably the most important in the development of Williams' poetry. In order to compose the Improvisations *he has asked himself all the artistic questions of the day, and in writing them he has most intimately come into contact with his gifts.*
—René Taupin on Williams (1929)[1]

I

Sometimes the explanations that William Carlos Williams gives of his own work explain very little. In his *Autobiography,* where he misplaces *Kora in Hell* (1920) in the sequence of his development, he tells us that the title represents the rout by the war of springtime,

[1] Moore, "A Poet of the Quattrocento," *Dial,* LXXXII (March, 1927), 215; Taupin, *L'Influence du Symbolisme Français sur la Poésie Américaine* (Paris, 1929), 284.

his own creative beginning and the resurgence of American letters with which he identified it. He does not mention the war—the First World War—in the fuller account of the book in *I Wanted to Write a Poem,* the autobiographical bibliography of his work; and the war, except perhaps as a pressure of the time leaving an indefinable imprint on the book, is not a part of it. He may have remembered (rewriting his own past, as so many writers do, from the evidence of others) that Gorham Munson had said of the book, in *Destinations,* that "Williams, suffering from the ghastly business of war, could yet try to reconstruct a springtime." Even then he may have remembered only the first and not the second phrase, which is closer to the spirit of the book as he delightedly recovers its intention in *I Wanted to Write a Poem.* Here he provides other and better clues. "I was feeling fresh," he remarks in reference to the cover design, an ovum, surrounded by spermatozoa, in the act of accepting one and being impregnated—a "beginning of life" that he thought a "beautiful thing" and wanted the world to see. And he himself was "Springtime," the Kora of the title his friend Ezra Pound had prompted: "I felt I was on my way to Hell (but I didn't go very far). This was what the Improvisations were trying to say."[2]

In this account of the book he also replaces the war of these war-years with a literary war closer to him. (The "Prologue" to *Kora in Hell,* published first in two installments in the *Little Review,* to which Pound had introduced the work of Joyce, Yeats, Eliot, Ford, and others, was one of Williams' heavy salvos.) For in these years, seven years before *The Waste Land* arrived to alter the literary landscape with what Williams always referred to as its atomic force, Eliot published "Prufrock." Williams confuses this poem with the title of Eliot's first book, *Prufrock and Other Ob-*

[2] *The autobiography of William Carlos Williams* (New York, 1951), 158; *I Wanted to Write a Poem,* ed. Edith Heal (Boston, 1958), 26–31; Munson, *Destinations* (New York, 1928), 112. In his *Autobiography,* Williams mistakenly recalls that a "dark" spermatozoa was accepted, a mistake in favor of his conception of the Beautiful Thing in *Paterson.*

servations, which appeared in 1917, the year in which his own third book of poems, *Al Que Quiere!,* was published. He remembers this accurately enough: "When I was halfway through the Prologue, 'Prufrock' appeared." And the violence of his response, the sense of the betrayal of his hope for the enterprise of modern art, was just as accurately remembered.[3]

The reason for this deep and enduring memory is not a petty one of recognition but a traumatic one of confirmation. *Prufrock and Other Observations* was noticed almost immediately in *Poetry* by Ezra Pound in a long unstinting review; this book was a major event, "the best thing in poetry since . . . ," Pound said, and he meant it. But *Al Que Quiere!,* an equally impressive work of force and originality showing clearly that Williams had found his way, was not so enthusiastically praised when it was reviewed by Dorothy Dudley in the same magazine in the following year. Williams was said to have the conscience but not yet the ease of a great artist (and in some poems this was true), and his task was perceptively identified with (and prefigured in) "Chicory and Daisies," a poem upon which he pointedly commented later in the "Prologue." Williams' arrival was not proclaimed, where Eliot's was, and this, not the publication and reception of *The Waste Land,* which only reminded him that his place in the galaxy of poets was still uncertain, stirred his deep, not wholly aesthetic, antipathy to Eliot.[4]

It is interesting to note that Williams did not take issue with "Prufrock" when the poem first appeared in *Poetry* in June, 1915.

[3] "Prologue," *Little Review,* V (April, 1919), 1–10, and VI (May, 1919), 74–80; *I Wanted to Write a Poem,* 30.

[4] Pound, "T. S. Eliot," *Poetry,* X (August, 1917), 264–71; Dudley, "To Whom It May Concern," *Poetry,* XII (April, 1918), 38–43; "Prologue to *Kora in Hell,*" *Selected Essays of William Carlos Williams* (New York, 1954), 17. Conrad Aiken, in reviewing Williams' *Collected Poems* in 1934, not only set Williams, the poet and the theoretician, squarely against Eliot, but praised *Al Que Quiere!* and *Kora in Hell,* books "obscurely published and poorly circulated," as his best, his "finest and sharpest" work. How consoling this may have been may be gathered from his well-meant praise of Williams as "still, at the age of fifty, a promising poet" and from Williams' very late poem "The Pink Locust," in *Journey to Love.* Aiken, *A Reviewer's ABC* (New York, 1958), 380–83.

Five poems of his own, under the covering title of "Root Buds," had been published there the previous month, among them "Sub Terra," the call for a new poetry with which he introduced *Al Que Quiere!*. He was aware of his humble emergence, but also confident, and even aggressive—the title of this book of poems means "To Him Who Wants It." But now, in 1917, Eliot's advent and Pound's annunciation of it (Williams assured Marianne Moore in 1918 of Pound's "unswerving intelligence in the detection of literary quality") shook his confidence and established the pattern of declaration and demonstration that ever afterward showed him to be hurt irreparably. Eliot did not destroy the root buds—did not touch the vital source of Williams' creativity. But because of Eliot he would, it seems, like the chicory, have over and over to lift his flowers "on bitter stems" out of the scorched ground.[5]

II

The composition of *Kora in Hell* immediately followed the publication of *Al Que Quiere!* and carried forward its themes and exuberant creativity. ("The Wanderer," placed at the end of the volume, was a summons to further creation.) The title suggests a downward turning of spirit, a descent, a phase of the rhythm of ascent-descent that marks the inner movement of Williams' work; and since every complete act of creation passes through these phases, the title suggests a descent of greater importance and profundity—descent as a conscious intention of the poet. Usually one turns in this direction in search of self-recovery and transcendence, because of defeat or creative impasse; it is the way of abandonment, of falling back on the deepest, the unconscious resources of the self, and on chaos, and hopefully a fertile one. It is the way of growth that Emerson enthusiastically endorsed in "Circles": "The way of life is wonder-

---

[5] Williams, "Root Buds," *Poetry*, VI (May, 1915), 62–66; *The Selected Letters of William Carlos Williams*, ed. John C. Thirlwall (New York, 1957), 42. For his remarks on his "inner security," see *Selected Letters*, 147.

ful; it is by abandonment." When Williams speaks of the "he and she of it"—what Emerson called intellect constructive and intellect receptive—"she" represents the phase of descent, the guardian spirit of formlessness and darkness, of creative night. Or passing beyond metaphor, "she" is the very "mother stuff," the ovum of the cover design; and here, as Williams wrote of it later in *A Voyage to Pagany,* he always retreated when he was beaten, to lie and breed with himself. Clearly the Kora he pursues in Hell is his own creative self, his feminine secret nature, the Beautiful Thing that the constructive or inventive work of art, by turning "the mind inside out," restores to the world. Nothing less than this generative passion, this dream of love and desire to release the self, moves him, an author who, Pound recognized, was primarily "concerned with his own insides." Where "The Wanderer," a ritual narrative of the realization of poetic vocation, celebrates the discovery of the female principle of his art, *Kora in Hell* celebrates his willing pursuit and the mating with himself that may account for his sense of the book's uniqueness and his remark that "it reveals myself to me."[6]

This is but one aspect of Williams' awareness of the profound processes of the imagination, an awareness justifying René Taupin's opinion that "Williams knows more about the work of the poetic imagination than any American poet today." In terms of the situation in poetry at the time, especially the conformity Williams derided, one of the most needed lessons provided by *Kora in Hell* is that nurture may be found in the ground of the self as well as in

---

[6] Emerson, "Circles," *The Complete Works of Ralph Waldo Emerson* (Boston and New York, 1903), II, 321; Williams, "How to Write," in Linda W. Wagner, *The Poems of William Carlos Williams* (Middletown, 1964), 147; "Night," *A Voyage to Pagany* (New York, 1928), 122–27, 277; *Kora in Hell* (San Francisco, 1957), 72; *Autobiography,* 288–89, where, in speaking of the "secret gardens of the self," he returns to the conceptions of "perfections" and "presence" first used in *Kora in Hell;* "Dr. Williams' Position," *The Literary Essays of Ezra Pound,* ed. Eliot (London, 1954), 398; *I Wanted to Write a Poem,* 26. See also "Revelation," *Selected Essays,* 268–71. In the manuscript of *Paterson IV,* now in the Yale University Library, Williams writes: "His other self, himself his woman"; he begins the "Prologue" by characterizing his imagination in terms of his mother's.

tradition. The poet shows how one might follow the directives of "Sub Terra" and "Ballet." His program, as Vivienne Koch says, translates the Emersonian ethic of self-reliance to the aesthetic sphere, though the actual descent into the self, the nurturing of self-reliance, owes little, I think, to Emerson and much to Whitman —and most, in this immediate instance, to Kandinsky. But *Kora in Hell* is not concerned solely with the "she" of it, though the title and subtitle suggest that it is. It also follows the compositional advice given in "To a Solitary Disciple" and brilliantly exemplifies the "he" of it, the constructive or formal means by which the self is again revealed and conformity again denied. For after the abandon of writing, Williams says, "one goes forward carefully." What descent discovers is made good in art, first by the intelligent acceptance of "the new and the extraordinary," and then by the invention of an appropriate form. *Kora in Hell* exhibits this double work. Its improvisations are not improvised.[7]

This may explain what Williams meant when he said that he was on his way to Hell but didn't go very far. Williams may have begun the book in a postpartum mood, as a loosening-up exercise following the difficult ascent of his recently completed book of poems. His prose experiments, especially *The Great American Novel,* the early prose portions of *Spring and All,* "Notes in Diary Form," and *A Novelette,* seem to have a function similar to that of *Kora in Hell,* which, Vivienne Koch says, was "preparation for a new poetic modus in his work." In *Spring and All* (1923), where he admits the faults of judgment in the "Prologue," he gives another account of *Kora in Hell* that merits quotation here:

> The Improvisations—coming at a time when I was trying to remain firm at great cost—I had recourse to the expedient of letting life go completely in order to live in the world of my choice.[8]

[7] Taupin, *L'Influence du Symbolisme Français,* 286; Koch, *William Carlos Williams* (Norfolk, Conn., 1950), 31; Wagner, *The Poems of William Carlos Williams,* 146–47. The poems from *Al Que Quiere!* are in Williams, *Collected Earlier Poems* (Norfolk, Conn., 1951), 117–18, 169–70, 167–68.

[8] Richard A. Macksey gives a valuable account of the tension of the book in "'A Certainty of Music': Williams' Changes," in *William Carlos Williams,* ed.

I let the imagination have its own way to see if it could save itself. Something very definite came of it. I found myself alleviated but most important I began there and then to revalue experience, to understand what I was at—

The virtue of the improvisations is their placement in a world of new values—[9]

Williams let the imagination go in a conscious attempt to test the organic theory of art set forth by Wassily Kandinsky in *Concerning the Spiritual in Art,* especially the notion of inner necessity that he later held up to "Ezra and Eliot" in the "Prologue." He let the imagination have its own way by writing down daily whatever came to mind, an automatic procedure that Kandinsky had suggested in his definition of an improvisation: "A largely unconscious, spontaneous expression of inner character. . . . This I call an 'Improvisation.' " There was nothing especially unusual in this procedure of expressionism except Williams' adoption of it—his willingness to experiment, not in a time of ebb or defeat, and in full awareness of the risk.[10]

What risk? The risk, as he puts it in the *Autobiography,* of "the longest leap, the most unmitigated daring, the longest chances"— the risk of discovering his "perfection," his inner necessity. In "The Basis of Faith in Art," he recalls that the first thing he learned as a writer was "that it isn't so easy to let yourself go." If conformity

---

J. Hillis Miller (Englewood Cliffs, N.J., 1966), 142–43. See Koch, *William Carlos Williams,* 33. See also *Selected Letters,* 52, and "The Black Winds," *Collected Earlier Poems,* 246: "How easy to slip/into the old mode, how hard to/cling firmly to the advance—." [9] *Spring and All* (Dijon, 1923), 43–44.

[10] Kandinsky, *Über das Geistige in der Kunst* was published in Germany in 1912, translated under the title, *The Art of Spiritual Harmony,* and published in London and Boston in 1914. The edition cited in this essay is *Concerning the Spiritual in Art* (New York, 1947). The formulation quoted by Williams is on p. 52 and is followed by Kandinsky's belief that "all means [forms] are sacred which are called for by internal necessity." Kandinsky's definition is on p. 77. Williams may have learned of Kandinsky from Marsden Hartley, who met the Blue Rider group in 1912, or from Pound's *Gaudier-Brzeska* (London, 1916). By 1923, he was critical of Kandinsky's Expressionism, calling it the "apotheosis of relief." See Williams, *The Great American Novel* in *American Short Novels,* ed. R. P. Blackmur (New York, 1960), 315.

("stereotype") hedged him on one side, chaos threatened him on the other: "If I ducked out of that I ran into chaos." Yet chaos was the only way, necessary, whatever the risk, to the creative sally; only that fluid condition, the occasion of so much terror in his work, released the mind. And so—to borrow words he would use in respect to Whitman—he set out "to discover . . . by headlong composition . . . what we can do."[11]

Marianne Moore remembered his recklessness and admired him for it—he had once written to her of his need to free himself by "violent methods." But Else von Freytag-Loringhoven, in a review of *Kora in Hell* that is a literary curiosity of the time, thought otherwise of Williams, whose favorite theme, acknowledged in a description of the hero of the autobiographical fiction, *A Voyage to Pagany,* was "the abandon of life and the—check," and whose choice of vocation and way of life, for all the benefit it conferred on his writing, was not, admittedly, a risky one. Still, as an act of the imagination, as a conscious pursuit of his imagination, his self—the pursuit of the imagination by the imagination, his great lifelong endeavor and theme—*Kora in Hell* represents a considerable risk. In it, Williams descended as far as he had ever gone into chaos, a fact corroborated, I think, by the compensatory nature, the check, of the composition. This book is the largest, most carefully realized formal achievement of these early years, the work in which he both hazarded most and discovered the saving virtue—and liberation—of form. The imagination, he found, was not only the substance and energy of the self (one of its erotic forces) but a plane of the self's existence upon which (or where) the self freely disposed of itself. Kandinsky had defined for him both the imperative to improvisation and the conscious compositional aspect of imagination that he followed. The virtue of the improvisations was their placement in

[11] *Autobiography,* 288; *Selected Essays,* 177; Wagner, *The Poems of William Carlos Williams,* 145; *Selected Essays,* 230. In *Paterson,* which in one respect is an autobiographical rehearsal of his poetic career, he writes: "Why have I not/but for imagined beauty where there is none/or none available, long since/put myself deliberately in the way of death?" *Paterson* (New York, 1963), 30.

this world of new values, the world of his choice, the world of art in which the artist, Kandinsky said, was free.[12]

III

This aspect of the book has been obscured by the tendency to see in *Kora in Hell* a derivative example of literary modernism. Williams, it is true, knew French well and, like most of the poets who shared with him the experimental work of *Others,* knew the current movements of the avant-garde. He was familiar with the writing of the Symbolists and with Dada, which Marcel Duchamp, one of his many artist friends in New York, had introduced there in 1916. The literary magazines to which he contributed, especially *Poetry* and the *Little Review,* having Ezra Pound for their foreign editor, were the most effective schools of writing and literature of the time; and chiefly because of Pound's insistent teaching, René Taupin could say without exaggeration in *L'Influence du Symbolisme Français* (1929) that "Poetry in America today speaks French." In this important early study of the American poets of his generation, Williams was recognized as a poet to be considered seriously along with Eliot and Pound. But the price of this recognition was Taupin's opinion, arrived at by comparing the Rimbaud of the *Illuminations* with the Williams of the *Improvisations* (a comparison endlessly perpetuated), that Williams was in the mainstream of French influence.[13]

In response to Pound's letter about his book, Williams himself had publicized the comparison in *The Great American Novel* (1923), a work published in France and of some consequence there. Employing Pound's comment, he writes in Chapter Three, "Take

---

[12] "Interview With Donald Hall," *A Marianne Moore Reader* (New York, 1965), 273; *Selected Letters,* 52; Else von Freytag-Loringhoven, "Thee I call 'Hamlet of Wedding-Ring,'" *Little Review,* VII (January–March, 1921), 48–55, and (Autumn, 1921), 108–11; *A Voyage to Pagany,* 211; Williams, "Three Professional Studies," *Little Review,* V (February–March, 1919), 36–44; Kandinsky, *Concerning the Spiritual in Art,* 77, 75.   [13] Taupin, *L'Influence du Symbolisme Français,* 288.

the improvisations: What the French reader would say is: *Oui, ça; j'ai déjà vu ça; ça c'est de Rimbaud.* Finis." But in the context of this exploratory work, the passage denies Pound's assertion, an assertion denied again in *A Novelette,* another exploratory work: "Kindly note that all I have ever done has been the one thing. Pound will say that the improvisations are—etc. etc. twenty, forty years late. On the contrary he's all wet. Their   excellence is, in major part, the shifting of category. It is the disjointing process."[14]

Pound was not entirely wet, as the persistent denial perhaps indicates, but too much concerned with literary influence, which was not, as Williams tried to point out, the significant influence in this work. It may be true, as Taupin says, that Williams is very much like Rimbaud in gifts, intelligence, and spirit; that, like Rimbaud, he has a talent for irony, an eye for minute detail, a predilection for the commonplace and vulgar, even a profound concern for the dance of the imagination. But likeness is not necessarily influence, and in the most important element of Taupin's comparison he is not like Rimbaud at all—in uniting the power to contact things with the freest and most visionary imagination.[15]

Williams is not a visionary poet. He is not a seer but the buzzard he mentions in *Kora in Hell* whose eyes are of "a power equal to that of the eagle's" and whose vision is not given to transcendental flight but to earthy things. Williams is aware that the mind itself is sufficiently visionary (his mother was a medium at spiritualistic seances) and, in the passage Taupin cites as evidence of his visionary concern, wishes to be rid of the *"floating visions of unknown purport"* that obstruct his sight:

[14] *The Great American Novel,* 312; *The Letters of Ezra Pound, 1907–1941,* ed. D. D. Paige (New York, 1950), 160; *A Novelette and Other Prose* (Toulon, 1932), 25; Pound, *Literary Essays,* 393. The citation in *A Novelette* is, significantly, in a chapter entitled "Juan Gris."

[15] Taupin, *L'Influence du Symbolisme Français,* 281–84. Munson, *Destinations,* 111–12, taking up the references to Rimbaud, considers *Kora in Hell* a deviation in Williams' development. This, I think, is not the case, though the following comment of Munson's is crucial and correct: "Rimbaud was an altogether different type, a prodigy who came to an end of skepticism and saw no way to make an affirmation."

*In the mind there is a continual play of obscure images which com-
ing between the eyes and their prey seem pictures on the screen at the
movies. Somewhere there appears to be a mal-adjustment. The wish
would be to see   not   floating visions of unknown purport but
the imaginative qualities of the actual things being perceived accompany their gross vision in a slow dance, interpreting as they go.*

Like the modern artists he admires most, Williams is a realist,
rigorous and intellectual—scientific, like the doctors he praises in *A
Voyage to Pagany*—in his search for truth. He wishes to sharpen
but not to derange the senses, for he wants the actual things that the
senses give him. "I want all my reactions," he declared at this time
in an autobiographical study which depicts a pure young man
(Thoreauvian, but hardly Rimbaldian) whose only passion is the
desire to write. "I want to write," he says. "It does not drug my
senses, it sharpens them. It is the holy ghost of that trinity: The
Senses, Action, Composition." Williams is a poet of the actual,
whose large freedom belongs to the inventive powers of the imagination, the power to dispose things on its own plane and thereby
make an art-object, a new, real thing. Here, in turning from the
artist as seer (the visionary imagination) to the artist as maker (the
constructive imagination), is the shifting of category of which he
speaks in *A Novelette*.[16]

The comparisons of *Kora in Hell* and the *Illuminations,* like
Pound's attribution of "opacity" to Williams' work, a quality Taupin believed to be "essentially a virtue of modern French poetry,"
are either superficial or misleading. They belong to a criticism that
praises by association, and makes association almost everything; this
is even true of Kenneth Rexroth's instructive essay, "The Influence
of French Poetry on American." Nearly everyone who has written
about *Kora in Hell*—Williams, too, in the preface of the recent City

[16] *Kora in Hell,* 75, 59–60. On the importance of the senses, see Kandinsky,
Concerning the Spiritual in Art, 23n.; "Three Professional Studies," 36–39. "Professional," here, relates to both medicine and poetry. For Williams' theory of the
emotional basis of poetry and knowledge see "Notes from a Talk on Poetry,"
Poetry, XIV (July, 1919), 211–16.

Lights reprint, where he admits familiarity but denies influence—refers to the precedents, usually French, of prose poetry. Karl Shapiro, for example, lists *Aucassin and Nicolette,* Baudelaire's *Small Poems in Prose,* the *Illuminations*—and "the abortive prose experiments of Eliot." He might have added, with, I think, as little usefulness, Stuart Merrill's translations of French prose poems, *Pastels in Prose,* or the work that Williams might have seen in the literary magazines—that, say, of Jean de Bosschère, John Rodker, Rabindranath Tagore, and Sherwood Anderson. Judging from Williams' writing, none of this work contributed in an essential way to his book. Even the "official precedent," as Shapiro calls *Varie Poesie* (Venice, 1795), the work of Pietro Metastasio that Pound left behind, perhaps for Williams' edification, only suggested how, by drawing a line between prose elements, he might arrange them.[17]

A work, however, from whose experiments he might have benefitted but may not have known at this time, was Gertrude Stein's *Tender Buttons* (1914), which faced "the problem . . . of a thing existing in itself, of an absolute and absolutely present literary work." This cubist work was in the spirit of contemporary French painting, the new art Williams had already seen at the Armory Show and at the gallery of Alfred Stieglitz. As the "Prologue" to *Kora in Hell* with its references to Walter Arensberg and to such painters as Duchamp, Gleizes, Man Ray, and Demuth indicates, this was an influence to which Williams enthusiastically responded.[18]

[17] Pound's comment on "opacity," *The Letters of Ezra Pound,* 124, was printed by Williams in the "Prologue," where Taupin, *L'Influence du Symbolisme Français,* 284, picked it up. What Pound had in mind was probably a quality countervailing the sentimentalism of American verse, the "Soft mushy edges" he mentions in his *Letters,* 90. Marianne Moore thought Williams' "exactness" and the "crisp exterior" of his work were like the French. See her review of *Kora in Hell* in *Contact* (Summer, 1921), 5–8. Williams' own comment in *The Great American Novel,* 312, is: "It [this novel] is Joyce with a difference. The difference being greater opacity, less erudition, reduced power of perception." For Shapiro, see "The True Contemporary," James E. Miller, Jr., Karl Shapiro, and Bernice Slote, *Start With The Sun* (Lincoln, Neb., 1960), 218.
[18] Donald Sutherland, *Gertrude Stein: A Biography of Her Work* (New Haven, 1951), 100. According to Kenneth Rexroth, Stein and Arensberg were the pioneer

IV

Although Williams employs the method of automatic writing associated with the surrealists, his work is not surrealist because it exists primarily for the writing itself. What he does in *Kora in Hell* is well-characterized in Donald Sutherland's comment on Gertrude Stein's procedure: "Anything inside or outside that 'happens to come' is as it were waylaid by the consciousness of the writer, and just as it is, with the writer's feeling about it and his angle of vision, it forms a composition in itself." The daily effort is made not so much for purposes of psychological investigation as for compositional experiment—imaginative exercise. Williams is not interested, to use Kenneth Burke's words of adverse criticism, in "the usual modern data of mental tests"; much of what he uncovered by automatic writing is familiar to us from *Al Que Quiere!*, and he himself rejected the "pure nonsense." If, in one respect, the result of his year's work is a diary of the unconscious, in another and more important respect, it is a diary of the imagination (what Robert McAlmon called "a portrait of Williams' consciousness"). It might be thought of as a sketchbook of free but carefully composed drawings comprising a composite portrait of the author—a good likeness if we accept as an essential feature of Williams' modernist awareness the criticism by Wallace Stevens of *Al Que Quiere!* that Williams countered in the "Prologue": "To fidget with points of

---

literary cubists and *Others* was the most advanced modernist magazine. See "The Influence of French Poetry on American," *Assays* (Norfolk, Conn., 1961), 154–55. Williams acknowledges his debt to the cubists in "Tribute to the Painters," *Pictures from Brueghel and Other Poems* (Norfolk, Conn., 1962), 135–37, and to painters in the Preface to *Selected Essays*. Williams does not speak of Arensberg's poetry, from which I think he could have learned little, but of his "sumptuous studio" and of the famous painting by Duchamp that was a nucleus of Arensberg's great collection of modern art. See *20th Century Art,* the catalog of the Louise and Walter Arensberg Collection, The Art Institute of Chicago, 1949. He might also have found instruction in the new art in *Camera Work,* Stieglitz's magazine, which published Gertrude Stein.

view leads always to new beginnings and incessant new beginnings to sterility."[19]

The work is not prose poetry, not, at least, the usual kind whose effect depends on the heavy rhythms of poetry. Its rhythmic quality is achieved by using direct speech and the cadences and contours of the phrase (in a humorous Steinesque example: "When beldams dig clams their fat hams . . ."). The foundation of rhythm in speech is clearly visualized in the spaces between phrases that guide one's reading, a kind of punctuation and notation that may have been suggested by Pound, whose "In a Station of the Metro" first appeared in *Poetry* with three widely-spaced phrasal units to the line, a prefigurement perhaps of Williams' triadic line, and by the poetry of Mina Loy and Robert Alden Sanborn in *Others*. We take this prose for poetry, I think, because it makes us intensely aware of language rather than rhythm (as in Amy Lowell's "polyphonic prose"); it has the non-expository presentational directness that modern painting and poetry have taught us to prize. This is the "poetry" of the prose that, along with compositional design, establishes its existence as art; this is the "opacity," the solidity of language, that presents to eyes unaccustomed to seeing words for what they are, an impenetrable surface. Once seen, the work, though not always explicable, is intelligible.[20]

The book is composed of blocks of prose, not single words, which Williams said later were too much the object of attention of those influenced by the "disintegrationists," Joyce and Stein. He was more concerned with the synthetic than with the analytic phase of cubism (his prosody, for example, as Shapiro says, involves the "total

[19] See "Prologue," *Selected Essays,* 12, for Williams' awareness of a method adequate to the speed and freshness of the emotions; Sutherland, *Gertrude Stein,* 88; Burke, "Heaven's First Law," *Dial,* LXXII (February, 1922), 198; this method contributed to an unfavorable opacity according to Munson, *Destinations,* 110–11; *I Wanted to Write a Poem,* 27; "Prologue," *Selected Essays,* 11–13; McAlmon, "Concerning 'Kora in Hell,'" *Poetry,* XVIII (April, 1921), 57–58.

[20] *Kora in Hell,* 37; Pound, "In a Station of the Metro," *Poetry,* II (April, 1913), 12. Mina Loy is praised for "freshness of presentation, novelty, freedom, break with banality" in the "Prologue," *Selected Essays,* 7.

form"; his touchstone among cubist painters is Juan Gris). In speaking of *Kora in Hell* he recalled that the frontispiece, "an impressionistic view of the simultaneous" by Stuart Davis, "was, graphically, exactly what I was trying to do in words, put the Improvisations down as a unit on the page." In the larger format of the original edition—the largest and most impressive work he had yet published—one more readily appreciates the distinctive constructivist quality of the visible form.[21]

Williams' description of this form as following the "A.B.A. formula" and his example of it in *I Wanted to Write a Poem* do not adequately represent the complexity of the work. Variations on a form by Metastasio more accurately describes it. There are twenty-seven chapters (or sketches), each composed of at least three improvisations and one interpretation, the latter set in italics and divided from the former by a line. More than half of the sketches are original designs, and even those that repeat the number and the relation of parts vary in respect to the size of the parts and their functions. Some are very complex, Chapter Four, for example, which is composed of the following: Part One—an improvisation, an interpretation followed by an improvisation, and another interpretation; Part Two—a two-paragraph improvisation; and Part Three —an improvisation and interpretation (without a dividing line). Sometimes a coda is added, and seldom is the interpretation, which itself exemplifies the fact that the presented improvisation cannot be reduced to a statement, simply interpretative. The numbering of chapters and sections is an essential visual element, formalizing the work and giving it a tidy appearance. It is also, curiously, an intrinsic formal agency, for although sequences can be made out, the serial or absolute order of the numbers is not significant—or only to the extent that, failing to help us keep order, they indicate a new relative order, the order of the imagination.[22]

---

[21] *Selected Letters,* 131; Shapiro, *Start With The Sun,* 211–13; *I Wanted to Write a Poem,* 29: *Kora in Hell* was published by the Four Seas Company, Boston, 1920.

[22] *Selected Essays,* 26; *I Wanted to Write a Poem,* 28.

This seemingly decorous form—compare its quiet visual order to the visual disorder of Williams' later experiments—allows anything to enter the world of imagination. It supports Williams' contention that "a poem can be made of anything" if only the imagination lifts it "out of the ruck." Like the Stuart Davis frontispiece, it presents, in the very act of lifting, in a dance of the imagination, the common everyday objects of the artist's world. The Hell of *Kora in Hell* is simply this ordinary world untouched (unexplored) by the imagination, a ruck similar to the American environment of *The Great American Novel, Life Along the Passaic River,* and *Paterson,* a place from which Kora may be rescued and that world saved (discovered and emotionally enjoyed) by the poet's art. This is a major theme that the book propounds and demonstrates as it discloses the full range of themes developed in Williams' lifetime. Among these, for example, are the important themes of the dream of love, which seems to have possessed him at this time, and of the discovery of America, which he mythicizes here, somewhat after the fashion of "The Wanderer," in terms of American "presences." These themes, as well as their presentation, may be considered in Chapter Sixteen.[23]

In the first improvisation of this chapter, the poet meditates the writing of a "happy poem" and imagines, as an actual present living experience, a "bare, upstanding fellow" swimming a river and breaking through thickets in chase of "a white flash over against the oak stems!" The interpretation that follows succinctly states the "meaning" and mythicizes it: *The poet transforms himself into a satyr and goes in pursuit of a white skinned dryad. The gaiety of his mood full of lustihood, even so, turns back with a mocking jibe.* The poet has become a sort of Pan and the dryad he pursues but never possesses is Beautiful Thing, the Diana of his imagination, the Kora of this book, which the dissolute Jacob Lou-

---

[23] *Kora in Hell,* 65, 11; *Selected Letters,* 130ff. The dream of love is treated in "The Ideal Quarrel," "Prose About Love," and "Love Song," *Little Review,* V (December, 1918), 39–40, and VI [*sic*] (June, 1918), 5–11.

slinger of Chapter One had already glimpsed while "bumming around the meadows": "Meadow flower! ha, mallow! at last I have you." The satyr-poet begins to learn what Williams expressed at the end of his life in *Paterson V,* where the satyrs and their tragic dance are invoked, that "The dream/ is in pursuit."[24]

The second improvisation, the " 'fallen' Olympiad" whose importance to *Paterson* was first recognized by Vivienne Koch, works downward, into the present, against but with the help of the mythicizing activity of the previous interpretation:

> Giants in the dirt. The gods, the Greek gods, smothered in filth and ignorance. The race is scattered over the world. Where is its home? Find it if you've the genius. Here Hebe with a sick jaw and a cruel husband,—her mother left no place for a brain to grow. Herakles rowing boats on Berry's Creek! Zeus is a country doctor without a taste for coin jingling. Supper is of a bastard nectar   on rare nights   for they will come—the rare nights! The ground lifts and out sally the heroes of Sophocles, of Aeschylus. They go seeping down into our hearts, they rain upon us and in the bog they sink again down through the white roots, down—to a saloon back of the railroad switch where they have that girl, you know, the one that should have been Venus by the lust that's in her. They've got her down there among the railroad men. A crusade couldn't rescue her. Up to jail—or call it down to Limbo—the Chief of Police our Pluto. It's all of the gods, there's nothing else worth writing of. They are the same men they always were—but fallen. Do they dance now, they that danced beside Helicon? They dance much as they did then, only, few have an eye for it, through the dirt and fumes.

Flexibility, movement, control—all are evident in the writing of this brilliant passage. Williams thereby restrains his passion, so easily sentimentalized, for things Greek, and transforms this passion, both by the careful composition of the passage itself and by what is juxtaposed to it, into a passion for the local. The significant glosses on this passage are his criticism of Hellenism in his reply to Hilda

---

[24] There are echoes here of the poetic impulse of his earliest work, an imitation of Keats's *Endymion; Paterson,* 259.

Doolittle in the "Prologue," an early poem, "An After Song," in which the sudden splendor of Apollo seems "strange" to him "in the modern twilight," a response developed in one direction by Eliot, and the letter to Kay Boyle in which he says that "the classic lives now just as it did then—or not at all." This epistolary essay shows us the close connection between Williams' concern for the local and for formal invention and, in conjunction with the doctor's outburst in *A Dream of Love* ("There's something in our day, common to them [the Greeks], that we can't even talk about!"), helps us understand his lifelong quest for Beautiful Thing, the ultimate "presence," the perfect realization of place.[25]

Following the intense present thought of this improvisation is a passage of flat, straight-forward prose in the past tense. The common narrative style of this interpretation is easily recognized—the interpretation, in fact, is the anecdotal situation of a short story about the Venus of the improvisation and exemplifies one way in which a writer now might embody her presence. To this end the interpretation purposely demythicizes. But the weakminded girl with the lust in her is still, for those with "quick eyes," the *Juana la Loca,* the queen, the Beautiful Thing, to whom the poet earlier sings his song.[26]

The third improvisation, about Homer in a butcher's shop, presents the poet's antipathy to the misuse of the classics. He will go his own way, please himself, as he also announces in the "Prologue." He will do what he has just done. To Ezra Pound's admonitions, represented in the interior dialogue by "Reading shows, you say," he replies, "Yes, reading shows reading." Homer's individual talent did not suffer for want of tradition. The literature of the past, conformed to, used for its "associational or sentimental value," is a

[25] Koch, *William Carlos Williams,* 35. For Hebe, see *Paterson,* 168; for Zeus, see "Old Doc Rivers," *The Farmers' Daughters: The Collected Stories of William Carlos Williams* (New York, 1961), 77-105; "Prologue," *Selected Essays,* 9-11; *Collected Earlier Poems,* 22; *Selected Letters,* 130ff.; *A Dream of Love* in *Many Loves and Other Plays* (Norfolk, Conn., 1961), 218.   [26] *Kora in Hell,* 45-46.

"carcass" (the butcher's shop is a library) and, as the flip interpretation suggests, has only the stink of death.[27]

V

Only close attention of this kind serves a text of the richness and complexity of *Kora in Hell*. As might be expected, the poet continues to treat recent themes, the themes of emergence, anti-success, and the common and the low that figured so prominently in *Al Que Quiere!*. He is the fool of the opening improvisation: "Fools have big wombs. For the rest?—here is pennyroyal if one knows to use it. But time is only another liar, so go along the wall a little further: if blackberries prove   bitter   there'll   be   mushrooms, fairy-ring mushrooms, in the grass, sweetest of all fungi." Here the assertion of the fertility of the irrational is followed by the natural things, the improvisations themselves, his leaves of grass. Some, like the pennyroyal, may be used as carminatives; others, for their sweetness (the doctor-poet knows folk medicine—and the natural is itself tonic). Such a "fool" is Jacob Louslinger, who, like the poet of "Pastoral," rejects middle-class security and order ("I would rather feed pigs in Moonachie and chew calamus root") and has gone afield to be rewarded by beauty ("the great pink mallow stand-[ing] singly in the wet"). His physical descent, like Boone's in *In the American Grain,* is lateral, a matter of space and freedom from conformity; but release may be found, as the juxtapositions in the terminal paragraphs of this unit also indicate, by going downward,

---

[27] "Prologue," *Selected Essays,* 10, 11. There is nothing picturesque in Williams' sketchbook. His view recalls that of Horatio Greenough, who advocated "Greek principles, not Greek things." Williams' statement that "the 'Greek' is just as much in Preakness as it was in Athens" seems to echo Greenough's statement that "the men who have reduced locomotion to its simplest elements, in the trotting wagon . . . , are nearer Athens at this moment, etc. . . ." See *Selected Letters,* 130, and *Form and Function,* ed. H. A. Small (Berkeley and Los Angeles, 1947), 22.

through the surface of respectable tidiness to the dark disorder and vitality of things.[28]

This is the difficult poetic way Williams chooses, difficult because he must first overcome the "secret arrogance" of his own gentility. The conventional tunes that impede him in Chapter Two are associated with success, with the treetops (with the robin of "Ballet" whom he had implored to "come down"). Yet he himself is beset by *"jumping devils,"* the *"images which he has invented out of his mind,"* which work against his desire for success and invite him *"to rest and disport himself according to hidden reasons."* This conflict ("You think you can leap up from your gross caresses of these creatures and at a gesture fling it all off and step out in silver to my fingertips")—this conflict is resolved temporarily when the spirit of gentility, the "lady" of this book, abandons him:

> Hark! it is the music! Whence does it come? What! Out of the ground? Is it this that you have been preparing for me? Ha, good-bye . . . . —and I? must dance with the wind, make my own snow flakes, whistle a contrapuntal melody to my own fugue! Huzza then, this is the dance of the blue moss bank! Huzza then, this is the mazurka of the hollow log! Huzza then, this is the dance of rain in the cold trees.[29]

These examples, so tightly knit, sometimes dramatic and sometimes serial in their development, represent the structure of the book. They begin the enactment of its theme: that imagination and desire, the quickest energies of being, cannot be restrained, not even by the natural seasons, the conditioning circumstances of life. *"There is neither beginning nor end to the imagination,"* we learn in Chapter Three, *"but it delights in its own seasons reversing the usual order at will."* White-haired Jacob Louslinger pursues a

---

[28] *Collected Earlier Poems,* 121. It is possible to see in Jacob Louslinger a disguised Whitman, the bard whom respectable people considered a tramp. His search for beauty represents the kind of heroism Williams admired in Columbus and Boone.

[29] The spirit of these passages is intensely Whitmanian; they provide a condensed version of the opening sections of "Song of Myself." See Williams on Whitman in *I Wanted to Write a Poem,* 5.

flower ("age's lust loose!") and Amundsen, in the anecdote of
Chapter Three, runs off with the girl at supper—both instances of
the "violent refreshing of the idea" that Williams, in the "Prologue," says is necessary to "love and good writing. . . ." When
"wiser and older," he too—or rather the narrator of *The Great
American Novel*—runs off with Nettie Vogelman, another notation
of the incident treated in *A Dream of Love*. And now, in Chapter
Four, he promises to be wiser: "Mamselle Day, Mamselle Day, come
back again! Slip your clothes off!—the jingling of those little shell
ornaments so deftly fastened—! The streets are turning in their
covers. They smile with shut eyes. I have been twice to the moon
since supper but she has nothing to tell me. Mamselle come
back! I will be wiser this time."

This lovely passage is Williams' equivalent of Emerson's "Days."
In it, the poet relinquishes the genteel symbolist imagination of his
Keatsean youth for an imagination of naked everyday reality—an
imagination of great power ("the streets are turning in their covers"
links it with the comparable forces in "St. Francis Einstein of the
Daffodils") and an imagination of the new world (the shell ornaments may link it with Pocahontas or the Indian spirit of place). In
any case, day has fled—Kora is in Hell—because the poet has been
inattentive or looking elsewhere. But now, in a passage indebted to
the fifth section of Whitman's "Song of Myself," he possesses her:
"If one should catch me in this state! —wings would go at a
bargain. But ah to hold the world in the hand then— Here's a
brutal jumble. And if you move the stones, see the ants scurry. But
it's queen's eggs they take first, tax their jaws most. Burrow, burrow, burrow! there's sky that way too if the pit's deep enough—
so the stars tell us." By descending, touching, burrowing, attending
to the particular things in the "brutal jumble" of the world, the poet
uses the imagination to seize the day. For Kora is not captive to the
seasons (much of the book is autumnal) but only to the poetic self
that has not yet learned what the closing interpretation of the book
again affirms—that *"The true seasons blossom or wilt not in fixed*

order" but according to the imagination itself, by whose agency an autumn day may have *"perfect fullness"* and be *"its own summer."* [30]

VI

When Williams wrote *Kora in Hell* he was about the same age and at about the same stage in his career as Whitman in "Song of Myself." In Chapter Twelve, he records his awareness of radical change: "The browned trees are singing for my thirty-fourth birthday [September 17, 1917]. Leaves are beginning to fall upon the long grass. Their cold perfume raises the anticipation of sensational revolutions in my unsettled life. Violence has begotten peace, peace has fluttered away in agitation. A bewildered change has turned among the roots." This change, the emergence of the poet's authentic self, is what *Kora in Hell* signifies as a literary gesture. In this, and in other ways, it is, I think, the modern work most closely related to "Song of Myself."[31]

In *Kora in Hell,* the poet had the luck he mentions in Chapter Twenty-three, the *"luck that gets the mind turned inside out in a work of art"*; in it, he found a form for his *"phallus-like argument."* Marianne Moore was one of the few critics to read the book in the requisite psycho-biographical way and to appreciate it as the work of a profound poet. She described it well when she spoke later of the "pressure configured" in Williams' work. For this is what the

---

[30] *Selected Essays,* 20; *The Great American Novel,* 338. See also *Autobiography,* 289; for "St. Francis Einstein . . ." see *Collected Earlier Poems,* 379–80. The two passages cited were printed without interpretations in *Little Review,* where a third passage completed the unit: "Lullaby! Lulla-by! the world's pardon writ in letters six feet high! So sleep, baby, sleep!" The second passage suggests "Sub Terra" and this passage "The Shadow," the poem closely following it. *Little Review,* IV (January, 1918), 4.

[31] Robert McAlmon used Whitman as the measure of his extravagant but nonetheless significant judgment that *"Kora in Hell* is immeasurably the most important book of poetry that America has produced," "Concerning 'Kora in Hell,'" *Poetry,* XVIII (April, 1921), 58.

imagination of his literary gesture discloses—an urgent need for release and for the free yet ordered space of the imagination. He wishes, as he said later in *Spring and All,* "To enter a new world, and have there freedom of movement and newness." This accounts for his otherwise curious identification with the visionary Poe, as well as for his identification with Whitman—poets, according to Williams, who had "to come from under." But he also wishes to create a new world, a new reality complete in itself. In another section of *Spring and All,* where the argument includes Juan Gris and his own desire to overcome "the fragmentary nature of his understanding of his own life," he writes of Whitman: "Whitman's proposals are of the same piece with the modern trend toward imaginative understanding of life. The largeness which he interprets as his identity with the least and the greatest about him, his 'democracy' represents the vigor of his imaginative life." Here, I think, we begin to see one of the most significant ways in which Williams, a romantic formalist, appropriated Whitman.[32]

Of course the most apparent indebtedness to Whitman is the "Prologue," which originally introduced *Kora in Hell* and was chosen later to begin the *Selected Essays.* Williams wrote it after he had completed the composition of the book and first published it with a subtitle that announced the book's achievement: "The Return of the Sun." He used it, as Whitman had the 1855 Preface to *Leaves of Grass,* to survey the literary situation and proclaim the departure of his own literary work—the "defiance advancing from new free forms." Although different in style, the essay has a similar declarative force (it belongs with such deliverances as "Belly Music" and the editorials of *Contact*). In it, Williams provides a modern

[32] Moore, "Kora in Hell," *Contact* (Summer, 1921), 5–8; Moore, "Things Others Never Notice," *Poetry,* XLIV (May, 1934), 103; *Kora in Hell,* 56: *"The act is disclosed by the imagination of it"; Spring and All,* 68, 36; *In the American Grain* (New York, 1956), 213. Another aspect of his identification with Poe is his quest of Beautiful Thing; *Spring and All,* 38; *Selected Letters,* 40: Williams wanted to suggest the democracy of *Al Que Quiere!* by calling it "THE PLEASURES OF DEMOCRACY."

version of the imagination that complements the imagination of the modern in *Kora in Hell*.[33]

This is why he repudiates the work of Eliot and Pound, "men content with the connotations of their masters," and ridicules Edgar Jepson, the English critic who considered Prufrock, "a New World type." Not Prufrock, but Williams himself, the poet of these improvisations, is the New World type. For *Kora in Hell* shows that he has fully understood the liberation from all absolutes that constitutes the essential nature of modernism and that for him the New World man is the poet-discoverer who possesses an imagination of this new world.[34]

[33] For "defiance . . . forms," see Whitman, 1855 Preface to *Leaves of Grass;* Williams, "Belly Music," *Others,* V (July, 1919), 25–32.

[34] "Prologue," *Selected Essays,* 21–22. See Jepson, "The Western School," *Little Review,* V (September, 1918), 4–9.

The Wanderer and the Dance:
William Carlos Williams' Early Poetics

JOSEPH N. RIDDEL

I

The modern poet's task, Williams never ceased to remind himself, was "through metaphor to reconcile/ the people and the stones." (CLP, 7)[1] The obligation suggests at once a life-style and a metaphysical attitude, a theory of the word and a commitment to the world to which he is bound both in fact and language. "Be reconciled, poet, with your world, it is/ the only truth!" (P, 103) he would admonish himself and his peers in the very moment of making *Paterson* an act toward reconciliation in a world where "divorce" (hence dualism) was the "sign of knowledge." (P, 28)

[1] Quotations from Williams' writings used in this essay are from the following volumes, and will be noted subsequently in the text: KH—*Kora in Hell: Improvisations* (Boston, 1920); SA—*Spring and All* (Dijon, France, 1923); GAN—*The Great American Novel* (Paris, 1923); CLP—*The Collected Later Poems of William Carlos Williams* (New York, 1950); CEP—*The Collected Earlier Poems of William Carlos Williams* (New York, 1951); SE—*Selected Essays of William Carlos Williams* (New York, 1954); ELG—*"Essay on Leaves of Grass," Leaves of Grass, One Hundred Years After,* ed. with introduction by Milton Hindus (Stanford, 1955); IAG—*In the American Grain* (New York, 1956); SL—*Selected Letters of William Carlos Williams,* ed. with introduction by John C. Thirlwall (New York, 1957); IWWP—*I Wanted to Write a Poem,* reported and edited by Edith Heal (Boston, 1958); PB—*Pictures from Brueghel* (New York, 1962); P—*Paterson* (New York, 1963).

But the recurring insistence on reconciliation affirms only the presence of alienation, of divorce, and urges the poet into action. His poetic act toward reconciliation lives off the reality of its opposite, and takes that reality as subject. Poetry thus becomes, in Wallace Stevens' phrase, the "subject of the poem" at precisely the moment poetry and the poetic act are thrust into the epistemological and moral dilemma of self-conscious experience: when one has to "reply to Greek and Latin with the bare hands." (P, 10) And so it is fundamental to understand the exact nature of this "subject" for Williams—in which the most modern of themes, poetry-about-poetry, makes its appeal to both a futurist and a primitive poetics.

There has been some controversy among critics recently about the significance of Williams' famous pronunciamento "No ideas but in things." Its disarming simplicity has been subjected to almost every kind of negative scrutiny, or to virtually unqualified approval for its innocent wisdom. But despite weighty logical evidence to the contrary, it is difficult to disagree with Hillis Miller that Williams meant just what it says, and that in effect he lived, or at least wrote, by its prescription—that it implies in one succinct phrase a rejection of the whole dualist tradition of Romanticism.[2] In that gesture (or nostrum?) Williams rejects the kind of poetry (dialectical, meditative, subjectivist) characteristic of Romantic and most post-Romantic poetry, which in turn denies the modern self its last sustaining illusion, its self-creativity. Williams' affinities first with Imagism, and later with what he called Objectivism, evidence, as Miller says, a new departure in poetic experimentation, not unrelated to Pound's yet intrinsically different, and in turn evidences a distinct metaphysical attitude toward the self, its nature and essence, and the world where it acts out its being.

Miller's argument is in effect the first to put Williams' early experiments and their subsequent evolution into a viable philosophical perspective. With one major qualification, I think that perspective basic to understanding the radical shift that Williams *thought*

[2] *Poets of Reality* (Cambridge, Mass., 1965), 285–359.

he was making, and the more modest originality he did achieve. The thing which primarily distinguishes Williams from his modernist peers, Miller argues, is that he resolved the heritage of Romantic dualism at the beginning, not the end, of his career. His simple denial of the metaphysical separation of self and world, subject and object, which was dramatized in his metaphorical initiation in the "filthy Passaic" at the end of his early long poem, "The Wanderer," portended a new poetics and a new style because it gave birth to a new self. The young poet is reborn to the reality of his essential "degradation" and washed through with the "black and shrunken" (CEP, 11) reality of a fallen world; yet he is purified at least of history because all of history and its corruptions had flowed through him, allowing him to accept its reality because he could henceforth ignore its teleological myths.

It is wrong, I think, to object as James Breslin does that Miller's view of Williams' plunge into reality implies a total resolution (and reconciliation) of either the philosophical or experiential problem.[3] Breslin argues that Miller denies Williams that essential sense of self which relates the modern poet to Whitman. But it is Miller's distinction, not Breslin's, that accounts for Williams' early poetics,

---

[3] Breslin, "Williams and the Whitman Tradition," *Literary Criticism and Historical Understanding* (New York, 1967), 178–79. Breslin is so intent on showing the line from Whitman to Williams that he ignores the extensive reservations that run through Williams' numerous comments on Whitman in the former's prose. The essence of Williams' strictures is that Whitman began, correctly, by discovering his affinity with the random thingness of his world, but that he quickly moved to absorb the distinctiveness of reality into his ultimately reductive idea of Democracy. He became "preoccupied with the great ideas of his time" (ELG, 23)—meaning Emerson's ideas—and this led him indiscriminately to define human and creative freedom as absolute and divine. He "was taken up . . . with the abstract idea of freedom," and he "went wild" (SE, 339), leading to a poetics based on cosmic rhythms, and not on the measure of a finite self to his local ground. Williams is acutely aware that the "measure consonant with our time" (SE, 339) cannot be the measure of Whitman's time (let alone the measure of Whitman's "ideas"). The modern poetic self, realizing itself in a full-fledged walk in reality, could not so much celebrate the flow of things into the One as manifest the objectivity of a self realized in its acts toward its limited field of reality. And this is what Miller implies when he states that Williams began by ignoring the subject-object problem.

and explains the role of the novitiate in "The Wanderer." For the Muse who lures the young poet into the Passaic, in that poem's intensely subjective drama, cleanses him of his distressing egoism (and thus his illusion of the possibility of self-transcendence), and marries him to his world both as native and alien. She initiates him, to become a "wanderer" with him—to make him whole, that is, as poet in an unholy world. The initiation does not resolve the condition of wandering; on the contrary it creates the condition, just as Daniel Boone, in *In the American Grain,* becomes in his "descent to the ground of his desire" a "wanderer" for life. (IAG, 136, 139) It is on this point that Miller's reading of "The Wanderer" does tend to confuse the kind of reconciliation, through "resignation to existence" (SL, 147), the poem dramatizes. The sacrifice of ego is not a sacrifice of self, nor is it any comfortable resolution of the poet's essential alienation. It makes him whole within his incomplete world, as Williams says in a letter emphasized by Miller, because it binds him to the world's "despair": "a despair which made everything a unit and at the same time a part of myself." (SL, 147) It begins by stripping down the self, thus closing the distance between its aspirations and its possibilities, its visions and its reality, its language and its actions.

A "resignation to existence" does radically alter the ratio of self to world, and with it the role of language which constitutes any subjectivist relation of self to other. By reducing the dimensions of the poetic self, it delimits the reality of his poetic world to the possibilities of an increasingly impoverished language; and hence it forces a reorientation of his action. It forces him to redefine his language, to reassess it—in Williams' terms, he has to re-invent it, or simply to "invent" it. This in turn leads him to look outside his ego for the exact referents of that language, the reality without which there is no language and hence no self. The world "outside myself" is real, he affirms in *Paterson,* because it is "subject to my incursions" (P, 57), and I realize myself because it is there as a place in which I can act. All of this activity, of resignation as a denial of the egotistical sublime and ultimately of idealism itself, is manifest so obviously in Williams' poetry that it hardly needs commentary—except that its simplicity has tempted critics to ignore the relevance of it as both a poetic and a metaphysical strategy.

Resignation, then, is not exactly reconciliation, nor is it a sufficient resolution to the subject-object problem either to emancipate or subsume the self. The poet of "The Wanderer" assumes the role of the title, rather than escaping it, through resignation. One notes he is not a quester, with the deliberately self-fulfilling plan implied by that term, but a "wanderer" seeking to harmonize himself with the given, whatever it may be. He is ruled by contingency, by immediacy, and thus by the present ground where he wanders. He may dream of futures, or ideals, of Beauty and resolution in the perfected poem, but that only sustains his wandering. And therein lies the key of Williams' modernist poetics.

Paradoxically, Williams the Objectivist shared with his peers the need for a poetry to resolve the multiple schisms of his world. And though he never meditated on the "ultimate poem" or "supreme fiction" as did Stevens, or dabbled with the calculus of transcendent vision as did Crane, like each of them and almost every other notable modern poet he justified his writing of "lesser poems" (Stevens' phrase) in terms of an ideal that lay beyond them—the recovery of beauty, and value, in his special post-Romantic sense of those terms. He recognized, with that double consciousness to which the modern poet seems condemned, that it was precisely his inevitable failure to write a self-transcending poem that justified the reality of his continuing attempts. *Paterson* begins by admitting that it must seek the "sum" by "defective means" (P, 11), a condition that persists to the very end. "Waken from a dream, this dream of/ the whole poem" (P, 234), Dr. Paterson reminds himself in a passage near the end of Part Four, which directly precedes his rejection of the sea (and death) as "our home." The "whole poem," either the holistic poem or the poem purified of its contingency and rendered a perfect thing itself, is purified of life—like the ultimate unity of the sea, it is deathly. To pursue it is to pursue one's own negation. And yet, the poet of *Paterson V* can quote from one of Williams' interviews to the effect that "a poem is a complete little universe" which "expresses the whole life of the poet." (P, 261) The contradiction incorporates his unceasing commitment and its existential dimensions. This "universe" or the "whole life" of the poet is coherent, but unlike Whitman's, it is not cosmic or divine.

Without a vision of self-transcendence, without the possibility of the "whole poem" or ultimate epic, the poet has no identity in the traditional sense. And should he achieve it, he has no further role. To be reborn a "wanderer," then, is not only a necessary beginning for the modern poet, but his end, the only answer to his question: "How shall I be a mirror to this modernity?" (CEP, 3) The essential quality of Williams' alienation is that it is manifest as the obverse of the egocentric poet's. The self closes with the other; it wanders in the intimacy of a world which like itself is governed by change, growth, and decay. Neither the self nor nature has an essence, except in the necessity of their relationships. This is what Williams' "resignation to existence" implies: to act without hope, to discover rather than receive value, to make something in the world that will be nothing more than itself, and to reject nothing, not even the stench and rottenness that surrounds the "wanderer" in reality: "As a reward for this anonymity I feel as much a part of things as trees and stones. Heaven seems frankly impossible. . . . I have no particular hope save to repair, to rescue, to complete." (SL, 147)

To begin by rejecting the dualism of subject and object is not to deny the self. On the contrary, it affirms both the finite self and its finite imagination. The Muse of "The Wanderer" comes to the young poet bare but not barren, unadorned except by the scent of "sweat"—"Ominous, old, painted" (CEP, 5), both (grand)mother and crone. And though the young man "fell back sickened," he is destined to be the one in whom the Muse-crone of modernity will "give her age youth." (CEP, 5) Committing him to his world,

denying him the beauty of some possible transcendent world, the
Muse gives him the only security he can know within contingency.
She gives him a role; he can, and must, speak to and for "my
people" (CEP, 8)—as Williams will repeatedly do later, for example, in "Tract." He can, and must, speak from the immediate
ground, and thus must speak its language. He must be intimate
with the other—with nature, with pain, with poverty, with ugliness
and beauty, with both the city and the garden. Intimacy with the
world gives him the language of that immediate ground and ties his
vision to local and natural rhythms—the idiom of an immediate, a
spoken language, a language emerging from contact with a place
that is therein raised to expression (see SL, 286) only because it is
not raised beyond itself, or made to stand to a dream beyond itself.
And yet that expression, in the poem, will be itself a transcendence,
a "world" in its illusion of wholeness—a thing itself made of words
to set apposite to the world as it is, reflecting not only the ugly of
that world but the minimal beauty an imagination may find there
after it forfeits the dream of ideal Beauty, that ultimate
abstraction:

> Good christ what is
> a poet—if any
>   exists?
> a man
> whose words will
>   bite
>   their way
> home—being actual
> having the form
>   of motion (CEP, 68)

This passage should lay to rest two canards about Williams'
Imagist phase and even about what he came later to call Objectivism: that it is non-subjective and absolutely self-denying; and that it
precludes a discursive poetry. Objectivism, if that term is truly
relevant to any one of Williams' phases, does not imply a strictly

visual or a static poetry, does not "copy" nature as Williams himself repeatedly warned, but "imitates" her, a relationship of one to the other like a "dance." (see PB, 109) Like Imagism, to use the distinction May Sinclair used very early, Objectivism presents rather than represents.[4] And like Imagism, then, it was not concerned with imagery in and for itself, as decoration; the poem itself is the object, a "made" thing as Williams often said, and as a made thing it takes its life not by picturing the world but by recreating in its own order the living *structure* of that world: "Nature is the hint to composition not because it is familiar to us and therefore the terms we apply to it have a least common denominator quality which gives them currency. . . . It is not opposed to art but apposed to it." (SA, 50) Nature-in-the-poem, nature presented in words, the "form/ of motion," is nature as experienced by an imagination which found an intimacy with her, and hence some form of being intimately related to her in both a structural and a vital sense. The poet's words must "bite" home, must have the *form* of *motion*, a phrase veritably echoing Pound's vorticist metaphors.[5]

II

"A poem is a small (or large) machine made out of words" (CLP, 4), Williams remarked in an introduction to *The Wedge*, continuing: "When a man makes a poem, makes it, mind you, he takes words as he finds them interrelated about him and composes them —without distortion which would mar their exact significances— into an intense expression of his perceptions and ardors that they may constitute a revelation in the speech that he uses." (CLP, 5) The subject, that is, is discovered, not given; it is discovered in the

[4] Sinclair, "Two Notes," *Egoist,* II (June 1, 1915), 88–89. She virtually repeats the distinction, and elaborates at length, in an essay on H.D. nearly a decade later: "The Poems of H.D.," *Fortnightly Review,* n.s., CXXI (March, 1927), 329–45.

[5] For an excellent study of the non-visual, presentational implications of Pound's Imagist and Vorticist theories, see Herbert N. Schneidau, "Vorticism and the Career of Ezra Pound," *Modern Philology,* LXV (February, 1968), 214–27.

random matter of random and contingent experience. If the objects of the poem are not prescribed by theme, then the raw language is limited only to the accidents of experience. The "exact significance" of the words, however, lies both in the words themselves, as they are and have been used, as well as in the intensity of the immediate experience they embody. Their interrelations are the state in which the poet "finds them." But the poet "composes," and "makes," he "drives" the prose into a "perfect economy." If the poem represents nature, then, it is the "perfect economy" of nature—its "intrinsic form." (CLP, 4) This is motion as felt by a pre-reflective consciousness and *composed* into a "form/ of motion." Williams throws out the reality of cognition of one sort; thus the poem has no abstract theme. But he cannot throw out the self, the vital self, which can both live and generate order. The expression of the poem thereby discovers the "intrinsic form," but not necessarily the "form" of some experience that precedes the poem. The "intrinsic form," and more importantly, the "intimate form" of the poem's "formal invention" (CLP, 5), would seem to be realized in the moment of its making, in the composing of speech as opposed to the speech as found. It is at once eternal, the duration of a human experience, and transient.

The ontological relevance of the theory notwithstanding for the moment, one can see in this position how a Williams poem may include both discursive and non-discursive elements. Those rhetorical poems, like Pound's Image and Vortex exercises as well as parts of *Mauberley* and the *Cantos* written in the spirit of his early theories, objectify and define the dynamics of an emotion or a feeling that can perhaps be enacted in no other way so as to be carried over to another ego and thus made real in the world.[6] A

[6] One has only to recall at this point the relation of Williams' poetics to vitalist concepts of "energy," to appreciate his interest in Charles Olson's theory of "Projective Verse," a part of which appears in Williams' *Autobiography,* and especially to such a dynamic view of the poem as energy unit, taking place at the point of contact between the poet's body and his immediate world, espoused by Olson.

poem like "Tract" manifests the "form" of an e-motion, a manifest irritation with man's ceremonious attempts to divorce himself from his mortality, just as a poem like "Young Sycamore" manifests the dynamic motion (the "intrinsic form") of a thing of nature intimately sensed in its relation to a pre-reflective consciousness that, as Sartre says, becomes conscious of itself. That is, the tree as other is itself; the tree that is the poem is the tree-as-perceived, felt and defined in terms of a perceiver's intimate relation to it. The poem superimposes both pre-reflective and reflective consciousness. Both poems imply a self, an imagination (even though "Young Sycamore" does it minimally, in the barely revealed hand of the composer). They manifest the presence of a "wanderer," a finite imagination in the moment of discovering his intimacy with the other or his involvement in the basic ceremonies of social life. Reality, then, for Williams, tends to imply communication, and hence an absolute intersubjectivity, in that the poem as object carries over an act of being-in-the-world to another consciousness, binding the two in the "intimate form": "In the imagination, we are from henceforth (so long as you read) locked in the fraternal embrace, the classic caress of author and reader. We are one." (SA, 3-4)

Moreover, this attitude indicates Williams' ahistoricism. History for him is not a succession of temporal events, but the simultaneity of "expressed" or composed events. History is dynamic because like a poem it is recorded in things which have the "form/ of motion." Men *make* history by doing, by making contact, by making an impression upon the grain of their world, for good or for bad. And Williams' only measure of the good or bad appears to be whether their making was an end in itself, a discovery made to endure and thus made for others, a discovery with a future because it gives the present duration; or whether the discovery was made as a means toward some abstract future, an exploitation of landscape or language. Columbus or Père Sebastian Rasles in the first instance, Alexander Hamilton in the second—for the imprints they made *In the American Grain*. The made poem implies a dynamics, a motion, and hence a transference of energy into "form/ of motion." The "form" is Williams' duration, the "instrinsic form" of a man's relationship with his local, the "intimate form" of humanity recorded in art as opposed to the exploitative or abstractive forms of efficient institutions or *isms*.

It is this sense of history as objective expression, of men expressing themselves in a field of events, that helps explain the avantgarde neo-primitivism of his poetics. One of his favorite images for the poem is the "dance" (not, by the way, the Romantic Image, to use Frank Kermode's phrase, but not unrelated to it either). The dance is at once motion and form, objective, intimate, and situational, since its rhythms depend on intensely composed relations. "We are reminded that the origin of our verse was the dance—and even if it had not been the dance, the heart when it is stirred has its multiple beats." (ELG, 23) The primitive order of the dance is synonymous with the intuited order of pre-reflective consciousness, of realizing the self by relation. Anterior to consciousness, it takes place in a world of innocence, its form dictated not by a prescribed choreography but by improvisation stimulated by the response of the whole self to another or to a thing. When Williams thinks of a poetic predecessor for this mode, he thinks of Homer interestingly enough—not the Homer whom Yeats in "Cool Park and Ballylee, 1931" welcomed into the brotherhood of the "last romantics" or whom, in "Vacillation," he claimed to be like all poets of the western world, an heir of "original sin." On the contrary, Williams' Homer is like old Mrs. Williams, described by her son in the "Preface" of *Kora in Hell* as having an Edenic imagination. (KH, 10) Williams' Homer was figuratively the last, before Williams' "resignation," to see things anterior to ideas, to see that the shifting relation of things in a field of action is both that action and its idea or revealed order.

There is a certain shock of recognition in the letter Williams wrote to Louis Martz in 1951, in which he confessed to have found in the *Iliad* what he had spent a lifetime seeking: "I have been able to 'place' the new in its relation to the past much more accurately. We have been looking for too big, too spectacular a divergence from the old. The 'new measure' is much more particular, much more related to the *remote past* than I, for one, believed" (SL, 299—my italics). "If we are to understand our time," he wrote in "Asphodel, That Greeny Flower," "we must find the key to it,/ not in the eighteenth/ and nineteenth centuries,/ but in earlier, wilder/ and darker epochs . . ." (PB, 162) His wild, dark epoch, his "remote past," antedates history; it is the duration not simply of innocence, what Stevens called the "ignorant man," but of vital energy. But when projected into the dance, into the "form/ of motion" of the poem that manifests being-in-the-world, its event becomes objective as a moment of history, at once in time and transcending time, an "illumination in the environment to which it is native" yet living in "an intrinsic movement of its own to verify its authenticity." (CLP, 5) In the same passage, Williams anticipated that some might call this "pre-art." But in his terms, a living art could be nothing else, lest it be separated from life and made to serve some claim for the ideal. Hence his experimental poetry exists as a preparation of some possibly "pure" thing itself, though that possible purity itself is ultimately of little consequence except as the life-urge that keeps the "wanderer" in reality going. Williams' early poetry gives us the "wanderer" *in extremis:* that cycle of "despair," "defeat," and "reversal," a "sort of renewal" he would dramatize in *Paterson II* (pp. 95–97) and elsewhere as the lone solace for the poet's Sisyphusean commitment:

> But somehow a man must lift himself
> again—
>   again is the magic word.
>   turning the in out (P, 162)

III

Williams' early poetry is characterized mainly by sharply juxtaposed incongruities, among which the poet—often to his astonishment—discovers congruities of a uniquely vital kind. There is the familiar "Pastoral" (more than one poem bears this parodic title) in which the community of hopping and "quarreling" sparrows reminds the poet of his own isolation and its attendant guilt, while the old man walking in the gutter (like Wordsworth's "leechgatherer," so at one with his world that he is beyond time) contrasts with the formal austerity of the "Episcopal minister/ approaching the pulpit/ of a Sunday" morning. The intimate form of this arrangement emerges as an epiphany: "These things/ astonish me beyond words." (CEP, 124) But the poem is a dance of words, the "form/ of motion" that reveals not only life as it is, but the idea of the good in the intimacy of self and things. The good, quite clearly, rests in the harmony of relationships, in the old man's identity with the ground; while the bad, if one wishes to call it that, is reflected in the alienation of the minister from this ground, his detachment from people and things in a form that denies both the world and himself. The old man needs no language, not being divorced. He is, indeed, the language of the place, since the contours of his motion is the place: the modern pastoral. The poet's astonishment closes the distance between him and the world, creates an intimacy denied by the minister's austerity. The poem's idea in the form of its relationships and revelation.

The poet realizes his self in his discovery, which is an act directed toward his world and a composition of the intimate form of that discovery. It is the invented world of "Danse Russe" (CEP, 148), where in the space of his loneliness the poet creates himself, as the "happy genius of my household." The dance of invention is a composition of space, and hence of self, the grotesquerie of isolation resolved in the spontaneous act ordering itself into form. The dance brings his body into consciousness, merging consciousness and body in the "mirror," thereby closing the space of consciousness-body-room. This in turn projects consciousness outward into the space of his moral relationships, merging the dancer with his wife and child in the total space of his "household." The dance generates a space of intimacy, with the self as center, as "genius." The motion of the dance is spatialized in the "mirror," into the form of motion that is the poem. The dance is at once the poem and the making of the poem, the actor realizing himself in his act, creating a living form of relationships. It is natural, spontaneous, yet a made form. Reflecting some years afterward on the figure which decorated *Al Que Quiere!* (1917), his first significant book of poems, Williams remarked on the aptness of the "effect of the dancer," which he called "a natural, completely individual pattern." It had been copied from a design on a pebble, yet it was somewhat too formal to suit him: "too geometrical; it should have been irregular, as the pebble was." (IWWP, 18) The making of a reality implies the making of a form out of what is already naturally there, a movement of the subject toward the object, as in a spontaneous rather than a rehearsed dance.

What I want to suggest here, then, is that the dance (that central figure in those masterful late poems) is no suddenly achieved resolution of Williams' last phase, not the figure of a perfectly achieved art transcending and mocking life. It is the making or composing of a thing, a reality, in space—the poem as object in the very sense of the poem as subjectivity turned inside out, into the world. The poet dances not toward some end or self-transcendence, but against the end: "There is nothing sacred about literature," he wrote in the "Prologue" to *Kora in Hell,* "it is damned from one end to the other. There is nothing in literature but change and change is mockery." (KH, 16) Williams thus rejects the romantic dilemma which, setting art against life, came to put an intolerable burden of transcendence on the perfection of the poem, the purification of language into the silence of blank spaces.

Kora, as Williams later recognized, was his most problematic (and in some ways, most revealing) early volume, his language experiment. The polemics of the famous "Prologue" complemented the reclusive improvisations in the sense, as Williams later noted, of a public style complementing a private style. In the "Prologue" Williams sets forth, *vis-à-vis* his contemporaries, the gist of his poetics, an aggressive apology for modern poetry's betrayal of its own ground. The "Prologue" links with the text proper in the way that, for Williams, prose sets particulars into logical sequences while poetry recomposes them into natural and lived durations. But in *Kora,* perhaps because of Williams' uncertainties about working in subjective isolation, the distinction doesn't quite hold. In fact, the argument of the "Prologue" disintegrates under the pressures of its contention and melts into the improvisations, to return again refreshed and reassured that both, saying the same thing, have not only proved a point but moved toward the affirmation of a new language. This rhythm, of evanescence and clarity, disappearance and return, is consonant with the greater structure of the book, and the implications of the title.

This, in fact, is the theme of the improvisations proper—the poet, or rather his imagination (female as in "The Wanderer") is in hell (total subjectivity), condemned there until he retrieves the language which will free him through speech into a new community. Williams has described the occasion of the improvisations as his jottings over a long, distressing winter during which he felt isolated from his world as person and, especially, as poet. The improvisations, which were composed on divergent occasions, are related not sequentially but texturally. Their substance is language pure and simple—the evocation of pre-reflective consciousness and thus a world anterior to meaning. They define a space of loneliness on the verge of turning itself inside out. They configure an imagination ready to reassume the world and its welter: "all manner of things are thrown out of key so that it approaches the impossible to arrive at an understanding of anything. All is confusion, yet, it comes from a hidden desire for the dance, a lust of the imagination, a will to accord two instruments in a duet." (KH, 21) This is one of the original interludes, transplanted into the "Prologue." It is a prophecy of the return from the chaos of the isolated ego to the order of a lived situation. But first the poet must use language in and for itself, must get its feel as it is without the encrustations of historical meanings. And this means also that he must accept the risks of using it with even its primal meanings, its original thingness, obscured.

The "Prologue" begins digressively, but quickly comes to focus on Williams' mother, his ideal of imagination. Old Mrs. Williams lives in isolated moments of time, not in the chaotic flow of history. Her approach to each experience is fresh, unconditioned by any previous experience. "She might be living in Eden" (KH, 10), he remarks: ". . . seeing the thing itself without forethought or afterthought but with great intensity of perception, my mother loses her bearings or associates with some disreputable person or translates a dark mood. She is a creature of great imagination. I might say this is her sole remaining quality." (KH, 11) Williams contrasts her imagination with the historical self-consciousness of Eliot's poetry, and with that of Wallace Stevens. Stevens' imagination, he argues, coerces reality into its own subjectively "fixed point of view." In contradistinction, he offers his "field theory" of imagination; the self is only a part of the field of reality, not its center and source: "The imagination goes from one thing to another. Given many things of nearly totally divergent natures but possessing one-thousandth part of a quality in common, provided that be new, distinguished, the things belong in an imaginative category and not in a gross natural array." (KH, 16)

The imagination has no being, no location. It acts toward the world, and realizes itself there like a shape-giving energy—"a force, an electricity or a medium, a place. It is immaterial which: for whether it is the condition of a place or a dynamization its effect is the same: to free the world of fact from the impositions of 'art.'" (SA, 92) "Dynamization" is the key word. The imagination lives in the new situations it makes. Its "place" is the locus of Williams' dance: "One may write music and music but who will dance to it? The dance escapes but the music, the music—projects a dance over itself which the feet follow lazily if at all. So a dance is a thing in itself. It is the music that dances but if there are words then there

are two dancers, the words pirouetting with the music." (KH, 51)
At this point, the imagination lacks a defined world. The reality of
Kora is the energy of its rhythm, not its meaning. The self anterior
to its assuming the world is its celebration.

The time of *Kora* precedes time; these are improvisations which
progress neither rhetorically nor dialectically, but move like counterpoint in a temporal relation that denies linear time: "The trick of
the dance is in following now the words, *allegro,* now the contrary
beat of the glossy leg." (KH, 58) The movement of the dance, in
other words, creates and composes an action into a spatial order that
is its very opposite: "Between two contending forces there may at
all times arrive that moment when the stress is equal on both sides
so that with a great pushing a great stability results giving a picture
of perfect rest. And so it may be that once upon the way the end
drives back upon the beginning and a stoppage will occur." (KH,
35) The hope is that a tension being achieved, the imagination will
return to the world as purified of reflection as is Mrs. Williams.

This movement toward stasis at the center of motion, imaged in
the dance, is the poet's aspiration for the poem: "permanence, in the
drift of nonentity." (SA, 69) For this purpose the poet has descended into the silence, the inarticulateness, of things, to forage for
the language through which to constitute their true stability because
it can survive both history and process.[7] One improvisation alludes
to a poet who sang in a beautiful music to his audience "of gross
matters of the everyday world such as are never much hidden from

[7] Implied here is the theory of language's total immanence that would allow
Williams to move from Objectivism to the poetics of *Paterson*. Language is action,
and all actions are "now," what Olson means by telling it as it is. That language
which survives (as hieroglyphic, or Mayan artifacts, or in the official records of
Paterson) manifests a consciousness of a particular place and time. But, more
important, that consciousness was a part of the on-going consciousness (energy) that
is human reality. An imagination is manifest in a place, but the form it makes there
is permanent only in the sense that there would be no "place" without the act of
imagination. Thus history is on-going, but a recurrent manifestation of the inexhaustible human energy. The poem as a "form/ of motion" likewise manifests that
paradox, which Olson and his followers insist is no paradox at all, because the
imagination acts through finite minds even as it refutes particular egos.

the quick eye." (KH, 60) But the audience saw only the gross matters, failing to hear their music, the harmony of their relation raised to expression. The audience, in other words, divorced words and things, and fell back upon *a priori* association. Books like *Kora in Hell* were necessary not because they were fully achieved works of art, but because they were prologue to poetry. They were the language experiment that might make poetry possible, by breaking the language loose from history's distancing and returning it to intimacy, a subjectivity turned outward into events. As far as possible suspending language from its ordinary uses, Williams hoped if not to purify it, then to indicate the possibility of refreshing it, of finding its residual objectivity: ". . . of old poets would translate this hidden language into a kind of replica of the speech of the world with certain distinctions of rhyme and meter to show that it was not really that speech. Nowadays the elements of that language are set down as heard and the imagination of the listener and of the poet are left free to mingle in the dance." (KH, 63) Its life, one notes, is that it binds two selves in a communal field, the "dance."

Williams himself acknowledges *Kora's* relation to the French prose poem, but the analogy stands up only for a limited number of the improvisations and hardly at all for its structure which includes a number of more or less clarifying notes. The notes and "Prologue" reveal the condition of divorce that necessitate the trip to hell, but they likewise affirm what is discovered and the future rebirth. His descent implies a return not anticipated in a visionary poem. His art becomes a preparation for poetry, yet his act of discovering the language becomes in the end his chief use of it. It is not really a matter of purifying language, especially not in the symbolist sense of refining out the pure music from the impure rhetoric. Rather, this "hidden language" is the roots of an objectivity, tying self to world. As he would conclude in *Spring and All,* "According to my present theme the writer of imagination would attain closest to the conditions of music not when his words are disassociated from natural objects and specified meanings but when they are liberated from

the usual quality of that meaning by transposition into another medium, the imagination." (SA, 92) Though "hidden" it is and always
has been present in the "speech of the world," the enduring objectivity within the subjective changes. It is the language of natural
and human immanence, like that of Williams' mother, literally
Edenic, immediate and not mediate. But *Kora in Hell* is not so
much a book realizing that language as rehearsal of the poet's quest
for it. *Kora* is a process poem. The improvisations occur at the inner
edge of consciousness, in a nearly pure subjectivity, at the margin
between sound and silence across which the imagination flows and
returns. It is the language of isolation, an inwardness seeking to
turn itself inside out.

A few years later, in that multifaceted joke *The Great American
Novel,* Williams again put the dilemma in terms of his national
situation. The American novel, having no generic precedent, is a
form to be discovered, not repeated. Williams enjoys the pun on
"novel," a form that exists in its moment of discovery. The great
American novel, and Williams relishes the cliché, is by definition a
work *to be* realized. America is a metaphor, as well as the locale, for
what Stevens called the "imagination's new beginning," the always
undiscovered country the wanderer pursues. But as Williams
argued in *In the American Grain,* the problem with America,
especially Puritan America, is that it adopted a language rather
than evolved the language of place. In *Paterson* he quotes Pound to
the effect that "American poetry is a very easy subject to discuss for
the simple reason that it does not exist." (P, 167) The joke, however, is turned against Pound, against an internationalist poetics.
American poetry doesn't exist, not simply because, as Pound said,
poetry and language transcend particular places, but because American poetry is a poetry to be discovered. The making of poetry is the
subject of the poem; American poetry would be pre-art.

"If I make a word I make myself into a word," the narrator of
The Great American Novel discovers. He thus makes himself available, objectively, to others, and in that act makes contact, like the

doctor of the narrative reaching out to his patient. This reemergence from subjectivity, turning the self inside out, is the dominant metaphor of *Spring and All,* the ascent which complements the descent of *Kora in Hell:* "In the imagination, we are from henceforth (so long as you read) locked in the fraternal embrace, the classic caress of author and reader. We are one." (SA, 3–4) So long as you read—the conditional implies the intersubjectivity of reality, rejects the isolation of *Kora.* For as Williams was to remark later, in the descent of *Kora* he had become "romantic": "I was having ideas." (SL, 267) That is, the improvisations were written to the tune of a theory, not in response to an imaginative act toward the world.

Spring and All, best known today as a series of twenty-eight diverse poems without the improvisational interludes of the first edition, has been in its totality a most unfortunately neglected book. It remains a primary source for Williams' poetics, and for the new directions he fathered. Out of their original context the poems stand as well individually as in series. A few are among Williams' best known. But with the interludes, the structure of the whole must be seen to emerge from *Kora in Hell* and to complete the first stage of Williams' development. The book is a total poem, characterized like *Kora* by an apparently casual intermingling of prose and poetry, argument and instance, the dividing line between the two scarcely ever clear. Nor is it meant to be. For that is the poet's worry and the poem's life: to present the dynamics of nature's rebirth as it impinges upon the activity of a consciousness in the world directed toward the world.

The first poem, beginning "By the road to the contagious hospital," is preceded by a sequence of prose variations (some polemical and direct, others private jokes, still others verbal exercises) that incorporates what is in effect a language in the process of emergence. The poetic process is apposite to nature's—as random and as formal—and its reality is like nature's the field of achieved relations. There is, of course, as much sense as nonsense in the prose, and an occasional concise phrasing of theory, but on the whole the effect is to suspend the obvious literal discourse by way of suggesting a truer language within. The structure emphasizes that moment in which prose fact is energized into an "intrinsic form," when the eternal language emerges from beneath the surface to manifest the music of a plural world. Hence the inverted paragraph headings, the dislocating of time and number sequences, the pastiche of concepts which at once mean and do not mean, and the assault on those Williams calls "The Plagiarists of Tradition"—all a kind of embryonic language for an emerging world of vital things.

But *Spring and All* remains a talky book, and Williams at one point acknowledges its hybrid quality: "So, after this tedious diversion—whatever of dull you find among my work, put it down to criticism, not to poetry. You will not be mistaken—Who am I but my own critic? Surely in isolation one becomes a god—." (SA, 36) His problem remains self-consciousness, having ideas, thus the danger of making nature serve as metaphor for man's will to order. But even at the outset a poet like Williams, eschewing tradition, had to be both creator and critic; his major efforts not simply poems, but also advertisements for himself. And while isolation fed the appetite of pride, to remain in the security of one's own willfully made world betrayed the very option for "reality" that demanded the journey to hell and back. One of the interludes in *Spring and All* refers pretty clearly to the crisis posed by *Kora:*

> The Improvisations—coming at a time when I was trying to remain firm at great cost—I had recourse to the expedient of letting life go completely in order to live in the world of my choice.
> I let the imagination have its own way to see if it could save itself. Something very definite came of it. I found myself alleviated but most important I began there and then to revalue experience, to understand what I was at—
> The virtue of the improvisations is their placement in a world of new values—
> Their fault is their dislocation of sense, often complete.
> (SA, 43-44)

The commitment that sent him into isolation ("dislocation" is a precise phrase) becomes the force of his release back into community; it helps him to extend "understanding to the work of others and to other things." (SA, 44) *Spring and All* celebrates the struggle of return—from the opening protestation that he has no auditors, through the joking threats that the imagination will rise to destroy the world (and its traditionalists), to the much-anthologized opening poem. What follows is a dance of prose and poetry: of theory (prose) laboring toward clarification under the pressures of an emerging new form (poetry). The whole implies a merging of distinctions, a blurring of genre and all other artifice of formal division, into one organic, objective order of process. The poems themselves—from that slow, painful birth of natural objects forced into definition (born in an atmosphere and into a consciousness where birth and decay are both imminent and immanent), to the fully blooming, fully composed "Black eyed susan," the concluding verse—register some of the possibilities inherent in the discovery. The first evidences the birth of individual and discrete things (a fragmention); the last, a fully composed thing, the whole flower alive in its radiance of colors and elements centered upon the dominant eye: "rich/ in savagery." But the "black eyed susan" offers no transcendent unity—the whole is identified in the relation of its parts. In between, the poems evoke variously the shifting interdependence of the emerging plural world, charged into a new field by the imagination, itself made manifest in the wholeness of its field. Poem seven is a revealing example. It begins by exploring the rose (now "obsolete," as symbol one supposes), discovering in the minutiae of its parts the flower's true universality:

> The rose carried weight of love
> but love is at an end—of roses
>
> It is at the edge of the
> petal that love waits . . . (SA, 31)

In the midst of the conventional phrase—"love is at an end" in the modern world of divorce in the same sense that the symbolic rose of literature and religion has become "obsolete"—the poem discovers the actuality of love's being at an "end." For love is precisely at the "end" or the "edge" of the rose, where cleavage ends and unity begins. The geometry of converging lines points outward to cosmic interrelations, affirming the mathematical harmony of relativity. Hence the universal in the particular:

> From the petal's edge a line starts
> that being of steel
> infinitely fine, infinitely
> rigid penetrates
> the Milky Way . . . (SA, 32)

An apparent dualism proves a unity; words abstractly meaning one thing, the "end," are discovered in the concrete to mean the opposite. From the particular, the movement or process of two toward one in the petal, an idea springs out to join world and universe. Love as emotion or idea is manifest in a space of language, as it is in the space of things, the infinite immanent in the processes of the finite. Penetrating space, the "rose" manifests unity as it cleaves.

Such are the poems of *Spring and All,* delicately or bluntly exploring the world of discrete yet related things, casting them into a new structure or focus, peeling away to their latent language. The "ball game" poem, for example, dares to entertain the cliché that life is a game. (SA, 39–40) But it succeeds rather in capturing a moment of isolation in community, the structure of a crowd at one in a contest which manifests to each the anxiety of his isolation. Yet the crowd is a unified plurality; its being is its singular consciousness directed at the single field of action, at the uselessness of the game which nevertheless is the "intimate form" of life itself. Reinventing reality means taking things "recognizable as the things touched by the hands during the day" and looking at them "in some peculiar way—detached." (SA, 34) The field of the game, like the poem, is the focus of random human relations. Detachment need not preclude the poet's angle of vision—the emotional focus even of his rhetoric—for every object exists in relation to another, including the object of a seer's body and the perspective of his consciousness without which relation has no human quality. The "rose" poem and the "ball game" poem are neither a rose nor a ball game, nor a picture of a rose or a ball game. They are structures—words which relate to things dynamized by a present sensibility, or imagination. They stand not only as commentary on the nativist (and communal) ground from which they have emerged and to which they are apposite, but as objects themselves—without which a world of change could never be known in its "intrinsic form."

Williams called *Spring and All* his book of imagination, that force which has its existence only in the duration of things it "invents." The imagination brings the self fully into the world of people and things, and not simply as a private voyager nor as a voyeur, but as a necessary part of reality's immanence. Williams accomplished in his poetry what his peers had largely failed to do—to include other people in their worlds. To do this, however, he had to reassess the role of his own person among others, the new role of the poet in the poem. His main obstacle was the willed isolation of a romantic age, the subjectivism which manifested itself in what he called divorce. He could not conceive of the poet as hero or prophet, but only as the voice of a place. Ironically, the poetry Williams wrote between *Spring and All* and *Paterson* has been remembered not as Objectivist but as discursive arguments and at times tirades against a world of divorce. Several of those most cherished, like "Impromptu: The Suckers," on the execution of Sacco and Vanzetti, or the elegy on Lawrence, are those into which the poet has projected his own subjective rage, in which the field is "dynamized" by his anger and compassion and love. In a sense, all of Williams' protest poems, as well as those like "Tract" and "The Yachts" which derive their power from a rhetorical stance, are poems set against divorce—blasts at the "pimps of tradition," against "abstract justice," catching the pathos of the "pure products of America" who "go crazy" because they have lost their roots. Their purpose is not to alter the world, but to tell it as it is, as it involves him both as subject and object.

For Williams, seeking the language of his place is an experimental act of making contact with his ever new and eternal ground. It must begin with a sacrifice of ego, but only by way of finding one's self. *Spring and All,* like *In the American Grain,* evidences the dangers of Williams' commitment—for the poet has become in both so much at one with his world that his own person is very nearly absorbed by it. "So much depends" on red wheel-barrows, etc.—perhaps the self de-pends there too, but that can only be inferred. The dominating person of the poet is there in *Spring and All* only in the aggressive interludes; in the poems he has almost too successfully achieved that union with his world he aspires toward: "The inevitable flux of the seeing eye toward measuring itself by the world it inhabits can only result in . . . crushing humiliation unless the individual raise [himself] to some approximate co-extension with the universe." (SA, 26–27—I amend the original to make sense.) To lose oneself as subject is to gain oneself as object—being-in-the-world.

The key to Williams, however, lies not in the fact that he transcended his beginnings but that he came to recognize their inevitable commitment. *Paterson,* whatever else one says about it, is a poem premised on its own limitations. To recognize divorce is not to resolve it, but to explore the conditions that might make resolution possible. The recurring theme of "dissonance" as the prelude to discovery is central, and the original four-part poem ends not with the ideal grasped nor the perfect poem (which Dr. Paterson aspires toward, as he aspires to embrace the "beautiful thing") achieved.[8]

---

[8] A. Kingsley Weatherhead, in his *The Edge of the Image* (Seattle, 1968), 129–36, offers a valuable commentary on Williams' incomplete poem, a poem for this modernity.

Turning back from the sea, Mr. Paterson somersaults back into reality. Near the end of the fourth part of *Paterson,* the poet inserts a verse on the theme "Virtue,/ . . . is a complex reward in all/ languages, achieved slowly," and goes on to recount the "legend" on a porcelain ash-tray given him by a now-departed friend. *"La Vertue/ est toute dans l'effort"* (P, 220-21), the "legend" read. In a sense, that is the meaning of *Paterson,* of the poet's struggle—not to give his local its final expression but to participate in its only life, the on-going process of its expression.

So when Williams turned in Part Five to a theme not continuous with Parts One through Four, but one which subsumes the others in its overview, he finds art to be that which survives death—but only in the sense that it manifests simultaneously the ideal (the "intimate form") which man lusts for and the quest for it in the natural world that is the life of that world. Art surrounds the void of ego with a "field" that is objective, real—in it alone does the imagination have being, like the unicorn in the tapestry, and process have a form, like Pound's vortex. And yet, art's ideal is only art's dream, violated in the catching. No virgin without the whore: "—every married man carries in his head/ the beloved and sacred image/ of a virgin// whom he has whored." (P, 272) And preceding this, the key to the poem, I think: "The Unicorn roams the forest of all true lover's minds. They hunt it down." (P, 272) The ideal of Beauty (and reconciliation) may be man's passion, but to capture it he must kill it, like whoring his virgin. To this the poet is condemned. He is condemned to write new poems, not to live in the old ones: "The dream/ is in pursuit." (P, 259) He must ever take a new measure of things: thus the satyric (a pun?) dance with which the poem concludes and the faith that art alone endures because it has come out of the self's "walk in reality." As Williams admitted to Cid Corman, the search for the "measure" would never really end. (SE, 340) The life of poems was in the search: as in the dance, the measure between any two things changes as they change. And so Williams discovered his end in his beginning (as *Paterson* mocks

Eliot's *Four Quartets*), in the living reality of the poem as a thing vital like the dance: "there are always two,// yourself and the other,/ the point of your shoe setting the pace,/ if you break away and run/ the dance is over . . ." (PB, 32–33)

Murder in the Cathedral:
The Limits of Drama
and the Freedom of Vision

MURRAY KRIEGER

It is difficult to speak, except problematically, about T. S. Eliot's *Murder in the Cathedral*. And this is the way the play's most significant commentators of three decades have invariably spoken. For one thing, there is the problem of relating its power as a poem to be read to its power as a play to be performed. For another, not altogether unrelated to the first, we must reconcile its character as an enclosed, self-sufficient work with its extenuating relations to the works of Eliot which follow upon it. Obviously, one can claim with all writers the problematic relation of any single work to the total corpus; but the case is special with *Murder in the Cathedral*. I am thinking, of course, of the *Four Quartets* generally, but especially of *Burnt Norton,* since this fine poem—opening the way to the later *Quartets*—is so largely a gleaning of leftovers from the play. Thus we can expect from the two, not only mutually illuminating thematic returns, but elaborations within a pattern of a common imagery, again mutually explicative. It is conceivable also that the larger, less restrictive domain of the poem can provide the ground for a freeing of vision, trapped but struggling to the end, in the drama. And it may prove rewarding for our fullest understanding of the play for us to read that visionary freedom back into the limitations of the stricter form. For while it is true that Eliot took the demands of the stage rather lightly and was anxious not to permit them to impose upon his material, still the limits of drama make themselves felt.

All this is to turn our concern from these other problems to the single issue I intend to treat here, one that is thoroughly thematic, involving the cluster of paradoxes surrounding the claims of saint-hood and the claims of dramatic character in the play. I want to circle once more the range of crucially difficult questions that pose the charges of the Fourth Tempter and the Fourth Knight (charges which we are to reject as Becket does) against the unquestionably sympathetic presentation of Becket's claim to sainthood. I must try to move beyond the flat acknowledgment of the fact that the charges of wilful pride are never answered in drama or dialectic but are merely rejected out of hand, by postulation. Yet there is nothing ambiguous about the fact that the charges *are* rejected and Becket's claim to sainthood held as authentic. The problem of will and of resignation—of the possible rationalization that permits us to read the former as the latter—remains to haunt us after the reassurances of Becket and his play. This problem carries with it the generic problem of sainthood for man, the generic problem of the imitation of Christ for him who is less than Christ, who is the Son of Man only. And lurking just behind is the fear of the demonism that prompts the false claim to sainthood, the extremities now fronting for each other once the safety of life at the center, in the common routine, is forsaken.

If we are reassured by the daringly affirmative vision behind the play, can we accept it within the dramatic terms created *in* the play *as* the play? Or do we accept—indeed reach for—the vision despite the play and the evidence earned by its dramatic totality? What is at issue for me here is the strange intertwining within and beyond the play of the visions that have been my concern: First, in Becket's daring transcendence of the ethical, his confrontation of his more-than-moral risk of demonism, he seems to be leading us into what I have treated as the tragic vision. But secondly, the presence of the women of Canterbury as Chorus, the "small folk," "living and partly living," whose "pattern of fate" entwines them with Becket's fate, brings us beyond the tragic and its extremity to the classic vision. But finally, in Becket's pretentious claim to have crossed over, without final doubt or qualification, from the tragic to the religious, we have a Christian vision, the Christ story anew that overwhelms human tragedy. It is this vision—with the leap that is its enabling motion—that I have elsewhere denied the power of being "earned" dramatically, of having access to dramatic categories.[1] Nor do even the persuasions, the amazing transcendence, of *Murder in the Cathedral* lead me to a different conclusion here. Yet we must account for the power and seeming authenticity of this play.

To the extent, then, that *Murder in the Cathedral* is seen as both a reflection and an evasion of these three visions, it comes to be seen as either the outermost limit of each of them or the threshold to a transcendent union among them. It could lead us to recognize the inadequacy of our discursive demarcations, as we respond to a literary (and existential) experience that leads our categories to break down. Yet the play, by its very self-conscious evasiveness (and I must argue that Eliot has in mind something like the cross-paradoxical overcomings of what I have been calling the tragic, the classic, and the Christian), can help to make visionary definition possible, despite the fact that it forces us to question the value of such limited entities as we are trying to define, when a single great work can produce such a collapse of categories. This transcendent emergence out of vision and merger of visions thus can help us—eschatologically, as it were—to make our definitions of our limited visions just as the end of history can help to define all that history has been. All this is a great deal to ask of a single work, however ambitiously affirmative its thematic pretensions. Still, we must look into the firmness of its answers.

[1] In Krieger, *The Tragic Vision* (New York, 1960), 209–10, 260, 263–64.

I. Becket and the Limits of the Tragic Vision

The endlessly taunting problem of sainthood—how to choose martyrdom without its being a wilful and prideful choice—has an
emphasis here that retains the Kierkegaardian blurring of demon
and saint ("true knight of faith"). It is thus proper, if not inevitable, that Eliot chose this as the issue with which to beard the blind
arrogance of the modern secularism that must declare the saint
madly arrogant and sainthood impossible. Yet he freely gives skepticism its voice. I recall being shocked at my *not* feeling shocked
upon learning that Eliot had found an occasion to make the Fourth
Tempter's lines his own. Then I discovered there had been no
reason to be shocked, but rather smugly assured at the sense of the
rightness of his choosing that role for himself. Surely there was no
one whose lines I would have preferred Eliot to have assigned
himself. Of course, the Fourth Tempter is not just or right; but
where do we find the play *showing* him wrong? Here has from the
first been the central problem for audiences struggling thematically
with this work, and perhaps for Eliot as both orthodox writer and
critical witness of his own writing.

Clearly it is only the Fourth Temptation ("To do the right deed
for the wrong reason") to which Becket can feel any vulnerability.
The first three were expected and are easily dispensed with. Properly, the fourth is the only Tempter Becket had not expected. But
the Fourth Tempter claims always to precede expectation, to be
already known to Becket, and to tell Becket only what is already
known by him. For the prideful seeking of the saint's glory, so
claims this Tempter, has been steadily at work in Becket's unconscious, an unsought-for rationalization conditioning his decisions.
The Tempter mockingly urges him to carry forth his arrogant quest
consistently, in conscious and purposeful awareness of his sinful
objective.

> Seek the way of martyrdom, make yourself the lowest
> On earth, to be high in heaven.

The "to be" clearly has the force of "in order to be"—in order to be high in heaven—introducing the sense of conscious purpose in what has been proposed. Thus the very presumptuous action ("make yourself") has in it the wilfulness that must contradict its supposed intention—saintly lowliness.

How is Becket convincingly to refute such charges? It is not possible once one submits to the rational procedure that sets them in motion and gives them their force. Every self-justifying claim conceals the taunting wink that suggests a further bit of self-deception. How can one become a saint without willing to be one? When all acts appear to be willed, how does one maintain the will he is setting in motion is not his, but God's? that what he does is not a temporal means to a more-than-temporal end, but reflects a will and an act taken totally "out of time"? Of course, what the Tempter beckons him to is the seeking of martyrdom as an utter act of will, insisting there is no other way. Becket recognizes in the Tempter's words the echo of his own desires ("Who are you, tempting with my own desires?"), words and desires equally "dreams to damnation," "damnation in pride." The Tempters together end by seeing him in terms befitting what I have elsewhere termed the tragic existent, creature of Kierkegaardian despair who has desperately "willed to be himself":

> This man is obstinate, blind, intent
> On self-destruction,
> Passing from deception to deception,
> From grandeur to grandeur to final illusion,
> Lost in the wonder of his own greatness,
> The enemy of society, enemy of himself.

How closely these words foreshadow those of the Four Knights (false knights without faith) in Part Two, especially the Fourth Knight's crude verdict of Becket's death as "suicide while of Unsound Mind." The anti-ethical tendency of Becket's apparent obsession is indicated by pleas of Chorus, who entwine their fate with his:

> O Thomas Archbishop, save us, save us, save yourself that
> we may be saved;
> Destroy yourself and we are destroyed.

His next words show his obliviousness to their common desperation in his own drivenness: "Now is my way clear, now is the meaning plain." Of course, he (through his action) is to become their partial savior, as Christ was. But he here acknowledges the justness (from their point of view) of the harsher, skeptic's judgment:

> What yet remains to show you of my history
> Will seem to most of you at best futility,
> Senseless self-slaughter of a lunatic,
> Arrogant passion of a fanatic.

Nevertheless, from his own new and transcendent resolve, such a judgment, fit for the tragic visionary, has the limits of vision—and the consequent blindness—of the fallen, empirical, Manichaean world that spawns it. And the Interlude, together with the second part to which it leads, rejecting such a vision and such a judgment, projects and extends the higher vision and the higher judgment which it justifies and celebrates. If, tragic visionaries ourselves, we choose not to be convinced, we must accept as our alternative the lowly skeptical judgment that is reduced in stature and seriousness from the fearful, austere brilliance of the Fourth Tempter to the shabbily pragmatic superficiality of the Fourth Knight.

II. BECKET AND THE LIMITS OF
THE CLASSIC VISION

What for a while seems to be Becket's ethical failure of the Chorus, what seems to be his wilful and wayward consulting only of his sense of his private destiny, points to the awesome gap between the common, communal role and the extraordinary requirements of the individuated creature chosen to be separated from the herd. Thus the way of the little people of history and the way of the single great persons, each way with its appropriate blessings and curses. The gap between the "two ways" was Eliot's constant concern, with the special prerogatives and risks of the saint's way an inherited existentialist problem for modern tragic and Christian visionaries, most dramatically posed for them by Kierkegaard. Eliot's conservative institutional allegiances do not make him less radical in his exploration of the alternatives. They are most explicitly formulated in the well-known speeches of Harcourt-Reilly to Celia in *The Cocktail Party:*

> I can reconcile you to the human condition,
> The condition to which some who have gone as far as you
> Have succeeded in returning. They may remember
> The vision they have had, but they cease to regret it,
> Maintain themselves by the common routine,
> Learn to avoid excessive expectation,
> Become tolerant of themselves and others,
> Giving and taking, in the usual actions
> What there is to give and take. They do not repine;
> Are contented with the morning that separates
> And with the evening that brings together
> For casual talk before the fire
> Two people who know they do not understand each other,
> Breeding children whom they do not understand
> And who will never understand them. . . .
> It is a good life. Though you will not know how good
> Till you come to the end. But you will want nothing else,
> And the other life will be only like a book
> You have read once, and lost. In a world of lunacy,
> Violence, stupidity, greed . . . it is a good life. . . .
> There *is* another way, if you have the courage.
> The first I could describe in familiar terms
> Because you have seen it, as we all have seen it,
> Illustrated, more or less, in lives of those about us.
> The second is unknown, and so requires faith—
> The kind of faith that issues from despair.

> The destination cannot be described;
> You will know very little until you get there;
> You will journey blind. But the way leads towards possession
> Of what you have sought for in the wrong place.

Of course Celia, unable like others in the play to settle for "the common routine," ends, though absurdly, in a Christ-like martyrdom of her own, "crucified very near an ant-hill."

If the embracing of extremity, whether with demoniacal or saintly frenzy—the product of despair or of transcendent bliss—leads either into the tragic or beyond the tragic to the religious, so the homely retreat from extremity found in the uncomprehending simplicities of "the common routine" leads to what I term the classic. Instead of the imitation of Christ, undertaken in pride or in submission, there is the rejection of all that would distinguish one and his destiny from the common destiny of the race. The routine march of history is not to be disrupted, turned into a series of discontinuous crises, by untimely intrusions from a non-temporal order through a temporal agent. The piety induced by the single fact of Christ need not justify it as a precedent for the discomfort of further eschatalogical punctuations. The quietly routine continuity of history, even with its routine sufferings, provides the common comfort of expectations, for better or worse, being met.

> We do not wish anything to happen.
> Seven years we have lived quietly,
> Succeeded in avoiding notice,
> Living and partly living.
> There have been oppression and luxury,
> There has been minor injustice.
> Yet we have gone on living,
> Living and partly living.
> Sometimes the corn has failed us,
> Sometimes the harvest is good,
> One year is a year of rain,
> Another a year of dryness,
> One year the apples are abundant,

Another year the plums are lacking.
Yet we have gone on living,
Living and partly living.

So it has always been and, so far as the small folk of history can know or want, ought always to be. It is the unique act, the isolated intrusion upon history's universal sequence, that surpasses their understanding, coming as it does from "out of time."

But now a great fear is upon us, a fear not of one but of many,
A fear like birth and death, when we see birth and death alone
In a void apart. We
Are afraid in a fear which we cannot know, which we cannot
face, which none understands,
And our hearts are torn from us, our brains unskinned like the
layers of an onion, our selves are lost lost
In a final fear which none understands.

It is the fear of the separateness and alienation, and of the consequent loss of the clustered comforts shared by the historical human community. Their negative response to the imitator of Christ who threatens their continuity is suspiciously similar to that of Dostoevsky's Grand Inquisitor (and the people he protects and represents) to the return of Christ to history (in order to supersede history). So they reject the role of the exceptional man who tears at the fabric of history's common march, reject it for themselves and others, as they seek to keep that fabric whole and intact—and to cover themselves with it.

The play is a kind of Christmas oratorio, if the musical metaphor can be applied, though of course far more tentatively than in *Four Quartets*. In the oratorio Becket is the only truly solo voice. All the characters are members of groups except Becket. Even others who sing singly—Priests, Tempters, Knights—are one among colleagues. And there is the centrally classic voice of the Chorus of women of Canterbury. In this play in verse, the classic vision, through its passive endurance, its resistance to action and even to firm moral commitment, is really a choral vision. But the choral harmony usually sings sad songs, out of their historical adjustment to the periodic infliction of history's sorrows.[2] Still, their poetry constitutes the finest passages in the play. However authentic the resonance of their lines, the play cannot rest in them, must try to move beyond the communal emptiness of their sorrows.

The choral vision, for all its mutual security, feels itself utterly separated from God, even as Becket—in his persistent separateness from the Chorus and their destiny—can claim a union with God as an instrument in His cosmic harmony. But their human fears, as classic rather than tragic existents, lead them to choose their frightening separateness from God rather than to pay the price of separating any one of themselves from the human herd. But toward the end, just before Becket's reckless embracing of his fate, the Chorus fearfully acknowledges the religious consequences of their human togetherness: the fading away into nothingness of the mundane objects that bind communal life to itself. Deprived of the homely rewards of the community that has turned them from Becket in his chosen isolation, they now shrink from the awesome chasm that human consolations have created to keep them from the union with God available to God's lonely man, His saint.

> Emptiness, absence, separation from God;
> The horror of the effortless journey, to the empty land
> Which is no land, only emptiness, absence, the Void,
> Where those who were men can no longer turn the mind
> To distraction, delusion, escape into dream, pretence,
> Where the soul is no longer deceived, for there are no
>   objects, no tones,
> No colours, no forms to distract, to divert the soul
> From seeing itself, foully united forever, nothing with nothing,
> Not what we call death, but what beyond death is not death,
> We fear, we fear.

[2] I speak of sadness rather than despair inasmuch as the latter, at least since Kierkegaard, has been reserved for the singular extremity and intensity of the tragic rather than the routine resignation of the classic.

Thus sing the small folk, the uncommitted ones of history, in consequence of their smallness and lack of commitment. How do these passive souls relate themselves to those foul deeds which are part of history's routine march? History's continuity can flow only with the choral complicity that refuses to see such deeds as creating discontinuity, that allows human misdeeds to be subsumed within the sequence of the natural order. What, then, of guilt within the need of the classic existent to retain his catholic receptivity to whatever comes?

How can the problem of guilt exist for those who, like the Chorus, the small folk, can only look on, who—in their early words —"are forced to bear witness"? Here, at the start of the action, with the wasting and revitalizing routine calendar of autumn and winter threatened with disruption by the advent of another Christ, "For us, the poor, there is no action,/ But only to wait and to witness." Still, the repeated language of soiling and cleansing indicates how even the witnesses are forced to become morally involved, are involuntary participants. The natural order, which is the order of the calendar that makes up their common routine in its historical march, is itself morally indifferent, countenancing human ill and human good alike. And choral man, in his "humble and tarnished frame of existence," appears to cooperate with this natural order and its moral consequences by moving in response to each season, answering with his needs to its demands.

Yet human evil, the terror of the singular malevolent act that can shock man out of the complacency wrought by continuity, *is* embedded in the very historical march that tries to pass it by. It shrieks for a special awareness of itself as a discrete entity, provocative of discontinuity, shrieks for the moral judgment which choral man must try to resist.

> And war among men defiles this world, but death in the Lord renews it,
> And the world must be cleaned in the winter, or we shall have only
> A sour spring, a parched summer, an empty harvest.

Between Christmas and Easter what work shall be done?
The ploughman shall go out in March and turn the same earth
He has turned before, the bird shall sing the same song.
When the leaf is out on the tree, when the elder and may
Burst over the stream, and the air is clear and high,
And voices trill at windows, and children tumble in front of the door,
What work shall have been done, what wrong
Shall the bird's song cover, the green tree cover, what wrong
Shall the fresh earth cover? We wait, and the time is short
But waiting is long.

Man and nature (ploughman and bird) are here united in the other-than-moral circularity of eternal recurrence. But here, by the start of Part Two, man has an other-than-natural, a Christian consciousness as well. And he waits, must wait again, wait to witness, and as witness who is morally a part of it all. These lines have shown us, after all, that the major Christian moments (Christmas and Easter) do become superimposed—as transcendent interruptions—on the circular continuity of the uninterruptable seasonal calendar. Choral man must find himself moved beyond the natural, historical calendar to the Christian one with what I have called its eschatological punctuations. The natural cleansing of the winter may be reflected in the hopes of what began on Christmas; but the wrong covered by bird's song, green tree, and fresh earth—joyous signs of the new year—may have to remain uncovered and still-happening in the Christian consciousness as chronological time turns static. Not unlike the blood-sacrifice, the dismembering of the child quietly sanctioned by the "children of the sun" in Thomas Mann's *The Magic Mountain,* nor unlike the tear of another dismembered child that taunts Ivan Karamazov in his rebellion against the earthly paradise, here too the unique "wrong" can never be finally covered by "fresh earth" for man—not even for choral man who, by thus allowing his history to be arrested, moves toward the gap between himself and Becket, his next Christian saint. And this is to close the gap between the classic and the Christian visions by announcing the insufficiency of the former.

The human, then, must use its saints to respond more than naturally to the wrongs absorbed by the natural cycle, to force itself to the recognition that it too is "soiled" by each "new terror." Otherwise, in their natural uncommitment, the Chorus can see "the young man mutilated,/ The torn girl trembling" (further dismemberment) and still go on living,

> Living and partly living,
> Picking together the pieces,
> Gathering faggots at nightfall,
> Building a partial shelter,
> For sleeping, and eating and drinking and laughter.

History and their classic historical role bring them, as the willing witnesses (willing in their acquiescence in history's march in order to preserve the comforts of the common routine), to complicity in history's sins. The play traces their increasing awareness of this complicity, enabling them, just before the murder, to confess the moral implications of their passivity.

> I have smelt them, the death-bringers; now is too late
> For action, too soon for contrition.
> Nothing is possible but the shamed swoon
> Of those consenting to the last humiliation.
> I have consented, Lord Archbishop, have consented.

Having partaken empathically in the death-dealings of nature, both killer and victim, they *have* known "What was coming to be."

> What is woven on the loom of fate
> What is woven in the councils of princes
> Is woven also in our veins, our brains,
> Is woven like a pattern of living worms
> In the guts of the women of Canterbury.

Becket attempts to exonerate them in their own eyes ("These things had to come to you and you to accept them") and promises that after the deed ("When the figure of God's purpose is made complete") a "sudden, painful joy" shall lighten their return to their household routine. But the murder itself seems to lift them out of history and its common routine for good. All the world is incurably soiled with the complicity of a Lady Macbeth; the natural cleansing power of time's circle is abrogated; time indeed must have a stop: stop the world, I want to get off!

> How how can I ever return, to the soft quiet seasons?
> Night stay with us, stop sun, hold season, let the day not
>   come, let the spring not come.
> Can I look again at the day and its common things, and see
>   them all smeared with blood, through a curtain of
>   falling blood?
> We did not wish anything to happen.
> We understood the private catastrophe,
> The personal loss, the general misery,
> Living and partly living;
> The terror by night that ends in daily action,
> The terror by day that ends in sleep;
> But the talk in the market-place, the hand on the broom,
> The nighttime heaping of the ashes,
> The fuel laid on the fire at daybreak,
> These acts marked a limit to our suffering.
> Every horror had its definition,
> Every sorrow had a kind of end:
> In life there is not time to grieve long.
> But this, this is out of life, this is out of time,
> An instant eternity of evil and wrong.

Nevertheless, the play closes with the hallelujah chorus—though finally it is a modest hallelujah—addressed to God, and at the last to Christ and to Becket as newly risen. The promise of Becket is fulfilled as the small folk, those who try vainly to clean ("the scrubbers and sweepers of Canterbury") and to accept history ("the men and women who shut the door and sit by the fire") at once acknowledge their guilt, present and past, ask forgiveness together with the power to return to their role with its further guilts. Their commonness, and the limitation of role which it permits, still must prevent even the most momentary union with God or Christ or even Becket. But the polar relation to Becket with which we began has been significantly closed, although the gap that remains is all-important and the closure cannot proceed further. Hence the separateness and emptiness are not even momentarily dispelled; but Becket, as resurrected, has become their divine intercessor. Their final lines call upon God and Christ to have mercy and upon Becket to pray for them. The imitation of Christ has worked and leads to divine consequences, even if their effects on "the common man" are limited by his continuing role as common man.

What we have been witnessing is the attempt to lighten the classic through the religious without that classic losing its essentially choral, routine, circular pattern. The play has moved from distance between Chorus and Becket to closeness with some crucial distance retained, as Becket's function turns out to serve, not only *his* service of God's pattern, but the needs of the Chorus and their self-awareness. They begin with a dedication only to history's amoral pattern and a resistance to all disruption of it; they move to an awareness of guilt and then to a total assumption of guilt, as they forego history's pattern for the Christian pattern, the soothing passage of time for the apocalyptic stoppage of time; and they close with a most uncommonly justified and uncommonly self-aware return to the common routine, together with a dedication to both time-patterns at once. Becket is the agent of this reconciliation of the two patterns, his action "out of time" taken by this man of his time. The pattern of his agency and his saint's role before Christ and God establish him as intercessor for the common man as he adopts the pattern of the risen Christ, the archetypal saint. The doubleness within the divine-human paradox clearly marks the pagan inadequacies of choral man, patterned only by the natural community in its common routine. The historical absorption of extremity denies the exceptional because of the terror produced by its risks. The greatest of such risks is the demoniacal probability lurking beneath the impossible self-assignment of sainthood. This is the fear we have observed: that the Christian is the deceiving mask for the tragic. We must return to grapple with Becket's dismissal of such fear.

III. BECKET AND THE IMPROBABLE POSSIBILITY OF CHRISTIAN VISION

In almost his very first words in the play, Becket instructs the Priests and the women of Canterbury in the passive condition in which we discover the Chorus. He uses the metaphor of the wheel to characterize the circular time they aimlessly travel. This passage establishes the terms for the problematics of will in this play.

> They know and do not know, what it is to act or suffer.
> They know and do not know, that acting is suffering
> And suffering is action. Neither does the actor suffer
> Nor the patient act. But both are fixed
> In an eternal action, an eternal patience
> To which all must consent that it may be willed
> And which all must suffer that they may will it,
> That the pattern may subsist, for the pattern is the action
> And the suffering, that the wheel may turn and still
> Be forever still.

The Aristotelian opposition between action and the suffering of action, between actor (or agent) and patient, is central. This terminology gives Eliot the opportunity for effective puns on "suffering" and "patient" in characterizing the receptive passivity of the "small folk." As patients, those acted upon rather than acting, their only virtue is their capacity to be patient; they must suffer the acts visited upon them by history as they must suffer from them. Aristotelian patience, then, breeds the classic need for patience as Aristotelian suffering breeds the routinely accepted suffering of the classic existent. It was in this double sense that I referred earlier to the line, "These acts marked a limit to our suffering," suggesting the crucial function of the common events of good and ill in keeping suffering finite ("Every horror had its definition") and in making possible the small folk's acceptance (suffering) of all that they must endure (suffer). Aristotelian and human patience, then, becomes both the motive and the consequence of human suffering as it becomes the equivalent of Aristotelian suffering. How many dimensions of meaning are thus locked in the paradoxical notion that "acting is suffering / And suffering is action." In this enigmatic relation between the mover and the moved is found the further puzzle of movement itself and its relation to stillness, to pattern. In effect it is the puzzle of the divine scheme and its relation to the endless motions of human history as we are returned to the two kinds of calendars we have been concerned with, the serial and the Christian, which is to say the historical and the eschatological: "that the wheel may turn and still / Be forever still." These words send us to *Burnt Norton,* that repository of unused lines from the play, where there is an important elaboration of the wheel image and its indispensable metaphorizing of movement and un-movement.

At the still point of the turning world. Neither flesh nor fleshless;
Neither from nor towards; at the still point, there the dance is,
But neither arrest nor movement. And do not call it fixity,
Where past and future are gathered. Neither movement from nor towards,
Neither ascent nor decline. Except for the point, the still point,
There would be no dance, and there is only the dance.
I can only say, *there* we have been: but I cannot say where.
And I cannot say, how long, for that is to place it in time.

In all these words, in play and poem, is enclosed the problem of the will—the very determination of the possibility of will—of acting and/or suffering action (and suffering *from* action). To return to the passage in the play, the endless repetitive movement along the rim would seem to produce the suffering patient who neither knows nor wills his being turned on the wheel. We recall Becket's early words,

We do not know very much of the future
Except that from generation to generation

The same things happen again and again . . . .
. . . Only
The fool, fixed in his folly, may think
He can turn the wheel on which he turns.

Those on the rim, then, may know their historical role but not the significance of it, since that would call for meta-historical knowledge, a true knowing of the pattern, the dance—a knowledge reserved for the hub. So, by contrast to the passively turning world along the rim, the source of all movement at the hub is the sublime agent, the knowing, willing, turning agent. The hub, as both the still point and the source of movement, is not mere fixity but rather that which transforms movement into dance, transforms action and suffering into "the pattern" of action and suffering, agent and patient becoming "fixed / In an eternal action, an eternal patience" which can unite the suffering with the willing of the suffering. Thus we come to the role of the saint as the spoke to run between rim and hub and thus to reconcile the two times, to reconcile the endless movement among unmarked moments with the movement as pattern, as dance, as tied to the sublime stillness of the wheel's hub.

In terms of the distinction between hub and rim, it would appear that no one who is subject to human time along the rim can safely take on the risks of the agent: acting, knowing, willing, turning the wheel. For, far from stillness and the origin of the pattern that is dance, he is by definition the patient: suffering and, neither knowing nor willing, being turned on the wheel. It is in this sense that the small folk are correct in their assessment of their historical role and that Becket is correct in his words about them. And that central problem of sainthood with which we began finally concerns itself with the possibility of the *active* existence of that connecting rod, the spoke, between that timeless first cause at the hub and the endless chronological effects along the rim. These are the risks that Becket, or Eliot behind him, assumes when he rejects the tragic and the classic (or the demoniacal and the choral) as his only alternative ways of action and bids for the assurance and authenticity of the Christian.

The metaphor of the wheel would seem normally to leave two mutually exclusive ways of action: either on the one hand the abject resignation to fate of the small folk, which is in effect a surrender of will and of an individuated sense of special destiny (perhaps akin to Kierkegaard's "not willing to be oneself" or, less, "not willing to be a self") or, on the other hand, the attempt to create one's private fate, to turn the wheel, which is the arrogant celebration of will (perhaps akin to Kierkegaard's defiant "willing despairingly to be oneself"). Becket's movement from Part One through the Interlude of the Christmas sermon to Part Two, as well as what we have seen him do for the Chorus as he moves them to their *Te Deum,* is clearly intended to reflect his miraculous discovery of the third way, the synthesis of agent and patient: the losing of his will in the will of God and his new capacity to act (or to suffer action) safely, in accordance with what he has found as a consequence of what he has willingly lost. The blessed resignation to the turning wheel allows him to will to have it turn as it does. The radiance is upon him, the power of radiating from hub to rim, the divine-human intermediary for the Chorus: their saint.

How persuasive can Eliot make this miracle, without which our skepticism forces us to fall back once more to the fearsomeness of the tragic on the one hand or the selfless passivity of the classic on the other? The Fourth Tempter had urged Becket wilfully to turn the wheel, at one point transposing the circular imagery to thread and skein:

> You hold the skein: wind, Thomas, wind
> The thread of eternal life and death.

This call to prideful self-will, disdained by Becket, is echoed by contrast in lines we have looked at before in another connection: a different manipulation of the image expresses the selfless passivity with which the Chorus later feels its union with the common horrors of the historical process.

> What is woven on the loom of fate
> What is woven in the councils of princes
> Is woven also in our veins, our brains,
> Is woven like a pattern of living worms
> In the guts of the women of Canterbury.

How successful can Eliot be in assuring us that Becket neither does what the Tempter urges in the first of these passages nor shares the fated quality of the Chorus in the second?

Most of the assurances come from Becket himself, first in his response to the Fourth Tempter, more firmly in his Christmas sermon, and absolutely as he faces his death. The most explicit statement is, of course, the statement in prose, the flat assertion in the Christmas sermon, in which all the doubts of Part One have, at least in Becket, been dispelled.

> A Christian martyrdom is no accident. Saints are not made by accident. Still less is a Christian martyrdom the effect of a man's will to become a Saint, as a man by willing and contriving may become a ruler of men. . . . A martyrdom is never the design of man; for the true martyr is he who has become the instrument of God, who has lost his will in the will of God, not lost it but found it, for he has found freedom in submission to God. The martyr no longer desires anything for himself, not even the glory of martyrdom.

Eliot clearly has made good use of the date of Becket's murder, the closeness with which it followed upon Christmas. This allows him to emphasize Becket as saintly imitator of Christ. Of course, the Christmas sermon prepares us for Becket's Easter, thus allowing Eliot also to unite the moment of martyrdom with the moment and promise of birth: to unite Easter with Christmas, mourning with rejoicing, end with beginning, all within a divine plan that enfolds the one in the other. Yet can we feel totally secure, after Becket's words, above, when he concludes his sermon by confessing his own confidence that his own martyrdom may be at hand? "I have

spoken to you today . . . of the martyrs of the past . . . because . . .
I do not think I shall ever preach to you again; and because it is
possible that in a short time you may have yet another martyr . . ."

Once he is this confident that his will has been re-formed in
accordance with a higher destiny, Becket can act, in Part Two, in
ways that make him seem amazingly anxious for martyrdom. And
these too shake our security about his freedom from the prideful
pursuit of sainthood. The challenges he repeatedly flings at the
Knights may seem really too provocative. Thus, among his less
antagonistic responses,

> At whatsoever time you are ready to come,
> You will find me still more ready for martyrdom.

A bit later, as the Priests plead with him to retreat from the
Knights, who have returned armed for the kill,

> All my life they have been coming, these feet. All my life
> I have waited. Death will come only when I am worthy,
> And if I am worthy, there is no danger.
> I have therefore only to make perfect my will.

Or,

> No life here is sought for but mine,
> And I am not in danger: only near to death.

When the Priests ask about the consequences upon themselves
("What shall become of us, my Lord, if you are killed?"), Becket's
answer reveals a sublime, if maddeningly anti-ethical, indifference:

> That again is another theme
> To be developed and resolved in the pattern of time.

His ecstatic longing knows no bounds:

> I have had a tremor of bliss, a wink of heaven, a whisper,
> And I would no longer be denied; all things
> Proceed to a joyful consummation.

When the Priests, having barred the door, rejoice in their safety,
Becket's reaction, in words he admits they will find "reckless, des-

perate, mad," is that they "unbar the doors! throw open the doors!" For he has "only to conquer / Now, by suffering. This is the easier victory."

Can we help worrying that it is too easy? With the Fourth Tempter behind us and so exaggeratedly extreme a performance before us, can we help retaining some of our skepticism? But then, as if to show us how thoroughly we have allowed our fallen, secular selves to be tricked, Eliot puts on stage the *reductio* of that secular skepticism in the argument of the Knights, especially the Fourth. His coarseness and shallowness of mind and temperament are simply the extension of our own ironic attitude to the action. If we accept our reasonable doubts, we have to accept him. And we discover that this is precisely why he is addressing us this way, that between him and us there is also the wink of fellowship. But against his sophomoric rationalism there are only those firm assertions of the frenzied Archbishop, heaven-bent (or hell-bent?) for fellowship with Christ. ("His blood given to buy my life, / My blood given to pay for His death, / My death for His death.") Those assertions, as ungrounded in action or argument as they are in their appeal to miracle, leave us free to believe or not to believe, in which latter case we must accept fellowship with the Knights. Having allowed us our smugness of unbelief, Eliot now uses the Knights as a mirror for our shame.

The fact is that Eliot has reinforced the inspired Becket's confident assertions by the ways in which he has allowed his play to develop. There is an upward movement in Becket and the Chorus that confirms his victory, matched by a downward movement in the dignity of opposing arguments that damns the skeptical denial of that victory. Becket moves from doubts to the absolving of doubts to absolute certainty; similarly, the Chorus moves from total alienation from Becket to a partial identity of goals with him, so that they find a new relation to him and, through him, to God and Christ. Thus there is for the Chorus incompleteness even at the end, with the modesty of the choral vision never altogether abandoned; but there is considerable advance toward momentary union also, even if there is retreat as well. But for Becket the closure with heaven is absolute, even as the meaning of this closure for the Chorus remains relative. Meantime, the force of the skeptic's counter-argument weakens significantly as we move from the dignity, the poetic brilliance, the awesome Mephistophelian mockery of the Fourth Tempter's lines downward to the offensive prosaic vulgarity of the several Knights. The daring lines of the Fourth Tempter seem to have tempted Eliot himself to mouth them, while our embarrassment at the end is occasioned by the leering inference that we ought to be mouthing the lines of prose with the Knights. So Eliot has strategically ordered the progression of the opposed lines of possibility, fashioning them as a rhetorical support for the desperate claims of Becket which we are to accept.

Yet what convincer do we have, after all, besides the explicit and more subtle manipulations of rhetoric? Since it is all presumably a matter of faith, however, what more dare we possibly expect to have? Nevertheless, whatever Becket may or may not be in terms of the metaphor of the wheel, as acting patient or patient actor, he is after all—on stage and in this play—the central agent, carrying on before our eyes causes that have cataclysmic effects. And it is when we must judge him as dramatic character, basing that judgment upon dramatic evidence, upon what seems probable, that we find our hopes to share Becket's faith in his special destiny sorely tried. Becket (like Eliot behind him) well knows they will be, as he acknowledges again and again the privateness of his sense of his vindication, his private sense of the sureness with which he has evaded the traps of demoniacal temptations. He can give us no more certainty, can no more communicate the authenticity of his vision —in defense against the charge that it is a self-deceptive, corrupting illusion—than could Kierkegaard's Abraham who was ready to sacrifice Isaac.

No one is more aware than Becket (unless it is the Eliot behind him) of the difficulty, if not the impossibility, of his movement, and of the easy danger that it must be confounded with the wilful pursuit of martyrdom. In my own terms, this difficulty results from the skeptic's claim that only the tragic or demoniacal and the classic or choral are authentic visions, and that the would-be Christian is a self-deceptive version of the first. Eliot shows us his awareness of this difficulty throughout the play, from the persuasiveness—never reasonably dispensed with—of the Fourth Tempter to the *reductio* of the Knights. Theirs is the appropriate response of the secular, rational-empirical mind to the evidence. It is, after all, Eliot himself who indulges the irony of putting into the mouth of the Fourth Tempter, in his final speech to Becket, the very words on acting and suffering, actor and patient, that we have seen Becket begin by speaking about the Chorus ("You know and do not know . . ." etc.). It is a savage mockery reducing Becket to one of the small folk—the only kind there are—and reminding him that these words can also be used to justify the ways of human will: that acting wilfully is also a way of existing that humankind must suffer. For the Tempter hurls these words of Becket's back into his teeth in response to the still doubting Becket's desperate questions:

> Is there no way, in my soul's sickness,
> Does not lead to damnation in pride?
> I well know that these temptations
> Mean present vanity and future torment.
> Can sinful pride be driven out
> Only by more sinful? Can I neither act or suffer
> Without perdition?

The Tempter is shrewd to answer by echoing Becket's words, telling him to suffer his need to act pridefully, to suffer this much perdition while using the small folk's excuse that removes moral responsibility. Yet Becket is shortly to resolve these doubts, whether or not we join him.

"Can sinful pride be driven out / Only by more sinful?" Becket has asked. Such circularity suggests an infinite regress as the charge of self-deceptive rationalization confronts and is confronted by

Becket's ambitious postulation of the union of his will with God's. Each new claim of victory over the earthbound temptation is made only to face the leering face of doubt again. An earlier Tempter, suggesting the hidden nature of Becket's collaboration, has said, "a nod is as good as a wink." And the sense of the wink persists long after Becket achieves his certainty until it becomes the downright smirk of the Knights. Thus the possibility of a new rationalization lurks behind each unrationalized rationalization to challenge the possibility of sainthood. Only the irrational leap beyond the evidence of human drama can dissolve the last and lasting doubt.[3]

These dangers in our response, and in our proper response, Eliot well knows, as he knows that he has put the Fourth Tempter into the play and Becket's words into the Fourth Tempter's mouth, at his peril. It is his way of foreclosing our skepticism by openly providing the basis for it himself. The Fourth Tempter, after all, has foreseen our skeptical response as well as that of the Fourth Knight when, speaking cynically about the antimiraculous role of "historical fact" in future judgments, he warns Becket of the time

> When men shall declare that there was no mystery
> About this man who played a certain part in history.

Similarly, Eliot warns us by having Becket warn, first the Chorus and later the Priests, that they (and we) will not be able to distinguish, through what they (and we) see, between the behavior of Becket as incipient saint and the behavior of Becket as wilful demon, between his claim of acting outside time and the dramatic reality of his action as a part of history (the word that is brilliantly rhymed here with "mystery," its opposed force). That is, the actions

[3] In its way, this infinite regress is a reverse of the similarly maddening one in Thomas Mann's *Doctor Faustus,* in which the sinner's self-conscious awareness of the challenge made to God by his depraved unrepentance must compete endlessly with the everlastingness of God's goodness. (See my discussion of this infinite regress of diabolical competition in *The Tragic Vision,* 100–102.) Such an inversion of competitions between Leverkühn and Becket is appropriate to the difference in their intended pretensions; Leverkühn's Christ-like imitation of the Antichrist and Becket's Christ-like imitation of Christ.

of Becket are identical with what they would be if the Fourth
Tempter were correct. The worst sin, Becket has told us, is "to do
the right deed for the wrong reason." But how can reason show us
his reason to be right or wrong? We have already seen him tell the
Chorus, at the end of Part One,

> What yet remains to show you of my history
> Will seem to most of you at best futility,
> Senseless self-slaughter of a lunatic,
> Arrogant passion of a fanatic.

And I have remarked that later, in answer to the Priests' sensible
plea that he should not pursue death so perversely as to refuse to bar
the door, Becket is himself aware that he is removed from all
sensible argument.

> Unbar the door!
> You think me reckless, desperate and mad.
> You argue by results, as this world does,
> To settle if an act be good or bad.
> You defer to the fact.

Surely this is also addressed to the beholder of the spectacle, the
necessarily empiricist audience bound by the facts that pass before
it.

Eliot thus *is* our Fourth Tempter, as through Becket he insists
that nothing his drama can show us can remove our doubts about
this desperate mode of Christian affirmation. Yet if we retain our
doubts, we must suffer our fellowship with the Fourth Knight.
We cannot quarrel with the factual accuracy of the Fourth Knight's
claim that Becket "used every means of provocation; from his
conduct, step by step, there can be no inference except that he had
determined upon a death by martyrdom." But we are struck by the
doubleness revealed by the possible significance of these words.
Does the Knight really know all he is saying, or is he merely saying
all he knows?

What Eliot has shown us is that his work must fail (is *intended* to fail) dramatically in order to succeed theologically; and its success as poem can be realized still since it is a more-than-dramatic work, if not indeed an anti-drama. We know somehow that Becket's vision as authentic *does* take shape here, that Eliot *has* worked it, although we must await the completeness of *Four Quartets* to find that vision earned in a way that is not at war with itself. It can come to us in *Four Quartets* because, musical rather than dramatic, there is no action there to cultivate extremity and its ultimate dilemma, so that purely metaphorical resolutions of the paradoxes leave us less divided.

At war with the fact and what facts allow, Eliot presses the uncompromising, seemingly anti-ethical extremity of Becket at the end in order to urge the phenomenal identity between Becket and the self-slaughtering "lunatic." The play's facts cannot *show* that we have one rather than the other. Yet the final hallelujah of the Chorus proves that they have been moved beyond dull empiricism and that his moving of them is a major part of Becket's gift: it is what the saint, in his intrusion upon history, does to lighten its common routine. Having failed dramatically to demonstrate his miracle, Eliot has managed to produce it in us after all.

It is as if the end of the play finds us sitting on the frame of our picture, looking both ways and noting its limits. The meta-dramatic leap of faith that affirms Becket's saintliness reveals the limits of the narrowly aesthetic by reducing the play to the secular skepticism, the brute empiricism, behind the Aristotelian doctrine of probability. For we must, despite Aristotle, open ourselves to the improbable possibility, however it violates our aesthetic convictions. As Christian visionary, Eliot becomes a denier of his own drama, of what he has—with tactical shrewdness—shown us. He can do no better and no more, if we refuse to join the final Chorus, except to leave us the absurd negations in the Knights' reductions—although, alas, these are not without justification in the action. We can say, then, that while "The Mortal No" chronicled by Frederick Hoffman is sustained by the limiting structure of Eliot's drama, the meta-dramatic vision yet can see beyond to an everlasting yea. Dare we say that this visionary thrust occurs *because* of the drama and not in spite of it? that the miracle succeeds even as it fails? that we are persuaded of it even as our skepticism reduces it? I believe we must. I believe that negation has worked a strange and special magic: that here, at the fringes of what literature can allow, the play, by pretending to earn a most ambitious vision it cannot earn, has earned it after all.

Virginia Woolf's All Souls' Day:
The Omniscient Narrator in Mrs. Dalloway

J. HILLIS MILLER

Critics commonly emphasize, properly enough, the newness of Virginia Woolf's art. They have discussed her use of the so-called stream-of-consciousness technique, her dissolution of traditional limits of plot and character, her attention to minutiae of the mind and to apparently insignificant details of the external world, her pulverization of experience into a multitude of fragmentary particles, each without apparent connection to the others, her dissolution of the usual boundaries between mind and world.[1] Such characteristics connect her work to that of other twentieth-century writers who have exploded the conventional forms of fiction, from Conrad and Joyce to contemporary French "new novelists" like Nathalie Sarraute. It might also be well, however, to recognize the profound connections of Virginia Woolf's work with the native traditions of English fiction. Far from constituting a break with these traditions, her novels may be defined as the fulfillment of them. They explore further the implications of those conventions which Jane Austen, George Eliot, Trollope, and Thackeray exploited as the given conditions of their craft. Such conventions, it goes without saying, are

[1] See, for one example of this, the chapter on a passage in *To the Lighthouse* in Erich Auerbach's *Mimesis*.

elements of meaning. The most important themes of a given novel are likely to lie not in anything which is said abstractly, but in significances generated by the way in which the story is told.

The novel is a form of literature which is especially fitted to investigate not so much the depths of individual minds as the nuances of relationship between mind and mind. If this is so, then a given novelist's assumptions about the way one mind can be related to others will be a generative principle lying behind the form his novels take. From this perspective the question of narrative voice can be seen as a special case of the problem of relations between minds. The narrator too is a mind, a mind usually endowed with special access to other minds and with special powers for expressing what goes on there.

The manipulation of narrative voice in fiction is closely associated with that theme of human time or human history which seems naturally developed by the form of the novel. In many novels, the use of the past tense establishes the narrator as someone living after the events of the story have taken place, someone who knows all the past perfectly. The narrator tells the story in a present which moves forward toward the future by way of a recapitulation of the past. This retelling brings that past up to the present as a completed whole, or it moves toward such completion. This form of an incomplete circle—time moving toward a closure which will bring together past, present, and future as a perfected whole—is central to the novel.

Interpersonal relations as a fundamental theme, the use of an omniscient narrator who is a collective mind rising from the copresence of many individual minds, *oratio obliqua* as the means by which that narrator dwells within the mind of individual characters and registers what goes on there, temporality as a determining principle of theme and technique—these are, I have argued elsewhere,[2] among the most important elements of form in Victorian fiction. Just these elements are fundamental to Virginia Woolf's

[2] In Miller, *The Form of Victorian Fiction* (Notre Dame and London, 1968).

work too. It would be as true to say that she investigates implications of these earlier conventions of form as to say that she brings something new into fiction. This can be demonstrated especially well in *Mrs. Dalloway*, first published in 1925.

"Nothing exists outside us except a state of mind"[3]—this seemingly casual and somewhat inscrutable statement is reported from the thoughts of the solitary traveller in Peter Walsh's dream as he sits snoring on a bench in Regent's Park. The sentence provides an initial clue to the mode of existence of the narrator of *Mrs. Dalloway*. The narrator is that state of mind which exists outside the characters and of which they can never be directly aware. Though they are not aware of it, however, it is aware of them. This "state of mind" surrounds them, encloses them, pervades them, knows them from within, is present to them all at all the times and places of their lives. It gathers those times and places together in the moment. The narrator is that "something central which permeate[s]," the "something warm which [breaks] up surfaces" (46), a power of union and penetration which Clarissa Dalloway lacks. Or, to vary the metaphor, the narrator possesses the irresistible and subtle energy of the bell of St. Margaret's striking half-past eleven. Like St. Margaret's, the narrator "glides into the recesses of the heart and buries itself." It is "something alive which wants to confide itself, to disperse itself, to be, with a tremor of delight, at rest." (74) Expanding to enter into the inmost recesses of each heart, the narrator encloses all in a reconciling embrace.

Though the characters are not aware of this narrating presence, they are at every moment possessed and known, in a sense violated, by an invisible mind, a mind more powerful than their own. This mind registers with infinite delicacy their every thought and steals their every secret. The indirect discourse of this registration, in which

[3] Virginia Woolf, *Mrs. Dalloway* (New York, 1925), 85. Further texts from this novel will be cited from this edition and will be identified by page numbers in parentheses after each quotation.

the narrator reports in the past tense thoughts which once occurred in the present moments of the characters' minds, is the basic form of narration in *Mrs. Dalloway*. This disquieting mode of ventriloquism may be found on any page of the novel. Its distinguishing mark is the conventional, "he thought," or "she thought," which punctuates the narrative and reveals the presence of a strange one-way interpersonal relation. The extraordinary quality of this relation is hidden only because readers of fiction take it so much for granted. An example is the section of the novel describing Peter Walsh's walk from Clarissa's house toward Regent's Park: "Clarissa refused me, he thought. . . . like Clarissa herself, thought Peter Walsh . . . . It is Clarissa herself, he thought . . . . Still the future of civilisation lies, he thought . . . . The future lies in the hands of young men like that, he thought . . ." (74–76)—and so on, page after page. If the reader asks himself where he is placed as he reads any given page of *Mrs. Dalloway,* the answer, most often, is that he is plunged within an individual mind which is being understood from within by an ubiquitous, all-knowing mind, a mind which moves at ease from one limited mind to another and in fact knows them all at once, speaks for them all. This form of language generates the local texture of *Mrs. Dalloway*. Its sequential structure is made of the juxtaposition of longer or shorter blocks of narrative in which the narrator dwells first within Clarissa's mind, then enters Septimus Smith's, then his wife Rezia's, then Peter's, then Rezia's again, and so on.

The characters of *Mrs. Dalloway* are therefore in an odd way, though they do not know it, dependent on the narrator. The narrator has preserved their evanescent thoughts, sensations, mental images, and interior speech. He rescues these from time past and presents them in language to the reader. In another way, however, the narrator's mind is utterly dependent on the characters' minds. It could not exist without them. *Mrs. Dalloway* is almost entirely without passages of meditation or description which are exclusively in the narrator's private voice. The reader is rarely given the narrator's own thoughts or shown the way the world looks not through the eyes of a character, but through the narrator's private eyes. The sermon against "Proportion" and her formidable sister "Conversion" is one of the rare cases where the narrator speaks for his own view, or even for Virginia Woolf's own view, rather than by way of the mind of one of the characters. Even here, however, the narrator catches himself up and attributes some of his own judgment of Sir William Bradshaw to Rezia: "This lady too [Conversion] (Rezia Warren Smith divined it) had her dwelling in Sir William's heart." (151)

In *Mrs. Dalloway* nothing exists for the narrator which does not first exist in the mind of one of the characters, whether it be a thought or a thing. This is implied by those passages in which an external object—the mysterious royal motor-car in Bond Street, Peter Walsh's knife, the child who runs full tilt into Rezia Smith's legs, most elaborately the skywriting airplane—is used as a means of transition from the mind of one character to the mind of another. Such transitions seem to suggest that the solid existing things of the external world unify the minds of separate persons because, though each person is trapped in his own mind and has his own private responses to external objects, nevertheless these disparate minds are unified by the fact that you and I, he and she, can all have responses, however different they may be, to the same event, for example, an airplane skywriting. To this extent at least we all dwell in one world.

The deeper meaning of this motif in *Mrs. Dalloway,* however, may be less a recognition of our common dependence on a solidly existing external world than a revelation that things exist for the narrator only when they exist for the characters. The narrator sometimes moves without transition out of the mind of one character and into the mind of another, as in the fourth paragraph of the novel, in which the reader suddenly finds himself transported from Clarissa's mind into the mind of Scrope Purvis, a character who never appears again in the novel and who seems put in only to give the reader a view of Clarissa from the outside and perhaps to provide an initial demonstration of the fact that the narrator is by no means bound to a single mind. Though he is bound to no single mind, however, he is dependent for his existence on the minds of the characters. He can think, feel, see only as they thought, felt, and saw. Things exist for him, he exists for himself, only because the others once existed. Like the omniscient narrators of *Vanity Fair, Middlemarch,* or *The Last Chronicle of Barset,* the omniscient narrator of *Mrs. Dalloway* is a general consciousness or social mind which rises into existence out of the collective mental experience of the individual human beings in the story. The *Cogito* of the narrator of *Mrs. Dalloway* is, "They thought, therefore I am."

One implication of this relation between the narrator's mind and the characters' minds is the fact that, though for the most part the characters do not know it, the universal mind is part of their own minds, or rather their minds are part of it. If one descends deeply enough into any individual mind one reaches ultimately the general mind, that is, the mind of the narrator. (The narrator, it goes without saying, is not Virginia Woolf.) On the surface the relation between narrator and individual goes only one way. As in the case of those windows which may be seen through in a single direction, the character is transparent to the narrator, but the narrator is opaque to the character. In the depths of each individual mind, however, this one-way relationship becomes reciprocal. In the end it is no longer a relationship, but a union, an identity. Deep down, the general mind and the individual mind become one. Both are on the same side of the glass, and the glass vanishes.

If this is true for all individual minds in relation to the universal mind, then all individual minds are joined to one another far below the surface separateness, as in Matthew Arnold's image of coral islands which seem divided, but are unified in the depths. The most important evidence for this in *Mrs. Dalloway* is the fact that the same images of unity, of reconciliation, of communion well up spontaneously from the deep levels of the minds of all the major characters. One of the most pervasive of these images is that of a great enshadowing tree which is somehow personified, a great mother who binds all living things together in the manifold embrace of her leaves and branches. No man or woman is limited to himself, but each is joined to others by means of this tree, diffused like a mist among all the people and places he has encountered. Each man possesses a kind of immortality, in spite of the abrupt finality of death: ". . . did it not become consoling," muses Clarissa to herself as she walks toward Bond Street, "to believe that death ended absolutely? but that somehow in the streets of London, on the ebb and flow of things, here, there, she survived, Peter survived, lived in each other, she being part, she was positive, of the trees at home; of the house there, ugly, rambling all to bits and pieces as it was; part of people she had never met; being laid out like a mist between the people she knew best, who lifted her on their branches as she had seen the trees lift the mist, but it spread ever so far, her life, herself." (12; see also 231, 232) "A marvellous discovery indeed—" thinks Septimus Smith as he watches the skywriting airplane, "that the human voice in certain atmospheric conditions (for one must be scientific, above all scientific) can quicken trees into life! . . . But they beckoned; leaves were alive; trees were alive. And the leaves being connected by millions of fibres with his own body, there on the seat, fanned it up and down; when the branch stretched he, too, made that statement." (32) "But if he can conceive of her, then in some sort she exists," thinks the solitary traveller in Peter Walsh's dream, "and advancing down the path with his eyes upon sky and branches he rapidly endows them with womanhood; sees with amazement how grave they become; how majestically, as the breeze stirs them, they dispense with a dark flutter of the leaves charity, comprehension, absolution . . . . let me walk straight on to this great figure, who will, with a toss of her head, mount me on her streamers and let me blow to nothingness with the rest." (85–87) Even Lady Bruton, as she falls ponderously asleep after her luncheon meeting, feels "as if one's friends were attached to one's body, after lunching with them, by a thin thread." (170)

This notion of a union of each mind in its depths with all the other minds and with a universal, impersonal mind for which the narrator speaks is confirmed by those notations in *A Writer's Diary* in which, while writing *Mrs. Dalloway,* Virginia Woolf speaks of her "great discovery," what she calls her "tunnelling process,"[4] that method whereby, as she says, "I dig out beautiful caves behind my characters: I think that gives exactly what I want; humanity, humour, depth. The idea is that the caves shall connect." (WD, 60)

Deep below the surface, in some dark and remote cave of the spirit, my mind connects with all the other minds, in a vast cavern where all the tunnels end. Peter Walsh's version of the image of the maternal tree ends nevertheless with an ominous note. To reach the great figure is to be blown to nothingness with the rest. This happens because union with the general mind is incompatible with the distinctions, the limitations, the definite edges and outlines, one thing here, another thing there, of daylight consciousness. The realm of union is a region of dispersion, of darkness, of indistinction, sleep, and death. The fear or attraction of the annihilating fall into nothingness echoes through *Mrs. Dalloway.* The novel seems to be based on an irreconcilable opposition between individuality and universality. By reason of his existence as a conscious human being, each man or woman is alienated from the whole of which he is actually, though unwittingly or at best half-consciously, a part. That half-consciousness, however, gives him a sense of incompletion. He yearns to be joined in one way or another to the whole from which he is separated by the conditions of his existence as a person.

One way to achieve this wholeness might be to build up toward some completeness in the daylight world, rather than to sink down into the dark world of death. "What a lark! What a plunge!"

[4] *A Writer's Diary,* ed. Leonard Woolf (London, 1953), 61. Henceforth this book will be cited as WD.

(3)—the beginning of the third paragraph of *Mrs. Dalloway* contains in miniature the two contrary movements of the novel. If the fall into death is one pole of the novel, fulfilled in Septimus Smith's suicidal plunge, the other pole is the rising motion of "building it up," of constructive action in the moment, fulfilled in Clarissa Dalloway's party. Turning away from the obscure depths within them, the characters may, like Clarissa, embrace the moment with elation and attempt to gather everything together in a diamond point of brightness: "For Heaven only knows why one loves it so, how one sees it so, making it up, building it round one, tumbling it, creating it every moment afresh . . ."; "what she loved was this, here, now, in front of her"; "Clarissa . . . plunged into the very heart of the moment, transfixed it, there—the moment of this June morning on which was the pressure of all the other mornings, . . . collecting the whole of her at one point." (5, 12, 54) In the same way, Peter Walsh, after his sleep on a park bench feels, "Life itself, every moment of it, every drop of it, here, this instant, now, in the sun, in Regent's Park, was enough." (119, 120) (This echoing from Clarissa to Peter, it is worth noting, is proof that Clarissa is right to think that they "live in each other.")

"The pressure of all the other mornings"—one way the characters in *Mrs. Dalloway* achieve continuity and wholeness is through the ease with which images from their pasts rise within them to overwhelm them with a sense of immediate presence. If the characters of the novel live according to an abrupt, discontinuous, nervous (one might say, feminine) rhythm, rising one moment to heights of ecstasy only to be dropped again in sudden terror or despondency, nevertheless their experience is marked by profound continuities.

The remarkably immediate access the characters have to their pasts is one such continuity. In one sense the moment is all that is real. Life in the present instant is a narrow plank reaching over the abyss of death between the nothingness of past and future. Near the end of the novel Clarissa thinks of "the terror; the overwhelming incapacity, one's parents giving it into one's hands, this life, to be lived to the end, to be walked with serenely; there was in the depths of her heart an awful fear." (281) In another sense, however, the weight of all the past moments presses just beneath the surface of the present, ready in an instant to flow into consciousness, overwhelming it with the immediate presence of the past. Nothing could be less like the intermittencies and difficulties of memory in Wordsworth or in Proust than the spontaneity and ease of memory in *Mrs. Dalloway*. Again and again during the day of the novel's action the reader finds himself within the mind of a character who has been suddenly invaded and engulfed by a memory so vivid that it displaces altogether the real present of the novel and becomes the virtual present of the reader's experience. So fluid are the boundaries between past and present that the reader sometimes has great difficulty knowing whether he is encountering an image from the character's past or something part of the character's immediate experience.

An example of this occurs in the opening paragraphs of the novel. *Mrs. Dalloway* begins in the middle of things with the report of something Clarissa says just before she leaves her home in Westminster to walk to the florist on Bond Street: "Mrs. Dalloway said she would buy the flowers herself." (3) A few sentences later, after a description of Clarissa's recognition that it is a fine day and just following the first instance of the motif of terror combined with ecstasy ("What a lark! What a plunge!"), the reader is "plunged" within the closeness of an experience which seems to be part of the present, for he is as yet ignorant of the place-names in the novel or of their relation to the times of Clarissa's life. Actually, however, the experience is from Clarissa's adolescence: "For so it had always seemed to her, when, with a little squeak of the hinges, which she could hear now, she had burst open the French windows and plunged at Bourton into the open air." (3)

The word "plunge," reiterated here, expresses a pregnant ambiguity. If a "lark" and a "plunge" seem at first almost the same thing, rising and falling versions of the same leap of ecstasy, and if Clarissa's plunge into the open air when she bursts open the windows at Bourton seems to confirm this identity, the reader may remember this opening page much later when Septimus leaps from a window to his death. Clarissa, hearing at her party of his suicide, confirms this connection by asking herself, "But this young man who had killed himself—had he plunged holding his treasure?" (281) If *Mrs. Dalloway* is organized around the contrary poles of rising and falling, these motions are not only opposites, but are also ambiguously similar. They change places bewilderingly, so that down and up, falling and rising, death and life, isolation and communication, are mirror images of one another rather than simply a confrontation of negative and positive penchants of the spirit. Clarissa's plunge into the open air is an embrace of life and its richness, promise, and immediacy, but it is, by the time the reader encounters it, already an image from the dead past. Moreover, it anticipates Septimus' plunge into annihilation. It is followed in Clarissa's memory of it by her memory also that when she stood at the open window she felt "that something awful was about to happen." (3) One is not surprised to find that in this novel, which is made up of a stream of subtle variations on a few themes, one of the things Clarissa sees from the window at Bourton is "the rooks rising, falling." (3)

The temporal placement of Clarissa's experience at Bourton is equally ambiguous. The "now" of the sentence describing Clarissa's plunge ("with a little squeak of the hinges, which she could hear now"), is the narrator's memory of Clarissa's memory of her childhood home brought back so vividly into her mind that it becomes the present of her experience and of the reader's experience. The sentence opens the door to a flood of memories which brings that faraway time back to her as a present with the complexity and fullness of immediate experience.

These memories are not, however, simply present. The ambiguity of the temporal location of this past time derives from the narrator's use of the past tense which is conventional in fiction and one of the

aspects of the novel which Virginia Woolf carries on unchanged
from her eighteenth and nineteenth-century predecessors. The first
sentence of the novel ("Mrs. Dalloway said she would buy the
flowers herself."), establishes a temporal distance between the narrator's present and the present of the characters. Everything that the
characters do or think is placed firmly in an indefinite past as
something which has always already happened when the reader
encounters it. These events are resurrected from the past by the
language of the narration and placed before the present moment of
the reader's experience as something bearing the ineradicable mark
of their pastness. When the characters, within this general pastness
of the narration, remember something from their own pasts, and
when the narrator reports this in that indirect discourse which is
another convention of *Mrs. Dalloway,* he has no other way to place
it in the past than some version of the past tense which he has
already been using for the "present" of the characters' experience:
"How fresh, how calm, stiller than this of course, the air was in the
early morning." (3)

The sentence before this one contains the "had" of the past
perfect which places it in a past behind that past which is the
"present" of the novel, the day of Clarissa's party, but still Clarissa
can hear the squeak of the hinges "now," and the reader is led to
believe that she may be comparing an earlier time of opening the
windows with a present repetition of that action. The following
sentence is in the simple past ("the air was"), and yet it belongs not
to the present of the narration, but to the past of Clarissa's girlhood.
What has happened to justify this change is one of those subtle
dislocations within the narration which are characteristic of *oratio
obliqua* as a mode of language. Indirect discourse always remains a
relationship between two distinguishable minds, but the nuances of
this relationship may change, with corresponding changes in the
way it is registered in words. "For so it had always seemed to
her"—here the little word "had" establishes three identifiable times:
the no-time or time-out-of-time-for-which-all-times-are-past of the

narrator; the time of the single day of the novel's action; and the time of Clarissa's youth. The narrator distinguishes himself both temporally and, if one may say so, "spatially," from Clarissa and reports her thoughts from the outside in a tense which she would not herself use in the "now" of her experience. In the next sentence these distances between the narrator and Clarissa disappear. Though the text is still in indirect discourse in the sense that the narrator speaks for the character, the language used is much more nearly identical with what Clarissa might herself have said, and the tense is the one she would use: "How fresh, how calm, stiller than this of course, the air was in the early morning." The "was" here is the sign of a relative identity between narrator's mind and character's mind. From the point of view he momentarily adopts, Clarissa's youth is at the same distance from him as it is from Clarissa, and the reader is left with no linguistic clue, except the "stiller than this of course," permitting him to tell whether the "was" refers to the present of the narration or to its past. The "was" shimmers momentarily between the narrator's past and Clarissa's past.

Just as a cinematic image is always present, so that there is great difficulty in presenting the pastness of the past on film (a "flashback" soon becomes experienced as altogether present), so everything in a novel is labelled "past." All that the narrator presents takes its place on the same plane of time as something which from the narrator's point of view and from ours is already part of the past. If there is no past in the cinema, there is no present in a novel, or only a specious, ghostly present which is generated by the narrator's ability to resurrect the past not as reality but as verbal image.

Virginia Woolf strategically manipulates in *Mrs. Dalloway* the ambiguities of this aspect of conventional storytelling to justify the power she ascribes to her characters of immediate access to their pasts. If the novel as a whole is recovered from the past in the mind of the narrator, the action of the novel proceeds through one day in the lives of its main characters in which one after another they go through a present experience, often one of walking through the city, Clarissa's walk to buy flowers, Peter Walsh's walk through London after visiting Clarissa, the walk of Septimus and Rezia to visit Sir William Bradshaw, and so on. As they make their ways through London the most important events of their pasts rise up within them, so that the day of *Mrs. Dalloway* may be described as a general day of recollection. The revivification of the past performed by the characters exists within the bringing back of that past inside another past (the present of the characters turned into a past) by the narrator.

If the pressure of all the other moments lies on the present moment which Clarissa experiences so vividly, the whole day of the action of *Mrs. Dalloway* may be described as such a moment on a large scale. Just as Proust's *À la recherche du temps perdu,* one of Virginia Woolf's favorite books, ends with a party in which Marcel encounters figures from his past turned now into aged specters of themselves, so the "story" of *Mrs. Dalloway* (for there is a story, the story of Clarissa's refusal of Peter Walsh, of her love for Sally Seton, and of her decision to marry Richard Dalloway), is something which happened long before the single day of the novel's present. The details of this story are brought back bit by bit for the reader in the memories of the various characters as the day continues. At the same time, the most important figures in Clarissa's past actually return during the day—Peter Walsh journeying from India and appearing suddenly at her door, then later coming to her party, Sally Seton, now married and the mother of five sons, also coming to her party.

The passage in *A Writer's Diary* about Virginia Woolf's "discovery," her "tunnelling process," takes on its full meaning when it is seen as a description of the way *Mrs. Dalloway* is a novel of the resurrection of the past into the actual present of the characters' lives. The tunnelling process, says Virginia Woolf, is one "by which I tell the past by instalments, as I have need of it." (WD, 61)

The "beautiful caves" behind each of the characters are caves into the past as well as caves down into the general mind for which the narrator speaks. If in one direction the "caves connect" in the depths of each character's mind, in the other direction "each [cave] comes to daylight at the present moment" (WD, 60), the present moment of Clarissa's party when the important figures from her past are present in the flesh.

Virginia Woolf has unostentatiously, even secretly, buried within her novel a clue to the way the day of the action is to be seen as the occasion of a resurrection of ghosts from the past. There are three odd and apparently irrelevant pages in the novel (122–24) which describe the song of an ancient ragged woman, her hand outstretched for coppers. Peter hears her song as he crosses Marylebone Road by the Regent's Park Tube Station. It seems to rise like "the voice of an ancient spring" spouting from some primeval swamp. It seems to have been going on as the same inarticulate moan for millions of years and to be likely to persist for ten million years longer:

> ee um fah um so
> foo swee too eem oo

The battered old woman, whose voice seems to come from before, after, or outside time, sings of how she once walked with her lover in May. Though it is possible to associate this with the theme of vanished love in the novel (Peter has just been thinking again of Clarissa and her coldness, "as cold as an icicle" [121, 122]), still the connection seems strained, and the episode scarcely seems to justify the space it occupies unless the reader recognizes that Virginia Woolf has woven into the text of what the old woman sings, partly by paraphrase and variation, partly by direct quotation in an English translation, the words of a song by Richard Strauss, "Aller Seelen," with words by Hermann von Gilm:

> Stell' auf den Tisch die duftenden Reseden,
> Die letzten rothen Astern trag' herbei,

Und lass uns wieder von der Liebe reden,
Wie einst im Mai.

Gib mir die Hand, dass ich sie heimlich drücke,
Und wenn man's sieht,—mir ist es einerlei,
Gib mir nur einen deiner süssen Blicke,
Wie einst im Mai.

Es blüht und duftet heute auf jedem Grabe,
Ein Tag im Jahr ist den Toten frei;
Komm an mein Herz, das ich dich wieder habe,
Wie einst im Mai, wie einst im Mai.[5]

Heather, red asters, the meeting with the lover once in May, these are echoed in the passage in *Mrs. Dalloway,* and several phrases are quoted directly: "look in my eyes with thy sweet eyes intently"; "give me your hand and let me press it gently"; "and if some one should see, what matter they?" The old woman, there can be no doubt, is singing Strauss's song. The parts of the song not directly echoed in *Mrs. Dalloway,* however, identify it as a key to the structure of the entire novel. "One day in the year" is indeed "free to the dead," "Aller Seelen," the day of a collective resurrection of spirits. On this day the bereaved woman can hope that her lover will return from the grave. Like Strauss's song, *Mrs. Dalloway* has the form of an All Souls' Day in which Peter Walsh, Sally Seton, and the rest rise from the dead to come to Clarissa's party. As in the song the lady's memory of her dead lover may on one day of the year become a direct confrontation of his risen spirit, so in *Mrs. Dalloway* the characters are obsessed all day by memories of the time when Clarissa refused Peter and chose to marry Richard Dalloway, and then the figures in these memories actually come back in a general congregation of figures from Clarissa's past.

[5] "Place on the table the perfuming heather, bring here the last red asters, and let us again speak of love, as once in May.
     Give me your hand, that I may secretly press it, and if someone sees, it's all the same to me. Give me but one of your sweet glances, as once in May.
     It is blooming and breathing perfume today on every grave. One day in the year is free to the dead. Come to my heart, that I may have you again, as once in May, as once in May."

Continuity of each character with his own past, continuity in the shared past of all the important characters—these forms of communication are completed by the unusual degree of access the characters have in the present to one another's minds. Some novelists, Jane Austen or Jean-Paul Sartre, for example, assume that human minds are opaque to one another. Another person is a strange apparition, perhaps friendly to me, perhaps a threat, but in any case difficult to understand. I have no immediate knowledge of what he is thinking or feeling. I must interpret what is going on within his subjectivity as best I can by way of often misleading signs—speech, gesture, and expression. In Virginia Woolf's work, however, as in Anthony Trollope's, one person often sees spontaneously into the mind of another and knows with the same sort of knowledge he has of his own subjectivity what is going on there. If the narrator enters silently and unobserved into the mind of each of the characters and understands it with perfect intimacy because it is in fact part of his own mind, the characters often, if not always, may have the same kind of intimate knowledge of one another. This may be partly because they share the same memories and so respond in the same way to the same cues, each knowing what the other must be thinking, but it seems also to be an unreflective openness of one mind to another, a kind of telepathic insight. The mutual understanding of Clarissa and Peter is the most striking example of this intimacy: "They went in and out of each other's minds without any effort," thinks Peter, remembering their talks at Bourton. (94) Other characters, however, have something of the same power of communication, Rezia and Septimus, for example, as he helps her make a hat in their brief moments of happiness before Dr. Holmes comes and Septimus throws himself out of the window: "Not for weeks had they laughed like this together, poking fun privately, like married people." (217) Or there is the intimacy of Clarissa and her servant Lucy: " 'Dear!' said Clarissa, and Lucy shared as she meant her to her disappointment (but not the pang); felt the concord between them." (43)

In all these cases, however, there is some slight obstacle between the minds of the characters. Clarissa does after all decide not to marry Peter and is falling in love with Richard Dalloway in spite of the almost perfect communion she can achieve with Peter. The communion of Rezia and Septimus is intermittent, and she has little insight into what is going on in his mind during his periods of madness. Clarissa does not share with Lucy the pang of jealousy she feels toward Lady Bruton. The proper model for the relations among minds in *Mrs. Dalloway* is that of a perfect transparency of the minds of the characters to the mind of the narrator, but only a modified translucency, like glass frosted or fogged to a greater or less degree, between the mind of one character and the mind of another. Nevertheless, to the continuity between the present and the past within the mind of a given character there must be added a relative continuity from one mind to another in the present.

The characters in *Mrs. Dalloway* are endowed with a desire to take possession of these continuities, to actualize them in the present. The dynamic model for this urge is a movement which gathers together disparate elements, pieces them into a unity, and lifts them up into the daylight world in a gesture of ecstatic delight, sustaining the wholeness so created over the dark abyss of death. The phrase "building it up" echoes through the novel as an emblem of this combination of spiritual and physical action. Thinking of life, Clarissa, the reader will remember, wonders "how one sees it so, making it up, building it round one." (5) Peter Walsh follows a pretty girl from Trafalgar Square to Regent Street across Oxford Street and Great Portland Street until she disappears into her house, making up a personality for her, a new personality for himself, and an adventure for them both together: ". . . it was half made up, as he knew very well; invented, this escapade with the girl; made up, as one makes up the better part of life, he thought—making oneself up; making her up." (81) Rezia's power of putting one scrap with another to make a hat or to gather the small girl, who brings the evening paper, into a warm circle of intimacy momentarily cures Septimus of his hallucinations and of his horrifying sense that he is condemned to a solitary death: "For so it always happened. First one thing, then another. So she built it up, first one thing and then another. . . . she built it up, sewing." (219, 221) Even Lady Bruton's luncheon, to which she brings Richard Dalloway and Hugh Whitbread to help her write a letter to the *Times* about emigration, is a parody version of this theme of constructive action.

The most important example of the theme, of course, is Clarissa Dalloway's party, her attempt to "kindle and illuminate." (6) Though people laugh at her for her parties, feel she too much enjoys imposing herself, nevertheless these parties are her offering to life, an offering devoted to the effort to bring together people from their separate lives and combine them into oneness: "Here was So-and-so in South Kensington; some one up in Bayswater; and somebody else, say, in Mayfair. And she felt quite continuously a sense of their existence; and she felt what a waste; and she felt what a pity; and she felt if only they could be brought together; so she did it. And it was an offering; to combine, to create." (184, 185) The party which forms the concluding scene of the novel does succeed in bringing people together, a great crowd from poor little Ellie Henderson all the way up to the Prime Minister, and including Sally Seton and Peter Walsh among the rest. Clarissa has the "gift still; to be; to exist; to sum it all up in the moment." (264) Her party transforms each guest from his usual self into a new social self, a self outside the self of participation in the general presence of others. The magic sign of this transformation is the moment when Ralph Lyon beats back the curtain and goes on talking, so caught up is he in the party. (258, 259) The gathering then becomes "something now, not nothing" (259), and Clarissa meditates on the power a successful party has to destroy the usual personality and replace it with another self able to know people with special intimacy and able to speak more freely from the hidden depths of the spirit. These two selves are related to one another as real to unreal, but when one is aware of the contrast, as Clarissa is in the moment just before she loses her self-consciousness and is swept into her own party, it is impossible to tell which is the real self, which the unreal: "Every time she gave a party she had this feeling of being something not herself, and that every one was unreal in one way; much more real in another. . . . it was possible to say things you couldn't say anyhow else, things that needed an effort; possible to go much deeper." (259, 260)

An impulse to create a social situation which will bring into the open the usually hidden continuities of present with past, of person with person, of person with the depths of himself, is shared by all the principal characters of *Mrs. Dalloway*. This universal desire makes one vector of spiritual forces within the novel a general urge toward lifting up and bringing together.

This effort fails. Peter Walsh's adventure with the unknown girl is a fantasy. Lady Bruton is a shallow, domineering busybody, a representative of that upper-class society which Virginia Woolf intends to expose in her novel. "I want to criticise the social system," she wrote while composing *Mrs. Dalloway*, "and to show it at work, at its most intense." (WD, 57) Rezia's constructive power and womanly warmth does not prevent her husband from killing himself. And Clarissa? Clarissa too is a failure. It would be a mistake to exaggerate the degree to which she and the social values she embodies are condemned in the novel. Virginia Woolf's attitudes toward upper-class English society of the nineteen-twenties are quite ambiguous, and to sum up the novel as no more than negative social satire is a distortion. Virginia Woolf feared, for example, while she was writing the novel that Clarissa would not seem attractive enough to her readers. "The doubtful point," she wrote in her diary a year before the novel was finished, "is, I think, the character of Mrs. Dalloway. It may be too stiff, too glittering and tinsely." (WD, 61) Nevertheless, Clarissa is in fact a snob, too anxious for social success, and her party is the perpetuation of a moribund society, with its hangers-on at court like Hugh Whitbread and a Prime Minister who is a sad fellow enough: "You might have stood him behind a counter and bought biscuits," thinks Ellie Henderson, "—poor chap, all rigged up in gold lace." (261) Moreover, even though Clarissa's party may create an atmosphere which facilitates an unusual communication among people, this communion is only momentary. The party comes to an end; the warmth fades; people return to their normal selves, and in retrospect there seems to have been something spurious about the sense of oneness with others the party created.

Moreover, Clarissa's power to bring people together seems paradoxically related to her reticence, her coldness, her preservation of an area of inviolable privacy in herself. Though she believes that each person is not limited to himself, but is spread out among other people like mist in the branches of a tree, with another part of her spirit she contracts into herself and resents intensely any invasion of her privacy. It almost seems as if her keeping of a secret private self is reciprocally related to her social power to gather people together and put them in relationship to one another. The motif of Clarissa's frigidity, of her prudery, of her separateness runs all through *Mrs. Dalloway*. "The death of her soul," Peter Walsh calls it. (89) Since her illness, she has slept alone, in a narrow bed in an attic room, and she cannot "dispel a virginity preserved through childbirth which [clings] to her like a sheet." (46) She has "through some contraction of this cold spirit" (46) failed her husband again and again. She feels a stronger sexual attraction for other women than for men. A high point of her life was the moment when Sally Seton kissed her. Her decision not to marry Peter Walsh, but to marry Richard Dalloway instead, was a rejection of intimacy and a grasping at privacy. "For in marriage a little licence, a little independence there must be between people living together day in day out in the same house; which Richard gave her, and she him. . . . But with Peter everything had to be shared; everything gone into. And it was intolerable." (10) "And there is a dignity in people; a solitude;

even between husband and wife a gulf," thinks Clarissa much later in the novel. (181) Her hatred of her daughter's friend Miss Kilman, of Sir William Bradshaw, of all the representatives of domineering will, of the instinct to convert others, of "love and religion" (191), is based on this respect for isolation and detachment: "Had she ever tried to convert any one herself? Did she not wish everybody merely to be themselves?" (191) The old lady whom Clarissa sees so often going upstairs to her room in the neighboring house seems to stand chiefly for this highest value, "the privacy of the soul" (192): ". . . that's the miracle, that's the mystery; that old lady, she meant . . . . And the supreme mystery . . . was simply this: here was one room; there another. Did religion solve that, or love?" (193)

The climax of *Mrs. Dalloway* is not Clarissa's party; it is the moment when, having heard of the suicide of Septimus, she leaves her guests behind and goes alone into the little room where Lady Bruton has a few minutes earlier been talking to the Prime Minister about India. She sees in the next house the old lady once more (this time going quietly to bed), thinks about Septimus, and recognizes how factitious all her attempt to assemble and to connect has been. Her withdrawal from her party suggests that she has even in the midst of her guests kept untouched the privacy of her soul, that still point from which one can recognize the hollowness of the social world and feel the attraction of the death which everyone carries within him as his deepest reality. Death is the only place of true communion, and Clarissa has been attempting the impossible, to bring the values of death into the daylight world of life. Septimus chose the right way. By killing himself he preserved his integrity, "plunged holding his treasure" (281), his link to the deep places where each man is connected to every other man. For did he not in his madness hear his dead comrade, Evans, speaking to him from that region where all the dead dwell together? "Communication is health; communication is happiness" (141)—Septimus during his madness expresses what is the highest goal for all the characters, but his suicide constitutes a recognition that communication cannot be attained in life.

Clarissa's corresponding recognition of this truth, her moment of self-condemnation, is at the same time the moment of her greatest insight and in a sense the instant of her salvation. The sentences describing this moment are the center of the novel and must be cited *in extenso:* "She had once thrown a shilling into the Serpentine, never anything more. But he had flung it away. They went on living . . . . They (all day she had been thinking of Bourton, of Peter, of Sally), they would grow old. A thing there was that mattered; a thing, wreathed about with chatter, defaced, obscured in her own life, let drop every day in corruption, lies, chatter. This he had preserved. Death was defiance. Death was an attempt to communicate; people feeling the impossibility of reaching the centre which, mystically, evaded them; closeness drew apart; rapture faded, one was alone. There was an embrace in death." (280, 281)

From the point of view of the "thing" at the center that matters most, all speech, all social action, all building it up, all forms of communication are lies. The more one tries to reach this center through such means the further away from it one goes. The ultimate lesson of *Mrs. Dalloway* seems to be that by building it up, one destroys. Only by throwing it away can life be preserved. It is preserved by being laid to rest on that underlying reality which Virginia Woolf elsewhere describes as "a thing I see before me: something abstract; but residing in the downs or sky; beside which nothing matters; in which I shall rest and continue to exist. Reality I call it" (WD, 132). "Nothing matters"—compared to this reality, which is only defaced, corrupted, covered over by all the everyday activities of life, everything else is emptiness and vanity: ". . . there is nothing," wrote Virginia Woolf during one of her periods of depression, "—nothing for any of us. Work, reading, writing are all disguises; and relations with people." (WD, 144)

It is easy to see that Septimus Smith's suicide anticipates Virginia

Woolf's own death. Both deaths are a defiance, an attempt to communicate, a courageous recognition that self-annihilation is the only possible way to embrace that center which evades one as long as one is alive. Clarissa does not follow Septimus into death (though she has a bad heart, and the original plan, according to the preface Virginia Woolf wrote for the Modern Library edition of the novel, was to have her kill herself). Even so, the words of the dirge in *Cymbeline* have been echoing through her head all day: "Fear no more the heat 'o the sun/Nor the furious winter's rages." Her obsession with these lines indicates her half-conscious awareness that in spite of her love of life she will reach peace and escape from suffering, only in death. The lines come into her mind for a last time just before she returns from her solitary meditation to fulfill her role as hostess. They come to signify her recognition of her kinship with Septimus, her kinship with death. For she is, as Virginia Woolf said in the Modern Library preface, the "double" of Septimus. In *Mrs. Dalloway,* she said, "I want to give life and death, sanity and insanity." (WD, 57) The novel was meant to be "a study of insanity and suicide; the world seen by the sane and the insane side by side." (WD, 52) These poles are not so much opposites as reversed images of one another. Each has the same elemental design, and the death by suicide Virginia Woolf originally planned for Clarissa is fulfilled by Septimus, who dies for her, so to speak, a substitute suicide. Clarissa and Septimus seek the same thing: communication, wholeness, the oneness of reality, but only Septimus takes the sure way to reach it. Clarissa's attempt to create unity in her party is the mirror image in the world of light and life of Septimus' vigorous appropriation of the dark embrace of death in his suicide: "Fear no more the heat of the sun. She must go back to them. But what an extraordinary night! She felt somehow very like him—the young man who had killed himself. She felt glad that he had done it; thrown it away." (283)

   Mrs. Dalloway seems to end in a confrontation of life and death as looking-glass counterparts. Reality, authenticity, and completion are on the death side of the mirror, while life is at best the illusory, insubstantial, and fragmentary image of that dark reality. There is, however, one more structural element in *Mrs. Dalloway,* one final twist of the screw which reverses the polarities once more, or rather which reconciles them. Investigation of this ultimate reconciliation will permit a final identification of the way Virginia Woolf brings into the open latent implications of the traditional form of English fiction.

I have said that *Mrs. Dalloway* has a double temporal form. During the day of the action the chief characters resurrect in memory by bits and pieces the central episode of their common past. All these characters then come together again at Clarissa's party. The narrator in his turn embraces both these times in the perspective of a single distance. He moves forward through his own time of narration toward the point when the two times of the characters come together in the completion of the final sentences of the novel, when Peter sees Clarissa returning to her party:

> It is Clarissa, he said.
> For there she was. (296)

In the life of the characters, however, this moment of completion passes. The party ends. Sally, Peter, Clarissa, and the rest move on toward death. The victory of the narrator is to rescue this moment and all the other moments of the novel permanently from death in that All Souls' Day at a second power which is literature. Time is rescued, however, into the region of death with which the mind of the narrator has from the first page been identified. This is a place of absence, where nothing exists but empty words, words which generate their own reality and do not refer to any reality outside themselves. Clarissa, Peter, and the rest can be encountered only in the pages of the novel. The reader enters this realm of vacancy when he leaves his own solid world and begins to read *Mrs. Dalloway.* The novel is a double resurrection. The characters exist for themselves as alive in a present which is a resuscitation of their dead pasts. In the all-embracing mind of the narrator the characters exist as dead men and women whose continued existence depends on his words. When the circle of the narration is complete—past joining present—the apparently living characters reveal themselves to be already dwellers among the dead. Clarissa's vitality, her ability "to be; to exist," is expressed in the present tense statement made by Peter Walsh in the penultimate line of the novel: "It is Clarissa." This affirmation of her power to sum it all up in the moment echoes earlier descriptions of her "extraordinary gift, that woman's gift, of making a world of her own wherever she happened to be": "She came into a room; she stood, as he had often seen her, in a doorway with lots of people round her. . . . she never said anything specially clever; there she was, however; there she was" (114, 115); "There she was, mending her dress." (179) These earlier passages, however, are in the past tense, as is the last line of the novel: "For there she was." With this sentence "is" becomes "was," and Clarissa along with all the other characters recedes into an indefinitely distant past. Life becomes death within the impersonal mind of the narrator, which is the place of communion in death. There the fragmentary is made whole, and there all is assembled into one unit. All the connections between one part of the novel and another are known only to the agile and ubiquitous mind of the narrator. They exist only within the embrace of that reconciling spirit.

Nevertheless, to return finally once more to the other side of the irony, the dirge in *Cymbeline* is sung over an Imogen who is only apparently dead. The play is completed with the seemingly miraculous return to life by the heroine. In the same way, Clarissa comes back from her solitary confrontation with death during her party. She returns from her recognition of her kinship with Septimus to bring "terror" and "ecstasy" to Peter when he sees her. (296) She comes back also into the language of the narration where, like Imogen raised from the dead, she may be confronted by the reader in the enduring language of literature.

It is perhaps for this reason that Virginia Woolf changed her original plan and introduced Septimus as Clarissa's surrogate in death. To have had a single protagonist who was finally swallowed up in the darkness would have falsified her conception. She needed two protagonists, one who dies and another who dies with his death (Clarissa vividly lives through Septimus' death as she meditates alone during her party [280]), and then, having died vicariously, returns to life, appearing before her guests to cause, in Peter Walsh at least, "extraordinary excitement." (296) It is not only that Clarissa's vitality, comes from her proximity to death. The novel as a whole needs for its structural completeness two opposite but similar movements, Septimus' plunge into death and Clarissa's resurrection from the dead, for *Mrs. Dalloway* is both these at once: the entry into the realm of communication in death and the revelation of that realm in words.

Though *Mrs. Dalloway* seems almost nihilistically to recommend the embrace of death, and though its author did in fact finally take this plunge, nevertheless, like the rest of Virginia Woolf's writing, it represents in fact a contrary movement of the spirit. In a note in her diary of May, 1933, Virginia Woolf records a moment of insight into what brings about a "synthesis" of her being: "how only writing composes it: how nothing makes a whole unless I am writing." (WD, 208) Or again: "Odd how the creative power at once brings the whole universe to order." (WD, 220) Like Clarissa's party or like the other examples of building it up in *Mrs. Dalloway,* the novel itself is a constructive action which gathers unconnected elements into a solidly existing object, something which belongs to the everyday world of other physical things. It is a book with cardboard covers and white pages covered with black marks. This made-up thing, however, unlike its symbol, Clarissa's party, belongs authentically to both worlds. If it is in one sense no more than a physical object, it is in another sense made of words which designate not the material presence of the things named but their absence from the everyday world and their existence within the place out of place which is the space of literature. Virginia Woolf's writing has as its aim bringing into the light of day this realm of communication in language. A novel, for Virginia Woolf, is the place of death made visible, and writing is the only action which exists simultaneously on both sides of the mirror, within death and within life at once.

Some Notes on the Technique
of Man's Fate

MELVIN J. FRIEDMAN

I

Most critics of the novel avoid talking about Malraux. He is not experimentalist enough to engage the attention of literary commentators who make it their business to talk about handling of point of view, displacement of chronology, tampering with levels of consciousness. Wayne Booth, in *The Rhetoric of Fiction,* for example, makes only two passing references to Malraux. This neglect is typical of the whole post-Jamesian movement in the theory of the novel. Even so good a novel as *Man's Fate* has little to say to a critic who is insistent on defining "scenic method" and finding "posts of observation" and "large lucid reflectors." We can substitute Malraux's name for Tolstoy's and quote to advantage a remark made recently by the distinguished Oxford don John Bayley: "Tolstoy makes the critic feel how superfluous his office can be."

Thus the "formalist" critics, who are attracted by the textural complexities of the inheritors of Flaubert and the French symbolists, have ignored Malraux and left him to the historians of literature and to those intent on defining the stages of a *Geistesgeschichte.* Yet there are in print several successful attempts to diagram the structure of Malraux's novels and discuss his imagery; mostly by

Malraux specialists rather than by theoreticians of the novel. W. M. Frohock's *André Malraux and the Tragic Imagination* (Stanford, 1952) goes through the novels systematically and gives them the loving textural care which is usually reserved for poetry. He studies *Man's Fate* with the same devoted attention to narrative point of view which Percy Lubbock gave the work which he considered the triumph of novel-writing, James's *Ambassadors*. Frohock has written not only the best book on Malraux but also the one which considers most convincingly his techniques as a novelist. In his introduction he defines the uniqueness of Malraux's method better than anyone else I know: "But in the art books we call this incoherence a defect and in the novels we call it an artistic technique. His craft is a craft of ellipsis." (p. x) Geoffrey Hartman's *André Malraux* (London, 1960) makes some interesting judgments about Malraux's working habits by studying closely several passages from his novels—including the brilliant opening scene of *Man's Fate*. The other book-length studies concentrate more on the ideology and less on the craft, although there are some excellent pages on imagery in Gerda Blumenthal's *André Malraux: The Conquest of Dread* (Baltimore, 1960) and on analogies between the novels and Sophoclean tragedy in Charles D. Blend's *André Malraux: Tragic Humanist* (Columbus, Ohio, 1963). A handful of articles are similarly concerned with matters of structure and metaphor but these are clearly in the minority.[1]

[1] Bert M-P. Leefmans, in his "Malraux and Tragedy: The Structure of *La Condition Humaine*," *Romanic Review*, XLIV (October, 1953), 208–14, considers, in convincing detail, the organization, time sequence, and "rhythm of classic tragedy" which carry through *Man's Fate*. R. M. Albérès makes some apt judgments about structure in his "André Malraux and the 'Abridged Abyss,'" *Yale French Studies*, No. 18 (Winter, 1957), 45–54. Albert Sonnenfeld speaks convincingly of the metaphors related to time in his "Malraux and the Tyranny of Time: The Circle and the Gesture," *Romanic Review*, LIV (October, 1963), 198–212. One can profitably turn also to the several articles by Rima Drell Reck, Brian T. Fitch, Paul West, and Walter Langlois and to early reviews of *Man's Fate* by Edmund Wilson, Malcolm Cowley, and William Troy. A book appeared after the completion of this essay which makes a serious attempt to confront Malraux's techniques as a novelist; see Denis Boak's *André Malraux* (New York, 1968). Boak suggests the connection

Frohock was quite right in noticing that "the cost of disregarding the character of Malraux's craft runs high." (p. x) He points to the October, 1948, issue of *Esprit* (devoted almost entirely to Malraux) as a crucial example of this neglect. Fortunately, the special Malraux issue of *Yale French Studies* (Winter, 1957) and the Twentieth Century Views *Malraux* (ably edited by R. W. B. Lewis) have partly righted the wrong.

Therefore, while the other phases of Malraux's achievement have been amply documented, there is still something left to be said about his methods as a novelist. While Malraux has tried hard to preserve the mystery of his whereabouts during certain crucial periods of his earlier years—in good B. Traven fashion[2]—he has certainly not intended that his devices as a novelist remain unexplained. Malraux has systematically acquainted us with his literary forebears and with his likes and dislikes. Thus we know what he thought of Flaubert, the darling of the formalists: he considered him more and more a "pale reflection" of Balzac.[3] R. M. Albérès, in his *Yale French Studies* article, is careful to distinguish the "cinematic 'abridgement'" and "telegraphic" structure of *Man's Fate* from the painstakingly narrated *Madame Bovary*. Indeed they are seemingly as unlike as two novels can be. The hectic pace and staccato rhythm of Malraux's novel is very different from the calm, leisured pace and almost still-born movement of Flaubert's. Flaubert's *coupes,* which make his sentences drop unexpectedly at the end, offer a tight coherence unrelated to what Albérès has called Malraux's "stylistic abridgements" and what Frohock called "craft of ellipsis."

---

with Jules Romains which I develop later in this essay. Attention should also be called to the fine chapter on Malraux in W. M. Frohock's *Style and Temper: Studies in French Fiction, 1925–1960* (Cambridge, Mass., 1967).

[2] The myths connected with B. Traven are even more elaborate. One of these, by chance, connects him with Malraux in a curious way: "He [Traven] was something big in some kind of pre-Communist international revolutionary underground." Anthony West, "The Great Traven Mystery," *New Yorker,* July 22, 1967, p. 82.

[3] See Charles F. Roedig, "Malraux on the Novel (1930–1945)," *Yale French Studies* (Winter, 1957), 39–40.

In one way, however, *Madame Bovary* and *Man's Fate* try for a similar effect: simultaneity. Flaubert uses his intermittent *tableaux,* we have been told many times, to slow down the forward movement of his novel and to offer the sense of juxtaposition we get from looking at a painting. *Man's Fate* also thrives on the illusion (and that is all it can be in literature) of simultaneity; it offers a modified example of what Joseph Frank, in his famous essay, has christened "spatial form."

We must qualify. The famous *comices agricoles* scene in *Madame Bovary* is pictorial and has a Bruegel-like density. The opening scene in *Man's Fate,* involving Ch'en's first murder, or the later scene when he throws himself under Chiang Kai-shek's car have a Goyaesque fluidity. (Malraux himself would appreciate this distinction and would want to be entirely on the side of Goya.) What I am saying is that there is a more restless, chaotic side to the Malraux scene than to the Flaubertian one. The following words seem to put the case for Malraux:

> I am not one of those people who find a bitter gratification in the contemplation of ultimate Incoherence. I am not addicted to the dilettantism of chaos. The world, no doubt, at any given moment of its existence, is anything you like to call it. But it is out of all this aimless dispersion, out of all these zigzagging efforts, out of all this disorderly growth, that the ideal of an epoch ends by disentangling itself. Myriads of human activities are scattered in all directions by the indifferent forces of self-interest, of passion, even of crime and madness; and they proceed to destroy themselves in their clashes or lose themselves in the void—or so it seems.

These words would have served handsomely as part of a preface to *Man's Fate.* Instead, they happen to be from the preface to a *roman-fleuve,* the first two volumes of which appeared the year before Malraux's novel: Jules Romains' *Men of Good Will* (1932–47). This preface supplies a coherent statement of Romains' doctrine of unanimism, which depends very much on what he calls "collective life." The one lesson Romains offers is that the unanimist novelist should "try to avoid reducing collective life to the dimensions of the individual and the individual consciousness." He warns against building a novel "around any central character," a practice that was fashionable in the nineteenth century. He does not use the word "mysticism" in this preface, but one of the keenest observers of contemporary French literature, Henri Peyre, has remarked pertinently that "Romains has secularized mysticism" and that he has "tried to raise unanimism to the plane of mysticism."[4]

The first volume of *Men of Good Will* is aptly titled *The Sixth of October*. We follow a group of Parisians, of different backgrounds, at various times on the day October 6, 1908. Several of the chapter headings reveal the time of day: Chapter One is called "Paris Goes to Work on a Fine Morning"; Chapter Three is called "Nine O'clock in the Morning at the De Saint-Papouls' and the De Champcenais'"; Chapter Eighteen is called "Introducing Paris at Five O'clock in the Evening." Romains' strategy is to watch these Parisians, quite unaware of the existence of one another, in a series of almost "mystically" connected scenes—creating the illusion of simultaneity. His interest is clearly more in the direction of "collective life" than of "individual consciousness."

We should keep this all in mind when we turn to *Man's Fate*. It seems to me that the structure of the novel is determined by a *variation* on unanimism. (It would be wrong to call Malraux a practitioner of unanimism. This is one of the rare *isms* which has not, to my knowledge, been attached to his name.) Malraux is even more scrupulous than Romains in acquainting us with times and dates. Part One and a large section of Part Two of *Man's Fate* occur on March 21, 1927. Malraux's day starts earlier than Romains': the first indication of time is "twelve-thirty midnight." There are frequent breaks in the text indicating a more advanced time of the day. About ten pages before the end of the second part we realize that Malraux's long day has come to an end: "The next day, four

---

[4] *French Novelists of Today* (New York, 1967), 54, 56.

o'clock in the afternoon." Malraux often manages several scenes, meant to be concurrent, within each of the time intervals.

Thus "twelve-thirty midnight," as the first block of time, has crowded within it Ch'en's murder of the sleeping man; the gathering at the phonograph shop with its famous moment of Kyo's failure to recognize a recording of his own voice; the scene in the *Black Cat* with the Falstaffian carryings on of Clappique; Kyo's confrontation with May about her recent infidelity. Now there is clearly forward movement here. Ch'en leaves the scene of his killing to join his comrades at the phonograph shop. Kyo goes from the shop to the *Black Cat* and then to the apartment he occupies with his father and May. All of this takes time. But there is a rhythm in conflict with this as Malraux gains the effect of partial simultaneity, of a series of concurrent scenes. Something resembling counterpoint is achieved: witness the sound of the phonograph confusedly mixing with the voices in the shop; the jazz music in the *Black Cat* cacophonically accompanied by Clappique's stuttering. This device runs counter to chronometric time with its linear advancing. Verlaine's famous warning to the poet, "take eloquence and wring its neck," should be translated into Malraux's terms: take *time* and wring its neck. Forward movement is at every turn frustrated; it is sacrificed to what Robbe-Grillet has recently called "private mental structures of 'time.'" (Ch'en lives in these rarefied spheres.) This attempt to abort the forward progress of the action is ironically underscored by Malraux's frequent mention of the time of day or night in strict chronological order.

To return to Romains and his doctrine, we recall his insistence on the "collective life," with its rejection of "the individual and the individual consciousness." The scenes in *Man's Fate* are almost all crowded. The opening scene, in which Ch'en is alone with the murdered man, rapidly turns into the crowded gathering in the record shop—with the revealing transitional sentence: "Now to return among men." But even when Ch'en is quite alone—with the man asleep under the mosquito netting or, at the end of Part Four, with the bomb—the aloneness is broken in upon at every turn. An alley cat relieves the solitariness of the first scene, for example.[5] There never seems to be any time in *Man's Fate* to explore an "individual consciousness." Instead of exploring Ch'en's consciousness at the moment before he commits his first murder, Malraux is content with some instant metaphysical editorializing: "Ch'en was becoming aware, with a revulsion verging on nausea, that he stood here, not as a fighter, but as a sacrificial priest. He was serving the gods of his choice; but beneath his sacrifice to the Revolution lay a world of depths beside which this night of crushing anguish was bright as day."[6] There are other similarly missed moments, when the "collective life" crowds in on the "individual consciousness." When Ch'en runs towards Chiang Kai-shek's car with his bomb (one of the moments in literature which comes closest to what Joyce means by an "epiphany"), Malraux can describe the scene with an aloof detachment: "He ran towards it with an ecstatic joy, threw himself upon it, with his eyes shut." (248) Even Dostoevsky, writing in the nineteenth century, felt compelled to enter Prince Myshkin's mind at the moment of "ecstasy" preceding the epileptic fit.

We are now ready to illuminate other aspects of Romains' unanimism. A novel which stays so forbiddingly remote from the consciousness of its characters, as *Man's Fate* does, tends naturally to treat fictional creatures in groups and avoid positing a "central character." Thus *Man's Fate* is genuinely "a novel without a hero," but in a sense quite different from the way Thackeray intended the expression in *Vanity Fair*. The heroics of Ch'en, Kyo, Katov, the wisdom of old Gisors, the qualified "villainy" of Ferral seem to

[5] Malraux, like Baudelaire and Verlaine before him, seems to have a fascination for cats. In this connection, there is a revealing sentence in the introduction to *The Metamorphosis of the Gods,* Malraux's latest foray into art criticism: "Let us suppose that a guardian devil (in the form of a cat) said to Baudelaire when he had just finished *Les Phares,* 'Come and see,' and led him into our present-day Louvre." *The Metamorphosis of the Gods* (Garden City, N.Y., 1960), 2.

[6] *Man's Fate,* trans. Haakon M. Chevalier (New York, 1934), 10. All subsequent references will be to this edition.

cancel one another out. Through the first four parts, Ch'en threatens to be the hero, but the rather wasted way in which he dies is eclipsed, first by Kyo's death from cyanide when all else fails, and then even more convincingly by Katov's self-sacrificing gesture of giving up his cyanide and dying more horribly in the boiler of the locomotive. So there is no "central character" in *Man's Fate,* just as Romains intended that there be none in *Men of Good Will.* (Malraux is probably more faithful, on this occasion, to Romains' dictum than he was himself; by the end of the twenty-seventh—and last —volume of *Men of Good Will,* Jerphanion has fairly well emerged as the central character.)

In certain ways, that other Romains trait, "secularized mysticism" (as Henri Peyre has called it), seems to emerge from this combination of fictional circumstances. In some of the most brilliant writing we have on *Man's Fate,* Frederick Hoffman tells of the secularization of the religious experience in Malraux's novel; the metaphors, he states, often remain the same but the experience occurs outside the church. Violent action becomes a substitute for contemplation and, "the sensation of death is close to resembling the mystic's experience of religious ecstasy."[7] Hoffman goes on to distinguish between Ch'en's and Kyo's reactions to "the absolute": Ch'en wishes to " 'taste it' " while Kyo views it "in terms of a life stream contained within the banks of human social organization." (115–16) This brings us back to Romains' unanimism which can be "mystical" only in terms of "human social organization." The unanimistic side of Malraux is not only decisive in determining the structure of *Man's Fate* but also in explaining the ultimate triumph of the Kyos over the Ch'ens; in other words (in Romains' terms) those who work for the "collective life" over those who represent "the individual and the individual consciousness."

There is still another statement in Romains' preface which has special relevance to *Man's Fate:* "I also face the fact that, in the

[7] *The Mortal No* (Princeton, 1964), 114. All subsequent references will be to this edition.

world as I see it, families are not of very much importance. They are in certain cases; but they are not in the common run of life. One can —indeed, one should—find a place for them in the picture. But confining oneself to depicting a family is not painting the present-day scene, nor is it interpreting its spirit." Malraux's world is not especially congenial to family life. *Man's Fate* is really the only one of his novels which bothers about it—and then only tangentially. We witness the destruction of Hemmelrich's family, which releases him for the life of action he so desperately craves. At the end of the novel, word comes back from Pei that Hemmelrich is employed in an electric plant and is meaningfully involved for the first time in his life. Family life had cruelly frustrated him. There is also a serious imperfection in the marriage of Kyo and May. Gisors feels uncertainties in his relationship with his son Kyo. Malraux could not help agreeing with Romains that "confining oneself to depicting a family is not painting the present-day scene." The intermittent view he offers of family life seems quite removed from the Weltan-schauung he is at pains to chronicle.

II

We have been speaking a good deal of attempts to depict the "collective life" and stifling individuality in *Man's Fate*. Malraux, however, has one device with which he tries to preserve the uniqueness of the characters.[8] Several of the significant people in the novel have some sort of peculiarity of speech. Clappique stutters. He keeps repeating as a kind of insane refrain: "Not a word" ("pas un mot!"). " 'Absolutely' found its way into all the languages that Katov spoke." (39) Katov, also, speaks in staccato fashion, swallowing certain vowel sounds. Valérie responds almost invariably in aphorisms, even in the bedroom scene with Ferral. Ch'en has difficulty with the French "on": he says "nong" and "distractiong" (this does not come across in the English translation). Justin O'Brien is

[8] This device was first brought to my attention by Professor Justin O'Brien of Columbia University in a course he gave on the twentieth-century French novel.

doubtless correct in explaining this phenomenon as Malraux's way of distinguishing among characters, many of whose names are sufficiently un-Western to defy recognition by Western readers. It might be troubling, in other words, on a first reading at least, to keep names like Kama and Katov apart if we did not know of Katov's fondness for "absolutely" and his slurring of vowel sounds. (The English translation to some extent tries to remedy the situation by printing a *dramatis personae,* following the contents page, to acquaint us with the names, nationalities, and occupations of the principal characters—as if we were about to read a play. Thierry Maulnier might have taken a cue from this 1934 translation when he turned the novel into a play in 1954.)

But there is probably another explanation, one which bears more crucially on Malraux's techniques as a novelist. These speech oddities might easily be justified as symbolical tags, or *leitmotivs;* a way of explaining character through symbolic suggestion. In good Wagnerian fashion, our attention is alerted to certain repeated patterns of language. Hesitancy of speech identifies Clappique and also says something about his mythomaniacal character. Katov's elliptically pronounced words and sentences warn the reader of his presence and also offer a key to his sense of urgency and intensity.

The device Malraux uses here is not much different from that of certain of his contemporaries. Two novels of the period immediately come to mind. In *As I Lay Dying* (1930) Faulkner is careful to connect each of the members of the Bundren family with a different symbol: thus we associate Vardaman with a fish, Jewel with a horse, Anse with a set of false teeth. At the mention of the symbol the character comes to mind. In *The Waves* (1931) Virginia Woolf, writing an extreme example of what has been called a "lyrical novel," uses poetic turns to identify each character. Thus we are reminded of Neville when "that wild hunting song, Percival's music" appears on the page. Louis comes to mind every time the qualifying description appears: "his Australian accent and his father a banker in Brisbane." Faulkner and Virginia Woolf use symbols and turns-of-phrase as their *leitmotivs* while Malraux relies on peculiarities of speech. The difference may be in the techniques of the novels: symbols and metaphors are essential to novels which depend on inner monologues (*As I Lay Dying* and *The Waves* are written entirely in monologue or soliloquy) while speech habits are the identifying principle underlining novels which depend heavily on dialogue (there are few novels in which colloquy figures as importantly as in *Man's Fate*). But the effects are much the same. One does not doubt the background of literary impressionism which helped form Faulkner and especially Virginia Woolf. There is this side also of Malraux which has been painstakingly studied by André Vandegans; he calls this Malraux's "inspiration farfelue."[9] The poetic frame of *Man's Fate* has been enlarged by the symbolical aspects of the speech peculiarities in much the way that *As I Lay Dying* and *The Waves* gain increased dimensions as poetry by the use of symbolic tags attached to the characters.

III

We have seen how *Man's Fate* employs a modified unanimism, tempered by a base in a certain kind of poetic practice. We have thus far compared *Man's Fate* with other works of the thirties. We should now look to a novel published in 1925, Gide's *Counterfeiters,* which has something in common both with Romains' unanimism and Virginia Woolf's impressionism. Literary history can help us out here. Malraux published a brief early essay on Gide, "Aspects d'André Gide," in *Action* (March–April, 1922), which Frohock felt was "too brief to permit even a guess as to how well Malraux knew Gide and Gide's work, or as to what specific aspects of the work appealed to him." (*André Malraux and the Tragic Imagination,* p. 30, note 3). Malraux knew Gide at Gallimard where Malraux started a lengthy association as art editor in 1927. Earlier, in Septem-

---

[9] See Vandegans, *La Jeunesse littéraire d'André Malraux* (Paris, 1964). This book studies Malraux's early work: *Lunes en papier* (1921) and *Royaume-Farfelu* (1928), as well as a fragment, *Écrit pour une idole à trompe.*

ber, 1924, Gide signed the petition which appeared in the *Nouvelles Littéraires* asking that the case against Malraux, in connection with *l'affaire des statues,* be dismissed—"to testify to Malraux's value to literature."[10] Gide makes intermittent references to Malraux in his *Journal.* Finally, Malraux reviewed Gide's *Les Nouvelles Nourritures* in the *Nouvelle Revue Française* for December, 1935.

These scattered hints of an association, although perhaps not a friendship, make it seem very likely that Malraux had read *The Counterfeiters* by the time he wrote *Man's Fate.* In any case, there are interesting similarities between the two books. The opening scenes are surprisingly alike. *The Counterfeiters* begins with Bernard alone in his parents' house having just finished reading the letter which confirms his illegitimacy. This is a moment which will decisively change the course of his life. Ch'en is alone, except for a sleeping man, at the beginning of *Man's Fate.* Instead of a letter he recovers a piece of paper. He must murder Tang Yen Ta, the sleeping man, to get it; this means killing for the first time, an act which will decisively change his life. In both instances the metaphysical implications far outweigh the events at hand, giving the events a kind of Dostoevskian gratuitiousness. One has the feeling that the restlessness of both Ch'en and Bernard has reached a kind of saturation point in these opening scenes and their respective pieces of paper are merely excuses for types of violence; there is the implicit irony in each case that these might have been blank pages. (Should we not be reminded somewhat of Mallarmé's "Sur le vide papier que la blancheur défend"?) In Ch'en's case, we recall, he was forced to return to the room after he killed his man because he had forgotten to take the paper—the ostensible reason for the murder. There is clearly an *absurdist* background to these scenes which sets a tone maintained through both novels.

If we are to compare the books further we should think of the

[10] See Janet Flanner, "Profiles—The Human Condition," *New Yorker,* November 6 and 13, 1954. This is probably the most accurate biographical testimony that we have of André Malraux.

positions assumed by old Gisors in *Man's Fate* and Edouard in *The Counterfeiters*. Both occupy passive but intrusive roles in the center of their respective novels. Victor Brombert has put the case decisively for Gisors: "And as for Gisors, it would seem that Malraux, far from disavowing him, has placed him at the very center of the novel: radiating tenderness and understanding, he is simultaneously outside the action and at the heart of the meaning of the novel. . . . He is the mirror where all action reflects itself, a conscience where all thought finds an echo and a prolongation."[11] Except for "radiating tenderness and understanding," this could easily be a description of Edouard's place in Gide's novel. Edouard hides behind his work-in-progress and his conflicting theories about the composition of a novel in much the way that Gisors disappears behind his opium pipe. Both are facile conversationalists and believers in Mallarmé's theory, "céder l'initiative aux mots."

Although there is no precise equivalent of Clappique in *The Counterfeiters,* one can easily imagine him in Gide's novel. In his role as "aventurier surréaliste,"[12] one can imagine him attending the Argonauts' banquet and even firing the pistol in good Alfred Jarry fashion. In fact, the description of Jarry at the banquet suggests Clappique: "Everything about Jarry, who was got up to look like the traditional circus clown, smacked of affectation—his way of talking in particular; several of the *Argonauts* did their utmost to imitate it, snapping out their syllables, inventing odd words, and oddly mangling others; but it was only Jarry who could succeed in producing that toneless voice of his—a voice without warmth or intonation, or accent or emphasis."[13]

The composition of the two novels makes for interesting comparisons. The rapid succession of scenes, relieved periodically by moments of violence (occasionally mock-violence in *The Counterfeit-*

---

[11] Brombert, "Malraux: Passion and Intellect," in *Malraux: A Collection of Critical Essays,* ed. R. W. B. Lewis (Englewood Cliffs, N.J., 1964), 138.

[12] This happy description of him is found in Marcel Savane's *André Malraux* (Paris, 1946), 78.

[13] *The Counterfeiters,* trans. Dorothy Bussy (New York, 1955), 275–76.

ers), characterizes both novels. Dialogue is plentiful in both books. When Claude-Edmonde Magny says about Malraux's novels that "the classic continuity of plot is replaced by a juxtaposition of sometimes simultaneous, more often successive scenes that unfold in various places and involve various characters. One passes without transition from one to the other, as in the projection of slides. . . ."[14] she could easily be speaking about Gide's *Counterfeiters*. Both novels, finally, have more than their share of "recognition scenes." Ch'en has two of them: when he kills for the first time and when he throws himself under Chiang Kai-shek's car with the bomb. Kyo has two: when he discovers May's infidelity and when he takes the cyanide. Katov has one before his heroic death. Ferral has two: when he discovers Valérie's deception and when he faces the financial powers-that-be back in Paris. Gide gives Bernard two: the opening scene with the letter and his struggle with the angel. Olivier's attempted suicide, inspired by some words of Dmitri Karamazov, is another.

We can go on with these *rapprochements* but the essential point has been made. Although the intentions of *Man's Fate* and *The Counterfeiters* are quite different, there are a variety of techniques and character types which they have in common. Romains' unanimism—which he first expressed coherently in *Le Bourg régénéré, conte de la vie unanime* (1906)—seems relevant to both novels as does "l'inspiration farfelue."

IV

In tracing the possible sources for the techniques of *Man's Fate,* the one part of the novel we have ignored is the seventh—which serves as an epilogue. Twentieth-century novels are notoriously lacking in epilogues. What happens to the characters after the action has ended (what little action there is) is rarely if ever bothered about.

---

[14] Magny, "Malraux the Fascinator," in *Malraux: A Collection of Critical Essays,* 121.

In the nineteenth century, however, especially among the Russians, there are final chapters which acquaint us with the subsequent doings of all the characters who survive the action. Thus we have this passage from Turgenev's *Fathers and Sons:* "We have reached the end, haven't we? But perhaps some reader or other may wish to learn what each one of the characters we have introduced is doing at present—the actual present. We are ready to satisfy his curiosity."[15] Turgenev then goes on for five pages filling in the information briefly for most of the characters, but giving an ironical portrait of Pavel Kirsanov in Dresden and dramatizing a fond pastoral scene of Bazarov's parents visiting his grave. This "epilogue" is considerably shorter than the one we find in most Russian novels.

The seventh part of *Man's Fate* runs twenty-five pages in the Modern Library edition and fairly well follows the nineteenth-century format. Bert Leefmans has interestingly pointed out that the indications of time in this final section are imprecise, indicating a slowdown in the movement. At the beginning of it we are given the vague "Paris, July" and fifteen pages later, merely "Kobe." (They offer quite a contrast to the nervously precise first indication of time, "March 21, 1927, Twelve-thirty midnight.") Under "Paris, July" Malraux gives us an ironical scene of Ferral back in Paris being crushed morally under the heel of the French financial Establishment. A group of directors, seated in plush chairs and chewing caramels, pass final and devastating judgment on the affairs of the recently returned Ferral. The caramels probably offer an unpleasant reminder of the sugar candies Katov is eating when we first meet him, the Katov who dies so heroically in the sixth part of the novel. We are no doubt meant to contrast the smugness of this scene which opens Part Seven with the heroic behavior of Kyo and Katov in the previous section.

The "Kobe" part is mainly an exchange between May and old Gisors about their future plans. May reads a letter written by Pei, reporting on his own and Hemmelrich's activities. Gisors, in this

[15] *Fathers and Sons,* trans. Bernard Guilbert Guerney (New York, 1950), 276.

final scene, renews his role as theoretician and passes judgment on all that has happened, especially to his son. He repeats the Dostoevskian remark he made earlier to Ferral: "Every man dreams of being god." (358)

Part Seven manages, then, to put us in touch with the characters who survive the deaths of Ch'en, Kyo, and Katov. Malraux moves from the ironical scene of Ferral's undoing to the serious exchange between Kyo's survivors, old Gisors and May, just as Turgenev moved from the ironical glance at the foppish Pavel Kirsanov to the serious moment of Bazarov's survivors (his parents) arriving at his grave. Malraux devotes more pages to his epilogue than Turgenev did but the effect is much the same.

It is clear from the preceding, I hope, that *Man's Fate* uses certain techniques and structural controls to considerable advantage. Malraux had to know a good deal about craft before he wrote it. One wonders—perhaps only half-seriously—whether the Malraux of *Man's Fate* is not really part-unanimist and part-symbolist disguised as a theorist of revolution.[16] His famous exchanges with James Burnham and Leon Trotsky give us one profile of Malraux. The one I have tried to present here is quite another.

[16] I am reminded of Malcolm Cowley's statement in his review of *Man's Fate* in the *New Republic* (July 4, 1934): "It is a novel written sympathetically about Communists by a man whose own mentality has strong traces of Fascism (perhaps this explains why it has been so popular in Italy) and a novel about proletarian heroes in which the technique is that developed by the Symbolists of the Ivory Tower." (214)

Part II

THE GROWING EDGE:
THEMES AND MOTIFS

The Inferno of the Moderns

OLGA W. VICKERY

In 1922 T. S. Eliot published *The Waste Land* and in his Notes to the poem drew attention to one of his major sources—Dante Alighieri. In 1963 LeRoi Jones chose as the title for his novel castigating society *The System of Dante's Hell*. The two dates, the two writers, seemingly so disparate, point up the special relevance of the *Inferno* to modern literature. The range of Dante's direct influence is, of course, wide. Not only Eliot and Jones have testified to their indebtedness but also Charles Williams, E. E. Cummings, Malcolm Lowry, Flannery O'Connor, Robert Penn Warren, Robert Duncan, and others. In addition, however, there is the issue of Dante's *Inferno* pervading the very structure of the modern imagination in such a manner as to function as a controlling metaphor of the human condition in the twentieth century. It is precisely here that the issue of an author's knowledge of Dante yields to the broader and more speculative question of the extent to which modern literature has been engaged in a radical secularization of the *Inferno* and its controlling images as a means of accommodating the imagination's religious impulse to its perceptions of the phenomenological universe. Though other names will come readily to mind, a suggestive perspective on this last issue emerges from considering figures like Stephen Crane, John Dos Passos, Paul Bowles, John Hawkes, and Ken Kesey. Rather than arguing for Dante's influence from internal evidence in their work, it might be more illuminating to read them and modern literature in general as mirroring that existential state historically forged in significant measure through Dante's powerful capacity to shape the modes and define the materials in which the twentieth century has found its identity.

It would obviously be absurd to claim that Dante was discovered or rediscovered by writers in our time and that the *Inferno* alone is fruitful as a source of concepts and images for a world in which all might and many do abandon hope. Neither Milton's Opulent Hell nor the Hell of fire and brimstone (so compellingly portrayed in *A Portrait of the Artist as a Young Man*) have been forgotten. In fact, in a *tour de force* F. Scott Fitzgerald is able to combine Milton's Hell and Dante's Inferno in a single locale somewhere in America though it is not to be found on any of its maps. In "The Diamond as Big as the Ritz" the ironically named Braddock Washington has built for himself a Satanic paradise, an inverted copy of Heaven, out of Earth's most precious material. But all guests of the Washington family are eliminated by one means or another. And in the midst of the splendor, there are men caged in holes in the earth: "Their upturned faces, lit with wrath, with malice, with despair, with cynical humor were covered by long growths of beard but with the exception of a few who had pined perceptibly away, they seemed to be a well-fed, healthy lot." From these "Malebolge" only one man has ever escaped. Significantly enough, he proves to be an "Italian teacher" who has been the occasion of considerable difficulties for Washington, an essentially Satanic figure. He quickly explains that the escape was a ghastly error: "But, of course," he adds, "there's a good chance that we may have got him. Perhaps he fell somewhere in the woods or stumbled over a cliff. And there's always the probability that if he did get away his story wouldn't be believed."

Yet the fact remains that it is Dante not Milton who speaks most cogently to the modern mind. For shorn of its theology, the *In-*

ferno gives us an image of our own civilization—a civilization made by man not by God. The very earth is hostile, the elements pitiless. That which should nourish man becomes a source of frustration and destruction. One needs only think, for instance, of John Steinbeck's *The Grapes of Wrath*. Here the sun creates its own deserts, the wind becomes a tornado, and the rain issues in floods. Further, the seasonal cycle of gradual modulation shrivels to searing summers and ice-bound winters. The promise of spring, the fruitfulness of autumn are seldom in evidence in works of this order. Only in artists such as Frost and Faulkner whose belief was in the land do they assume a major place, and even then they are cast in an aura of nostalgic memory and elegiac loss. For most of the others, the land as such was almost obscured by the cities, overcrowded, constricting, soul-destroying—in brief, a stunning re-creation in brick and mortar of Dante's City of Dis.

Balancing this situational metaphor is the Dantean strategy of perspectival independence. While demanding of himself the fullest self-discipline, Dante also demanded full freedom for himself as an artist. He took the freedom to castigate his society for its errors, its vices, its stupidities. And in doing so, he felt free to comment on people, some not identified, some public figures whether alive or dead, and some friends, however close or distant. It is essentially this technique that Dos Passos makes full use of in his *U.S.A.* trilogy when he combines the stories of fictional characters with the "Newsreels," factual records of contemporary events, and "Biographies," brief portraits of men, living or dead, who had become part of their country's history.

The artist, as Dante demonstrated, must also be free to choose his cast of characters from the damned to the blessed. But in the *Inferno* he wrote only of the doomed and damned: murderers, suicides, pimps, whores, hypocrites, perjurors, and betrayers. Obviously writers from the beginning of time or at least from the beginning of recorded literature have fought for these freedoms, from Rabelais to Chaucer to Flaubert to Henry Miller. But it is in the *Inferno* as created by Dante that the modern writer finds an archetype of a world into which his confused, wretched men without hope can fit. There is no Beatrice drawing the quester from the depths of Hell; in the modern novel, for instance, she is much more apt to be a memory of what might have been but never was. There is no *Purgatorio* since suffering has been relinquished to the psychologists, and the *Paradiso* is a long since relinquished dream to which only a few can still cling with much real conviction.

Again appealing to our time, the *Inferno* has an unerring sense of structure while giving the initial impression of total discontinuity. Quite disparate and often frequently contrasted in mood and tone, each scene presents a view of a crowd which then dissolves in cinematic fashion to focus on one or two major characters. But Dante, of course, was less interested in the technique than in those characters who emerged out of the crowd. As his own protagonist, he can feel pity for the adulterous lovers Paolo and Francesca, sorrowful affection for Ser Brunetto Latini, contempt for Pope Nicholas III, and moral outrage as he adds to Bocca Degli Abbati's torment by pulling out his hair in handfuls. The centrality of *The Waste Land* and Pound's *Cantos* to the modern tradition is unequivocal, and so is their organizational approximation to Dante's poem. Out of the crowd of the dead flowing over London Bridge emerge the Hyacinth girl, Mr. Eugenides, Elizabeth and Leicester, and Christ, each as indelibly rendered and responded to as the figures in the *Inferno*. With that very centrality has come the acceptance of the Dantean habit of verbal economy suspended in shifting perspectives that range from the near to the middle distance, an acceptance that has elevated it to one of the chief modes of the modern literary imagination.

Dante's final act of artistic freedom lies, then, in the use of language. While at times he soars and resounds with the majesty of Milton's verse, at other times he is much closer to Chaucer's irreverence for propriety. Dante's Thaïs, a whore, "scratches herself with dungy nails"; the seducers find themselves in "a river of excrement / that seemed the overflow of the world's latrines." A simoniac has "soles all ablaze and the joints of the legs quivered and writhed about." A Sower of Discord is ripped in half; "Between his legs all of his red guts hung / with the heart, the lungs, the liver, the gall bladder, / and the shrivelled sac that passes shit to the bung." This combination of pathology and scatology is not new, as the recollection of Swift suggests, but it certainly has been found of paramount importance to the twentieth century. Joyce's Molly Bloom will not be forgotten whatever the fate of *Tropic of Cancer, Naked Lunch,* or *Last Exit to Brooklyn.*

The confluence of all these strands suggests that the modern world in many ways stands forth as a displaced existential projection of Dante's *Inferno,* a hell created by man not God and therefore an exact archetype of the radical truncation of the imagination. It is man who has polluted earth, air, and water only to be punished by so doing. It is man who has built his own cities of Dis and has found himself trapped by them. He has traced his own circles of the Inferno, his own Malebolge, by separating group from group, man from man, imprisoning them in the loathsome squalor of clichés, stereotypes, and egocentricity. He has created his own monsters and submitted himself to them. He has endured pain, but apparently without empathy he has inflicted it on others. He is indeed the fallen man who has, through centuries, created for himself what Dante describes as "The City of Woe," of "Forsaken People," of "Eternal Sorrow." The means by which he had done so constitute, among other things, a conspectus of the chief figures and forms of twentieth-century literature.

In a very loose sense the war novel always embodies the infernal principle, though in most cases the relationship to Dante's *Inferno* is tangential at best. Generally speaking, war novels seem, like Norman Mailer's *The Naked and the Dead* or James Jones's *The Thin Red Line,* to fit most easily into the realistic or naturalistic tradition. Thus, they reject the traditional romantic concept of the hero fighting for a cause in an epic struggle. Instead they echo Ezra Pound whose soldiers "walked eye-deep in hell" and died "non 'dulce' non 'et decor' ":

> There died a myriad,
> And of the best, among them,
> For an old bitch gone in the teeth,
> For a botched civilization.

The emphasis is on the soldier as victim, who surrenders his freedom of choice upon the moment of his induction. He must automatically obey all, question nothing, and believe that everything is meant for his own good. Like one of Dante's sinners, his is the torture of enforced immobility interspersed with periods of hectic activity. His is the leaden weariness, the hunger and the thirst, the exposure to the elements. His also the wounds that will not heal, the dismemberment or the disembowelment as vividly portrayed as Dante's presentation of the Sower of Discord. Furthermore, he is at the mercy of his officers with unlimited power to punish and little inclination to forgive. Both are part of a self-perpetuating system as *From Here to Eternity* or *The Caine Mutiny* indicate. It may be a system created by man, but *sub specie aeternitatis* it is Dante's Inferno.

Two novels in particular, however, come even closer to the *Inferno* and in ways that have scarcely been recognized: *The Red Badge of Courage* and *The Cannibal*. It has been documented that Stephen Crane had neither participated in nor observed a war at the time that he wrote *The Red Badge of Courage*. He had, of course, done considerable historical research—it has been suggested that he re-created the scenes and experiences of the Battle of Chancellorsville. But the novel's effectiveness depends on the reader's impression that the action takes place on no recognizable terrain. Moreover, though the action takes place in time and presents a plot sequence—Henry Fleming runs from battle, a self-confessed coward, returns and becomes a hero not only in the eyes of his comrades but in his own estimation—the war itself has no beginning and apparently no ending. One side, distinguished only by the color of their uniforms, and driven furiously by their officers, can claim a momentary victory. But there is always the subsequent confrontation, punishing and being punished, running in fright, or attacking in mindless fury. And dominating all is the agonizing death of Jim Conklin and the sight Fleming has of a dead soldier: "The eyes, staring at the youth, had changed to the dull hue to be seen on the side of a dead fish. The mouth was open. Its red had changed to an appalling yellow. Over the gray skin of the face ran little ants. One was trundling some sort of bundle along the upper lip."

The concept of an endless war, as well as specific scenes, are reminiscent of Dante. But perhaps even more important is Crane's use of imagery. Critics have commented on various strands—imagery of color, of animals, of the mechanical, for example. But providing an emotional unity for the book as a whole are the infernal images. To mention but a few, one finds throughout the novel demonic elements like the following: "dark shadows that moved like monsters," "two serpents crowding from the cavern of night," "the black forms of men [who] make weird and satanic effects," "swirling battle phantoms," "the red god of war." It is small wonder that Henry Fleming sees his camp in the early light of dawn as "a charnel place.": "He believed for an instant that he was in the house of the dead, and he did not dare to move lest these corpses start up, squalling and squawking." In brief, irrespective of sources and influences, *The Red Badge of Courage* continues to compel our attention because it is in the tradition of Dante's Inferno —the powerful blending of realism and imagination.

John Hawkes's *The Cannibal* deals not with war but with its aftermath. Spitzen-on-the-Dein is indeed an inferno, a city of the living dead. Having no communication with the outside world, it is completely self-contained. Since no one has a watch, it is also existing outside of time. For the inhabitants, the main task seems to be to burn out "the pits of excrement, burning the fresh trenches of latrines where wads of wet newspapers were scattered, burning the dark round holes in the black stone huts where moisture travelled upwards and stained the privy seats." Nearby is a swamp "filled with bodies that slowly appeared one by one from the black foliage, from the mud, from behind a broken wheel."

In this land of barren earth, barren women, and impotent men (the Census taker is out of a job), dying animals abound. A particularly vivid scene is that at the local asylum from which the patients have fled but left behind them frozen monkeys strewn over the grounds: "One of the monkeys seemed to have grown, and frozen, was sitting upright on the bodies of the smaller beasts, tail coiled about his neck, dead eyes staring out through the gates." In this grotesque figure it would appear Hawkes is implying that those who are punished, those who are fixed in Dante's lowest circles of the Inferno are the ones who have returned to animality.

Situations and images continue to recall Dante's Inferno. The characters are, of course, victims, each enduring his own agony, but each is quite capable of victimizing, even torturing others for the sake of his own wretched survival. Jutta, one of the main characters, becomes a nymphomaniac; Ernst becomes a worshipper of wooden images, neglecting his wife Stella who enslaves Balamir as her lover. Sinking into lust is matched by the drive for power as Zizendorf supervises the murder of Stintz and Leevey in order to gain control of Spitzen-on-the-Dein.

But the lowest regions of Dante's Inferno have not been reached —Ugolino and Ruggieri, one sinking "his teeth into the other's nape / at the base of the skull, gnawing his loathsome dinner." Whether or not Dante was actually listing cannibalism as one of the unforgivable sins, Hawkes picks up the gambit. The Duke, otherwise unidentified, becomes convinced that Jutta's son is a fox and kills him. He finds his prey very hard to skin, since it "was not a deer or a possum." After much effort, he manages to skin, dismember, cook, and share it with Jutta who partakes of the unusual meat dish with great relish. The scene is horrifying, as horrifying as Procne feeding her child to her husband for supper: "She watched him while he ate; and then told him what he had feasted upon." But it is Hawkes's fusion of realistic detail, psychological acumen, and controlled fantasy that constitute his originality.

There is no question but what the war novel generally aligns itself with the upper levels of Dante's Inferno. While some individuals may sink much lower, the essential emphasis is usually on the opportunists, the lustful, the wrathful, and the sullen—in short, on those who populate the first circles of damnation in Dante. By the same token the lower depths of *The Inferno* generate their own novel transmutations which even more fully capture the existential concerns of the age, as the number of city novels indicate. The City of Dis has been fully recognized and powerfully re-created in such fiction as *Manhattan Transfer* and *The System of Dante's Hell*.

After the conventional though promising *Three Soldiers,* the very unconventional *Manhattan Transfer* commanded a great deal of attention. Dos Passos had apparently found his theme and his medium, both of which possessed striking resemblance to Dante that simultaneously defined both the continuity of the tradition and also the twentieth century's innovations in it. Initiating the pattern, Dos Passos' protagonist, wandering aimlessly, crosses water (by ferry) and finds himself in Manhattan, a place of constriction and isolation, a place where souls cannot survive, and no one really cares for anyone else. There are, in addition, punishing extremes of weather. And above all there is violence whether accidental or intentional. A fourteen-year-old boy confesses to killing his aged and crippled mother; a firebug sets fire to an apartment: "Something black had dropped from a window and lay on the pavement shrieking." In a cab a man jerks a revolver up to his mouth and dies on the curbstone "vomiting blood, head hanging limp over his checked vest." Elsewhere seductions, rapes, and abortions are taking place. In a subway one character, concerned with the possibility of throat cancer, sees the other passengers "green faces in the dingy light. . . . A trainload of jiggling corpses, nodding and swaying." With almost ingenuous irony, Dos Passos underlines the correspondence between his existential world and Dante's theological. One character complains: "The trouble with me is I cant decide what I want most, so my motion is circular, helpless and confoundedly discouraging." The complacent response is: "Oh but God decided that for you. You know all the time, but you won't admit it to yourself."

As Jimmy Herf attempts to orient himself in this Manhattan of human indifference and perpetually shrieking fire sirens, he is told by a stranger: "Walk east a block and turn down Broadway and you'll find the center of things if you walk far enough." The parallel of this to Dante's directed journey through the Inferno to its center is clear. More important, since Manhattan like the Inferno is itself coterminous with the bounds of the novel, Dos Passos can and does use an incredibly large cast of characters. Some simply fill out a scene; others, of course, become prominent. In the course of this panoramic view of Manhattan, Dos Passos articulates a contemporary version of Dante's itemized list of sinners: the gluttons, the drunkards, the virtuous pagans, the murderers, suicides, seducers, frauds, flatterers, and counterfeiters. Not to be forgotten are the treacherous and the cold of heart as exemplified in Ellie, a woman who becomes frozen into an Elliedoll, a non-person.

Still following the pattern of the *Inferno,* Dos Passos has Jimmy Herf become the only man to leave the Inferno of Manhattan. He travels at night, the only passenger on a ferry which is significantly met by "a brokendown springwagon loaded with flowers." On land, he climbs a hill, stops to look back at Manhattan, and then becomes conscious of himself as a living human being, a man returned from the living dead: "He can see nothing but fog spaced with a file of blurred arclights. Then he walks on, taking pleasure in breathing, in the beat of his blood, in the tread of his feet. . . . Gradually the fog thins, a morning pearliness is seeping in from somewhere." Like Dante's star, which he sees as he emerges from the Inferno, the "morning pearliness" is a symbol of a hope devoid of certainty that there are no more crooked paths to be encountered.

LeRoi Jones's *The System of Dante's Hell,* like *Manhattan Transfer,* ostensibly consists of disconnected scenes and random thoughts or observations. Some early reviewers asserted that Jones used a pretentious title as an appeal to intellectuals. Yet, with meticulous precision, with broken but somehow poetic sentences, Jones does expose a Hell, a black ghetto thriving on incontinence, violence, and fraud, surrounded by "white monsters" who add to the torment of the Inferno and prevent escape. As his own protagonist, Jones, like Jimmy Herf, has penetrated the very depths of Hell—Newark Street: "This is the center I mean. Where it all, came on. The rest is suburb. The rest is outside this hole. Snakes die past this block. Flames subside."

Yet in a very real sense Jones believes that he belongs in the Inferno which he himself has helped to build. He has witnessed and participated in the basest evil: "heresy against one's own sources, running in terror, from one's deepest responses and insights . . . the denial of feeling." He walks away from a woman who offers him her warmth, her affection, her body, in order to return to the army. And he does so not from a sense of discipline but fear. There he participates in a gang sexual attack on a black woman who screams for mercy not for herself but for them—she is diseased: "She screamed and screamed, her voice almost shearing off our tender heads. The scream of an actual damned soul. The actual prisoner of the world." Without mercy or compassion they throw her out of the moving car: "She smashed against the pavement and wobbled on her stomach hard against the curb." In this urban Inferno the victims are not only tormented by their environment and their monsters but by each other, thereby removing the last trace of humanity. It is a city dominated by the Gorgon of Despair.

With the therapeutic community where everything is being done for the inmates' own good we penetrate into the lowest region of Dante's the *Inferno*—the Malebolge, the region where the sinners are fixed in the earth or in ice. A curious example here is E. E. Cummings who has acknowledged his own close study of Dante but who employs as the basic analogue for *The Enormous Room* not the *Inferno* but *Pilgrim's Progress*. Like Bunyan's Pilgrim, Cummings, first accompanied by his friend and then alone, recognizes the evils of Vanity Fair, rejects both bribes and threats, is reassured by his vision of the Delectable Mountains, and finally reaches the safety of his father's house. Nevertheless, his pilgrimage takes place in a world much closer to Dante than Bunyan, though with the former's legitimate values and hierarchy mindlessly inverted and rendered ironic. Like the other prisoners, he has been suddenly and arbitrarily removed from the "decent God-fearing community." Like the others, he is urged to confess his crime, admit his guilt, and acknowledge the justice of his punishment. There is no way out of his dilemma—confessing means merited punishment; not confessing means added punishment. The index of this pervasive irony is perhaps most clearly seen in the fact that the Cummings protagonist is merely released from prison instead of moving on into the *Purgatorio* and *Paradiso*. On this confessional basis the prisoners can be assigned to one of two groups. Though both are confined and tormented, the "accommodators" are useful. The "incorrigibles" (some of whom coincide with Cummings' "Delectable Mountains") are dispensable. The latter can be consigned to the *cabinot* (as close an approximation to Dante's Malebolge as one can get): "Within the stone walls of his dungeon (into which a beam of light no bigger than a ten-cent piece, and in some cases no light at all, penetrated). The culprit could shout and scream his or her heart out if he or she liked, without serious annoyance to His Majesty, King Satan."

Among the monsters, "His Majesty, King Satan" is himself the most terrifying, perhaps because he is relatively seldom seen. When he does appear, he is described as "shaking a huge fist of pinkish, well-manicured flesh, the distinct, cruel, brightish eyes sprouting from their sockets under bushily enormous black eyebrows, the big, weak, coarse mouth extended almost from ear to ear and spouting invective, the soggy, brutal lips clinched apparently upward and backward showing the huge horse-like teeth to the froth-shot gums." With capricious will and unchecked sadism he keeps order. For example, he makes sure that male and female are separated (whether or not they be husband and wife), but both are expected to attend the Sunday service not to join in faith and hope but to suffer the combination of nearness and separation, of desire and frustration. No wonder an eleven-year-old girl suddenly passing by him staggers, "sobbing and shaking, past the Fiend—one hand held over her contorted face to shield her from the Awful Thing of Things." The situation, the language are Dante's not Bunyan's.

A similar displacement of Dante's *Inferno* into the secular technological hell of twentieth-century existence is operative in Ken Kesey's *One Flew over the Cuckoo's Nest*. Cummings deployed Dante's *Inferno* by superimposing it on *Pilgrim's Progress*. Kesey, on the other hand, works in a fashion less of amalgamated literary forms than of ironic cultural juxtapositions. His book derives its ultimate impact from its fusion of the contemporary and the traditional, the technology of our period and the imaginative formalism of Dante's. It is, of course, clear that Dante's Inferno is filled with "sinners" judged by God, LeRoi Jones's with criminals judged by whites, Cummings' with prisoners disposed of by military judges, and Kesey's by misfits examined by psychiatrists. In each case, the very parallels magnify the irony—the irony which deepens when it is the individual that is at issue.

In Kesey's novel each individual, as long as he is capable of talking, has exercised his free will time and time again by rehearsing his sins, accepting his punishment, and indeed inflicting it on himself. At least one prisoner continually burns himself with any cigarette or stub he can obtain in a psychotic ritual that is a demonic parody of Dante's Christian vision of moral judgment. Thus, each is encouraged to recognize his sin and guilt, thereby demonstrating his free will, and to compensate, for his own sake, by yielding his complete, unquestioning obedience to authority. Yet the authority itself is secular, human, and simplistic rather than sacred, divine, and replete with moral subtlety.

If Kesey has stressed the parallel ironies between commitment to the Inferno or to a "modern" asylum, he strengthens the parallel by describing the way in which each inmate is assigned to a group, apparently for life. At the top, Kesey like Dante, places an ambulatory group, the "Acutes." They are able to move, to talk to each other, to make jokes at one another's expense. But they are also quite capable of spying and tale-telling, of increasing someone else's torment for a moment of their own surcease. They are the footlickers, the toadies, the traitors. They are not mad, insane; they are simply "still sick enough to be fixed,"—and as such they must be for a time or forever taken out of human society. Only in such cases, not God but the psychiatrist makes the decision.

Below these are the "Chronics," who are defined in a technological metaphor: "Machines with flaws inside that can't be repaired, flaws born in, or flaws beat in over so many years of the guy running into solid things that by the time the hospital found him he was bleeding rust in some vacant lot." The physical details of the description echo LeRoi Jones, but they refer to the "Chronics," who however they got to the asylum are precisely subdivided in terms of their immobility. The "Walkers" can still get around and show some slight signs of individuality providing they are helped with their feeding. Even the "Wheelers," though utterly dependent on machines or on others for their survival occasionally recall some sense of their identity. The "Vegetables," however, are as totally fixed as Dante's "sinners" bound by earth or ice. Forcibly fed by "a twisting motion of the spoon, like coring a rotten apple," they are totally immobile, consigned to a world of excrement, indifference, and at times sadism. Unlike Dante, however, Kesey does not stratify his characters in a moral hierarchy; he does not find the "Vegetable" more reprehensible than the "Chronic." For him, the demonic world receives its values from the psychiatrist who has taken over the task of examining, judging, and prescribing.

Yet even the psychiatrist knows that he is under the directions of the Big Nurse. Dr. Spring, a well-intentioned man who does care for his patients, is rendered impotent; a little "birthmarked swing-shift nurse" does have "compassion but not courage." The others follow the orders of the Big Nurse without question. She is the symbol of supreme authority in the institution; she is the dispenser of awards and punishments; and she is, for the patients at least, both omnipotent and omniscient. And in fulfilling these roles she reveals her full monstrosity. The Indian inmate, apparently with enough sanity to convince his keepers that he is "deaf and dumb," tells us he sees her slide "through the door with a gust of cold and locks the door behind her and I see her fingers trail across the polished steel—tip of each finger the same color as her lips. Funny orange. Like the tip of a soldering iron. Color so hot or so cold that if she touches you with it you can't tell which."

She is capable of controlling the elements, as the Indian narrator observes, and thus to produce fog at a moment's notice. She has pills for every occasion, almost any emergency. Above all she has her "black boys" (Dante's monsters) to keep her patients in line. Clad in immaculate hospital white, "they are tall and sharp and bony and their faces are chipped into expressions that never change like flint arrowheads. Their eyes come to points. If you brush against their hair it rasps the hide right off you." At best they are cruel, at worst sadistic. And they have been trained, thoroughly trained by the Big Nurse. With such supervision and knowing what treatment is in store for them, it is no longer strange that so many of the inmates confess to sins, real or imaginary, that they find a relief in confession and a desire for punishment. As recorded in the Big Nurse's Log Book, the list of sins is endless: "I tried to take my little sister to bed. . . . I—one time—wanted to take my brother to bed. . . . I killed my cat when I was six. . . . I lied about trying. I did take my sister. . . . So did I! So did I . . . And me! And *me*!"

Kesey's is a brilliant fusion of the contemporary mechanical and the traditional theological—God as I.B.M. His is the brilliant exploration of a world that has accepted mechanization as progress and tradition as nonsense. He has made his readers see that the individual can be described but never typed; he can be punished but never relieved of his freedom. That, in effect, is what God gave to man. In the end, the Indian has to decide whether the Big Nurse has established her Log and various other phenomena through magic or science. Sooner or later he has to believe in her powers and defy them if he is to exist.

Many live in the Inferno for eternity. A few are crucified in it—the sacrificial victims, each meaning everything or *nada*. Such is Jim Conklin in *The Red Badge of Courage,* a man whose death, not life, parallels that of Christ's. No one has seriously challenged R. W. Stallman's list of parallels. The difference, of course, as Conklin's physical death agony seems to project so vividly, is that he has no powers of redemption or salvation. There is no connection between his death and Henry Fleming's return to camp and further engagement in the war. In terms of the novel as a whole, Crane is simply exploring the myth of the hero as man and as a divine being, and contemplating the distance between them with wry irony: a man who dies, dies in the likeness of Christ, wounded, forbidden to be touched, forbidden to be followed. But with Dantean attention to physical detail, while there is "something ritelike in these movements of the doomed soldier, the agony of dying is emphasized." At one time he is the man "waiting with patience for something he had come to meet"; at another time he is like "an animal kicking and tumbling furiously to be free." In no sense is he Christ as redeemer, in many ways he is Christ the scapegoat, a scapegoat barely witnessed and officially ignored. In the Inferno the Christ figure can be either ignored or inverted.

McMurphy in Kesey's novel is a particularly contemporary version of the Christ figure. The parallels between McMurphy and Christ are as clear as those between Faulkner's Corporal and Christ. He is the man of the earth—the con man, the miracle worker. He is able, after much persuasion, argument, and confrontation to take twelve of his comrades as well as Dr. Spring on a fishing trip. Though he himself shows little but weariness, the fish multiply. Somewhat later, he is able to provide a wedding feast or at least drink for a "Momma's boy" Billy, who is totally satisfied but, with help from the Big Nurse can only return to Momma and the Big Nurse as a child-like tell-tale who describes how McMurphy transformed water into wine for the sake not of an orgy, as the nurse believes, but of a ritual coupling.

From the beginning marked as a rebel by his language and disrespect for authority, accused by Billy, he suffers his martyrdom, his hands locked to each side. As he is about to be given shock treatment, already documented as having destroyed several minds, he comments with final irony: "Anointest my head with conductant, do I get a crown of thorns?" After the therapy he is a "vegetable." His actual death is a *coup de grace* by the Indian narrator, who because of McMurphy has gradually discovered a sense of his own manhood and of life. Immediately after McMurphy's death, there are convictions that "he will be back." His is the material for legends not simply because he defied the Big Nurse and, at least once made her look ridiculous, but because he carried human values into a non-human, mechanistic world.

Out of this modern Inferno, some—a very few—seem to escape and when they do, it is in diverse fashions. Crane's Henry Fleming leaves the field of battle believing in his own heroism, barely aware of the fact that he has lasted through a battle not a war. Dos Passos' Jimmy Herf is most aware of the fact that he is still alive and functioning as such, "feeling the tread of his feet on the pavement." Zizendorf in *The Cannibal,* having accomplished the death of the American overseer and taken possession of his motorcycle, has no doubts about the future. Such representative figures reveal that these emergences range from the marginal and physical through the mistaken and illusory to the non-existent and insane. These, each in his own way and degree, belong in the Inferno.

Others, apparently like Dante, are privileged to emerge from the Inferno and report on its dimensions. McMurphy may be dead, but his disciple, the Indian, once inarticulate, is able to tell his story. LeRoi Jones, not quite sure whether he personally is inside or outside the Inferno, can reflect: "Once, as a child, I would weep for compassion and understanding. And Hell was the inferno of my frustration. But the world is clearer to me now, and many of its features more definable."

For Crane, for Dos Passos, for Faulkner—for any number of writers who have observed our scene, our life, and found it an inferno, Jones speaks not only the epitaph but the possibility of resurrection, of a new life, a new man, a new world bound but not tied to tradition: "Hell is actual, and people with hell in their heads. But the pastoral moments in a man's life will also mean a great deal as far as his emotional references. One thinks of home, or the other 'homes' we have had. And we remember w/ love those things bathed in soft black light. The struggles away or towards this peace is Hell's function." Jones has his own reasons for recognizing the innocence of childhood and the fallen world of man. They may be more cogent but no more compelling than ours. We all admit that we have long fallen from grace, we all admit that we are living in an Inferno. But Dante had his Beatrice—his symbol of faith. The rest of us are left in a void, a limbo, at best, or with growing apprehension we recognize around us the familiar landmarks of the *Inferno*.

The Impact of French Symbolism
on Modern American Poetry

HASKELL M. BLOCK

These are still early days for the study of twentieth-century American poetry. We have learned to think of literature not as a dead past but rather as a living presence, whose meaning does not remain fixed and definite, but is itself subject to the mutations of time and of human values. We cannot predict what needs will animate the study of poetry in a later time or what modifications the poetry itself will undergo in human consciousness. The Virgil of the twentieth century is no more the Virgil of the Middle Ages than of Augustan Rome. As with the ancients, so with the moderns. Particularly in the study of so large and complex a subject as the impact of French symbolism on modern American poetry, it would be well to keep a word of caution in mind. Our view of the French symbolists has undergone vast change since the days of Arthur Symons' *The Symbolist Movement in Literature* or Edmund Wilson's *Axel's Castle,* and the same process will surely operate in our view of American poets of the past half-century. The student of modern poetry, whether of Europe or America, cannot escape the fact that there are large areas of uncertainty and ambiguity in our understanding and appreciation of the literature of the recent past. If the following discussion seems to raise more questions than can possibly

165

be resolved, it is in large part because so little has been done by way of systematic analysis and interpretation of the problems at hand.

The pioneering study of the subject is René Taupin's dissertation of 1929, *L'Influence du Symbolisme français sur la poésie américaine (de 1910 à 1920)*. Pioneers are perforce obliged to submit to the corrections of those who follow in their paths. It is not difficult to list the weaknesses of Taupin's study: a narrow and mechanical conception of influence, typical of comparative studies of an earlier time; an understandable tendency to see French symbolism everywhere on the American poetic scene of the early twentieth century; a somewhat hasty examination of the diffusion of the symbolists in the American periodicals of the 1890's; and too limited a view of the interaction of aesthetic and historical values in the individual work of art. Quite apart from these inadequacies, the year 1920 was plainly an unfortunate cut-off date, for American poets continued long after 1920 to respond imaginatively to the achievements of the French symbolists. Indeed, in relation to the symbolist tradition, the work of the major American poets which appeared after the publication of Taupin's study is even more important than their earlier writings. Taupin's study was a courageous undertaking, and it remains valuable within its limits, but, for a variety of reasons, it needs to be redone. In the meanwhile, students interested in the subject can find a number of recent essays that point toward a fresh approach. The most provocative studies are: Harold Rosenberg's suggestive summary, "French Silence and American Poetry," reprinted in *The Tradition of the New* (1959); Kenneth Rexroth's more ambitious survey, "The Influence of French Poetry on American," reprinted in *Assays* (1961); and the broad philosophical overview of Frederick J. Hoffman, "*Symbolisme* and Modern Poetry in the United States," in *Comparative Literature Studies,* IV (1967), 193–99. In addition, there are, of course, a large number of useful studies dealing with individual poets, chiefly T. S. Eliot and Wallace Stevens.

Although the description of a unified group of French poets as symbolist does not gain common currency until 1886, from our present vantage point we may view the symbolist movement as extending approximately from 1850 to 1920 and embracing three generations of French poetry, from Baudelaire through Mallarmé to Valéry. Yet, just as the roots of this tradition may be found in a variety of literatures besides the French, so the heritage of symbolism, as C. M. Bowra has convincingly shown, is part of western literature generally. Moreover, despite a common tendency to confine symbolist poetry to the later nineteenth century, it is clear that the origins of the movement lie in a continuous Neoplatonic and mystical tradition in western thought and expression, and also that the movement did not come to an abrupt end shortly before or after the First World War. While all terms employed to describe historical or literary periods are vague and approximate in character, they generally help to define the assumptions and norms underlying the work of a large number of writers, and they should be used with what precision they will allow.

The distinguishing elements of symbolist poetry may be seen in a distinct poetic theory and style. The poetics of the movement were set forth by Baudelaire, notably in his essays on Poe and on Wagner, as well as on such French contemporaries as Gautier and Hugo. According to the principle of correspondences, which Baudelaire derived mainly from Swedenborg, the world is a vast dictionary wherein objects are signs or symbols, emblems or hieroglyphs. Through the unique power of the imagination, the poet is able to perceive the secret relation of the visible and invisible planes of reality, grasped through correspondences and analogies. As Baudelaire declared, the visible universe is but a storehouse of images and signs to which imagination gives their relative place and value. The imagination is thus the "queen of faculties," the supreme reality, the power by which objects are apprehended as symbols.

The insistence of Poe on the autonomy of poetry, its musical and magical suggestiveness, and its essential difference from prose, was expanded by the symbolists into a complex theory of poetic language. For Mallarmé, this language consisted not of statement but suggestion. In keeping with Poe's doctrine of effects, he asserted that the poet must depict not the thing itself but the effect which it produces. Mallarmé's poetics and poetry are marked by the same concern with mystery and magic that we may see in Baudelaire, but with a more complex interiorization of experience as the groundwork of expression. With the passage of time, Mallarmé has emerged as the great synthesizer of the symbolist movement, in his dense and subtle critical essays as well as in a series of great poems. In his invocation of the values of dream and spirituality in a language of rich concentration and suggestiveness, Mallarmé radically enlarged the plane of poetry. In so doing, he moved toward a polarization of poetry and ordinary discourse. It should be added, despite the claims of hostile critics to the contrary, that Mallarmé did not repudiate either concrete human experience or the perceptual world. Nevertheless, it is from Mallarmé rather than from Baudelaire that the notion of symbolist poetry as abstract and perforce difficult poetry derives, with its insistence on a necessary obscurity. For Mallarmé, who saw the sole duty of the poet as the orphic explanation of the Universe, a poem is a mystery for which the reader must seek the key. Philosopher and seer, the poet reveals through the magical power of language the mystery and wonder of our being.

Mallarmé's preoccupation with the crises and cleavages of inner experience should not be viewed as an escape from life or an evasion of its problems. Indeed, it may be claimed that no poet of any time or place was more deeply involved in the actual and human character of existence. Nevertheless, the poet's bold experimentation and his tendency toward metaphysical or mystical abstraction served to widen the distance between poetry and mundane reality. It was the achievement of Mallarmé's follower, Valéry, to render the techniques and values of symbolism more immediate and accessible to the reader, without abandoning the claims of vagueness, musicality, and complex introspection. For Valéry's Jeune Parque as for Mallarmé's Hérodiade, the self is the universal image of contemplation. The theme of solipsism moves hand in hand with the image of Narcissus in symbolist poetry, an image endowed by the symbolists with new mythical value. The symbolists' Narcissus mirrors the acute and anguished consciousness of the mind's enforced preoccupation with itself. Yet, Narcissism is no final resting place for any of the major symbolist poets. In his best poems, such as "Le Cimetière Marin," Valéry gives utterance to a passionate and moving awareness of the claims of physical experience on the individual. His art, like that of his great predecessors, fittingly weds intellect and sense, the abstract and the concrete, the private and the universal.

Despite their marked individual differences, Baudelaire, Mallarmé, and Valéry are all part of a continuous poetic tradition which may be defined as the main axis of the symbolist movement. There are, to be sure, other figures who have been commonly viewed as symbolists. At the end of the nineteenth century, the representative poet of the new movement was held to be not Mallarmé but Verlaine, and it could be plausibly contended that, although Mallarmé's importance has been far greater in our own day, Verlaine had a much wider impact at the turn of the century when symbolist poetry was frequently identified with his languorous musicality and sound-play. His art of delicate nuance and evocative mood creation was accompanied by a direct outpouring of personal feeling that represents a distinct, though muted return to a Romantic style. The more characteristic symbolist poets are at once more impersonal and intellectual, yet without abandoning the awareness of deeply-felt personal experience. Even more marginally symbolist than Verlaine is Jules Laforgue, whose ironic and conversational idiom, for all of its engaging liveliness, is at some remove from the poetry of correspondences and analogies. Laforgue was far more symbolist in his aesthetic thought than in his poetry, and it is possible that had he lived longer, his art might have moved toward a more recognizably symbolist style. We can see the new style in the work of a number of young writers who grouped themselves around Mallarmé: Régnier, Dujardin, Rodenbach, Van Lerberghe, Mockel, Vielé-Griffin, Merrill, the early André Gide, and a host of others; but it will not do to consider every French poet of the later nineteenth century—Rimbaud, for example—as a symbolist poet. Despite striking affinities, notably in his occultism and his experimentation with synaesthesia, Rimbaud's style is far more violent and explosive than we may find in any of the major symbolists, and his impact on subsequent poetry has been in a markedly different direction.

When we survey modern American poetry against the background of the main line of the French symbolist tradition, we must remember that this tradition is itself, in part, an extension of values of earlier American literature, most notably in the work of Poe. To some extent, the discovery of the French symbolists in the United States was a return to a temporarily neglected aspect of the native American tradition. It has been common to see two principal lines of development in modern American poetry, one stemming from Poe and expressing an intellectual and coterie view of poetry; the other stemming from Whitman and expressing an emotional and populist view—but a less schematic approach would see the poetry of twentieth-century America as marked by an astonishing diversity which rejects the imposition of any fixed patterns.[1] It would therefore seem difficult to speak of an "Ecole symboliste américaine" even among the early poets of American modernism,[2] to say nothing of their successors. All the same, the symbolist tradition has been a significant force in the poetry of the United States, often entering into the mainstream of our poetry in a vital, formative role, not only as a source of experimentation and of freshness of language,[3] but as a quest for formal purity and spiritual transcendence.[4]

---

[1] See F. O. Matthiessen, "American Poetry, 1920–40," *Sewanee Review,* LV (1947), 24–55.

[2] René Taupin, *L'Influence du Symbolisme français sur la poésie américaine (de 1910 à 1920)* (Paris, 1929), 45.

[3] Harold Rosenberg, "French Silence and American Poetry," *The Tradition of the New* (New York, 1959), 87–95.

[4] Cf. Glauco Cambon, *The Inclusive Flame* (Bloomington, 1963), 50.

This is not to deny the simultaneous presence of other forces moving poets in the same direction as the symbolists. The affinities between French symbolists and modern American poets are often quite independent of any conscious derivation or influence.

The Mauve Decade saw the introduction of the symbolists in the United States, in large part through British writers such as George Moore and Arthur Symons.[5] An earlier and more direct interaction was provided by Stuart Merrill, whose father was American Consul in Paris. After returning to the United States to study law at Columbia University in 1884, Merrill went back to France in time to experience the full impact of the formalization of symbolist doctrine. His awareness of the new emphasis on reverie and mood creation is reflected in *Pastels in Prose,* a volume including rhythmic prose translations of Baudelaire and Mallarmé as well as of several lesser symbolists, published by Harper's in 1890 and virtually ignored. Merrill left America for the last time in 1892, to remain in France where he became a significant member of the young symbolist generation. Despite the fact that he seems to have had no impact on the American poetry of his day, Merrill has recently been praised as "the greatest American poet of the turn of the century."[6] He was unmistakably among the most cosmopolitan American poets in an age of insularity, and his work in English merits sympathetic reappraisal.

Perhaps the first article published in the United States to deal at all extensively with symbolism as a literary current was T. S. Perry's "The Latest Literary Fashion in France" (*Cosmopolitan,* July, 1892). Perry based his general remarks chiefly on Jules Huret's *Enquête sur l'évolution littéraire* (1891), and emphasized the work of Verlaine and Ghil. He translated part of Maeterlinck's *L'Intruse* and cited a poem, "Rêverie," of Stuart Merrill. Perry's comments on Mallarmé are largely negative, and his essay offers little by way of

---

[5] See Bruce A. Morrissette, "Early English and American Critics of French Symbolism," *Studies in Honor of Frederick W. Shipley* (St. Louis, 1942), 159–80.

[6] Kenneth Rexroth, "The Influence of French Poetry on American," *Assays* (New York, 1961), 147.

constructive generalization concerning the new impulse. Somewhat more significant was the essay by Theodore Child, "The New Poetry" (*Harper's,* August, 1892), for it offers the first definition in English of symbolism as a literary movement: an effort to interpret "the relations, correspondences, and affinities between certain sounds, forms, and colors, and certain states of soul."[7] As far as this definition goes, it is excellent, but the context is largely pejorative, and throughout the essay any praise for the symbolists is carefully qualified. Far more knowledgeable as well as sympathetic was the essay of Aline Gorren, "The French Symbolists" (*Scribner's,* January–June, 1893). While drawing in part on George Moore and Arthur Symons, her essay offers much that is new, including an extended discussion of Laforgue, a good account of the Wagnerian vogue in France, and a serious attempt to relate symbolist poetry to contemporary painting. Despite an undue stress on alleged preciosity and on minor writers, the author plainly knows who the major figures are and writes out of a genuine imaginative sympathy with the new tendency.

By 1895, articles popularizing the symbolist movement were appearing in American periodicals with some frequency.[8] Some early essays, such as that of Richard Hovey on Maeterlinck, combined knowledgeable description with lavish admiration.[9] Vance Thompson's contributions to *M'lle New York,* later collected in his *French Portraits,* reveal an almost incredible familiarity with the symbolists for the time, but it has been convincingly shown that Thompson's exposition of Mallarmé's theories was cribbed from Wyzewa's *Nos maîtres.*[10] Many of the early essays set forth a pejorative definition of Arthur Symons' formulation, in *Harper's* for November, 1893, of "The Decadent Movement in Literature." Thus, B. W. Wells de-

---

[7] Cited by Morrissette, *Studies in Honor of Frederick W. Shipley,* 168.

[8] See Taupin, *L'Influence du Symbolisme français,* 32–40.

[9] Hovey, "Impressions of Maurice Maeterlinck and the Théâtre de l'Oeuvre," *Poet Lore,* VII (August, 1895), 449.

[10] Bruce A. Morrissette, "Vance Thompson's Plagiarism of Teodor de Wyzewa's Articles on Mallarmé," *Modern Language Notes,* LXVII (1952), 175–78.

clared in the *Sewanee Review* for November, 1895, that Baudelaire's work was "a house built on sand." Applying rough and ready moralistic canons of criticism, Wells dismissed the symbolists as "decadent and deliquescent," marked by a "morbid singularity," and he warned against the power of bad foreign influences "to cultivate in enervated minds the diathesis of indefinite mysticism." The university public seems to have been slow to respond positively to the symbolists, although a measure of understanding may have been acquired from the visit and lectures of Henri de Régnier in 1900.[11] Mention should also be made of the role of a young instructor at Harvard a few years later, Pierre La Rose, in stimulating interest in the symbolists among his students.[12] Of course, we may assume that the more adventuresome university poets of that time discovered the symbolists by themselves. The early critical essays in the literary journals of the day helped to create a sense of the importance of the new poetry of France, which was sustained most notably in the following decade in the criticism of James Gibbons Huneker.[13]

It has been all too easy to disparage American poetry of the period 1890–1910, but a more balanced view would suggest that the poetry of these decades was far from mediocre. It should be recognized that many of the most promising poets of the turn of the century, notably Richard Hovey, Trumbull Stickney, and William Vaughan Moody, all died while comparatively young. Hovey was particularly active on behalf of the symbolists in America. He had traveled in France in 1891–92, and soon afterwards published two volumes of translations of the plays of Maeterlinck. Most of Hovey's verse consists of official or patriotic poetry of a purely ceremonial character—he is best known for originating the phrase, "Remember

---

[11] Taupin, *L'Influence du Symbolisme français*, 41.

[12] Malcolm Cowley, "Laforgue in America: A Testimony," *Sewanee Review*, LXXI (1963), 63.

[13] Cf. Taupin, *L'Influence du Symbolisme français*, 43–44. For comments on Huneker's symbolist prose poems, see Arnold T. Schwab, *James Gibbons Huneker* (Stanford, 1963), 96.

the Maine"—but his collection of 1898, *Along the Trail,* includes several translations of Mallarmé, including "Apparition" and the "Scène" from *Hérodiade.* A captious reviewer remarked of Hovey's Mallarmé translations: "They have no lasting value as poetry, but neither have their originals, and they do reproduce something of the striking verbal effects at which the poet chiefly aimed."[14] A few of Hovey's somewhat cloying love lyrics, such as "My Lady's Soul" or "The Thought of Her" seem to reflect symbolist techniques, but without the sureness of control that we find in Hovey's French forbears. His last collection, *To the End of the Trail* (1908), also includes some translations of the symbolists, as well as a short fragment, "A Mallarmé," presumably written on the occasion of the poet's death.

Far more gifted than Hovey and closer in style and spirit to the symbolists was the classical scholar, Trumbull Stickney. Born in Switzerland, educated at Harvard and the Sorbonne, his knowledge of contemporary French poetry and criticism was probably unequalled by any other American poet of his time. Stickney died in 1904 at the age of thirty. His poetry is to be found in two volumes, *Dramatic Verses* (1902) and *The Poems of Trumbull Stickney* (1905). Both collections are books of promise rather than fulfillment, but their best poems combine classical, Elizabethan, or symbolist elements with a deeply felt *inquiétude,* rendered in a language of vivid clarity. The sonnet, "Tho' inland far with mountains prisoned round," invokes the values of dream and infinite aspiration amid the immensity of nature. Many of his other poems are tender nostalgic lyrics in the mood and tone of Verlaine.[15] In a review published in 1901 of a study of contemporary French poetry by Diego Di Roberto, Stickney displays a considerable familiarity with the symbolists and their contemporaries. He chides Di Roberto

[14] William Morton Payne, "Recent Poetry," *Dial,* XXVI (April 16, 1899), 277. For a detailed discussion of Hovey's relationship to Mallarmé, Maeterlinck, and other symbolists, see Allan H. MacDonald, *Richard Hovey* (Durham, 1957), 155–80.

[15] See Edmund Wilson, " 'The Country I Remember,' " *New Republic,* CIII (October 14, 1940), 530.

gently for leaning too heavily on the adverse critical judgment of Brunetière, and for an excessive valuation of Coppée along side of Mallarmé, Verlaine, and the young writers of the *Revue Blanche*.[16] Some of Stickney's poems are marked by an intense and poignant sense of suffering and loss, often charged with dramatic intensity by sudden bursts of violence, as in the pastoral, "On Rodin's 'L'Illusion, Soeur d'Icare.'" Cut off before he could develop a harmony of vision and style, Stickney deserves far more sympathetic critical attention than he has received.[17] Had he continued to develop, he may have altered in a significant way the character and force of symbolist influence on modern American poetry.

In retrospect, we can see the establishment of *Poetry: A Magazine of Verse* in Chicago in 1912 as the beginning of a Renaissance of poetry in the United States. Under the leadership of Harriet Monroe and with the aid of vigorous corresponding editors in London and Paris, the magazine did much to create a new cosmopolitanism and sophistication in the American literary scene.[18] In response to the program of Ezra Pound and kindred spirits, *Poetry* played a leading role in promulgating the tenets of Imagism: an insistence on the exact word, on a maximum of concentration, on bareness, speed, and concreteness, on the autonomy of the image as the center of poetic value, on composition "in sequence of the musical phrase, not in sequence of a metronome."[19] In *Poetry* for November, 1912, Harriet Monroe described the Imagists as poets who tried to "attain in English certain subtleties of cadence of the kind which Mallarmé and his followers have studied in French."[20] There are unmistakable analogies between symbolist and Imagist poetry, notably in

---

[16] Stickney's review of Diego Di Roberto, *Poeti Francesi Contemporanei* appears in *La Cultura* (Roma), XX (15 febbraio, 1901), 60–61.

[17] See Horace Gregory and Marya Zaturenska, *A History of American Poetry, 1900–1940* (New York, 1947), 32–37, and especially James Reeves and Seán Haldane (eds.), *Homage to Trumbull Stickney* (London, 1968), 1–24, 85–90.

[18] A good summary of the significance of the founding of *Poetry* and the work of Harriet Monroe may be found in Gregory and Zaturenska, *American Poetry*, 141–49.

[19] Cited by Stanley K. Coffman, Jr., *Imagism* (Norman, Okla., 1951), 9.

[20] *Ibid.*, 7–8.

rhythmic experimentation, as reflected in the early poetry of Pound.[21] Despite the Imagists' rejection of the obtrusive musicality of sound-play, they drew considerably on Verlaine's art of mood creation and wilful fragmentation. Some Imagist poetry, such as Amy Lowell's *Pictures of the Floating World* (1919), combines styles of Verlaine and oriental poetry, admittedly with more concern with description and decoration than is found in either of these models. Overtones of the fragility and delicacy of Verlaine may also be found in many other American Imagist poems, as in some of the early experiments in concentrated suggestiveness of William Carlos Williams.[22] Beyond these affinities with Verlaine, there would not at first glance seem to be any deeper relationship between Imagism and symbolism. The Imagists aimed at concreteness, precision, and objectivity. The symbolists under the aegis of Mallarmé tended toward abstraction, vagueness, and subjectivity. Nevertheless, as Warren Ramsey has recently suggested, there are important common elements that co-exist along with very real differences.[23] Foremost among these common elements is the passion for order, the ideal of construction. From this standpoint, it is quite possible that Pound might have found Baudelaire and Mallarmé far more congenial both as theorists and poets than he recognized. The symbolist preoccupation with vagueness and suggestiveness is, at its best, an art of maximum precision which in no way excludes the presence of powerful visual images. Indeed, despite the very considerable contribution made by Imagism to the creation of a new and fresh poetic language at a time when this was badly needed, the Imagist poets might have achieved even more than they did had they shared the symbolist quest for wholeness of experience, for a totality of poetic vision embracing both visible and spiritual realms of being. Lacking such totality of aspiration, Imagist poetry found its characteristic

---

[21] See William Van O'Connor, *Sense and Sensibility in Modern Poetry* (Chicago, 1956), 71–72.   [22] Cf. Gregory and Zaturenska, *American Poetry,* 210.
[23] Ramsey, "Uses of the Visible: American Imagism, French Symbolism," *Comparative Literature Studies,* IV (1967), 177–91.

style in fragments, often striking and arresting in themselves, but without any larger promise or relation. Of course, some of the poets most active in the promulgation of Imagism, such as F. S. Flint, Amy Lowell, and John Gould Fletcher, fused Imagist and symbolist values freely in their art, as did Wallace Stevens in his poems written around World War I, and Hart Crane in some of his early lyrics. Thus, the poem "Legend" in Crane's *White Buildings* begins:

> As silent as a mirror is believed
> Realities plunge in silence by . . .

Similarly, in the still life "Garden Abstract," the preoccupation with dream and suggestiveness points simultaneously to symbolist reverie and Imagist concentration. These poems are not typical of Hart Crane's early manner, which was at once more personal and more turbulent in imagery than we may find either in symbolist or Imagist poetry, but Crane was a highly eclectic poet and both of these styles enter to some extent into his art. Imagism, like symbolism, came to be rapidly assimilated into the resources in both theory and technique available to the modern poet, and the two tendencies often intersect in the work of poets who were neither symbolists nor Imagists in any strict sense.

It is a commonplace that the most typical and clearest expression of a particular literary movement or style is often found in the work of secondary or distinctly minor figures. Truly great poets make what they borrow their own. All the same, the diffusion of new poetic resources is in itself an important part of the dynamics of literary creation, and consciously derivative art is not necessarily mediocre simply because of its transparent dependence on the work of others. Perhaps the nearest approximation to symbolist poetry in American writing of the early years of the present century is the work of Walter Conrad Arensberg. A Harvard classmate and friend of Wallace Stevens, Arensberg has received a modest degree of attention in recent years from readers of Stevens interested in that poet's early sources and contemporary affiliations. Robert Buttel has called attention to some impressive thematic and verbal parallels between the poetry of Stevens and Arensberg.[24] Along with other French poets, Arensberg translated Nerval, Baudelaire, Mallarmé, and Verlaine. His collection *Idols* (1916) is of special importance for its fine translation of "The Afternoon of a Faun: Eclogue by Mallarmé," accompanied by an elaborate "Note" which present-day interpreters of Mallarmé might well consult with profit. Arensberg declares of the poem: "It is a dream within a day-dream—a sort of solipsistic drama in which the dreams are the symbols which the dreamer has invented for his desires, and which he strives by all the human means of logic, art, and action to endow with actual existence."[25] Arensberg has caught the central movement of the poem in an act of inner transformation. He sees the reconciliation of the dreamer and the dream in the silence beyond the "threshold of unconsciousness" towards which the words move. Both the translation and the commentary are a landmark in the sensitive interpretation of Mallarmé in English, and are altogether remarkable for their time.

Arensberg was not a daring innovator and his poetry lacks a powerful personal idiom. Nevertheless, it is a significant expression of characteristically symbolist themes and values, and points the way to further developments of symbolist style by other and greater American poets. One of Arensberg's representative poems is "Voyage à L'Infini," which appeared in *Others* for September, 1915:

> The swan existing
> Is like a song with an accompaniment
> Imaginary.
>
> Across the glassy lake,
> Across the lake to the shadow of the willows,
> It is accompanied by an image,

---

[24] Buttel, *Wallace Stevens: the Making of Harmonium* (Princeton, 1967), 96–99.
[25] Walter Conrad Arensberg, *Idols* (Boston, 1916), 78.

—As by Debussy's
"Reflets dans l'eau."

The swan that is
Reflects
Upon the solitary water—breast to breast
With the duplicity:
"The other one!"

And breast to breast it is confused.
O visionary wedding! O stateliness of the procession!
It is accompanied by the image of itself
Alone.

At night
The lake is a wide silence,
Without imagination.

The Narcissus-like swan contemplating its own image is both an object of physical beauty—a work of art—and an analogue of human consciousness entrapped by the limits of its operation. The recurrent musical comparisons along with the muted description and gradual revelation of the swan's *état d'âme,* all serve to sustain an evocation of mystery culminating in silence. The poem lacks the dramatic tension and deep philosophical probing that we find in the great poems of Mallarmé—for example, in his swan sonnet, "Le vierge, le vivace et le bel aujourd'hui"—but it is by no means a poor poem, and it will bear favorable comparison with much of the Imagist poetry that was being published in the United States at the same time.

By the end of the First World War, young American poets interested in the symbolists could find a number of translations and essays of popularization dealing with both major and minor French poets. Amy Lowell was a particularly important force in enhancing the appreciation of the symbolists, notably through her lectures in Boston in 1915 on the poetry of Verhaeren, Samain, Gourmont, Régnier, Jammes, and Fort, published that same year with accompanying translations as *Six French Poets.* Imagist poets like John

Gould Fletcher consciously emulated at times the mistiness and reverie of the symbolists, as in *Irradiations* (1915):

> The spattering of the rain upon pale terraces
> Of afternoon is like the passing of a dream
> Amid the roses shuddering 'gainst the wet green stalks
> Of the streaming trees . . .

It is reported that when Fletcher read *Irradiations* at a London dinner party, Amy Lowell exclaimed, "Why, my dear boy, you have genius"—to which Fletcher replied, "You will find that if you read Baudelaire, Mallarmé, Verlaine, Rimbaud, and Verhaeren carefully, that I am not so original as you think."[26] Fletcher's poems in the symbolist vein are of limited historical import, but his late and often terrifying religious poetry deserves attention in its own right.

When we approach the major American poets of the twentieth century from the perspective of French symbolism, it is difficult to see any clear pattern of relationships. As in other times and places, different poets seem to respond to the same impulse in strikingly different ways. Particularly in view of the modern emphasis on originality and individualism, the conscious emulation of a single recognizable style is the exception rather than the rule. This does not mean, as has been contended, that our subject must necessarily be confined to "the most obvious borrowings and surface similarities."[27] A poetic vision reflects a poet's total experience, including the poetry he has read, re-read, and assimilated. The eclecticism and at times bewildering variety of styles present within the work of a single poet—or even within a single poem—makes the evaluation of the role of any particular style extremely difficult. Surface similarities are sometimes signs of deeper affinities between poets, but for most students of modern poetry, obvious elements of resemblance

---

[26] Cited by Ralph Behrens, "John Gould Fletcher and Rimbaud's 'Alchimie du Verbe,'" *Comparative Literature,* VIII (1956), 46. For a fuller discussion of symbolist aspects of Fletcher's work, see Taupin, *L'Influence du Symbolisme français,* 193–210. Also see Calvin S. Brown, "The Color Symphony before and after Gautier," *Comparative Literature,* V (1953), 304–307.   [27] O'Connor, *Modern Poetry,* 66.

are much less interesting than convergences in poetic vision and style, even when these convergences are themselves part of a complex mixture of styles. Examples of direct influence and of conscious borrowing, if they matter at all, point to a participation in a common literary tradition. It may be rash to speak of "American symbolist poets" or to contend that all or even most of our major twentieth-century poets were greatly affected by the symbolist example; but there can be no doubt of the presence of a symbolist tradition of poetics and poetry in twentieth-century America, and of its operative power in the art of a number of our foremost poets.

For many readers, the outstanding poet of our time is T. S. Eliot. F. O. Matthiessen was unquestionably correct in calling Eliot "the most influential poet of the nineteen-twenties."[28] His first book, *Prufrock and Other Observations* (1917), revealed an unusual awareness of the main traditions of both English and European poetry. Eliot's early poems reveal his particular fondness for colloquial and conversational idiom in the ironic manner of Corbière and Laforgue, and for striking and often bizarre images in the manner of Donne and other metaphysical poets. These poems also display some kinship with Baudelaire in occasional borrowings and in the common concern with the sordid aspects of private life in the modern city; but the principal symbolist poets do not seem to have had any significant impact on the Eliot of "Prufrock" and *The Waste Land*. All the same, Eliot was keenly aware of the stylistic experimentation of the symbolists, and he sought at one time to establish a parallel between metaphysical and symbolist poetry, even contending that Donne and Mallarmé are essentially kindred spirits.[29] The example of the symbolists was reflected more clearly in Eliot's poetic theory of the 1920's than in his poetry, most strikingly in certain broad similarities to the poetic theory of Valéry. In particular, Eliot's impersonal theory of poetry, his rigorous distinc-

---

[28] Matthiessen, *Sewanee Review*, LV, 24.
[29] See my essay, "The Alleged Parallel of Metaphysical and Symbolist Poetry," *Comparative Literature Studies*, IV (1967), 145–59.

tion, in his early criticism, between poetry and prose, his insistence on precision in language and on conscious control as opposed to spontaneous inspiration in the act of composition, all constitute important elements of affinity between the two poets. In a memorial tribute to Valéry published in the *Quarterly Review of Literature* in 1946, Eliot expressed reservations concerning the universal validity of Valéry's view of the composition of poetry, but he also declared, "I have found again and again that his analyses of the poetic process corresponded to my own experience, and brought much to light of which I had been but obscurely aware." To some extent, both Eliot and Valéry are part of a common symbolist heritage, sharing a conscious intellectuality, a preoccupation with unity and order, an ideal of composition. The occasional parallelism in their poetic thought and art is the result not so much of deliberate borrowing by the American poet from the French, as of a kindred response to a common set of poetic imperatives.

We may see this presence of symbolist values in Eliot's poetic theory most markedly, perhaps, in the essay of 1942, "The Music of Poetry." No twentieth-century poet approaching the subject thoughtfully could easily escape the force of the symbolists' long and probing concern with music and its relation to poetry. Valéry, indeed, defined the whole symbolist enterprise as the endeavor of a group of poets to take back from music what was rightfully theirs —"de reprendre à la musique leur bien."[30] For Mallarmé, music and poetry are inseparable: just as harmonic relationships are a residual element of our spiritual being, so music, as the rhythm of these relationships, is necessarily present in poetry.[31] Fundamental is Mallarmé's conviction that the music of poetry is not external but structural; to write poetically is perforce to write musically as well. Similarly, in Eliot's discussion of "The Music of Poetry," this music is contextual, a harmonious intersection of immediate and associative values: "the music of verse is not a line by line matter, but a

[30] Paul Valéry, "Situation de Baudelaire," *Œuvres* (Paris, 1957), I, 612.
[31] See Mallarmé, *Œuvres complètes* (Paris, 1956), 367–68.

question of the whole poem."[32] Eliot shares with the symbolists an awareness of the complex analogy of poetry and music in rhythm and structure, and his account of its possible modes of expression is of deep significance for our understanding of his own late poetry:

> There are possibilities for verse which bear some analogy to the development of a theme by different groups of instruments; there are possibilities of transitions in a poem comparable to the different movements of a symphony or a quartet; there are possibilities of contrapuntal arrangement of subject-matter.[33]

Late in life in the course of a public lecture, Eliot remarked, "Today I read Mallarmé more than I do Laforgue." Whether or not he read Mallarmé's Oxford lecture, "La Musique et les Lettres," in connection with the writing of "The Music of Poetry" is beside the point. Eliot's essay sets forth an essentially symbolist view of his subject, all due allowance made for the individuality of the poet and his deep roots in English poetic theory and practice.

We may see a similar presence of symbolist values in Eliot's last major poem, *Four Quartets*. The very title is suggestive of a symbolist view of poetry. This is not to say that *Four Quartets* is a symbolist poem. The presence of recurring symbols is common to all poetry. Eliot's poem embodies an intricate pattern of symbolic configurations, but we should not confuse symbolic expression and symbolist style. Just as all poets have perforce employed metaphoric language, so all poetry is a mode of symbolic statement. This generic symbolization is not the exclusive property of any particular group of poets. When we consider *Four Quartets* in relation to the values of dream, reverie, the evocation of an *état d'âme*, the revelation of the mystery and wonder of the universe, we cannot view it essentially as symbolist poetry. At once autobiographical and highly personal, it reflects a far more tangible and concrete sense of reality than we may find in symbolist poetry of the later nineteenth century. Moreover, the insistent didacticism and religious exhortation

---

[32] Eliot, *Selected Prose* (London, 1953), 64.   [33] *Ibid.,* 67.

of the poem—part sermon, part confession and prayer—are at once
at a far remove from the symbolist repudiation of discursive values
in poetry. These are important differences, but it must also be
recognized that along with these differences, there are significant
areas of convergence that bear witness to Eliot's thorough assimilation of symbolist poetics and poetry.

On the purely verbal level, the complex allusiveness of Eliot's
poem, replete with citations from Eliot's own earlier works as well
as from great poetry of both the distant and recent past, includes
recognizable restatements of lines from Mallarmé. The opening of
Section II of "Burnt Norton," "Garlic and sapphires in the mud,"
may be a modified transposition of line ten of Mallarmé's sonnet,
"M'introduire dans ton histoire": "Tonnerre et rubis aux moyeux";
and the recollection of the dead master in "Little Gidding"—"Since
our concern was speech, and speech impelled us/To purify the
dialect of the tribe"—is an obvious rendering of line six of Mallarmé's "Le Tombeau d'Edgar Poe": "Donner un sens plus pur aux
mots de la tribu." The office of the poet as a purifier of common
language is a commonplace symbolist notion, and Eliot's citation
points to a more pervasive affinity in his recurrent preoccupation in
Four Quartets with the nature and function of poetic language.

If Eliot shares the symbolist conviction that poetry is made not
with ideas but with words, he also views words not as denotative
and referential signs, but as repositories of supernatural mystery and
wonder. The evocative and magical power of language embraces
both the visible and the invisible. Thus, the music of poetry is an
intimation of silence; the poet, as Mallarmé suggests in "Sainte," is
"Musicienne du silence." This same view of the co-existence of
words and music moving toward the realm of silence is given poetic
utterance in the final section of "Burnt Norton":

> Words, after speech, reach
> Into the silence. Only by the form, the pattern,
> Can words or music reach
> The stillness, as a Chinese jar still

> Moves perpetually in its stillness,
> Not the stillness of the violin, while the note lasts,
> Not that only, but the co-existence, . . .

Indeed, the passage may be viewed as a transmutation into poetry of the symbolist poetics of Eliot's essay, "The Music of Poetry." Music itself is here conceived as a movement toward the absolute purity of silence, "music heard so deeply/That it is not heard at all," as Eliot puts it in "The Dry Salvages." The musicality of language is derived, for Eliot as for the symbolists, from the supernatural power of the Word, in keeping with the Christian conception of the *logos* as the revelation of God in and through language. As Baudelaire declared, language is in its very nature *sacred:* "Il y a dans le mot, dans le *verbe,* quelque chose de *sacré* qui nous défend d'en faire un jeu de hasard."[34] The quest for precision of expression, for exact control of language, is crucial to both Eliot and the symbolists. Thus, in the final section of "Little Gidding," Eliot envisages the poem as a complete harmony of its linguistic elements:

> And every phrase
> And sentence that is right (where every word is at home,
> Taking its place to support the others,
> The word neither diffident nor ostentatious,
> An easy commerce of the old and the new,
> The common word exact without vulgarity,
> The formal word precise but not pedantic,
> The complete consort dancing together) . . . .

Yet, this harmony and precision is an ideal far more than an actual account of poetic expression. Eliot, like the symbolists, recognizes that the poet cannot have absolute control over language, that his art is perforce subject to the vagaries of chance:

> And so each venture
> Is a new beginning, a raid on the inarticulate
> With shabby equipment always deteriorating

[34] Baudelaire, "Théophile Gautier," *Critique Littéraire et Musicale* (Paris, 1961), 257.

> In the general mess of imprecision of feeling,
> Undisciplined squads of emotion.[35]

The same awareness of the disorder and potential chaos inherent in the brute givenness of language, closely echoing Mallarmé's concept of "le hasard," is vividly expressed near the end of "Burnt Norton":

> Words strain,
> Crack and sometimes break, under the burden,
> Under the tension, slip, slide, perish,
> Decay with imprecision, will not stay in place,
> Will not stay still.

Just as the "Word in the desert" is assailed by discordant voices, so the elemental disorder and instability of language mocks the poet's loftiest endeavor.

Four Quartets may fittingly be described as poetry of the ineffable, as a complex orchestration of the interplay of time and timelessness, fixity and flux, being and not being, the human and the divine. In large measure these are themes of symbolist poetry, but they are given a particular context and application through the uniquely personal experience of the poet. Similarly, the language of *Four Quartets* is that of a poet who has assimilated the symbolist heritage but has also gone beyond it in the merging of formal and conversational idiom, of abstract and highly concrete expression. The descriptive and narrative elements of Eliot's poem are far more immediate and tangible than we may find in most nineteenth-century symbolist poetry. Here, as in other aspects of his art, Eliot exhibits a closer relation to Valéry than to Baudelaire and Mallarmé, in the concretization of symbolist values. We will look in vain among the symbolists for Eliot's poetry of active faith, or for any poem of similar complexity and magnitude concerned simultaneously with the here and now and the hereafter. The powerful dramatic quality of Eliot's poem, particularly in "Little Gidding," along with much of its religious symbolism, reflects the author's life-long preoccupa-

---

[35] Eliot, "East Coker," Section V, *Four Quartets* (London, 1962), 22.

tion with Dante. The legacy of the symbolists is but one of many forces entering into Eliot's mature poetic vision, yet the presence of this legacy is unmistakable as a significant part of the poet's achieved composition.

In his late critical essays and notably in the essay "From Poe to Valéry" (1948), while displaying a remarkably sure sense of symbolist historiography, Eliot took some care to dissociate himself from what he viewed as an extension of the claims of poetry beyond the capacities of human apprehension. For him, the obsession with purification of means in the effort to separate rigorously the poetic and the non-poetic had issued in an involution and abstraction remote from human needs and purposes. In Valéry, he felt, the symbolist tradition had reached a final point of development, with no further possibility of significant prolongation. Whether the symbolist tradition did in fact reach a point of exhaustion in the early years of the present century is open to serious question. In any case, Eliot's attitude late in life represents to some extent a conscious turning away from one of the vital sources of his own development, and may have been a response to what he considered a bleakly nihilistic view of both life and art in the thought and poetry of Valéry. In spite of these reservations, Eliot in both his criticism and poetry offers an important illustration of the nature and scope of the impact of French symbolism on modern American poetry. Eliot's work serves to define and extend the symbolist tradition, even as it selects and modifies what the poet regarded as the most congenial and usable elements of the tradition.

It is interesting to note that Eliot was not alone in his view of the symbolist movement as part of a completed past rather than a living present. This perspective is central to the account of symbolism in Edmund Wilson's *Axel's Castle* (1931), probably the most influential single source of knowledge and awareness of the symbolists in the American literary scene of the 1930's and 1940's. In restrospect, Wilson's book is a challenging but greatly over-simplified and journalistic survey, deficient in both knowledge and imaginative sympathy in its view of the symbolists, and far more valuable for its discussion of English and American writers than for the French. Wilson's study has the merit of a broad comparative approach, and it recognizes the kinship between the symbolist poets and certain novelists such as Proust and Joyce; but Wilson's historical generalizations are loose and imprecise, and his critique of the symbolist poets is based on the application of an aesthetic and social philosophy totally unrelated to the assumptions animating the symbolists. *Axel's Castle* reflects throughout its author's conviction that the symbolist movement is "the last and ultimate stage in an evolution which is *now finished.*"[36] He saw symbolist poetry as an expression of the withdrawal of the poet from the world, with the result that poetry was stifled by its own exclusiveness. Like T. S. Eliot, he considered Valéry as the end of a tradition, the architect of a dehumanized poetry.[37] Wilson's inaccurate and unfair appraisal of Valéry was corrected for the English reader by C. M. Bowra in *The Heritage of Symbolism* (1943), which insists quite properly on the role of both abstract thought and concrete sensuous experience in Valéry's art. A more direct criticism of *Axel's Castle* was made by Allen Tate in his essay "Yeats' Romanticism" (1942), in which he contends that Wilson inevitably saw in the heirs of symbolism "an evasion of the reality that he, Mr. Wilson, was looking for."[38] And Tate adds, pointedly, "If you are looking for pins you do not want needles, though both will prick you." Wilson's easy dichotomies and simplified generalizations are responsible for a good deal of the misunderstanding of the symbolists in American criticism of recent decades, yet paradoxically, he made the symbolist poets important and thereby helped to impel many readers to come to know the symbolists in the original texts. With all of its limitations, *Axel's Castle* is of large importance as part of the continuing diffusion of symbolist values in American literary thought and expression in our time.

[36] Cited in Sherman Paul, *Edmund Wilson* (Urbana, 1965), 78.   [37] *Ibid.*, 83.
[38] Tate, *The Man of Letters in the Modern World* (New York, 1955), 228.

Even while some American poets and critics were contending that the symbolist movement was exhausted as a creative impulse, others were consciously exploiting and enlarging its resources, finding in them a stimulus of their own originality. Of all modern American poets, Allen Tate has probably been the most conscious of the legacy of Poe and the symbolists in his own work. Tate's poetry, like that of most of his contemporaries, is marked by a variety of styles, and it would not do at all to describe Tate as a symbolist poet. His poetry is distinguished by a clear and precise use of language, often employing simple and direct words and images to express highly abstract ideas. The witty intellectuality and sudden juxtaposition of discordant figures characteristic of metaphysical poetry is more apparent in Tate's work than the musical suggestiveness of the symbolists, and at first glance there would seem to be little direct indebtedness of Tate's poetry to that of Baudelaire and his followers. Their impact, however, is not to be measured simply in the study of sources or parallel passages; rather, it must be apprehended as an assimilated part of Tate's poetic vision. His keen awareness of the symbolist tradition and his conscious reliance on its resources is a salient aspect of his art.

Tate's familiarity with the symbolist poets dates from the beginnings of his career as a poet.[39] Like many of his fellow "Fugitive" poets, he combined a passionate sense of the history of the South and its present-day cultural mission with a rigorous aesthetic formalism that included a deep respect for traditional prosody and verse form. At the same time, however, Tate recognized that the innovations of the symbolists had immensely widened the modern poet's range of activity. In an essay in *The Fugitive* in April, 1924, Tate declared that the poetic idiom rooted in the Romantic notion of spontaneous expression was inadequate and must be discarded: "Today the poet's vocabulary is prodigious, it embraces the entire range of consciousness. . . . Baudelaire's Theory of Correspondences—that an idea out of one class of experience may be dressed up

[39] Cf. Louise Cowan, *The Fugitive Group* (Baton Rouge, 1959), 65.

in the vocabulary of another—is at once the backbone of Modern poetic diction and the character which distinguishes it from both the English Tradition and free verse."[40] At about the same time that Tate was urging a new fluidity and metaphorical richness of language based on the theory and example of Baudelaire, he was also translating Baudelaire's "Correspondances," which he published in *The Fugitive,* December, 1924, not simply as a translation but as an original poem patterned on the French model:

> All nature is a temple where the alive
> Pillars breathe often a tremor of mixed words;
> Man wanders in a forest of accords
> That peer familiarly from each ogive.
>
> Like thinning echoes tumbling to sleep beyond
> In a unity umbrageous and infinite,
> Vast as the night stupendously moonlit,
> All smells and colors and sounds correspond.
>
> Odors blown sweet as infants' naked flesh,
> Soft as oboes, green as a studded plain,
> —Others, corrupt, rich and triumphant, thresh
>
> Expansions to the infinite of pain:
> Amber and myrrh, benzoin and music condense
> To transports of the spirit and the sense!

We can see that Tate is obliged on occasion to depart from a strictly literal rendering of Baudelaire's poem in order to preserve the verse form, yet this formal symmetry is an essential part of the meaning of the poem. In spirit, the translation conforms fully to the original, despite occasional divergences in detail. Thus, while "forest of accords" in line three does not quite approximate "forêts de symboles," it embodies a large part of the original meaning without doing violence to it. The second stanza departs more freely from the text and justifies the poem's title: Allen Tate, "Correspondences" (from the French of Charles Baudelaire); but the final sestet not only retains the rhyme scheme, but captures accurately both the

[40] Cited *ibid.,* 151.

spirit and sense of the French poem. Tate's re-creation of Baudelaire's poem is easily among the best of the many renditions attempted by modern American poets, and it should be better
known.[41] In translating Baudelaire's sonnet, Tate surely recognized
that "Correspondances," more than any other single poem, defines
and illustrates the fundamental assumptions of symbolist poetry.

In both his subsequent poetry and literary criticism, Tate repeatedly invoked Baudelaire's correspondent vision, not only for the
interplay of natural and supernatural reality, but for its support of a
lively employment of synaesthetic metaphor. We may find many
examples of fluidity of imagery derived from the blending of diverse modes of sensory experience in Tate's poetry, in such lines as
"The heaving jelly of my tribal air" ("Causerie"), or "The bleak
sunshine shrieks its chipped music" ("Death of Little Boys"). In his
essay on John Peale Bishop, Tate declares that the symbolist poets
gave a new significance to the mixture of the genres when they
began "to push the borders of one sense over into another."[42] While
the symbolists clearly did not invent vertical correspondences in
poetry, they were much bolder in their experimentation in figurative language than earlier poets had been. Tate recognizes the risk
of formal destructiveness inherent in such experimentation, but also
insists on the importance of the deeper understanding of the symbolizing processes of poetry made possible by Baudelaire and his
followers. Tate's fullest statement of this importance occurs in his
essay on Dante published in 1951 entitled "The Symbolic Imagination"·

> The symbolic imagination conducts an action through analogy, of
> the human to the divine, of the natural to the supernatural, of the low
> to the high, of time to eternity. My literary generation was deeply
> impressed by Baudelaire's sonnet *Correspondances,* which restated the
> doctrines of medieval symbolism by way of Swedenborg; we were
> impressed because we had lost the historical perspective leading back
> to the original source.[43]

[41] The text is included in Tate, *Poems 1922–1947* (New York, 1953), 205.
[42] Tate, *Man of Letters,* 275.   [43] *Ibid.,* 96.

It is significant to note Tate's awareness of the deep historical and religious roots of symbolist poetics, as well as his insistence on the necessity for the poet to translate the correspondent vision into the poet's experience of "the body of this world": "If the poet is able to put into this moving body, or to find in it, a coherent chain of analogies, he will inform an intuitive act with symbolism; his will be in one degree or another the symbolic imagination." Clearly, the symbolic imagination is not here viewed as the exclusive property of any particular group of poets, but it is derived by Tate in large measure from Baudelaire's conviction that the poet, by dint of his power to decipher analogies and correspondences, possesses unique knowledge of the ultimate oneness of all things. The imagination, which Baudelaire described as the queen of faculties, is the source and center of the poet's spiritual vision. For Tate as for Baudelaire, the working of the imagination is perforce a symbolizing act.

If Tate sees symbolist values as common to all poetry, he also recognizes that the form-consciousness and studied intellectuality of "the trained man of letters, the cunning poet in the tradition of Poe and Mallarmé,"[44] is a unique condition of our own times. The modern poet is "the specialist in symbol," but this does not mean that symbolic expression lacks a direct relationship to life. Baudelaire's poetry, Tate insists, is marked by "sensation as direct experience,"[45] and even the poetry of Mallarmé may have at least an indirect, but no less tangible, relation to society and to personal conduct.[46] While unsympathetic critics of symbolist poetry have viewed it as an evasion of the claims of common reality, Tate properly sees this remoteness as at best a matter of degree, contending that even the most complex and seemingly hermetic poetry is nonetheless capable of exerting a profound impact on the reader's response to the world around him. The main deficiency of the symbolists according to Tate would seem to lie in their religious values, in their conception of God as analogy rather than essence, in what Tate calls "the angelism of the intellect," most markedly

[44] *Ibid.*, 13.   [45] *Ibid.*, 202.   [46] *Ibid.*, 32.

present in Poe and Valéry, but characteristic by implication of the whole symbolist tradition.[47] Despite these reservations, it should be clear that Tate's formation and development as both poet and critic owes much to the symbolist example. His essays constitute a striking illustration of an essential accord between symbolist poetics and the values of the "New Criticism," particularly in their common assault on Romantic self-expression, and their preoccupation with a poetry of abstract thought set forth in complex and "difficult" figurative language.

While Tate is not often considered among the major American poets of our century, his best poetry represents a high order of accomplishment. In its variety of styles, Tate's work mingles Latin poetry, Dante, the metaphysicals, Poe, and the symbolists—to name only some of the more obvious formative elements. Much of Tate's art is perhaps unduly cerebral; his poetry may not always adequately combine intellect and emotion, and it may occasionally seem unduly parochial in its expression of the burden of southern history. Yet, at its best, Tate's poetry can be profoundly moving, particularly in those poems which fuse the poet's act of historical location, through the invocation of an ancestral past, with themes and circumstances common to all men regardless of their historical and geographical affiliations. His best poem, "Ode to the Confederate Dead," both embodies and transcends the defeat of the South in the Civil War. Its subject is dialectical and universal: the interplay of past and present, time and timelessness, the living and the dead, being and becoming, the self and the external world. This large philosophical preoccupation points to a kinship with many contemporary poets, most notably T. S. Eliot, but also Paul Valéry, especially in "Le Cimetière Marin." Tate's ode is not simply an American adaptation of Valéry, but the reader familiar with both poems cannot help noting pervasive similarities: both poems consist of meditations before a cemetery; both begin on the plane of objective description, move swiftly to introspection, and proceed through a

[47] *Ibid.*, 130–31.

mounting tension to a climax followed by a partial and incomplete resolution, open rather than closed, in keeping with an insistently interrogative tone. The drama in both poems is essentially a drama of the mind, in which immediate visual experience is rapidly converted into philosophical reflection. Both poets invest similar traditional images with new meaning by juxtaposing abstract and concrete diction, combining vivid sensuous imagery with impassioned intellectual argument. The concourse of the living and the dead— the presence of the absent dead and the positive value thereby conferred on absence as a condition of being—is a natural consequence of the circumstances out of which both poems arise. Even particular allusions have a common thematic function. Thus, at the lowest point of dejection in "Le Cimetière Marin," the speaker, protesting his entrapment and consequent suffering as a fragile and mutable being longing for permanence and fixity, alludes to the paradoxes of Zeno as an analogue of his condition:

> Zénon! Cruel Zénon! Zénon d'Élée!
> M'as-tu percé de cette flèche ailée
> Qui vibre, vole, et qui ne vole pas!
> Le son m'enfante et la flèche me tue!
> Ah! le soleil . . . Quelle ombre de tortue
> Pour l'âme, Achille immobile à grands pas!

Similarly, Tate's observer at the gate of a Confederate graveyard cries out against the destructive force of time and change, a cry animated by his consciousness of the frustration of his longing for an order of pure being:

> You know the rage,
> The cold pool left by the mounting flood,
> Of muted Zeno and Parmenides.

The paradoxes of the Eleatic need not be elaborated in Tate's poem. The allusion suffices to oppose the observer's passionate desire for certitude and the impossibility of its attainment.

In his essay "Narcissus as Narcissus" Tate points out that his

"Ode to the Confederate Dead" is an exemplification of the extreme introspection of our time. "Le Cimetière Marin" is also a Narcissus poem, although less solipsistic than Mallarmé's "Hérodiade" or Valéry's "La Jeune Parque," but similarly concerned in large part with the mind's contemplation of itself. In Tate's poem the Narcissus image is transformed into the violence and frenzy of a mind unable to break free of its self-made prison: ". . . like the jaguar leaps/For his own image in a jungle pool, his victim. . . ." As Tate has remarked, this figure is "the only explicit rendering of the Narcissus motif in the poem,"[48] but the inability of solipsism to sustain the faith and glory of the southern past is manifest throughout. The ode ends with the image of the serpent, "the ancient symbol of time," and with the dominion of death over all. The "heroic age" is gone; the Confederate dead are truly dead, and the turbulent historical vision gives way to the solitary landscape of the mind. As Tate reminds us: "The scene of the poem is not a public celebration; it is a lone man by a gate." In its final lines the poem moves beyond the unresolved drama of consciousness to solitude and silence.

A sympathetic reader of Tate's poem is bound to concur with the judgment of F. O. Matthiessen: "Despite too numerous echoes of Eliot and Valéry, Tate's structure and rhythm have attained here a rare elevation and dignity."[49] Nothing else that Tate has written approaches the ode in intensity and depth, nor need one be a descendent of the Confederate dead in order to share the poem's imaginative power. The presence of symbolist values in the poem in no way detracts from Tate's originality. His "borrowings" are far more a matter of poetic vision than of particular words and images, and whatever he has borrowed, he has made his own. The pressures of a specific time and place, or a particular historical and cultural setting, are not those that operate in Valéry or in any other poet. In poems of large endeavor and achievement, tradition and originality move hand in hand, each enhancing the other.

[48] *Ibid.,* 344.   [49] Matthiessen, *Sewanee Review,* LXXI, 41.

The deep awareness of the legacy of Poe and the symbolists that we have seen in the work of Tate is present in no diminished sense in the poetry of his close friend, John Peale Bishop. Perhaps more than any other poet of his time, Bishop responded warmly to the symbolist tradition. In the course of his long residence in France, he acquired a close familiarity with the art of the symbolist poets, notably of Baudelaire and Verlaine, but also of Mallarmé and Valéry. Many of Bishop's early sonnets and light verses echo Baudelaire, while the early poem, "Losses," with its epigraph from Verlaine, is, in its first stanza, virtually a translation from *Sagesse.*[50] Bishop's later poetry is generally more concrete and objective than we may sometimes find in the symbolists, yet many of his poems reflect at least elements of symbolist inspiration, as in the close of "Speaking of Poetry," 1925:

> The ceremony must be found
>
> Traditional, with all its symbols
> ancient as the metaphors in dreams;
> strange, with never before heard music; continuous
> until the torches deaden at the bedroom door.

The notion of poetry as rite and invocation, a magical and musical evocation of dream and mystery, points clearly to the poet's symbolist affinities. Even more striking in this respect is the poem "Narcissus," written in 1935, one of several sustained studies in mood creation marked by the same musicality and fluidity of metaphor that we find in the symbolists, and moving to the final destruction of an obsessive self-consciousness:

> What could he do above the mirroring stream,
> Matching desire with his virginity,
>   What could he do but burn
> Into a contemplation, marvelling
> That his own body was become a whirling
> Mirror of death? Stark in dissolution

---

[50] Cf. Bishop, *Collected Poems* (New York, 1948), 208.

Stare at swifter shadows flooding, that charged
All changing objects with raging delight?

Bishop's Narcissus is caught between being and non-being, rapt and helpless before the compulsive power of his image, simultaneously losing and discovering his identity. The poem will bear close comparison with Valéry's "Narcisse parle" as a hymn to an embodiment of contemplative beauty lost in the obsession with his own image.

There are other, no less compelling expressions of Bishop's awareness of the art of the symbolists. Joseph Frank has rightfully called attention to his indebtedness to Valéry in poems of the middle 1930's such as "The Saints" and "Divine Nativity."[51] Valéry lent powerful support to a consciousness of the exigencies of formal structure that is characteristic of Bishop's art.[52] The employment of a taut and compressed line in his meditative shorter poems, as well as an elaborate color symbolism, as in the final stanza of "A Subject of Sea Change," are further examples of Bishop's symbolist inclinations. These find large expression in his prose as well. In his notes under the heading "Diction," Bishop wrote: "Office of the poet: Donner un sens plus pur aux mots de la tribu."[53] The function of the poet as well as the definition of poetry are derived squarely and explicitly from the symbolists. Bishop's analysis of the structure of poetry and his distinctions between words and statements, the real and the arbitrary, are remarkably close to the poetics of Valéry.[54] The impact of symbolist aesthetics seems to find its fullest expression in Bishop's masterful essay of 1938, "The Discipline of Poetry." The essay is in large part a generous tribute to the symbolist movement which, Bishop insists, "did, as a matter of fact, produce an extraordinary amount of poetry, much of it, even today, admirable, and some of it indubitably great."[55] Baudelaire is singled out as the originator of a new form-consciousness and musicality in poetry which has entered vitally into the art of American poets: "Neither

[51] Frank, "Force and Form: A Study of John Peale Bishop," *Sewanee Review*, LV (1947), 106.   [52] Cf. Tate, *Man of Letters*, 271.
[53] Bishop, *Collected Essays* (New York, 1948), 368.   [54] *Ibid.*, 17.   [55] *Ibid.*, 99.

T. S. Eliot nor Allen Tate would be today what they are had it not been for Baudelaire."[56] Bishop modestly omits reference to himself, but clearly, he is part of the same tradition. Indeed, it has been reasonably contended that Bishop "represents the best in the perfection of the symbolist style in English."[57] His poetry merits far more sympathetic attention than it has received. He was gifted too in art criticism as well as literary criticism, and his interest in the interplay of poetry and painting reinforced his concern with suggestiveness, spirituality, and correspondent vision. Bishop's work is not exclusively the consequence of his attraction to French poetry from Baudelaire to Valéry; he was a poet of wide experience and large literary culture, with a keen sense of involvement in American life and literature. His art is that of an American poet passionately aware of the cleavages and imperfections in our culture, the decay of tradition, the rootlessness of the individual, the absence of belief. His admiration for the French symbolists was in large part a response to their awareness of form and tradition, and he sought, in both his poetry and criticism, to extend this awareness in twentieth-century America. We need not describe Bishop as a symbolist poet to recognize the role of symbolist elements in his art. The symbolist analogies and affinities which we have cited are altogether proper to the work of a sensitive, solitary, and contemplative poet of our time.

Perhaps the most complex of all American poets in his symbolist affinities is Wallace Stevens. Clearly among the major poets of our century, Stevens developed a vivid personal style that at times reflects but also unmistakably transcends the art of any antecedent group of poets. As he declared late in life, "While, of course, I come down from the past, the past is my own."[58] Stevens was unusually well-read in both modern French and American poetry. A keen interest in the symbolists was among his life-long preoccupations.

---

[56] *Ibid.,* 100.

[57] Robert Wooster Stallman, "Preface" to "John Peale Bishop: A Checklist," *Princeton University Library Chronicle,* VII (1945), 62.

[58] Wallace Stevens, *Letters* (New York, 1966), 792.

To study Stevens' relation to the symbolist tradition, one must take full account of the poet's rich individuality, of the freedom of his art from any narrow dependence on the poetics and poetry of others, and of his rare ability to assimilate and transform his literary experience. The study of the impact of French symbolism on modern American poetry necessitates a concentration on a single aspect of Stevens' art; a wider view of the poet's work would do full justice to the variety of traditions it reflects and to the powerful originality of Stevens' poetic vision.

Stevens' awareness of the French symbolists probably dates from the period of his studies at Harvard, 1897–1900. More important early interests were the Elizabethans, the Romantics, and the Pre-Raphaelites, but through friendships with classmates of kindred spirit and through wide reading, Stevens apparently came to know the work of many of both the major and minor symbolist poets. It is possible too that he attended the series of lectures given by Henri de Régnier at Harvard in the spring semester of 1900, describing the new tendencies in French poetry.[59] Stevens' poetry during his college years is marked by a vague religiosity and a somewhat cloying sentimentality, but with occasional symbolist overtones as in the "Sonnet" published in the *Harvard Monthly* for July 1899, to which Stevens affixed the pseudonym of "John Morris, 2nd."[60] The earliest symbolist poet to influence Stevens was probably Verlaine,[61] for whom he expressed his admiration in a letter of 1908.[62] Several of the poems subsequently published in *Trend* in 1914 are brief evocations of fleeting experience or intimations of a mystical density akin to that of the symbolists, as in "Tides" (1908):

> These infinite green motions
> Trouble, but to no end,
> Trouble with mystic sense
> Like the secretive oceans,
> Or violet eve repining

[59] Buttel, *Wallace Stevens,* 6.   [60] *Ibid.,* 12.   [61] *Ibid.,* 56–64.
[62] Stevens, *Letters,* 110.

Upon the glittering rocks,
Or haggard, desert hills,
Or hermit moon declining.[63]

This misty supernaturalism and mood creation was to give way in
Stevens' subsequent poetry to a more precise and concrete interplay
of the visible and invisible. His first published poems after leaving
Harvard, "Carnet de Voyage," printed in *Trend* for September,
1914, clearly reflect the subtle intellectuality and correspondent vision of the symbolists. "An odor from a star" suggests Mallarmé's
"Apparition" with its enveloping progression and striking employment of synaesthesia and color symbolism:

An odor from a star
Comes to my fancy, slight,
Tenderly spiced and gay,
As if a seraph's hand
Unloosed the fragrant silks
Of some sultana, bright
In her soft sky. And pure
It is, and excellent,
As if a seraph's blue
Fell, as a shadow falls,
And his warm body shed
Sweet exhalations, void
Of our despised decay.[64]

Here we see Stevens moving beyond the evocation of external
nature to an embodiment of beauty as absolute purity, at once
material and spiritual, appealing to sight, touch, and smell in a
series of delicate yet precise delineations. The beauty invoked by the
poet is both beyond and within the world we inhabit.

There can be no question of the importance of the symbolists in
Stevens' art from the beginning of his career as a poet. No doubt,
this importance has been overstated on occasion,[65] and it has not

[63] Cited Buttel, *Wallace Stevens,* 53–54.   [64] Cited Buttel, *Wallace Stevens,* 104.
[65] For some representative generalizations, see Hi Simons, "Wallace Stevens and
Mallarmé," *Modern Philology,* XLIII (1946), 235.

always been assessed with due regard to the essential values of the poetry of either Stevens or the symbolists. Most students of the subject have emphasized Stevens' relation to Mallarmé, and it has been persuasively argued that Mallarmé's influence on Stevens was "strong and continuous, from at least as early as 1914."[66] Stevens himself seriously questioned claims of his dependence on the French symbolists, but his statements about his own early development were made at a distance of two or three decades, and while they resolve some problems, they raise others. Thus, in a letter to Hi Simons on July 8, 1941, Stevens replied to a query concerning his reading of Mallarmé, Verlaine, Laforgue, Valéry, and Baudelaire: "I have read something, more or less, of all the French poets mentioned by you, but, if I have picked up anything from them, it has been unconsciously. It is always possible that, where a man's attitude coincides with your own attitude, or accentuates your own attitude, you get a great deal from him without any effort. This, in fact, is one of the things that makes literature possible."[67] It is, of course, extremely difficult to separate conscious from unconscious derivations. By pointing to the possibility of an essential agreement in attitudes, Stevens seems to suggest that his relationship to the symbolists is one of affinity far more than of influence, but he adds that affinity facilitates influence. His reply recognizes too that unconscious appropriations are no less real for being unconscious. Earlier, Stevens disclaimed any significant dependence on Valéry, declaring in a letter of 1935, "I have read very little of Valéry, although I have a number of his books and for that matter, several books about him."[68] Here again, however, he admits the possibility of an unconscious relationship. Stevens returned to the subject in a letter of May, 1949, by way of commenting on Hi Simons' study, "Wallace Stevens and Mallarmé":

Mallarmé never in the world meant as much to me as all that in any direct way. Perhaps I absorbed more than I thought. Mallarmé was a good deal in the air when I was much younger. But so were other

[66] Buttel, *Wallace Stevens*, 104n.   [67] Stevens, *Letters*, 391.   [68] *Ibid.*, 290.

people, for instance, Samain. Verlaine meant a good deal more to me. There were many of his lines that I delighted to repeat. But I was never a student of any of these poets; they were simply poets and I was the youthful general reader.[69]

Stevens persistently refused to endorse any view of his art which made it dependent on that of any other poet. On the other hand, he recognized as very real the possibility that he may have assimilated many of the elements of symbolist poetry. The problem is a complicated one and it will not yield to easy and ready-made solutions.

We can readily understand the recurrent tendency to identify Stevens and the French symbolists. Thus, René Taupin declared of Stevens: "Il est symboliste par son art de l'évocation, sa recherche des correspondances, des mots qui font image et des mots qui font écho."[70] This same view is implicit in a number of quips concerning Stevens, such as the statement that he wrote French poetry in English, or Gustave Cohen's description of the poet as "le Valéry américain."[71] At the opposite extreme, some students of Stevens' poetry insist that he is not a symbolist at all.[72] In a series of thoughtful and stimulating essays, Michel Benamou has argued for an essential difference between Stevens and the symbolists, even while admitting what he considers to be largely verbal affinities.[73] There is no question that similarities between Stevens and the symbolists are to be found throughout his work, not only in his poetry, early and late, but also in his prose, especially in the statements of poetics reprinted in *The Necessary Angel* (1951) and in *Opus Posthumous* (1957), to say nothing of Stevens' experiments in symbolist drama

[69] *Ibid.*, 636.   [70] Taupin, *L'Influence du Symbolisme français*, 277.

[71] See *Trinity Review*, VIII (May, 1954), 24.

[72] Cf. Joseph N. Riddel, *The Clairvoyant Eye* (Baton Rouge, 1965), 178. I should add that Mr. Riddel is keenly aware of the complexities of the question of Wallace Stevens as a symbolist poet. Cf. *ibid.*, 186–88.

[73] The following essays by Michel Benamou are of special importance for our subject: "Beyond Emerald or Amethyst: Wallace Stevens and the French Tradition," *Dartmouth College Library Bulletin*, n.s., IV (December, 1961), 60–66; "Sur le prétendu 'Symbolisme' de Wallace Stevens," *Critique*, 175 (décembre, 1961), 1029–1045; "Wallace Stevens and the Symbolist Imagination," *ELH*, XXXI (1964), 35–63.

and his markedly symbolist dramatic theory. The problem is further complicated by the poetic character of Stevens' literary prose on the one hand, and the use of poetry for explorations in aesthetics and literary criticism on the other. Here again, Stevens shares an essential affinity with the symbolists. The notion of the poet as critic, which is central to the literature of our time, has perhaps its boldest elaboration in Baudelaire's essay on Wagner, wherein Baudelaire declares, "il est impossible qu'un poëte ne contienne pas un critique," and he adds: "je considère le poëte comme le meilleur de tous les critiques."[74] Mallarmé referred to the prose essays which he collected in *Divagations* as constituting a new form, the "poème critique."[75] The interpenetration of poetry and criticism is as evident in the work of Stevens as in the French symbolists, and it is understandable that many of his poems, particularly those written late in life, should be read in large part as statements of a theory of poetry.

The study of Stevens' relation to the symbolists depends first and foremost on perspective. It would not be difficult to point out verbal similarities and parallelisms in the poems of Stevens and the symbolists.[76] The same could no doubt be done for Stevens in relation to other poets. The isolation of parallel passages is of little value in and of itself, but parallelisms in themes and techniques may point to deeper affinities. One of the most commonly cited examples of symbolist expression in Stevens is the poem "Peter Quince at the Clavier," first published in *Others* in August, 1915. Dominated by a conscious enlargement of the music of the keyboard to that of the spirit, the poem reveals the permanence of beauty in the body and in the realm of the infinite. It may be read as a hymn to the music of poetry, defined as "feeling, then, not sound;" and finding its origin not in instrumental performance but in human feelings and relations. Not many of the poems Stevens collected in *Harmonium*

---

[74] Baudelaire, *Critique Littéraire*, 373. [75] Mallarmé, *Œuvres complètes*, 1576.
[76] See Hi Simons, *Modern Philology*, XLIII, 237; also, William York Tindall, *Wallace Stevens* (Minneapolis, 1961), 16–18.

reflect the vagueness and suggestiveness of landscape that we associate with the symbolist *paysage,* but a striking example may be seen in "Sea Surface Full of Clouds," a poem which combines scene painting and subtle mood creation with rich color symbolism; however, the mock-exaggeration of the emotional reverberations of the sea points to a parody as well as a statement of symbolist values. Given the playfulness and irony of many of the poems of *Harmonium,* this simultaneous parody and statement is by no means contradictory. *Harmonium,* a small reed organ, is itself a correspondent title, but the symbolist affinity becomes even more striking when we note that Stevens orginally proposed to his publisher that the book be called: "THE GRAND POEM: PRELIMINARY MINUTIAE."[77] It is difficult to escape the inference that Stevens was familiar with Mallarmé's concept of the GRAND ŒUVRE as the totality and culmination of a poet's work and indeed of all poetry.[78] The universe itself is viewed in this sense as a great poem of which the poet's individual work is a fragmentary manifestation. Despite this symbolist conception of poetry, it must be conceded that very few of the poems of *Harmonium* are written in a symbolist style. We may see a more striking example of symbolist expression in a poem of about 1916, "Blanche McCarthy," with its intimation of invisible powers, "symbols of descending night," and "the glare of revelations going by!"[79] Stevens apparently decided not to publish the poem, perhaps because it was too obviously symbolist in manner, lacking the fanciful inventiveness and physical immediacy of most of the poems of *Harmonium.* The most striking symbolist elements in Stevens' early poetry are his conscious musicality, his occasional vague and misty evocations of landscape, his elaborate color symbolism, and his movement toward a poetry of ambiguity and abstraction that was to become characteristic of his later work.

[77] Stevens, *Letters,* 237.

[78] See Mallarmé, *Œuvres complètes,* 662–63. For a thoughtful discussion of the concept, see A. R. Chisholm, *Mallarmé's* GRAND ŒUVRE (Manchester, 1962).

[79] Stevens, *Opus Posthumous* (New York, 1957), 10.

It is in his mature poetry and prose far more than in *Harmonium* that the force of the symbolist tradition is most evident in Stevens' art.

For an increasing number of Stevens' admirers, his late, longer poems constitute the triumph of his achievement. "The Man with the Blue Guitar," "Esthétique du Mal," "Notes toward a Supreme Fiction," and "An Ordinary Evening in New Haven"—these are at once his most ambitious and most complex endeavors. Their complexity is due in large part to the poet's preoccupation with the theory of poetry in his poetry, and particularly with the relation of the imagination to reality. Both the problem and the definitions of it in Stevens' poetry reflect an essential kinship with the symbolists. The constant interrogation into the relationships of being and seeming, of appearance and reality, of the imagined and the real, is central to symbolist poetry, even if the resolutions of their interplay are not wholly identical to those, for example, in "L'Après-midi d'un faune" or "La Jeune Parque." The concern with the identity of the self, the nature of consciousness, and the processes of inner transformation, is fundamental in the major poems of both Stevens and the symbolists. This is not to imply that Stevens explored these themes as a deliberate emulation of the symbolists; it may well be, rather, that Stevens' view of the poet's situation and function, and of the great themes of poetry, accorded with that of the symbolists, but was developed by him without any conscious reliance on the work of any predecessor.

It has been argued that despite verbal similarities, the concept and representation of reality in Stevens marks a central difference between him and the symbolists in that the symbolist notion of reality is equated with "le néant" or with pure abstraction, while Stevens sees reality as present in the world we inhabit. Thus, it is argued, "Mallarmé seeks a land of the mind beyond reality; Stevens a land beyond the mind, as part of reality."[80] It is correct to hold that

---

[80] Michel Benamou, *ELH*, XXXI, 35; cf. Riddel, *The Clairvoyant Eye*, 187.

Mallarmé is more mystical than Stevens; indeed, Stevens had little patience with mystical doctrine of any sort. However, we do the symbolists less than justice if we view their poetry as a rejection or destruction of the world of concrete experience. If Mallarmé's poems were as dehumanized or as sterile as some critics have contended, it would be difficult to account for their continuous hold on three generations of readers. One need only read Mallarmé's magnificent series of "Tombeaux" as evidence of the poet's deep involvement in the here and now, in the exigencies of the human condition in the world that all men inhabit. We should question seriously the contention that the symbolist poets viewed words and the world as incommensurate, or that their poetry is lacking in richness and fecundity. There are, of course, differences as well as similarities between Stevens and the symbolists, just as there are important differences between the individual symbolist poets, or between any two poets who might be studied side by side; but it should be possible to take due account of a poet's relationship to other poets without thereby impugning his originality or misinterpreting his art.

In Stevens' late poetry, "reality" is generally defined in one of three ways: first, as objective things or events located in the world around us; second, as the subjective appropriation of things and events, in their image in the mind; third, as imagination, a universal principle both within and around us. These definitions are not mutually exclusive. For Stevens, imagination embraces both objective and subjective experience. Reality encompasses not simply the empirical realm but also the life of the mind and spirit:

> We seek
> Nothing beyond reality. Within it,
>
> Everything, the spirit's alchemicana
> Included, the spirit that goes roundabout
> And through included, not merely the visible,

The solid, but the movable, the moment,
The coming on of feasts and the habits of saints,
The pattern of the heavens and high, night air.[81]

In symbolist terms, Stevens' concept of reality as the province of imagination is at once material and spiritual. Objects are both things and metaphors, existing in their individual concreteness, but also relationally, as part of a totality. Things are not merely inert objects; they are signs or emblems in a world swarming with metaphysical changes in the physical acts and places of living. The life of the mind, or what Stevens sometimes calls the idea, is a central part of reality. Hence, the necessary abstraction of poetry. The poet's province is "the metaphysical streets of the physical town."

Stevens' late poems not only glorify the world around us; they celebrate even more fully the life of the mind and its transforming power. The mind itself is a great poem, at once subject and object of poetry, rendering through metaphor the processes of transformation operative both in things and in ourselves, seizing the object as "The centre of transformations that/Transform for transformation's self,"[82] capturing "The freshness of a world" as "The freshness of transformation."[83] Stevens' perception of life or nature as theatre also expresses this awareness of reality as dynamic process. In its misty coalescence of changing objects, the description in "The Auroras of Autumn" evokes a symbolist landscape or an impressionist painting:

It is a theatre floating through the clouds,
Itself a cloud, although of misted rock
And mountains running like water, wave on wave,

[81] Stevens, "An Ordinary Evening in New Haven," *Collected Poems* (New York, 1957), 471–72.   [82] Stevens, "Human Arrangement," *ibid.*, 363.
[83] Stevens, "Notes toward a Supreme Fiction," *ibid.*, 397–98.

Through waves of light. It is of cloud transformed
To cloud transformed again, idly, the way
A season changes color to no end,

Except the lavishing of itself in change, . . .[84]

The transformation of landscape is part of the essential process of change which the poet re-creates. The park in which he sits, like the landscape he observes, constitutes a "Theatre of Trope":

The water of
The lake was full of artificial things,

Like a page of music, like an upper air,
Like a momentary color, in which swans
Were seraphs, were saints, were changing essences.[85]

The poet's awareness of the musicality and suggestiveness of objects and his evocation, in correspondent imagery, of their capacity for fluid transformation, illustrate once more the kinship of Stevens' poetic vision and that of the symbolists.

Stevens' passion for totality and order in his late poetry also reflects the symbolists' preoccupation with construction, with the disposition of the parts in relation to the whole. This preoccupation is, of course, not limited to the symbolists, but from Poe to Valéry, the idea of composition has been a conscious and dominant concern. The wholeness of the poem, its "huge, high harmony," is invoked by Stevens most strikingly, perhaps, in "A Primitive Like an Orb," as inherent in the nature of poetry, "The essential poem at the centre of things" to which "lesser poems" give expression.[86]

The central poem is the poem of the whole,
The poem of the composition of the whole,
The composition of blue sea and of green,
Of blue light and of green, as lesser poems,
And the miraculous multiplex of lesser poems,
Not merely into a whole, but a poem of

[84] *Ibid.*, 416.   [85] *Ibid.*, 397.   [86] *Ibid.*, 440.

>   The whole, the essential compact of the parts,
>   The roundness that pulls tight the final ring.[87]

The miracle of the "lesser poem" resides in its architecture as microcosm of "the central poem," the gigantic poem of the universe. The imagination, in conferring value on reality, necessarily invests reality with order. In "The Idea of Order at Key West" the poet recognizes this "rage for order" as "Blessed," as a sanctification of the imagination, a glorification of the poet's ordering of words.[88] Stevens gives similar expression to a symbolist conception of the poet's ordering of experience in the poem of 1934, "Hieroglyphica," when he suggests that the poet pieces the world together "with holy magic."[89] His most elaborate assertion of a symbolist theory of language, of description as revelation, the word as an analogue of the *logos*—"The thesis of the plentifullest John"—occurs in "Description without Place," as a celebration of the role of language in "the making of the world," in the shaping and ordering of experience.[90] For Stevens, the exactness and rightness of language are essential elements of the absolute order of the "supreme fiction," the poem.

Our consideration of the themes and implications of Stevens' late poems may suggest that the mature poet placed an unusual emphasis on abstract thought. Abstraction, as Stevens insists in "Notes toward a Supreme Fiction," necessarily follows from the interplay of imagination and reality, but it is "an abstraction blooded,"[91] surrounded by vivid and concrete particulars and invested with deep human pertinence. A strikingly similar relationship between poetry and abstract thought informs the work of the French symbolists. Stevens' late poems, like the major poems of the symbolists, invest abstraction with feeling, creating a music of ideas marked by both intimacy and intensity, clarity and wonder. His mature poetry expresses the poet's ceaseless interrogation into the mystery of our being, in a language not of cold ratiocination but of impassioned

---

[87] *Ibid.*, 442.   [88] *Ibid.*, 130.   [89] Stevens, *Opus Posthumous*, 75.
[90] Stevens, *Collected Poems*, 345.   [91] *Ibid.*, 385.

meditation, fusing things and ideas in the figurations of a powerful and compelling poetic vision.

Stevens' conviction that "the theory/Of poetry is the theory of life" underlies not only the interdependence of poetry and philosophy,[92] but also the special importance of the theory of poetry in his poetry. When we examine his formal statements of poetic theory, especially in *The Necessary Angel,* we find a remarkable degree of convergence between Stevens and the symbolists. In contending that "reality is the central reference for poetry,"[93] Stevens sets forth a view of reality not as mechanical and fixed, but as metaphorical and correspondent. Stevens uses the phrase, "resemblance between things," in the same way as the symbolists would employ analogy or correspondence. Resemblances bind things together not through statements of identity, but through metaphorical relationships. "Poetry," Stevens declares, "is a satisfying of the desire for resemblance."[94] Thus, the pleasure derived from the archetypal image of Narcissus expresses the pleasure we find in seeking out resemblances. Despite his refusal to admit any mystical elaboration of his theory of resemblances, Stevens recognizes that "metaphor has its aspect of the ideal."[95] This ideal character of figuration is developed substantially in the essay, "Effects of Analogy," wherein Stevens defines images as part of analogies, and poetry itself as a transcendent analogue:

> It is a transcendence achieved by means of the minor effects of figurations and the major effect of the poet's sense of the world and of the motive music of his poems and it is the imaginative dynamism of all these analogies together. Thus poetry becomes and is a transcendent analogue composed of the particulars of reality, created by the poet's sense of the world, that is to say, his attitude, as he intervenes and interposes the appearances of that sense.[96]

Despite certain differences in emphasis, Stevens here sets forth a theory of analogies and correspondences which the symbolists would have recognized as tantamount to their own.

[92] *Ibid.,* 486.   [93] Stevens, *The Necessary Angel* (New York, 1951), 71.
[94] *Ibid.,* 77.   [95] *Ibid.,* 82.   [96] *Ibid.,* 130.

The preoccupation with the nature and function of language that we have seen in Stevens' poetry is also a central concern in his prose. Poetry he defines as "the imagination manifesting itself in its domination of words."[97] His sharp opposition between the language of the press and the language of poetry recalls Mallarmé's similar polarization of poetry and "l'universel *reportage*."[98] For Stevens, as for the symbolists, "above everything else, poetry is words"; or again, "Poetry is a revelation in words by means of the words."[99] The poet is distinguished first and foremost by his absolute authority over language; hence, the crucial importance of precision and control in the selection and disposition of words. Despite Stevens' love of ambiguity in poetry, his syntax is much closer to that of Valéry than to Mallarmé; however, he shares with both poets a love of the constructive power of poetic language both in itself and as part of a larger totality. In his "Two Prefaces" to *Dialogues* of Paul Valéry (1955), Stevens declares: "Mallarmé and Valéry announce a new climate of thought. They want clear enigmas, those that are developable, that is to say, mathematical."[100] In speaking of Rilke's pleasure in Valéry's language, Stevens indirectly intimates his own. His praise of *Eupalinos* for its "extended and noble unity, . . . large and long-considered form," reflects his own similar values as a poet. Stevens could write so perceptively and admiringly of Valéry because he was steeped in the same tradition and responded to the same imperatives.

This similarity is perhaps most apparent in Stevens' recurrent concern with pure poetry. In *The Necessary Angel,* he declares: as for the social obligation of the poet, "He has none."[101] Rhetoric must necessarily make for bad poetry. Similarly, in letters to Hi Simons, Stevens declared, "The purpose of writing poetry is to attain pure poetry"; or, again, "The idea of pure poetry, essential imagination, as the highest objective of the poet, appears to be, at least potentially, as great as the idea of God, and for that matter, greater, if the

[97] *Ibid.,* viii.   [98] Cf. Mallarmé, *Œuvres complètes,* 368.
[99] Stevens, *The Necessary Angel,* 32–33.   [100] Stevens, *Opus Posthumous,* 279.
[101] Stevens, *The Necessary Angel,* 27.

idea of God is only one of the things of the imagination."[102] By "pure poetry" Stevens meant what Valéry meant: absolute poetry, that is, poetry in which all that is non-poetic has been purged. Despite his anti-mystical bias, Stevens insists, in an essay of 1936, "Pure poetry is both mystical and irrational."[103] Here, Stevens is referring to the theories of Abbé Brémond, derived in large measure from Valéry. Like the latter poet, Stevens would surely have agreed that "pure poetry" is in fact a term applicable to poetry as such. All poetry for Valéry and Stevens is "pure poetry."

The large agreement between Stevens and the symbolists on the nature and function of poetry reflects their common rejection of a supernatural sanction of belief. As Stevens remarked in his notes entitled "Adagia," "God is a symbol for something that can as well take other forms, as, for example, the form of high poetry."[104] The absence of belief in God and a concomitant skepticism, Stevens declares, forces the mind in on itself to examine its own creations.[105] In this process, aesthetics may come to displace religion. For both Stevens and the symbolist poets, the recognition that the heavens are empty and that human life is finite and evanescent leads to the enlargement of poetry to the plane of a secular religion, as a glorification of both man and the cosmos in the face of a bleakly pessimistic and even nihilistic view of the human condition. In the poet's sense of things, Stevens declares, "the significance of poetry is second to none."[106] It is in poetry that man's ultimate grandeur resides.

The affinities between Stevens and the symbolists are so large and pervasive that it is altogether understandable why some have considered him a symbolist poet. Clearly, the convergences of Stevens and the symbolists in their poetic theories are very great. Stevens declares in his "Adagia," "The poet is the priest of the invisible."[107] Baudelaire would not have put it differently. On the other hand, just as there are important differences in poetic art between all of the principal French symbolist poets, so are there striking differ-

---

[102] Stevens, *Letters*, 363–64, 369.   [103] Stevens, *Opus Posthumous*, 222.
[104] *Ibid.*, 167.   [105] *Ibid.*, 159.   [106] *Ibid.*, 245.   [107] *Ibid.*, 169.

ences between them and Stevens. The isolated juxtaposition of the poetics and poetry of Baudelaire, Mallarmé, or Valéry with that of Stevens is not nearly as revealing as the examination of Stevens' mind and art against the background of the whole symbolist tradition. His embodiment of that tradition heightens rather than diminishes his originality.[108] In our consideration of Stevens against the background of French symbolism, we must not lose sight of the fact that he was an intensely American poet. In one of Stevens' last compositions, the magnificent prose poem "Connecticut" (1955), he declares that to return to the places of his state "is a question of coming home to the American self in the sort of place in which it was formed. Going back to Connecticut is a return to an origin."[109] Similarly, the poem of pure reality moves straight to the object, "A view of New Haven, say, through the certain eye,"[110] but the object for Stevens includes nothing less than everything. It makes little difference that Stevens is not a symbolist poet in precisely the same way as Mallarmé or Valéry. He is unmistakably part of the heritage of symbolism, a heritage which he assimilated and, in a highly personal and distinctly American way, enlarged. The question of conscious or unconscious assimilation, of deliberate dependence or accidental convergence, is at bottom not important. Undoubtedly, some elements of all of these relationships are present. The large community of poetic values shared by Stevens and the symbolists is among the noblest of tributes to the continuing vitality of the symbolist tradition in the twentieth century, and the unique capacity of one of the major American poets of our time to enrich this tradition.

American poetry since the Second World War is on the whole less consciously literary in its origins and affiliations than was the case during the years between the wars. There may be European antecedents and parallels for such recent developments as "Beat

---

[108] See the sensitive discussion of Warren Ramsey, "Wallace Stevens and Some French Poets," *Trinity Review*, VIII (May, 1954), 36–40.

[109] Stevens, *Opus Posthumous*, 296. [110] Stevens, *Collected Poems*, 471.

poetry" or "jazz poetry," but they are assuredly not symbolist. Even poetry which employs traditional diction and syntax tends to be simpler, more visual, and more immediate in both subject and style than was the case for American poetry of the preceding generation. There may also be a conscious turning away from any European models in a new wave of regionalism and nationalism. The assessment of the conflict in modern American poetry between formalism and a revolt against traditional forms made by Robert Lowell in 1961 still holds good at the present time: "We have had a run of poetry as inspired, and perhaps as important and sadly brief as that of Baudelaire and his successors, or that of the dying Roman Republic and early Empire. Two poetries are now competing, a cooked and a raw."[111] Underlying the opposition between "cooked" poetry and "raw" poetry are the legacies of Poe and Whitman, even though the opposition, both historically and stylistically, reflects more of an emphasis than an absolute. Recent studies of Whitman have shown convincingly that his sprawling and strident poems are indeed intricately ordered and form-conscious, while the poetry of subtle nuance and calculated effect that stems from Poe is by no means deficient either in imaginative freedom or emotional power. Moreover, in the work of our most gifted poets, "cooked" and "raw" poetry may be found side by side, even in the same poem. Nevertheless, these divergent tendencies deserve to be recognized, for they are very much a part of the current poetic scene.

The poetry of Robert Lowell reflects a keen and sustained awareness of the legacy of the symbolists and of post-symbolist European poetry. In addition to translating symbolist poetry,[112] Lowell has written a number of adaptations or "imitations" which take their departure from poems of the symbolists, such as "Charles the Fifth and the Peasant" in *Lord Weary's Castle,* a poem based on Valéry's

[111] Cited in Hugh B. Staples, *Robert Lowell: the First Twenty Years* (New York, 1962), 13.

[112] See Lowell's translations of six poems from *Les Fleurs du Mal, Partisan Review,* XXVIII (March–April, 1961), 192–200.

"César"; or "Commander Lowell" in *Life Studies,* which evokes Mallarmé's "Brise Marine" by way of contrast. Lowell's re-creations of poems by Rilke, Montale, and Pasternak as well as many other modern European poets attests to his consciousness of the importance of large literary experience in the development of his art. In his poems, both early and recent, which express an intense personal suffering in a language of relative clarity and directness, Lowell is probably closer to Baudelaire than to that poet's symbolist followers, but it must be added that Lowell's poetic style and vision, at least to date, reflects an assimilation of symbolist poetry as but one of many resources in the shaping of his art rather than a commitment to symbolist techniques and values. The same broad recognition of the importance of the symbolists is present in the poetry of many of Lowell's contemporaries,[113] again without any particular sense of dependence or affiliation. The roots of almost all of our most recognized younger poets are distinctly American and, for the most part, remote from the symbolists, but the symbolist tradition remains in perpetual readiness for assimilation as one of the many resources open to the young poet. It is still altogether possible that we may have symbolist poetry of a high order produced in the United States during the second half of the twentieth century.

The modern poet in both France and the United States has been to a large extent a *déraciné,* and his preoccupation with the realm of inner and often highly personal experience reflects to some extent his awareness of his rootlessness and alienation in the larger social environment. The response of the poet has often been to find a sense of community and common participation in his relation to other poets, of the past as well as of the present. The symbolist idiom has been especially suitable to an introspective and meditative poetry rather than, for example, a poetry of social protest or of public celebration. If we view the effort of both French and American poets of the recent past as constituting in large part "a siege against the cliché,"[114] it is noteworthy that the quest for a new literary

[113] For some examples, see O'Connor, 76–78.   [114] Rosenberg, 87.

language and for a poetic strategy in accord with the demands of
the poet's time and place, has been animated in large measure by
the symbolist example. This has not been generally recognized by
American students of poetics and poetry. Wallace Stevens properly
complained of the exclusive concern with English and American
critical values and their spokesmen in Stanley Edgar Hyman's *The
Armed Vision;* "the great source of modern poetics," Stevens in-
sisted, "is probably France."[115] Not many American poets of our time
reflect Stevens' awareness of the immense importance of the French
symbolists in the enlargement of the frontiers of poetry, but those
who spent a good part of their lives in universities or who were
attracted to the French language and its literature were bound to
respond, at least to some extent, to the impact of the symbolists.
Even American poets who knew no French and who had little
personal interest in modern French poetry, unconsciously absorbed
some elements of symbolist thought and expression. There can be
no doubt that modern American poetry would be the poorer without its embodiment of symbolist values.

   At the same time, we must recognize that not many major
American poets of the twentieth century display the same awareness
of the symbolists as do T. S. Eliot or Wallace Stevens. Indeed, a list
of the names of important modern American poets not discussed in
this essay would be rather long. Ezra Pound's poetry, except for
some of his early work, is in open opposition to the symbolist
tradition, and the same can be said for William Carlos Williams
and Hart Crane, despite the latter's warm response to the poetry
and poetics of Rimbaud. We do wrong to both Rimbaud and Crane
to view their work as essentially within the symbolist context, in
spite of common elements of occultism and mysticism in the case of
Rimbaud, and an awareness of the transcendent power of language
in the poetry of Crane. In its open assertion of personal feeling and
experience, and in its metaphorical fluidity, Crane's poetry represents a turning away from the symbolist tradition. As Frederick J.
Hoffman properly concluded, Crane's great poetry "comes only

[115] Stevens, *Letters,* 598.

incidentally from the *symbolistes*."[116] The isolation for purposes of study of the symbolist tradition in France and the United States is bound to result in a certain limitation and narrowing of focus. The same would be true were we to attempt to isolate the impact of Whitman or of Imagism or of any other single aspect of modern American poetry. The symbolist presence is only one of many forces shaping this poetry, but it is a significant force, fully deserving of detailed consideration.

Any assessment of the impact of French symbolism on modern American poetry must be accompanied by a recognition of the limits as well as of the very real scope of this impact. The mere presence of symbolist themes and techniques does not make a poem a masterpiece, and it must be conceded that much of the American poetry written under the direct influence of the symbolists, particularly in the early decades of the century, was mediocre. Moreover, the great achievements of some of the American poets influenced by the symbolists were not always their poems that were most obviously in the symbolist manner. Nevertheless, it is hoped that our discussion of the work of several important American poets, some of them indisputably great, has shown conclusively that the symbolist tradition has been a significant part of modern American poetry. It must be added that those major American poets who were attracted to the symbolists, drew on them chiefly for ways of asserting their own originality. One may contend, indeed, that in poetry of the highest excellence, the presence of the individual poet clearly overweighs the presence of a literary tradition—but the tradition is present too, within the art of the poet. In the last analysis, the legacy of the symbolists, not only in France and in the United States, but wherever poetry is written, matters not as a distinct and now distant movement or moment in the history of poetry, but as part of the permanent property of poetry. It remains in perpetual readiness for further assimilation and transformation by poets who write to be re-read.

[116] Frederick J. Hoffman, *"Symbolisme* and Modern Poetry in the United States," *Comparative Literature Studies,* IV (1967), 198.

Mythopoesis and Modern Literature

JOHN B. VICKERY

I

Twenty years ago Northrop Frye observed that an age marked by the angels of Rilke, the hermaphrodites of Proust, the ivory tower of James, and the dying gods of Eliot was clearly a great mythopoeic period.[1] The intervening years have only strengthened this view. The more critics of twentieth-century literature have come to understand its historical roots as well as its significant texts the more its central activity is seen to involve the adaptive use of a wide variety of myths to the enduring aesthetic needs of men. So diverse are the artistic strategies and so multiform the causes of this fresh interest in myth that to attempt either a full-scale critical analysis or a complete historical explanation would be foolhardy. A more modest approach may serve us better here. To that end I should like in the following pages to focus on a particular aspect of modern literature's mythopoeic character. Elsewhere I have explored facets of the part played by Sir James G. Frazer's *The Golden Bough* in the twentieth-century interaction of myth and literature. Here I wish to look at some Frazer-inspired mythic perspectives and recur-

[1] Frye, *Fearful Symmetry* (Princeton, 1947), 423.

ring literary strategies which reveal the inexhaustible vitality and resourcefulness of the mythopoeic imagination. In the process it will also be clear that *The Golden Bough* has been and continues to be of seminal importance both for the forging and understanding of twentieth-century literature.

When one compares the arrangement of *The Golden Bough* with the prevailing qualities of modern literature's mythology, it is impossible not to be struck at the congruity exhibited. Though writers did not set out to create a literature that accurately mirrors Frazer's major work, something very like that seems to have occurred. Thus, what may be called the "anthropoetic" mythology of contemporary literature underscores most of the features that stand out from the welter of details that makes up such a large part of *The Golden Bough*. Frazer dwells at length on such issues as magic and its implications for the safety and survival of the human soul, the centrality of fertility deities in the history and psychology of man's religious consciousness, the rapt engrossment of original man with the natural vegetative scene, the strangeness and significance of specific ritual customs, and finally the implications of all these when viewed from the standpoint of the comparative method for the origin, development, and future of religion. Each of these topics delimits a precise aspect of the modern mythology informing twentieth-century literature. Naturally this does not mean that these topics all appear in literary form with exactly the same emphasis and intonation as they possess in Frazer's essentially rationalistic, dispassionate scholarship. But that he is the major informing presence and tutelary genius for the modern mythopoeic imagination, the starting point and ground base for the artists' explorations and compositions, is evident.

One of the clearest indications of the closeness with which Frazer's anthropology and modern literature's mythology are associated is the extent to which *The Golden Bough* figures not only as influence but as participant in the imaginative world scene of literature. The novels of Richard Aldington afford a most instructive instance of Frazer's contribution to an accurate sense of the time and context of the period presented fictively. They indicate in striking fashion the extent to which Frazer dominated the minds and conversations of many areas of society in the 1920's and 1930's. A novel like *All Men Are Enemies* (1933) does, in a measure, for anthropology what other writers were doing for psychoanalysis. It uses the language and ideas of *The Golden Bough* as part of both the work's setting and point of view. In so doing it reveals a major shift in the cultural sensibility of the age, which marks it off in unmistakable fashion from its predecessor. For instance, one of the male characters observes a woman clutching her breasts as though, he thinks, "she wanted to tear them like the wild mourners for Thammuz."[2] And elsewhere certain of the characters are said to "live on these pictures, like mistletoe on a tree." (75) These allusions testify not so much to Aldington's trying to establish symbolic or archetypal levels in his novel as to his reflecting faithfully the prevailing interests and attitudes and expressions of his own world. Both the dying god and the parasitic mistletoe had, in effect, become household words as a result of the impact of *The Golden Bough.*

The prevalence of Frazer's role in the cultural life of the time is revealed throughout Aldington's other works. An earlier novel, *The Colonel's Daughter* (1931), develops the ironic view of many aspects of modern civilization first shown in *The Death of a Hero* (1929). When a wedding is touched on, Aldington observes: "The wedding of Tom and Lizzie . . . might have provided entertainment and instruction to an anthropologist studying the persistence of magical practices and ceremonial costumes in civilised communities."[3] The Maypole is called "that cheery phallic emblem" (174) and economic capital is referred to as "that sacred totem which

---

[2] Aldington, *All Men Are Enemies* (New York, 1933), 207. Subsequent references are indicated in the text.

[3] Aldington, *The Colonel's Daughter* (New York, 1931), 161. Subsequent references are indicated in the text.

compels poor boobs to work for us." (177) And later one of the character's efforts to free himself from the bondage of religious belief is viewed sceptically as scarcely worthwhile for "he immediately fell into the much older and more nauseous bog of magic." (265) Here Aldington clearly reflects Frazer's view that magic preceded religion in the development of culture. More importantly, however, the novel accentuates the ironic attitude implicit in Frazer's comparative method and the anthropological perspective generally. Thus, magic is seen not so much as a primitive phenomenon but rather as a contemporary one whose form is naturally different. Instead of spells and incantations it is found to reside in "gadget-worship" and for one character to be "inextricably woven with the primitive feminine worship of trinkets." (265)

Perhaps the most unequivocal reflection of Frazer's shaping role in the imagination of the twentieth century occurs in *Very Heaven* (1937). One of the characters, Chris Heylin, is an assiduous student of anthropology, comparative religion, and pre-history, as well as psychology. The affinity between character and author is underscored by the informed specifying of Chris's textbooks: "On the mantelpiece stood some of the honoured ones: Frazer, Budge, Petrie, Breasted, Sayce, Hall, Wooley, Breuil, Moir, Elliott Smith, Childe."[4] As with so many others of the period who had pondered *The Golden Bough* and similar works, Chris feels the need to bring his knowledge to bear on his own contemporary scene. In a letter to one of his friends he remarks: "I ought to have brought a team of psychologists and ethnologists with me. Without such interpreters I'm all at sea, and don't even know where to begin. I wish Rivers and Malinowski were available. I'm more and more convinced that ethnology should begin at home." (34) The irony at the follies in the modern world revealed by the anthropological perspective is here tempered by a desire also to find answers, explanations, and where necessary new formulations and solutions. Thus, he tests

---

[4] Aldington, *Very Heaven* (New York, 1937), 145. Subsequent references are indicated in the text.

marriage in the light of arguments concerning Briffault's thesis that it was a wholly economic institution. He relates the exhilaration felt at cutting free from an old life to commence a new one to the stress that ancient religions placed on rebirth. In addition, he puzzles over the origins of civilization and wonders whether all myths and religions have a common psychological basis and what it might be. Perhaps the most representative of his view is his feeling that anthropology can provide the illumination necessary to removing the society's imperfections: "The world is filled with irrational beliefs and destructive prejudices. Now, if it can be shown that these things are not innate, but have their origins in dead religion or magic, we've taken the first step towards correcting them." (91)

Something very like this view of Chris's dominated the thinking of many creative artists in the twentieth century, especially after World War I. For many the war was the great traumatic revelation of Frazer's insistence that the savage lay very close beneath the skin of civilized man. Rendered so aware, they quickly found further evidence of this in the forms and manners of society and in its controlling attitudes. Chris's feeling that recognizing the historicity of man's irrational and destructive impulses is the first step to eradicating them persisted in the culture at large. Among artists, however, this quickly became subordinate to a more sceptical and ironical temper. To them the central issues became whether Western culture as it had been known could survive and whether art would have a significant place in whatever equivalent substitute might develop. While there are countless ramifications of this particular issue, they all come to a head in the increasingly intense problem of the relation between art and science. Insofar as the latter seemed to many artists to epitomize the secular, factual, technological character of their civilization, they saw themselves as an embattled cultural minority bereft in substantial measure of their traditional role of moral and spiritual educators. The scientific habit of mind appeared, at this time in the century at least, to exclude the poetic and imaginative faculties from contributing knowledge of any order. Confronted by such apparent challenges to their autonomy and very right to existence, artists, critics, and those seriously concerned about the nature of aesthetic matters began, frequently unwittingly, a serious reexamination of the nature and grounds of their craft.

Interesting and important though *The Golden Bough* is, the fact of its influence is less central than the question of the precise character of its impact on the mythopoeia of modern literature. Casual consideration usually leads us to feel that myth and works which encourage literary interest in it are likely to issue in quasi-religious attitudes and generally idealistic philosophic views. Eliot's concern with primitive nature myths as a matrix for Christianity and Cassirer's stress upon the nature and function of mythical consciousness are often taken as comprising not only the major but also the only possible dimension myth may impart to literature. In point of fact, twentieth-century writers have found both more varied and pragmatic uses for myth in their works than the examples of the great modernists, like Eliot, Yeats, and Joyce alone would suggest. And in doing so, they are, from all the available evidence, largely indebted to *The Golden Bough* for the flexible and multiform perspective it generates with regard to myth and related matters. In the present essay only a few representative uses can be illustrated and examined, but they will suffice to show that myth is a more flexible literary device and technique than ordinarily supposed. Modern writers have deployed myth to create verbal structures of an essentially contextual nature, to make diagnostic cultural analyses, to dramatize and participate in psychological dynamics, and to achieve philosophical positions of existential detachment. And it is to instances of these, their specific traits, and general implications that we now turn.

II

One poet drawn to Frazer and the creation of poems of context is T. Sturge Moore, the brother of the famous Cambridge philosopher G. E. Moore. Like that of his friend Yeats, Sturge Moore's career extended from the nineties through the first quarter of the twentieth century. In so doing it paralleled that of Frazer whose first edition of *The Golden Bough* was already being widely discussed when Moore published his *The Vinedresser and Other Poems* (1899). Even more than Yeats, Moore was attracted to classical and mythological themes and situations. It is perhaps too much to say that this was due to the influence of Frazer. Yet it does seem likely that this interest was reinforced and also moulded by Moore's awareness of the developments in anthropology and comparative religion spearheaded by Frazer. Thus, in glancing over Moore's entire poetic corpus, one cannot help but be struck by the way in which his attention is continually drawn to classical and biblical subjects. In dealing with these, Moore by his absorption in the myths, rituals, and history of the two gives the impression of being engaged in a poetic version of *The Golden Bough's* comparative treatment of religions and customs.

Even more striking evidence of Frazer's influence appears in the classical deities Moore mentions most frequently and from the characteristics he attributes to them. Adonis as the god beloved and mourned by women, Hyacinth as a later version of the dying god Adonis, Marsyas as Apollo's victim, Zeus as the sky-god, Bacchus or Dionysus as a deity of both wine and agriculture whose worship has spread through all Asia, Aphrodite and Artemis as contrasting symbols of virginity and sex, Astarte as a moon goddess and harlot figure worshipped by the Tyrians, and Demeter and Persephone as corn goddesses, all reflect points underlined by *The Golden Bough*.[5] Moore as well as Frazer viewed them as participating in an immense drama of love, fertility, and death which was of incalculable importance to those men and women who were their worshippers. Moore also resembles Frazer in that while concentrating on classical and Mediterranean myths and rituals, he is aware of others such as

---

[5] Moore, *The Poems* (London, 1931–33), I, 18, 240, 243; II, 57ff., 139, 165; III, 60, 61, 65, 162, 171. Cf. Frazer, *The Golden Bough* (London, 1907–13), VI, 23; VII, 216, 258, 263; IX, 390. Subsequent references to Moore's poetry are indicated in the text.

the Scandinavian. Indeed, when they look north, both focus on the myth of Balder the Beautiful and particularly his death at the hands of Loki. Thus, Moore in his poem *To Loki* observes, "Thou lovely Balder by their hands didst kill" because "content thou dost abhor." (I, 21) For the speaker, Loki is "passionless desire" and "divine mobility" which he asks to "enter our life once more,—force us to live!" (I, 20) In other words, he thinks of the half-divine Loki as still present in the world ranging over its surface not only as "Mischievous Lob, or lanthron Jack" (I, 21) but also as a gipsy. This unmistakably echoes Frazer's contention that much of contemporary folklore and superstitious custom possesses an intimate connection with the great myths and beliefs of the past. At the same time, the poet betrays Moore's sense of the diminution of modern life and of its need for revivification. In particular, he finds it is in man's heart where "fade the once bright myths of heaven and hell!" (I, 94) His plangent nostalgia for the loss of ancient myths identifies Moore's perpetuation of much late nineteenth-century poetry where the concern was more with the mythological than with the mythopoeic. For such poets myth was essentially the product of higher civilizations and thus a kind of iconographic cultural shorthand which could be used to communicate and create anew the splendors, beauty, and moral power of the past. It is in this spirit that many of his poems take up not so much the recreating as the contemplative retelling of myths like that of Zeus and Semele, Danae, Leda, Orpheus and Eurydice, and Omphale and Herakles.

Yet Moore is considerably more than a belated nineteenth-century poetic mythographer. His work testifies emphatically to the subtle yet emphatic effect *The Golden Bough* had on the deployment of myth in poetry. Though much of Moore's work is ostensibly traditional in mythic attitude, it is nevertheless clearly post-Frazerian in concentration. There is a greater stress on ancient myths' involvement with fertility themes, with their reflecting and growing out of a sustained body of primitive customs, and with their being preeminently the means of apprehending the past as real and alive in all its strangeness and otherness. Thus, in his loosely allegorical treatment of Danae he shows "the painted goddess, its lewd sign,/ Soused by the hiccuping roysterers, drip with wine." (I, 218) And in one of his biblical poems, "Jonathan," he associates the protagonist's cry with pagan fertility rituals:

> loud as heathen maids,
> To hail that star they worship, shuddering cry,
> Because they deem it virile and a god
>   Prompt to take umbrage at their virgin state. (II, 170)

Such comparisons function in the same way as Frazer's larger and more sustained parallels between the so-called higher religions and primitive rites. And also like *The Golden Bough,* Moore's poetry frequently sets the myths and rituals of great ancient civilizations in a context of primitive custom. Thus, the poems embody in their dramatic fabric such beliefs as that of the dead's exacting rites from witches, the soul's being like a butterfly and escaping from the body via the mouth and thereafter being capable of helping or harming living persons, the need for injunctions against naming the dead or men in battle, and the necessity of having a wizard for any attempts to raise the dead. In so doing, Moore embodies the view of the ancient world Gilbert Murray described near the end of the nineteenth century. The serene classical Hellene and the aesthetic fleshly Pagan no longer persist in their original clarity. Ancient man and his world are seen anthropologically as close kin of contemporary savage tribesmen. Moore continues to believe in and celebrate both earlier nineteenth-century views, but at the same time he is receptive to the insights afforded by Frazer. The result is a poetic rendering of the transitional state occupied by classical studies as anthropology of a Frazerian caste came to impinge upon it.

Even more germane to the temper of the age is *The Golden Bough's* shaping power in the imaginative secularization of religious experience. Here, too, Moore affords an instructive gloss in the modern sensibility's struggles of reconstruction and accommodation. His long dramatic narrative "Judas" takes up the story on the night of the Last Supper and follows it through to Judas' suicide. In it Moore draws explicitly on *The Golden Bough's* discussion of the parallels between Christ's crucifixion and certain Jewish rituals. A Glossary appended to the poem has two entries of considerable interest. The first deals with Barabbas of whom he says:

> Means "Son of the Father," the title of Marduc (=Mordecai) who is crowned to represent the power of renewed increase in the vegetable and animal kingdoms, in his father's stead, when Ariman (=Haman), the previous Son of the Father, dies in his stead. The king of the country was originally slain every year, but in time one of his sons was substituted, and still later any criminal received the title and ruled for a brief symbol of the year, to die in his turn at the next year's feast. (II, 331)

The stress on vegetative fertility, the king's annual sacrifice, and the gradual process of sacrificial substitution, all suggest the closeness of Moore's acquaintance with *The Golden Bough,* which elaborates each of these points with a wealth of illustration. Any lingering doubt as to Frazer's impact on Moore is removed by the second glossary passage, which deals with the festival of Purim. It reads:

> Sir James Frazer, in "The Golden Bough," suggests that possibly Jesus may have died as Haman in the celebration of the Feast of Purim. It seems certain that the Book of Esther is a pious travesty of the myth of Ishtar (=Esther) and substitutes a patriotic import for the original magic. The celebration of the Feast of Purim (=Sacaea) was a custom brought back from the captivity in Babylonia, the native home of this cult. Sir James' suggestion enhances the poetical and religious significance of the story of the Passion. Outworn notions of substitution and redemption would thus have conspired in the tragedy out of which more spiritual forms of those ideas were to be evolved. It is possible that pious Pharisees were shocked by this pagan celebration, and that the Sadducees were cynically indifferent to it, and hence efforts to suppress and revive it led to much irregularity in its celebration about this period. (II, 333)

Clearly Moore's dramatic poem is, like Graves's *King Jesus,* a myth-opoeic rendering of the cultural adaptability of the dying and reviving god figure. Both works reverse the traditional emphasis on the uniqueness of the Crucifixion. They argue instead that its importance is actually enhanced by recognizing it as a particularly prominent historical instance of a ritual rooted in the archetypal myth of the dying god whose proliferation throughout the world testifies to its importance and perdurability. The value of the Crucifixion as a religious symbol lies for them not in its individuality so much as in its commonality. In turn, the contemporary relevance of Jesus consists preeminently in his having been a superior man capable of accepting the awesome obligation of enacting a ritual of fatality and of shaping history into a mythic form and therefore a felt reality. Thus, both "Judas" and *King Jesus* exemplify modern literature's inclination to either replace or redefine the concept of transcendence as a spiritual metaphor.

For Moore, the poetic interest in myth is part of the human effort to apprehend the essential nature of the past. Myth is largely dedicated to discovering the felt truth about men and societies whose deaths in a remote time have conferred on them an aura of mystery that is a subtle compound of secular curiosity and religious awe. At the same time, Moore's style with its languorous rhythms and deliberate archaisms suggests that for him the world of myth and comparative religion is also an aesthetic construct in which refuge may be sought from the pressures of contemporary dilemmas. His long, mythological dramatic poems become, then, barometers of the mythopoeic imagination's efforts to resolve these dialectical tensions. Their length affords him both the necessary scope in which to fully explore the past and his relation to it and also the luxury of prolonged withdrawal from the modern world.

Both Aldington's novels and Moore's poetry exemplify forms of contextualization, though with significant differences. Aldington concentrates on limning in as part of the fictive texture and density of the immediate social scene the intellectual presence of *The*

Golden Bough. For him, Frazer is a socio-cultural *donnée* with which both fictional and real characters of the twentieth century must come to terms as part of the process of living. Moore, on the other hand, makes myth, its *figurae,* and actions generate a universe of artifice in which release from the dialectic of time is sought in a remote verbal eternity. Where Aldington aims at creating the conditions of the historical present, Moore seeks to produce an ideal context out of present desires projected on to an infinitely remote past.

III

Two other species of contextualization are worth noticing for the sense of mythopoeic flexibility they convey. Each provides, as it were, an instructive qualification on one of the contextual modes mentioned above, almost, one might say, by a process of cross-pollination. In the first of these, myth and ritual emerge as a transcription of historical reality, as a poetic equivalent to Malinowski's functionalism which sees myth as a hard-working cultural force concerned with the fundamental business of living and its perpetuation. In contrast to the focus of this mode on the past, the second species of contextualization utilizes Frazer's anthropological vision of the primitive past to crystallize the enduring dilemmas of the cultural present. What both of these modes make clear is that not all artists have been primarily concerned to effect radical alterations or accommodations of the dying god or other mythic emblems so that Frazer's images subserve their own dominant metaphors.

One poet who responds to *The Golden Bough* not with efforts at imaginative displacement or extrapolation but with narrative mirroring is F. L. Lucas. His *From Many Times and Lands,* subtitled *Poems of Legend and History,* exemplifies the transcriptive mode. A poem entitled "The First Yule" tells a story of a tribal king who annually halts the dying sun's mid-winter decline by ostensibly magical means, who ultimately loses his powers with old age, and in consequence is ritually slain by his people, and who is supplanted by his son who restores the sun to health, and tribal life to a fertile state. Any doubt as to the poem's indebtedness to *The Golden Bough* is removed by a footnote referring explicitly to specific pages in four different volumes of the third edition. The central concern of the poem is not to exploit the metaphoric potential of the king whose life is bound up with the fertility of his tribe and its land. Rather it is to render as vividly and simply as possible a past reality that conditions, however allusively and tangentially, our life today. The emphasis, therefore, is on scene and action rather than character and symbol. Narrative pace and simplicity of image allow Lucas to make of Frazer's material a vignette from pre-history whose reality and remoteness carry considerable emotional reverberation.

In this regard this sort of poem comes closest perhaps to finding an imaginative equivalent for the prose of *The Golden Bough* and the function it sought to fulfill. Like Frazer, Lucas is concerned to render the scene with maximum fidelity and to keep his interpretations of its significance to a minimum. Only in the opening and closing stanzas does he produce his version of Frazer's speculative and reflective comments. Thus, the poem begins:

> Askest why, stranger,
> We stamp, we sing,
> And black round the cavern
> Our shadows spring?
> Because we are mighty,
> Who once were nought,
> By the wisdom that Ung,
> Our grandsire, wrought.[6]

Here Frazer's theory that human progress depends on the actions and intelligence of outstanding individuals who learn more quickly than most how to bend both nature and man to their desires is

---

[6] Lucas, *From Many Times and Lands* (London, 1953), 20. Subsequent references are indicated in the text.

given poetic form just as the bulk of the poem derives from Frazer's scenic images and ritual actions.

More reflective in tone is the final stanza which suggests his central and yet how tragic ritual is to man's perpetuation:

> *My* turn, ere many
> A moon be run,
> To rule the Rain
> And bind the Sun.
> I too shall be mighty,
> Who once was nought,
> By the wisdom that Ung
> My grandsire wrought.
> On with the dance!
> Tread hard the floor!
> Who knows if we meet
> Next Yule once more? (25)

The speaker of the poem proves to be the grandson of Ung and hence the successor to his own father, the present king and wizard, whose knowledge provides the religio-magical assurance of the persistence of the sun, spring, warmth, and fertility. Implicit in the material from Frazer, in the subject itself, is the fact that tribal survival and cultural advance involve not merely an easy sense of achieved progress but an equally strong awareness of the grim sacrifices it entails. Such a poem, then, functions as a mirror or window on the anthropological scene depicted by *The Golden Bough*. The resonance it generates is that of Frazer's mythopoeic imagination rather than that of the poet so that the reader is brought to a state of reflective contemplation on the dimmest and most remote realities of human history.

The last mode of contextualization to be considered also reflects *The Golden Bough*'s deployment of scenic mythopoeia. It appears in the contemporary poet Robin Skelton. In 1960 he published a poem "The God," first written in 1956, which is based on the chapter in *The Golden Bough* dealing with sundry forms of animal worship and its connection with totemism and taboo. Like Lucas, Skelton strives to render the scene in all its anthropological immediacy as a kind of genetic cultural vision. But unlike Lucas, Skelton is more concerned to shape his verse in the prevailing contemporary idiom while still preserving narrative clarity. He also is prepared to make more sustained, if implicit, efforts to develop the theme's relevance to the human condition and particularly to the idea of man as a creature of the present.

Central to Frazer's treatment of the primitive worship of the bear, as in the cases of the American Indians and the ancient Ainos, is the puzzling fact of the ambiguity surrounding their feelings about the animal. On the one hand, for the greater part of the year it is regarded with profound veneration, and firmly grounded taboos against slaying it are scrupulously observed. On the other hand, at a particular moment in the year, solemn religious obligation to slay the bear is enjoined as part of a ceremonial ritual of sacrifice and propitiation. It is just this ambiguity that Skelton emphasizes when he begins:

> Feed the beast
> that you weep for, having killed.
> Garland the great bear
> of the wood and hill.
> Make him enter each house
> with blessing snarl.[7]

The contradictions inherent in the tribal behavior are rendered even more pointedly when the bear is described as "the body bayed and torn,/ worshipped and fattened." (28) And at the approximate middle of the poem the polarization of worship and sacrificial sacrament is made explicit:

> he was the hunting god
> the body's rage

[7] Skelton, *Begging the Dialect* (London, 1960), 28. Subsequent references are indicated in the text.

could recognize
and worship in his cage,

and weap and feast upon. (29)

Skelton's poem represents an advance in modernity of mythopoeia over that of Lucas in its greater sense of the problematic and
of that state's impingement upon the present. For one thing, Skelton, like Robinson Jeffers, utilizes the irony resident in man's killing those creatures, the gods, whom he has created in order to save
him. For Jeffers, the principal irony revolves around the inevitabil-
ity and indeed the desirability of suffering. For Skelton, it consists
by implication of man's having created for himself a ritual analogue
of vegetative time, a cycle of recurrence that perpetuates the mystery without providing the meaning:

> The seasons turn
> stiffly upon
> the dying and the born,
> looking for him they killed
> to come again
>
> in the same shape
> from the bestial Spring. (29)

The slain god is seen throughout the poem as moving via his ghost
or spirit into the land of ancestors, called "the fathers." This end,
however, is as riddling as the genesis of man, with which, in a
strange way derived from the researches of Frazer and Jane Harrison, it is identified. That is, the death of an individual is thought to
entail a return to an ancestral matrix—what Harrison calls "alcher-
inga" time—from whence issues in turn the living creature. Skelton's poem presents this as the problematic condition confronting
man. The region of the fathers is an impenetrable mystery to the
living:

> The unknown
> returns no message back
> but the unknown,

and the seasons turn.
What pity have
the gathered centuries
across the grave
to send no more
than this for rage and love— (30)

Here the slain god—"clumsy, rank, matt-haired,/ with slavering jaws," (30)—ultimately stands forth as the final inhuman mystery which challenges many by posing the irreducibility of the unknown against his desire for knowledge. Thus the poem closes with the image of "the new caught god" who "awaits our knives and prayers" set over against the query "What meaning is there?" (30) In such a question we see both the extent to which Skelton moves beyond Lucas in investing the narrative pattern of *The Golden Bough* with thematic point and also the manner in which his poem captures one of the central motifs of modern literature, namely, the irony of man's passionate need for fertility and the lengths to which his search for its emblems and signs takes him.

For a more sustained effort to bring myth to bear on the agonies of contemporary life while utilizing the form of the long poem and the mythological drama one has to turn to Robinson Jeffers. Moore's poetic career began in 1899 and was substantially over by the time of the publication of his collected poems (1931–32). Jeffers' first volume appeared in 1912, though it was really with the Tamar collection of 1924 that he achieved his characteristic manner, and continued into the middle of the century. Thus, Jeffers provides an apt and instructive development of Moore's interest in the extended poetic treatment of myth. They resemble one another in their comparatist interest in the myths of a number of cultures, but they differ significantly in their motives and hence in their use of these myths. The work of Moore and Jeffers reveal how the central figure and motifs of *The Golden Bough* may be utilized for aesthetic escape and existential confrontation respectively. By calling on the resources of anthropology and the aura of pre-history, Jeffers does

not so much build a context as engage in diagnostic cultural analysis.

By his own admission, Jeffers has been concerned to explore the
sources of contemporary Western civilization.[8] Since this exploration involves attending to the interaction of myth and history in
particular cultures, it both resembles and derives in all likelihood
from Frazer's interest in the genesis of society and the reconstruction of the past. Jeffers acts mythopoeically on the Hebrew-Chris-
tian, the Greek, and the Teutonic sources of our modern civilization
in *Dear Judas, The Tower Beyond Tragedy,* and *At the Birth of an
Age* respectively. The last mentioned is of particular interest for our
purposes, for it makes extensive use of the symbol of the self-tor-
tured god who hangs himself on a gallows for a number of nights
in order to gain wisdom of all things. The pertinence of Odin, the
Scandinavian deity, to *The Golden Bough*'s figure of the dying god
would be apparent even without Frazer's many references to him.
At one point Gudrun even speaks of "the hanged God/ that my
childish blood loves," while later a stage direction capitalizes the
entire phrase by way of indicating Jeffers' associating of the particular Scandinavian deity to his archetypal function in comparative
religion.[9] Gudrun's hypnotic attraction to the hanged god is the
achievement of self-knowledge "in the flame of reality." (77)

At least part of the knowledge acquired through the reality of
suffering and pain is precisely that the hanged god is, as Moore
observed of the goddess in his *Medea,* a creature of many aspects.
Jeffers, however, intensifies the comparative cultural perspective by
having his heroine take a more emphatically Frazerian stance:

> Ah Sigurd that I was mourning Adonis
>   the mistletoe lance,
> Hoegni nail hard
> The hero's hands

[8] Jeffers, *Selected Poetry* (New York, 1937), xviii.
[9] Jeffers, *Solstice and Other Poems* (New York, 1935), 76. Subsequent references
are indicated in the text.

> To the eagle wings, make him more than a man,
>   die for me Christ,
> Thammuz to death,
> Dermot go down.
> What boar's tusk opened God's flank,
>   what enemy has bound his wrists,
> Nailed him on the eagle
> Wave of the mountain? (82)

The effect of this, of course, is to universalize the god's death. In Moore the goddess Delia appears as Orthia, Hecate, Cynthia, Artemis, and Selene, that is, as more or less local versions of one expression of a single culture's deity. But in Jeffers the dying god encompasses a plurality of cultures. Like *The Golden Bough,* Jeffers shows that the pattern of godhead conceived by mankind is substantially the same.

In Jeffers' case, the fact that he regards the hanged god as the genetic paradigm of Western civilization becomes of the utmost importance. Eliot sees in the multiplicity of dying gods evidence of the evolution of religious consciousness and of Christianity's uniqueness through history's working out of the *praeparatio Christi*. Jeffers, on the other hand, finds the hanged god to be a profoundly ironic revelation. The irony, however, is less directed at the fact of man's insistence on killing his gods—though that certainly is a powerful motif in much of modern literature—than at the nature of his fate's revealing the ultimate reality that man's existence creates for himself. The hanged god himself articulates this revelation in response to the anguished cries of dead and dying warriors:

> Pain and their endless cries.
> How they cry to me: but they are I:
>   let them ask themselves.
> I am they, and there is nothing beside.
> . . . .
>   Without pressure, without
> conditions, without pain,

Is peace; that's nothing, not-being; the pure night,
  the perfect freedom, the black crystal.
  I have chosen
Being; therefore wounds, bonds, limits and pain;
  the crowded mind and the anguished nerves,
  experience and ecstasy.
. . . .
  I am the nerve, I am the agony,
I am the endurance. I torture myself
To discover myself. (88–89)

Here the hanged god emerges not as a transcendent power incarnated in human form in order to save mankind but as the concentrated essence of self-aware humanity. Being, for Jeffers, is ineradicably human, living, and suffering so that the dying god ultimately is man engaged in inflicting on himself the pain inherent in existence. Like Yeats, Jeffers construes transcendence as an imaginative act of knowledge directed at the phenomenological universe. Where the two poets differ, of course, is in the greater attention given by the latter to sheer physical endurance and the inflicting of violations on the human body and mind. Thus, in Jeffers' mythopoeia the man-god is the embodiment of both the universal and perennial human condition and also of the particular cultural age that worships him. In his foreword to *At the Birth of An Age* he suggests that the present age suffers from self-contradiction and self-frustration "bred from the tension between its two poles, of Western blood and superimposed Oriental religion." (1) The poem as a whole works out in dramatic terms this analysis of what Jeffers calls the Christian age, so that finally the hanged god of Frazer becomes the sinister emblem of cultural disintegration at the same time as his "heroic beauty of being" (91) and its power to compel worship are acknowledged. Indeed, it is the very conjunction of imaginative force and inappropriate cultural context that makes him in Jeffers' eyes such an inevitable guarantee of the fate of the civilization. For him, the dying god is what civilization does and becomes: a magnificent human creation of a divine self-crucifixion.

IV

The authors so far considered have exemplified *The Golden Bough's* adaptability to the mythopoeic creation of works of socio-cultural context and of probing genetic analysis. Because of the concentration on phenomenological constants such as imagery and conceptual frames such as narrative patterns, these works are marked by a higher degree of clarity and simplicity than is commonly the case in modern literature. This, however, does not mean that either myth as a literary factor or *The Golden Bough* as a shaping force is restricted to traditional techniques or static ideas. The third chief use of mythopoeic materials to be discussed here amply demonstrates this, for it dramatizes the psychological dynamics involved in the interaction of the twentieth-century ego with the world that is both its womb and its prisonhouse. A recent extended illustration of this use is provided by John Wain in his long poem *Wildtrack*.

His strategy of deploying *The Golden Bough* for mythopoeic purposes is significantly more emphatic and experimental than any hitherto discussed. To some extent, it derives from the radical poetic of *The Waste Land, The Cantos,* and *The Bridge* though with a rather different concentration of interest. In a manner that obviously owes something to William Carlos Williams' *Paterson,* Wain includes direct prose quotations from *The Golden Bough* as part of the fabric of the poem itself. For Williams, of course, this technique is an integral part of his poetic involving as it does the whole issue of the relations between prose and verse and between artifice and reality. In Wain's case this doesn't seem as central an issue, though the poem does exhibit a certain variety of styles ranging from the elliptical and colloquial to the formality of the sonnet. His interest in this technique seems more nearly thematic. Both *The Golden Bough* quotations and others from Dostoevsky, Johnson, Boswell, and eighteenth-century newspapers stress their subjects, which then are made the focus for poetic extrapolations, comments, comparisons, and allusions.

Precisely how this operates in the instance of *The Golden Bough* is best seen in the section, near the middle of the poem, entitled "Adventures of the Night-Self in the Age of the Machines." The poem as a whole—as the epigraph from Joseph Campbell's *The Hero with a Thousand Faces* suggests—explores the twentieth century's concentration of wonder and mystery in man rather than the natural world. It begins from Blok's Revolutionary poem "The Twelve," which epitomizes the clash of ego and society. Wain then develops the dialectic of day-self and night-self through which man works out his pattern of death by crucifixion and then resurrection.

The poet engages in a sustained effort to relate the social and individual or personal issues of the age to one another and to suggest their interaction. The section dealing with Frazer thus begins with a sonnet delivered by the possessed man who spoke to Jesus in the Gospel of St. Mark, and then moves on to deal with *Hamlet* and other topics that in a variety of ways develop the motif of kingship. Immediately following the initial sonnet, Wain declares:

See now,
the reverent burlesques begin.

Man worships by parody.
The outward miracles of Christ, the inward miracles of the Buddha:
on the fourth day, the noose and the two razors.[10]

This inaugurates the theme of the king's office as incarnational, sacrificial, and parodic simultaneously. The English people of both the Renaissance and the eighteenth century were "crazed with their sufferings." (21) Hence they accept the king's proximity to the divinity as reason for regarding him as capable of magically healing their ills. For them, "The king is their best magic." (22)

[10] Wain, *Wildtrack* (London, 1965), 21. Subsequent references are indicated in the text.

By juxtaposition with passages from *The Golden Bough* it is suggested that the genesis and ground of this view lies in Frazer's discovery that primitive man both held his king in religious reverence and also ruthless watchfulness. The king's vigor and good health were essential to the fertility of the land, the people, and their animals. When the king's health and virility begin to fail, he is put to death. In this there is a profound indifference to the individual and his physical welfare for the sake of the larger communal good, and it is out of this context that the oblique razor reference in the above passage is clarified:

> The piety of the Shilluk teaches how
> to disregard the flesh. If the king's soul leaks out
> through mouth or nostril, it wanders unattended.
> A sorcerer might trick or imprison it. And even
> without sorcerers, how can the people be sure
> the soul that keeps them safe will be transferred
> to the rightful body of the king's successor?
>
> In some tribes of Fazoql the king had to administer justice
> daily under a certain tree. If from sickness or any other
> cause he was unable to discharge this duty for three whole
> days, he was hanged on the tree in a noose, which contained
> two razors so arranged that when the noose was drawn tight
> by the weight of the king's body they cut his throat.
> Frazer, ibid.

On the fourth day, the noose and the two razors. (23)

In a way this poetic technique represents a fusion of the two imaginative modes of poems like *The Waste Land*. The notes that Eliot later appended to his poem are here incorporated into the text itself. As a result the device of thematic and symbolic allusion is both used and identified, giving thereby an increased sense of the imaginative interrelation of fact and poem. Eliot saw poetry as a dramatic distillation of experience and so conceived of the allusive technique as a means of condensing and multiplying literary contexts so as to achieve the maximum of imaginative power. Wain, however, as befits the 1960's, treats poetry less as a medium of concentration and more as an opportunity for imaginative reflection. Thus, immediately following the above passage, he goes on to observe:

> Primitives, of course. The seventeenth century
> looking back on the tenth. Edwardian Cambridge
> comparing the field notes of anthropologists.
>
> It is said that Frazer was allowed
> to keep his Cambridge fellowship just so long
> as he drew no conclusions from his evidence.
>
> On the fourth day, the noose and the two razors. (23)

The reference to the seventeenth and tenth centuries suggests *Hamlet*'s perspective involves a retrospective view of the period when Hamlet was supposed to have engaged in his own scrutiny and ritual of kingship. It leads on to and stands within the larger comparative view afforded by Frazer's contemplation of his ancient peoples from the ostensibly sophisticated vantage point of nineteenth-century English academic life. Both the poet and the anthropologists are, Wain suggests, detached chroniclers of man's ritual of survival and supremacy. In both cases the initial sense of cultural superiority is subjected to ironic involvement which reveals its own subjection to the primitive ritual of adoration and sacrifice. Frazer, as much as the primitive king of the Shilluk or Fazoql, is subjected to taboos prescribing the kind of conduct requisite to his high office.

The net effect is to extend Frazer's ironies concerning the relation of primitive and higher cultures one century further so that he himself moves from his role of detached chronicler to that of ritual victim. Now it is the twentieth-century poet who becomes the clairvoyant eye surveying the cultural eddies and whirlpools of civilization's historical development. Thus, he carries the exploration of kingship as a socio-religious ritual on from the Renaissance into the eighteenth century of Swift and Johnson. And toward the

end of the section, the poet renders his evaluative definition of the
psychic structure of kingship and its magical base:

> belief in magic keeps
> humanity from devouring its
> own entrails.
> > Swift went
> mad because he saw too clearly
> where dreams end and wakefulness
> begins.
> > In a healing dream
> the lady in black touched Sam's face.
> He lived. Shilluk and Fazoql
> panoplied their kings in love and
> death. Their dream
> in the frightening jungle
> was no different from that licensed
> by Dr. Swinfen.
> > > Night-self and day-self!
> The ribboned ceremony and the dark
> creaturely sty of sleep,
> where motives are littered and
> tug at the ranged nipples in the mud!
>
> To have a king is to say:
> *We will dream of a magic person, and*
> *when we wake that person shall*
> *still, by our will, be magic.*
> > > Dean Swift,
>
> You never understood! (30)

Here Wain implicitly suggests the similarity of magic and poetry or
art. The figure of the king is the living fusion of the two selves (the
night and day forms) in a realized prolongation of human desire
that forestalls individual madness and societal catastrophe. It is the
very imperative of magic coupled with its capacity to alter the
world and man's perceptions of it that for Wain implicitly makes it
a symbol of the poetic act, such as he himself is engaged upon in
Wildtrack. Thus, his efforts to unify and reconcile the two selves

through poetic meditation upon the cultural drift of the twentieth century is his form of magical exercise complementary to that of the ritual gestures and customs of the primitive tribesman chronicled by Frazer in *The Golden Bough*.

V

This final mode of mythopoeia to be considered is that by which the poet achieves a posture of existential detachment through an ironic perspective that views with a compassionate lucidity both fact and metaphor, brute experience and myth, reasoned constraint and imaginative exuberance. Probably the most significant illustration of this handling of myth occurs in the poetry of Louis MacNeice. Throughout his long career MacNeice's primary bent has been the topical, the occasional reflection on social issues and the individual's wry relation to them. Consequently, even his use of mythopoeic materials is sceptical and detached, poetic rather than dogmatic. As such the prevailing temper of *The Golden Bough* was particularly congenial to his own perspective. This appears in incidental remarks, such as likening the Ionic columns of the British Museum to "totem poles—the ancient terror"[11] beneath which refugees from the contemporary barbarism of Hitler murmur sorrowfully, as well as in more sustained evocations of the world of myth and ritual. The two best instances of this last occur in the volumes *Ten Burnt Offerings* (1952) and *Autumn Sequel* (1954).

The second poem in the former, "Areopagus," adopts the basically Frazerian strategy of a comparative approach which ironically reduces religious and cultural claims of uniqueness. Thus, the Virgin Mary is likened to "those other Virgins/ Long brought down to classical earth" (288), a parallel analogous obviously to Frazer's of Mary and Isis and with much of the same point. The chief difference is that Frazer generally inclined to see the primitive genesis of

[11] MacNeice, *The Collected Poems*, ed. E. R. Dodds (New York, 1967), 161. Subsequent references are indicated in the text.

Christian figures as evidence of their antiquated irrelevance to contemporary life. MacNeice, like many other mythopoeic artists, uses the comparison, on the other hand, to underline the plangent effects of time in overlaying the past with ghosts that blur and dislocate the present. Thus, he suggests that Paul "scouring the market found an altar/ Clearly inscribed but between the words/ Was the ghost of a Word." (288)

The same essential point is made more concretely in the poem's next section where anemones and almonds, traditionally identified, as Frazer points out, with Adonis, are linked to Christ's crucifixion:

> After anemones, after almond,
> Pitiless heaven, enamelled sea;
> The Furies plumped the grapes with blood,
> Their living rock was the death of sea.
> As Christ's dead timber fired by blood
> Was to blossom bright as peach or almond.
>
> The Unknown God? Judge or saviour?
> The unknown goddesses—Cursing or kind?
> Shall we have neither? Either? Both?
> The dark prehistory of their kind
> Hung over Jews and Greeks and both
> Found, of their kind, a likely saviour. (289)

Here the images of crucified Christ, pagan dying gods, and natural vegetation are interrelated in a dramatic continuity that exactly matches the historical one developed by Frazer in the course of *The Golden Bough*. In the poem the three images function to create a cycle whereby Christ, the most recent of dying gods, summons up the earliest emblematic form of the primitive deity, namely, the natural vegetative symbols of fertility. At the same time, the Frazerian comparative perspective of MacNeice creates a kind of Spencerian deity, a formative spiritual power that takes the shape demanded by the cultures in question. What differentiates MacNeice from Spencer in this regard is that the poet sees the spiritual form of the deity as generated by "the dark prehistory of their kind." That is, like Frazer, he finds the sacral character of the so-called high cultures determined by the events, compounded of ritual and accident, of their primitive past. Thus, while both the poem and *The Golden Bough* seem to deal with the human necessity of having a deity, they also make it a wholly human and immanent affair. The god is generated out of the cultural context, which essentially consists of the phenomenological realities impinging on the imaginative consciousness of the individual. In neither poet nor anthropologist is there an assumption of transcendent reality investing or incarnating itself in the natural order.

The chief difference between the two is that Frazer is more content, in theory at least, to accept a rational humanism, which looks forward to the ultimate disappearance of religion. MacNeice, on the other hand, recognizes that such a course is ultimately stultifying and disastrous for poetry since it would eliminate one of its richest sources of image and symbol. His solution is to base his beliefs and attitudes upon a poetic rather than a philosophy, upon the primacy of metaphor as a linguistic mimesis of an infinite variety of ontological conditions. Essentially this is what he does when in the last section of "Areopagus" he declares:

> The body may be a tomb
> Yet even the beggar's body is bread, is wine, is flowers in bloom. (290)

Or when the Furies are associated with Christ and are called ripeners of "crop and flock" and "yeoman and bride" who ward off evil and blight.

The same basic deployment of metaphor to make real and viable some of the central myths endemic to the primitive mind of mankind appears also at the end of the volume. In a poem directed to his wife and her primacy in his world, he observes that "what was/ The earliest corn-and-fire dance is your hair." (323) Here the metaphor assists in the identification of primitive fertility ritual with a contemporary human being in a transformation of action into an entity. It also suggests the metamorphosis of ritual function undergone between the ancient past and the present world. This knife edge of difference broadens elsewhere to a full scale sense of the imaginative diminution separating past and present, the extraordinary and the normal:

> Back to normal; the ghosts in the pinetrees
> Have dwindled to lizards; primaeval brows
> Lined with a myriad drystone terraces
> Smiles in the sun; the welded blue
> Of sea and sky is the tenure of legend;
> Far; near; true. (304)

The most sustained instances of Frazer's and myth's shaping force on MacNeice's topical and historical verse probably occur in *Autumn Sequel* and the third poem, "Cock o' the north," in *Ten Burnt Offerings*. The former deals with a number of MacNeice's friends, especially Dylan Thomas. MacNeice, however, is at pains to render the historical incidents and experiences in an archetypal or mythic pattern. Thus, a number of primitive deities, like Isis, Thor, and Pan, are invoked as symbols of man's drive for life and truth. And in Canto VIII, it is from the midst of the historical preciseness of September 25, 1953, and the facticity of an art gallery that he articulates the inexpungability of the mythical quality from the human heart:

> When painters changed their theme
> From myth to bistro, something mythical
> Still dogged their hands like an abandoned dream
>
> That dares come back in daylight; rational
> Behaviour may ignore the cloven hoof
> But hoof prints in the heart remain indelible. (362)

Such a conviction, of course, squares with the evidence if not the contentions of *The Golden Bough*. Given this conviction, however, it is understandable to find Thomas represented as the archetypal poet and to learn that at least some of his imaginative entourage are mythic and Frazerian:

The poet will not be bought, he has powerful friends
Who are his own inventions—the one-eyed hag
Whose one is an evil eye, the maiden goddess who sends
Her silver javelin straight, the Knave of Fools
Who cocks his snook and blows his dividends. (338)

Hag and maiden, as Robert Graves has argued frequently in both verse and prose, are forms of the great female fertility deities whose rituals and myths are elaborately traced in *The Golden Bough*. For Thomas, or Gwilym as he is called in the poem, to have them as "powerful friends" suggests, at least by implication, that he is a fusion of the poet and the dying god, the consort of the fertility goddess. When one takes into account Thomas' biographical escapades, one is not surprised to find his early loves being called "deep-bosomed goddesses of corn" (403) and he a "bow-tied Silenus" who was "well aware/ That even Dionysus has his day/ And cannot take it with him." (404)

Yet because *Autumn Sequel* is essentially in the same topical vein as *Autumn Journal*, it never really seeks to establish the identification of history and myth, of Thomas' twentieth-century life and Dionysus' archetypal pattern. Instead it explores the possibility of observing the similarities and parallels and of entertaining their relationship as metaphor. Consequently, the poem as a whole introduces both the connection and the disparity between Thomas and Dionysus so that the reader sees not only the individual given an archetypal definition but also the mythic figure redefined to achieve a more concrete and less remote quality. Back of this is the implication that the myth figure stands forth less as a historical phenomenon than as a more than historical creature, one who lives in history but who so seizes the imagination that he assumes an aura larger than life. In effect, the mythopoeic process MacNeice inaugurates here implicitly leads on, as Wallace Stevens shows us, to a dramatic description of the mythopoeic process itself as it unfolds in the human imagination.

Ten Burnt Offerings is of a more formal and reflective order, less determinedly chatty. This allows MacNeice, when he chooses, to be more sustainedly archetypal or mythical when the situation warrants. The best instance of this is, as has been remarked, in "Cock o' the north." This poem deals largely with Byron and his death in Greece. Though much of the poem maintains the jaunty and ironical rhythms of the series, MacNeice also develops an imagery pattern that conflates Byron, Christ, Adonis, and Meleager into a single composite figure of sacrificial death. This is inaugurated in the conclusion of the first section of the poem where the advent of Easter is anticipated:

> Scarlet flowers from a far-off tomb,
> *Christos! Christos aneste!* (291)

In the second section Byron and Meleager are brought into conjunction through the ritual imagery appropriate to the myth—the boar, death by fire, and the life or soul deposited in the log. At the same time, MacNeice is careful to so present the animal antagonist as to make it possible for it to be associated with both Meleager and then in the next section with Adonis:

> The boar was black
> Like the after-life of an Ethiop; his tusks
> Flashed curving through the forest like the Milky Way
> And his small eyes were death. (292)

The deliberate multiplicity of reference achieved by this image is clearly indicated by the use of blackness. For not only does this intensify the sinister nature of the boar's role, but it also links it with the cropped black sow that figures so prominently in the Celtic world of both MacNeice and Yeats. Indeed, this creature is explicitly mentioned by MacNeice in *Autumn Sequel.* There the association with the Celtic antagonist is part of a childhood scene in which the children play their innocent games unaware of a more ancient realm that surrounds their cozy country kitchen. This same feeling of the boar and god as part of a distant, departed era, and of their at the same time being associated with childhood and its fantasies and dream terrors, occurs in *Ten Burnt Offerings:*

> The boar is dark in the night of the wood,
> The boar is dead in the glens of myth,
> There is only a flame in the back of the mind
> Consuming a log . . . . (293)
> . . . .
> The dogs i' the nicht are ill at ease
> For they snuff the boar i' the reed-banks.
> His white tusks curve like a Turkish sword—
> Back to the nightmare! Back to the nursery!
> Our Lady o' Death has all assured
> And her board is spread for Adonis. (294)

In the fourth section of this poem (as the above passage indicates) MacNeice assumes a dialect designed to point up Byron's Scots ancestry. It also identifies the speaker here as Byron himself lamenting the death of Meleager and associating himself with those poets and gods who have sacrificially died for Hellas as a ritual act of triumph through death:

> I maun burn my body to clear my een,
> Yon withered bough maun blossom.
> To fell yon boar means death by fire—
> Calydon saved and Calydon ruined. (294)

It is in this linking of the poet, the dying god, and the legendary man that MacNeice finds his most sustained and most powerful deployment of *The Golden Bough*'s controlling image. To associate poet and god alone would be to adopt a more Romantic view of the dilemmas facing the poet in the modern world than MacNeice is prepared to accept. By the same token, to restrict the metaphor to god and human being would be to ignore his own central imaginative commitment—the art and act of writing poetry. It is precisely because MacNeice can see his affinities with all three, with the existential condition of mankind and with the imaginative states of poet and dying god, with ecstasy and dissolution alike, that he is able to carve out for himself a twentieth-century version of the middle style and an attitude that is one of mildly depreciatory irony toward both the benefits and liabilities of living.

The "Conscience" of the New Literature

NATHAN A. SCOTT, JR.

Those hucksters who make it a business in our literary life to sniff out and then to advertise *Tendenz,* whether at the level of the *Partisan Review* or of our Sunday supplements, appear, rather curiously, not to have noticed one interesting development of the last few years. For the increasing commerce between the disciplines of theology and literary criticism has very largely gone unremarked, outside a relatively small circle. But, though unadvertised and without celebrity, the recent inclination of these two fields of thought to move towards a point of convergence makes a significant circumstance of the present time: it may not constitute what Lionel Trilling would call a "cultural episode," but it is at least a development which, if carefully attended to, may have the effect of revealing some of the emerging landmarks of what Harold Rosenberg terms "the tradition of the new."

On the side of theology, the enormous prestige which the modern literary enterprise has come to have may in part perhaps be a consequence of an eagerness to descry some sort of disguised *preparatio evangelica* amidst all the clanging heterodoxy of this century's poetry and drama and fiction. Undoubtedly, what was once called "apologetics" or what we now speak of as "theology of culture" represents an endeavor which is to some extent controlled by a desire to disallow the possibility of any cultural force or movement being untouched by religious meaning of a positive kind. And most of our younger theologians have, at one time or another, displayed a most remarkable expertise in the art of turning up Tillich's "God above God" in cultural materials which were themselves very emphatically committed to secular modes of statement. But, in the transaction they have attempted to negotiate between themselves and the modern artist, the "apologetic" interest has by far been superseded by the intention to "listen" to the news the arts can bring us about what the jargon of our period calls the Human Condition.

Very often, one suspects, without being aware of its ancestry, the theological community (under the influence of thinkers like Maritain and Berdyaev and Tillich), in its dealings with literature and the arts, has been guided, perhaps most basically, by an idea which first took hold of the modern imagination in the late eighteenth and early nineteenth centuries, during the high period of the Romantic movement. It is the notion, descending from Lessing and Hegel through Herder to Madame de Staël and Taine, that the great function of art as a cultural institution, and most especially of literary art, is that of providing a very sensitive kind of barometer of the *Zeitgeist,* or of what Taine, in his famous trinity, spoke of as "race," "moment," and "milieu." And when the American Protestant theologian Amos Wilder tells us that we may find in the literature of the modern period "our best clues to the diagnosis of men's hearts and the deeper movements of the age,"[1] we recognize an emphasis which is often present today in theological analysis of cultural life, and we feel, too, that the Hegelianism of a Taine is not far distant—the sort of sentiment to which Hegel himself gave concise expression, when he said in his *Aesthetik:* "Every work of art belongs to its time, its people, and its environment" (*So dann*

---

[1] Wilder, *Modern Poetry and the Christian Tradition* (New York, 1952), xi.

gehört jedes Kunstwerk seiner Zeit, seinem Volke, seiner Umgebung).

Now the kind of Hegelian aesthetic of the Time-Spirit which has tended to govern recent theology in its method of approaching imaginative literature has appeared, of course, over a long period to find a very considerable sanction in the general style of the modern writer's pursuit of his vocation. Indeed, the fundamental aim of modernism might be said to have been (if I may lift out of its context a phrase of the English critic John Holloway) that of "living in the whole present."[2] Or perhaps a phrase of Stephen Spender's is even more apt, for he speaks of the distinctively modern vision in literature as a "vision of the whole."[3] And this makes, I believe, for an exact specification. For in the last hundred years or so the literary imagination has been overtaken by a most acute seizure of fascination with our metaphysical poverty, with what Wallace Stevens calls "the spectacle of a new reality." And this new reality is, of course, the catastrophic dishabilitation of that "whole/Shebang"[4] which was once considered to be a providentially ordered world. Not only has there disappeared that structure of archaic cosmology which Rudolf Bultmann speaks of as "the three-storied universe,"[5] but so too has the whole framework of the *philosophia perennis* suffered an irreversible collapse. Modern mentality simply has not beheld the world, and cannot behold it, as a hierarchy of orders intellectually appropriable by way of a metaphysical ascent through "the degrees of knowledge" to the Divine Principle which reigns at the apex of the whole. For nearly two hundred years we in the West have been an incorrigibly non-metaphysical people, at least in the sense of being unable—except by way of scholastic *tour de force*—to construe reality in terms of two realms. The whole

[2] See Holloway, *The Colours of Clarity* (London, 1964), Chap. 1.

[3] See Spender, *The Struggle of the Modern* (Berkeley and Los Angeles, 1963), Chap. 2 of Part 2.

[4] Stevens, "The Comedian as the Letter C," *The Collected Poems*, 37.

[5] See Bultmann, "New Testament and Mythology," in *Kerygma and Myth*, ed. by Hans Werner Bartsch and trans. by Reginald M. Fuller (New York, 1961), 1–44.

procedure whereby it has been natural since the Enlightenment for men to make sense of themselves and their world has been one which has effectively undermined the old supposition that progress towards "the really real" moves along an upward path, along some sort of analogical ladder, from the public world of natural and historical phenomena to a spiritual or noumenal world of pure Being. Indeed, all the pre-Kantian certainties of the *fides perennis* have long since disappeared—and their death might be said to be the central event of modern history: the linchpin of that entire conceptual scheme is simply gone: though it once carried cogency, it does so no longer, for, as Wallace Stevens says, "A tempest [having] cracked on the theatre," what is now most real is

> The rip
> Of the wind and the glittering . . .
> In the spectacle of a new reality.[6]

In short, as Léon Bloy said many years ago, "Modern man has been brought to bay at the extremity of all things."[7] And, in this severe situation, the literary artist has felt obliged to seek a "vision of the whole"—or at least the writers whom we now regard as classically incarnating the period-style of modernity are those who risked some comprehensive judgment of "the whole present."

"What has happened," said the late R. P. Blackmur, "[is that] almost the whole job of culture has been dumped on the artist's hands."[8] And, judging from the many similar testimonies that have come from virtually all the focal strategists of the modern movement, it would indeed appear to have been felt to be the case, that a vast job had been dumped on the writer's hands. In this connection, one could bring forward relevant declarations from so diverse a group of representative figures as Arthur Rimbaud, Matthew Arnold, Henry James, William Butler Yeats, Rainer Maria Rilke, An-

---

[6] Stevens, "Repetitions of a Young Captain," *The Collected Poems*, 306.

[7] Quoted in Stanley Romaine Hopper, *The Crisis of Faith* (New York and Nashville, 1944), 15.

[8] Blackmur, *The Lion and the Honeycomb* (New York, 1955), 206.

dré Breton, Jean-Paul Sartre—but T. S. Eliot's famous testimony, in
the review that he published in the *Dial* in 1923, of Joyce's *Ulysses,*
makes as good an exhibit as any other. And here the significant
thing is, of course, that, as Eliot undertook to confront and assess
Joyce's astonishing accomplishment just a few months after the
book's appearance, what he was impressed by, above all else, was
the extent to which Joyce, in using an Homeric paradigm, "in
manipulating a continuous parallel between contemporaneity and
antiquity," had found "a way of controlling, of ordering, of giving a
shape and a significance to the immense panorama of futility and
anarchy which is contemporary history." It was, he suggested, such
"a step toward making the modern world possible for art" as could
be taken only by those who had "won their own discipline in secret
and without aid, in a world which offers very little assistance to that
end."[9] The implicit assumption was that inherited systems of reference had broken down, that, in order for the spectacle of the new
reality to be mastered, the artist had to take on "the whole job of
culture"—raiding dead tradition for the still viable remnant of
meaning, minting out of his own untrammeled inventiveness new
world-hypotheses, and so ordering it all as somehow to give a shape
and a significance to a world which itself offers very little assistance
toward the attainment of a coherent vision of human existence.
What was implicitly assumed was that, in a late and difficult time,
the artist's natural effort will be that of finding a "whole present" in
which to live and that any "vision of the whole" which he achieves
will have been managed by a discipline won "in secret and without
aid."

Now, despite the brevity of Eliot's early account of the meaning
of Joyce's achievement, it has today a classic status, and we have
long since discerned the marvelous accuracy with which it expressed the modern writer's sense of his own situation and charted

---

[9] Eliot, "Ulysses, Order and Myth," first appeared in *Dial,* November, 1923;
reprinted in John W. Aldridge, (ed.), *Critiques and Essays on Modern Fiction:
1920–1951* (New York, 1952).

the course which he was undertaking. For the people who incarnate the idea of modernity—the Pound of *Mauberley* and the *Cantos,* the Joyce of *Ulysses,* the Eliot of *The Waste Land,* the Rilke of the *Duino Elegies,* the Pirandello of *Six Characters,* the Yeats of *The Tower* and *The Winding Stair,* the Faulkner of *The Sound and the Fury*—are all artists who felt what Wordsworth called "the weight of all this unintelligible world." Knowing themselves to be disinherited of an effective metaphysical machinery for the ordering of experience, they proceeded to improvise into existence new systems of meaning and faith. And thus, however untouched they may have been by the usages of orthodoxy, there is in their work, we feel, an austere religious grandeur that is an expression of the stringent honesty and courage with which they move through tracts of the spirit left darkened by the recession of older codes and beliefs. It is, indeed, a literature drenched in the passions of metaphysics and theology. And thus it should be no occasion for surprise that that vanguard in criticism which has undertaken to plot and to explicate the established canon of the modern movement should so frequently have had to enter an area of theological reflection. Nor is it any less strange, given the general shape and tendency of modern literature, that the most alert professional theologians should be deeply drawn, as they have been, to this whole body of art, as a kind of unconsecrated scripture arising out of the innermost chambers of the heart in a straitened age.

Many years ago, early in the first decade of this century, Santayana suggested that literature always reveals a special sort of "piety" or "conscience": for, said he, "it cannot long forget, without forfeiting all dignity, that it serves a burdened and perplexed creature."[10] And it might be said that the distinctively "modern" element in modern literature was in part an affair of the consistency with which the "conscience" of that literature prompted the artist to compete with that "immense panorama of . . . anarchy" of which

[10] George Santayana, *The Life of Reason,* Vol. IV of *Reason in Art* (New York, 1905), 84.

Eliot spoke in his review of *Ulysses*. Haunted by an "enormous dream of . . . the mortality of [the] gods"[11] and of the consequent disarray of the human City, the literary imagination undertook to find a stay against the confusion in new myths and metaphysics. Whether one turns to Joyce or Mann or Broch, or to Rilke or Yeats or Eliot, one feels that what is being proffered, at bottom, is some vast metaphor or parable about Time and Destiny, about History and the Human Prospect. The *analogia fidei* no longer being available as a way to ultimate affirmation, the modern artist turned then to a new method of reflection, proceeding by way of what might be called the *analogia extremitatis*. And, if this dialectical route did not yield a new *analogia entis,* at least the radicalism with which the writer spanned the great frontiers of modern experience gave an immense vibrancy and poignance to metaphysical perplexity and had the effect, we feel, of expressing that peculiar form and pressure which constituted "the very age and body of the time."

Indeed, it is just as we remember the audaciousness and urgency with which the classic literature of our period was competing with reality, it is just as we remember its passion to face into and alter the course of history, that we are bound to be put in mind of how great is now the distance that already separates the contemporary landscape from the modern tradition: it is just here that we begin to sense how deeply literature has already moved into a post-modern phase. One doesn't know quite where to locate the point at which the transition began. Perhaps the search for origins might go back to Rimbaud's fascination with "the voluptuousness of nirvana,"[12] or to Mallarmé's disenchantment with "the literary game," or to Kafka's curious aesthetic of indeterminacy which made his fiction so astonishing when it first began to be widely read thirty years ago. But wherever may be the point which is to be identified as that at which the modern period in literature begins already to be drawing

---

[11] Ihab Hassan, "The Dismemberment of Orpheus: Reflections on Modern Culture, Language and Literature," *American Scholar,* XXXII (Summer, 1963), 463.

[12] Marcel Raymond, *From Baudelaire to Surrealism* (New York, 1950), 33.

to a close, there is, early on in Robert Musil's novel *The Man Without Qualities,* a sentence which can now be seen to have been prophetic of the new turn which the literary imagination was to take in its post-modern phase. It is the sentence in which Musil tells us that "no serious attempt will be made to . . . enter into competition with reality." And his meaning is that the simple sequentiality of literary narrative—and then, and then, and then—is no longer a true simulacrum of human experience: however comforting its illusion of order and necessity may once have been, the illusion has lost its beguiling power, and both Musil and his hero Ulrich take it for granted that "everything has now become non-narrative." The concrete experiential material of the world, in this very late season, has somehow become so intractable, so radically contingent, as to make any attempt to the artist to "compete" with it not only futile but inauthentic, and even fraudulent. And he therefore best "serves a burdened and perplexed creature" by relegating to the discard as utterly specious the old illusions, the mistaken supposition that literary art can give "a shape and significance to the immense panorama of . . . anarchy" which is our present situation. What the "conscience" of the artist must now require, Musil wants in effect to say, is that the work of art simply be, in its own tenuous fragmentariness and indeterminacy, an image of the actual world to which man is condemned. And, in his manifest impatience with the logic of traditional narrative order, it would in fact seem that it was such an image that he was himself attempting to create in *The Man Without Qualities.* For, given the "mere anarchy [which] is loosed upon the world," it is a novel which wants only to provide an illustration of that chaos.

Now this refusal to compete with reality—which marks what may well be the central impulse of the post-modern movement in literature—undoubtedly reaches well back into the nineteenth century, and most especially into those French Romantics who, as Mario Praz says, exalted "the artist who does not give a material form to his dreams—the poet ecstatic in front of a forever blank page, the musician who listens to the prodigious concerts of his soul without attempting to translate them into notes."[13] "It is romantic," Praz suggests, "to consider concrete expression as a decadence, a contamination,"[14] and this is at least the feeling represented by that French line that runs, crookedly, from Rimbaud through Mallarmé and Valéry to Maurice Blanchot. But there are, of course, still other antecedents of the contemporary refusal of that imperial imagination so typical of classic modernism—which was beautifully expressed by Yeats when, in a famous phrase, he expressed his desire to hold together reality and justice in a single thought. In, for example, those baffling arabesques of Kafka's, one senses a deep disposition of the artist to forswear that structurally enclosed kind of autonomy which was so much the intention of traditionalist modernism: the ambiguity which this poet of the novel experienced in his encounter with the world was so radical that, far from dreaming of his art as a way of subduing the anarchy and of holding together reality and justice, he could only create a tantalizingly opaque fiction whose meanings were deliberately left unresolved and open. And it is a similar procedure that is also noticeable in Gide's *The Counterfeiters,* in Ford Madox Ford's *The Good Soldier,* in Djuna Barnes's *Nightwood,* in Ivy Compton-Burnett's *A House and Its Head,* in Nabokov's *Pale Fire,* in Bellow's *Seize the Day*—a procedure which has the effect of conveying the writer's sense of the world's so far surpassing the framing devices of art as to render both futile and fraudulent the attempt, were he to make it, to enter into any very strenuous competition with reality.

Or, again, a kind of disavowal of modernism's ambitiousness for the large reconstructive effort is to be felt in the fleeting deliquescence and vague, shadowy mistiness so much cultivated by Virginia Woolf—who proposed, in her much-quoted manifesto of 1919 (on "Modern Fiction"), to "record the atoms as they fall upon the mind in the order in which they fall." This was the only pattern she

[13] Praz, *The Romantic Agony,* trans. Angus Davidson (Cleveland and New York, 1956), 15.   [14] *Ibid.*

wanted to trace—"the pattern, however disconnected and incoherent in appearance, which each sight or incident scores upon the consciousness." And there is no doubt a fairly straight line leading from the Virginia Woolf of *To the Lighthouse* through the Djuna Barnes of *Nightwood* to the Malcolm Lowry of *Under the Volcano* and the Nathalie Sarraute of *Tropismes*. For these are writers—and the list could be enlarged—who adhere to something like the sort of standard Virginia Woolf was herself embracing. Their characters, for example, as one of Mrs. Woolf's critics has remarked of her own, "are not characters" but are left somehow "unfinished, spreading as the ripples of a lake spread in the sunlight."[15] And they give the impression of being unfinished, because they have been dissolved into psychological tropisms, into (in Mrs. Woolf's phrase) the "incessant shower of innumerable atoms" that fall, disconnectedly and incoherently, upon the mind.

But the impulse which is so much a part of the life of literature in our immediate time—the refusal in any way to transfigure or to reconstruct or to try to impose a new order on the human reality—was expressed precursively not alone in the area of the novel. For, in poetry too, there was a marginal tradition contemporaneous with the classic modern movement that wanted only to be, in Carlos Williams' phrase, an "approximate co-extension with the universe."[16] And in the *témoignages* of René Char and Henri Michaux on the French scene, or in the *collages* of Charles Olson and Williams himself on the American scene, we discern expressions of that anti-Platonic current in our century's poetry which is distinguished by the poet's habit of apprehending the world as simply *there* and as in no way itself proposing any sort of transfiguration. For William Carlos Williams a kitchen spigot is simply a kitchen spigot, and a wheelbarrow touched by rain is nothing other than itself: nor does *poiesis* involve any metaphysic of transubstantiation: it is simply a technique of resignation to the sheer welter of exist-

---

[15] Bernard Blackstone, *Virginia Woolf: A Commentary* (London, 1949), 10.
[16] Williams, *Spring and All* (Dijon, France, 1923), 27.

ence: and, in this, Williams was at one with such writers as Jorge Guillén and St.-John Perse, for whom Wallace Stevens may be regarded as having spoken, when, in "An Ordinary Evening in New Haven," he said, "We seek/Nothing beyond reality."

Nor is traditionalist modernism in the theatre without its anticipations also of post-modern tendency. For to move from Büchner's *Woyzeck* to Strindberg's *A Dream Play* and from Jarry's *Ubu Roi* to Pirandello's *Six Characters in Search of an Author* is to scan early and significant instances of the dramatic imagination finding in the imbalances and unresolved tensions of an open kind of form a way of circumventing any rigorous effort at giving a shape to the immense panorama of modern reality.

But it is chiefly in the years since, roughly, World War II that the avant-garde in recent literature has taken an emphatically post-modern form. Here, as so often in the past, the French have played a decisive role, and it is the brilliant virtuoso Alain Robbe-Grillet who presents the crucial case. For the novels which he has been producing since the early 1950's comprise the most widely publicized and perhaps the most important exhibit of that *nouveau roman* whose practitioners (Claude Simon, Michel Butor, Marguerite Duras, Nathalie Sarraute) represent today one major phase of the post-modernist insurgency. But, in addition to his considerable novelistic gifts, M. Robbe-Grillet has a genius for programmatic statement, and thus the essays which make up his little book *Pour un Nouveau Roman* (1963) constitute a notable landmark of the present time.

Robbe-Grillet's basic rejection—on which his whole theory of literature is based—is a rejection of what he considers to be the inordinate anthropomorphism of the inherited literary tradition. The tradition of Homer and Dante and Shakespeare and Tolstoi and Proust is, for all of its variousness, a tradition which, in his estimate of things, is deeply rooted in the old "cult of the 'human,'" and its method or system is an affair of analogy. It speaks, for example, of the weather as "capricious" or of the mountain as "majestic" or of the sun as "pitiless," as though the furniture of the world were drenched in human sentiments and moral values—and this analogical attribution of fancy *profondeurs* to the data of physical reality, this throwing of bridges across the gulf between man and the world, has the effect of suggesting, say, that "Mont Blanc has been waiting for me in the heart of the Alps since the tertiary era, and with it all my notions of greatness and purity!"[17] But if there is no "metaphysical pact" between man and the world—and Robbe-Grillet takes it for granted that there is none—then, he contends, it is simply fraudulent for the literary artist to render reality as if it were all an affair of "signification."

And not only must all analogical procedures be, therefore, discarded, but so too must the writer forswear essentialism of every kind, taking objective, phenomenological description as his legitimate and appropriate task. For, as he says, that dubious "interiority which Roland Barthes has called 'the romantic heart of things' " is in truth a "pseudo-mystery."[18] Nor is man himself in fact omnipotent: the world is not his "private property, hereditary and convertible into cash":[19] indeed, what is most remarkable about the world is simply that it *is*. "Around us, defying the noisy pack of our animistic or protective adjectives, things *are there*. Their surfaces are distinct and smooth, *intact*, neither suspiciously brilliant nor transparent."[20] And what lucidity requires is that we achieve the ability to *see*, "through entirely unprejudiced eyes," without camouflaging everything with "a continuous fringe of culture."[21] "Man looks at the world, and the world does not look back at him,"[22] for, contrary to the traditional humanist illusion, the world itself is not bathed in "signification": it is outside man, irredeemably "other," and a truly mature literature is one which undertakes "to measure the distances —without futile regret, without hatred, without despair."[23]

So M. Robbe-Grillet wants to propose—and most especially for

---

[17] Alain Robbe-Grillet, *For a New Novel: Essays on Fiction*, trans. Richard Howard (New York, 1965), 56.   [18] *Ibid.*, 21.   [19] *Ibid.*, 29.   [20] *Ibid.*, 19.   [21] *Ibid.*, 18.   [22] *Ibid.*, 58.   [23] *Ibid.*, 74.

the novel which is his chief concern—that literary art in our time be submitted to a very drastic surgery. His declaration is that, given its general stagnation, it needs to be radically purged of all the old eloquence, the old "myths of 'depth,'" the old anecdotalism, if it is to become anything more than "mere literature," if it is to become (in Giraudoux's phrase) "an evening school for adults." Total objectivity, "total impersonality of observation," may not, as he admits, be easily achievable. "But *freedom* of observation should be possible"[24]—such a freedom, that is, from conceptual encumbrances as will permit us lucidly to behold the world in its brute factuality and in its unyielding resistance to our conventional habits of ordering and apprehension. "Since it is chiefly in its presence that the world's reality resides, our task is now to create a literature which takes that presence into account."[25]

But the creation of such a literature will entail not only a strict attentiveness to the fact that the objects of the world are *"there* before being *something,"* will entail not only a refusal of the old anthropomorphism: it will also entail full recognition of the fact that what is primarily true about the human presence itself is simply its *thereness.* Not only must the world itself not be rendered as if it were merely a vague reflection of the human spirit, but the "one serious, obvious quality" of man himself must be shown to be simply his *presence,* his *thereness.* The traditional hero is very largely a creature of the author's commentary and interpretation, of what M. Robbe-Grillet calls "psychological analysis." But *le roman objectif* will forswear the old "sacrosanct psychological analysis," the old anthropocentrism; and it will exclude from itself what has traditionally been denominated as "character," for the sake of inviting the reader to reflect that human personality is not indeed "the means and the end of all exploration," that the person is not in fact omnipotent, and that the old "cult of the 'human'" is, therefore, an obsolete irrelevance. And just as rigorously will *le roman objectif* expunge from itself what a traditional poetic of fiction calls "story."

[24] *Ibid.,* 18.   [25] *Ibid.,* 23.

For to tell a story which has a beginning and a middle and an end is to impose such an order upon the world as has the effect of domesticating it within an atmosphere of *human* value and sentiment: and not only is the old anthropomorphic fallacy thus reinstated, but the whole machinery of reversals and recognitions, of climaxes and denouements, does also have the effect of implying what is in fact a lie—namely, that events do but mask the "hidden soul of things" and that there are "depths" in experience which call for some sort of metaphysical transcendence. So Robbe-Grillet's prescription for what he takes to be the present malaise of fiction requires the extrusion of both "characters" and "stories," and his intention, says the French critic Bernard Dort, is "to stick to zero":[26] he would have the novelist convert the world and the reality of man into a kind of frozen "still life" about which nothing at all really is to be *said,* about which no judgment is to be made—which is simply to be *looked* at, with "entirely unprejudiced eyes."

Now M. Robbe-Grillet is not the sole theorist in the *nouveau roman* circle in France today: Michel Butor has produced two volumes of critical essays, and Nathalie Sarraute, whose own fiction is not always easily associable with the group has given many of the circle's aims impressive formulation in her book *L'Ere du Soupçon.* But it is the pungent insolence and brilliant intensity of Robbe-Grillet's rhetoric which have given his manifestoes a quasi-official status. And, however much the essays in *Pour un Nouveau Roman* were originally written, as he himself admits, in justification of his own novelistic practice, they do, nevertheless, present a remarkably useful summary of the general ethos made up by the fiction of such writers as Butor and Beckett and Mme. Sarraute and Jean Cayrol and Claude Simon, and numerous others—though, of course, since Robbe-Grillet is in no formal sense a legislator for the group, his theoretical work provides no exact chart of a movement representing a good deal of lively variousness and diversity.

Robbe-Grillet's novel of 1959, *Dans le Labyrinthe,* is an extreme

[26] Dort, "Are These Novels 'Innocent'?" *Yale French Studies,* (Summer, 1959), 24.

example of this literature—a book which wants its reader, as the Preface tells us, "to see in it only the things, gestures, words, and events that he is informed about." An unnamed soldier, exhausted and ill, is lost in a strange city through whose snow-blanketed streets he wanders at night, having forgotten the name of the particular street for which he is looking. He carries a cardboard box which contains the last remaining possessions (a watch, a sheaf of letters, a ring, a bayonet) of one of his comrades who was killed at the front, and, since their forces have been defeated, he wants to deliver this package to a relative of the dead soldier before the enemy's occupation troops arrive in the town. But he has forgotten not only the street and the address for which he is headed but also the name of the person to whom his parcel is to be given and the appointed hour of their meeting. So his search goes on in a labyrinth, the progress of it moving through street after street after street of the snow-covered city. At a certain point he is led to an inn by a small boy, and, at another point, he is taken in and given refreshment by a young woman. A restless night is spent in a sort of hostel for disabled soldiers. And, finally, he is fatally wounded by a reconnoitering patrol of the enemy forces. He dies, however, not on the streets but in the apartment of the young woman—who takes him in a second time; and to her he gives his package the contents of which are sorted out by a physician who says that he was too late to help the dying man. And it is the physician's use of the possessive adjective of the first person ("my") to speak of his visit to the young woman's apartment which enables us to identify him with the "I" who, at the beginning of the novel, speaks in a closed room —on one wall of which there is an engraving that pictures a café-scene containing the very characters (the soldier, the little boy, etc.) whom we are to meet in the course of the novel.

So, despite the book's appearing to have been written from the standpoint of an impersonal omniscience, it seems that the narrative point of view is really that of the physician, and the exploration of this puzzle yields some interesting and valuable insights into

Robbe-Grillet's basic intention. But all that I want to remark at this point is the dominant and over-riding impression which the novel leaves us with—which, as we remember the lost soldier's uncertain progress through the strange, dark city, is an impression of the maze-like geometry of deserted streets bisecting and intersecting one another, one intersection leading into another, this avenue being broken by that, one road being cancelled out by another, the whole labyrinth being eerily illuminated by street-lamps which dimly reveal façades that seem all to be identical. And nothing seems to be explained, nothing seems to be connected with anything else: the whole is simply a "multiplicity of still-shots,"[27] like the script which Robbe-Grillet prepared for Alain Resnais' film *L'Année dernière à Marienbad.* And the stillness in his novels, as in those of Beckett and Butor, makes one feel that Claude Mauriac is right in suggesting that a certain silence has descended upon much of the new *alittérature:*[28] it is, indeed, in Roland Barthes' phrase, a *degré zéro de l'écriture.*[29]

So we are now at a very considerable distance from the modern movement. For that was a great effort—in the novel, in poetry, occasionally in the theatre—to give order and form to what was felt to be the essential formlessness of modern reality. Indeed, in the careers of men like Joyce and Mann and Eliot and Rilke, it was an effort so grand in its scope and so moving in its intensity as to have provided a generation with its chief model of the very idea of the imagination. For, in attempting to say what we mean by the term "imagination," when we hark back to the language of Coleridge's *Biographia* and speak of what he called "esemplastic power," the power of giving form to the immense multifariousness of the world, it is, I suspect, these great heroes of the modern movement that we have most immediately in mind. And if the making of order be considered to involve a process whereby the mind gives its consent

[27] Ben F. Stoltzfus, *Alain Robbe-Grillet and the New French Novel* (Carbondale, Ill., 1964), 93.   [28] See Mauriac, *L'Alittérature contemporaine* (Paris, 1958).
[29] See Barthes, *Le Degré Zéro de l'écriture* (Paris, 1953).

to some ruling myth which itself in turn confers intelligibility and coherence upon the whole of experience, then the central passion that lay behind classic modernism may be said to have been a great mythicizing passion.

But what we now face—say, in the work of so representative an artist as Alain Robbe-Grillet—is a violently mythoclastic literature which is guided by a "conscience" that tells the writer that he best "serves a burdened and perplexed creature" by refusing in any way at all to "compete" with the immense panorama of reality in our own late time. And, as it is made by many of those who express today the central impulse of the post-modernist insurgency, this is a refusal, it might be said, which situates the contemporary writer somewhere between Antioch and Alexandria.

The conjunction of the names of these two great cities of the Roman Empire does, of course, immediately put us in mind of the great controversy that raged in the early centuries of Christian history between the two principal "schools" of exegetical theory. Alexandria, in northern Egypt, from a very early time was deeply affected, in its theological tradition, by the distinguished Jewish Hellenist, Philo, whose eclectic tendencies had led him to hellenize Scripture and to find much of Greek philosophy in the Old Testament. And, by the third century, under the influence of Philo's allegorism and as a result of its further development by such Christian exegetes as Clement and Origen, Alexandria had become the major center in the ancient Church of the employment of allegorical methods of scriptural exegesis. The Alexandrians were, on the whole, an urbane group of thinkers who tended to be warmly responsive to Greek intellectual tradition, most especially to the Platonic sense of the preeminence of the spiritual world. And, given their eagerness to find "spiritual" meanings in the Old and New Testaments, the allegorical method commended itself to them as the most fruitful way of explicating the Bible's mysterious language of parable and metaphor.

The Antiochenes, on the other hand, were convinced that the

allegorism of the Alexandrians was calculated to do nothing other than evacuate the biblical tradition of its solid historical reality. The basic theological tendency of the Church of Antioch, in other words, was Aristotelian rather than Platonist and historical rather than speculative and mystical. So its principal exegetes—men like Diodorus of Tarsus and Theodore of Mopsuestia and John Chrysostom—instead of looking for arcane "spiritual" meanings in scriptural texts, wanted rather to emphasize the historical reality of the biblical revelation and to ground all exegesis firmly in the letter of Holy Writ. Their historicism led them to offer a vigorous resistance to what they took to be the Gnosticizing tendencies of the Alexandrians. And, following the Council of Nicaea, the sharp divergences between the two schools became something enormously explosive in the great Christological controversies of the fourth century, in which the Alexandrians very radically stressed the eternal and divine element of the Incarnation and the Antiochenes, with equal radicalism, stressed the human and historical side.

Now, if this bit of history be itself allegorized, in Alexandrian fashion, then these two cities of the ancient Middle East, Antioch and Alexandria, may be thought of as standing for two countries of the mind, two perennially opposed perspectives on the relative weight which is to be accorded the claims of history as against those of the imagination. If one's allegiance is to Antioch, one turns then to the concrete materialities of the objective world as the locus of the real, and it is assumed that all imaginative construction must be corrigible by norms which are firmly grounded in the things of actual history. But, if one's allegiance is to Alexandria, then one regards the human spirit as having its proper residence in what Henri Focillon calls *la vie des formes,* and man's highest capacity is held to be the "esemplastic power," the power of giving order and form to the contingency of historical existence. In Antioch, the prevailing attitude is one of profound respect for the rough and ragged contingencies of the world, since here, it is believed, in the unhewn givens of concrete experience, we encounter the reality that

Henry James defined as "the things we cannot possibly not know." But, in Alexandria, the prevailing interest is in designing (in I. A. Richards' phrase) "speculative instruments" whereby a shape and a significance may be given to the immense panorama that lies before us. And the distance between the two cities is immense indeed.

But the interesting thing about the protagonists of the new modernism in our literary life today is that they are to be located in neither Antioch nor Alexandria. They are, to be sure, not inclined to enter into any sort of competition with reality, and the refusal of a writer like Alain Robbe-Grillet to replace Reality with Myth or to attempt any sort of transfiguration of the historical concrete would seem to indicate a firm rejection of Alexandria. But, then, such books as *Le Voyeur* and *Dans le Labyrinthe* do not, on the other hand, give us a sense of saturation in historical actuality: each is a skillfully contrived arabesque that has its limited fascination, but, amidst the complicated geometry of M. Robbe-Grillet's *chosisme,* we descry too much of the stuff of our experience being left out to be able to regard these books as doing any kind of adequate justice to the human life-world. So determined, in short, is the artist not to compete with reality that reality ends up being very much left behind, and thus the writer's position appears, finally, to be equidistant *between* both Antioch and Alexandria—neither for Reality nor for Myth.

Now this middle region, between the two cities, is being colonized today not alone by the *nouveau roman* circle of Alain Robbe-Grillet in France. These writers, to be sure, have, many of them, determinedly staked out this territory. But they have neighbors, the most immediate no doubt being those artists who work chiefly not in the area of the novel but in the theatre and whose stage Martin Esslin has taught us to speak of as the Theatre of the Absurd.[30] Mr. Esslin's umbrella reaches over a number of Englishmen (Harold Pinter, Norman Simpson) and Americans (Edward Albee, Jack Gelber, Arthur Kopit); but the chief figures, again, are those who

[30] See Esslin, *The Theatre of the Absurd* (Garden City, N.Y., 1961).

write in the French language (a group so diverse, however, as to include the Irishman Beckett, the Rumanian Ionesco, the Spaniard Arrabal, and the Russian Adamov).

Here, too, such properties of traditional literary fiction as character and story are very often relegated to the discard, for this is a dramatic imagination which, since it finds existence inexplicable and unjustifiable, is unwilling to use a theatrical machinery that might have the effect of suggesting that the world is in fact amenable to the ordering of dramatic *mythos*. Indeed, the theatre of playwrights like Beckett and Adamov and Ionesco is, as Mr. Esslin says, very largely an affair of " 'pure theatre' and abstract stagecraft" —an affair, that is, simply of "exits and entrances, light and shadow, contrasts in costume, voice, gait and behavior, pratfalls and embraces, all the manifold mechanical interactions of human puppets in groupings that suggest tension, conflict, or the relaxation of tensions."[31] No discursively formulable generalization about anything is advanced. People are not shown moving into and through the rhythms of fate and destiny, and what they do is not done out of rationally analyzable considerations of motive and intent. This stage does not even admit onto itself those passional conflicts arising out of the opposed purposes of men. What it presents instead is a radically situational tableau of happenings, but of happenings strung together on a temporal continuum which is simply an unending transition between "one damn thing after another," so that, if you ask what will happen next, the answer, as Mr. Esslin reminds us, is likely to be that *anything* may come next, since we are moving through an imaginative universe in which conventional probabilities have been suspended. So in such a play as Beckett's *Godot,* for example, we do not get the gradual revelation of a basic principle or the gradual completion of a unifying pattern, but, rather, we are given a series of spectacles, a series of happenings and of concrete

[31] Esslin, "The Theatre of the Absurd," in *Theatre in the Twentieth Century,* ed. Robert W. Corrigan (New York, 1965), 230.

images, and it is their very concreteness which the dramatist, it seems, is principally concerned to render.

Mr. Esslin has perhaps too great a penchant for the usual counters of fashionable journalism, when it is dealing with one or another variety of existentialist radicalism. And one regrets this, for the whole apparatus of the Absurd and the Human Condition entails a semantic which tends to suggest that in a play like Beckett's *Godot* or Ionesco's *The Bald Soprano* or Adamov's *Ping-Pong* we are really encountering a *pièce à thèse* all over again: and thus it may be that the real intent of these dramatists is to some extent betrayed. For they too, one feels, are often inclined to make a testimony something like Alain Robbe-Grillet's, that "the world is neither significant nor absurd,"[32] that it simply *is*. But, though Alexandria is thus bypassed, Antioch itself is not visible, either, on this horizon. For, in so representative a case as *Waiting for Godot,* despite the play's abundant allusiveness to the Passion story of the New Testament, one cannot but be impressed by how untouched it is by the kind of vibrant historicity that Erich Auerbach found to be so notably characteristic of the biblical narrative.[33] Again, the artist's position seems to be at a point *between* Antioch and Alexandria.

Nor should it be supposed that this is, in any singular way, the position in our time of the Continental avant-garde. My chief examples, to be sure, have been European, but the general tendency I have been wanting to remark is not a singularly European phenomenon. I cannot, of course, in brief compass undertake any full conspectus of the present scene in literature. But, having now spoken of the *nouveau roman* movement and the Theatre of the Absurd, both of which are largely European developments, I should perhaps also mention, even if hastily, a somewhat parallel movement in the United States, chiefly by way of suggesting how perva-

[32] Robbe-Grillet, *For a New Novel,* 19.
[33] See Auerbach, *Mimesis: The Representation of Reality in Western Literature* (Princeton, N.J., 1953), Chapters I–III.

sive is the basic impulse which appears to define post-modernist enterprise in contemporary writing.

What is here in view is a particular development in the American novel of, roughly, the last decade, and it is one which splays out in so many diverse directions as to make very difficult a quick notation: nor has it been given that sharpness of programmatic definition that the *nouveau roman* movement and absurdist theatre have received in the numerous manifestoes which their various advocates have issued. But, nevertheless, in the work of such writers as Thomas Pynchon and John Barth, James Purdy and Richard Stern, Bruce Friedman and Joseph Heller—and John Hawkes ought perhaps also to be included here—we can discern a particular current of sensibility, a kind of highly stylized vision, which establishes these novelists as constituting a distinctive force on the present scene, however reluctantly they may themselves regard one another as expressing a common tendency.

This movement has not yet received any widely recognized name. Its designation has sometimes been made in the terminology of absurdism, but such a nomenclature tends to associate these writers too closely, perhaps, with their European contemporaries. And, again, they are sometimes referred to as specialists in "black humor" —a term whose clarifying power may be more apparent than real. Yet the tag "black humor" does at least have the effect of calling attention to what is one of the primary qualities of this literature— namely, a sort of dandyism of ironic preposterousness and larky, outrageous joking. And, as a term of specification, it may also emphasize the tendency of such writers as Barth and Pynchon and Heller to create a fiction in which tragic and comic modalities jostle each other with enormous briskness and animation.

The predilection of these novelists for the commingling of tragic and comic form does, of course, express a deep inclination toward the abolition altogether of formalizing structures. In an interview published shortly after the appearance of *The Adventures of Augie March* in 1953, Saul Bellow said: "I kicked over the traces, wrote catch-as-catch can, picaresque. I took my chance."[34] And it is a similar sort of chance that the Barth of *The Floating Opera* or the Heller of *Catch-22* appears to have taken: they are novelists who do not want greatly to fidget over "the art of the novel," for, given their sense of how largely the world itself is indeterminate and astonishing and intractable, their feeling seems to be that one had better write catch-as-catch can, not bothering overmuch about controlling forms but trusting to the luck of the improviser, throwing the farcical together with the horrific, the arcadian with the gothic, the bitter with the sweet, and allowing one's fictions garrulously to sprawl out into the untidy formlessness of primary existence. In Thomas Pynchon's *V.*, in J. P. Donleavy's *The Ginger Man*, in John Barth's *The Sot-Weed Factor*, in Thomas Berger's *Reinhart in Love*, in Joseph Heller's *Catch-22*, we face, in short (in Leonard Meyer's phrase), an "anti-teleological art,"[35] an art which, taking it for granted that the world is without discoverable purposes or goals, devotes itself therefore to random procedures, to the methods of improvisation, giving up any highly "structured syntax of pattern and form,"[36] in order that it may be truly open to the turbulent incoherence of reality.

So, as one contemplates many of the characteristic styles of the post-modern movement in literature of the present time—and I have barely even begun to catalogue the relevant evidence that might be marshaled—it does indeed appear that Saul Bellow's Augie March is expressing the new sensibility of the age, when, towards the end of his tumultuous adventures, he says: "To tell the truth, I'm good and tired of all these big personalities, destiny moulders, and heavy-water brains, . . . big-wheels and imposers-upon, absolutists." For it is something very much like this that seems to be felt today by many of the most interesting writers on

---

[34] Harvey Breit, "Talk with Saul Bellow," *New York Times Book Review*, September 20, 1953.

[35] See Meyer, "The End of the Renaissance?: Notes on the Radical Empiricism of the Avant-Garde," *Hudson Review*, XVI (Summer, 1963), 169–86.   [36] *Ibid.*, 175.

both the European and the American scene. They look back upon
the classic modern movement of the great early decades of the
century, and they face the various massive structures of meaning
which that movement attempted to impose upon what Eliot called
"the immense panorama of . . . anarchy which is contemporary
history"—and, recalling this whole adventure, their feeling seems to
be that, for all of the courageousness of spirit and brilliance of mind
that distinguished the innovating pioneers of forty or fifty years
ago, these big personalities, these destiny moulders, these imposers-
upon, do not any longer embody an authentically contemporary
style. For these were writers—a Yeats, a Mann, a Pound, an Eliot—
who were proposing, in a great way, to "compete" with what one of
Bellow's characters calls "the reality situation." But now, as it is felt,
deep in our post-modern era—and at a point equidistant between
Antioch and Alexandria—we cannot extricate ourselves from that
general condition which Nathalie Sarraute speaks of as "suspicion."

"We have now entered upon an age of suspicion," says Mme.
Sarraute[37]—by which she means the skepticism felt by the contemporary reader when the writer undertakes to offer him something
more than simple, direct reports on matters of fact; and she also
means the disbelief that is felt by the writer himself in the integrity
of his own medium, when he finds its being used to purvey something like Goethe's "the beautiful, the good, the true." It is, in other
words, such a suspicion as requires the literary enterprise being
placed in the service of nothing more fancy or complicated than
facts, *little* facts—"the first blade of grass . . . a crocus not yet open
. . . a child's hand nestling in the hollow of my own": for, says
Mme. Sarraute, "believe me, that's all that counts." And it is such a
reverence for *l'actuelle,* for the radical hecceity of the concrete,
which constitutes the prompting force behind the recent abdication
from any large "competitive" effort. But, as we have seen, this
ostensibly Antiochene position is itself often held in too radical a

[37] Sarraute, *The Age of Suspicion: Essays on the Novel,* trans. Maria Jolas (New
York, 1963), 57.

way to yield any genuinely profound re-appropriation of the *whole* fabric of the experienced world, and thus the result has tended to be a condition of exile from the two great Cities of the imagination, *both* Antioch *and* Alexandria being left uncolonized.

So it was inevitable that the new literature should seem, as it often does, to be short-circuiting the kinds of theological concerns that traditionalist modernism did so actively advance. And thus a formal theology that, through its encounter with the literary imagination, had found itself quickened not only in its sense of the modern climate but in its own self-understanding as well is bound to feel somewhat frustrated now, as it confronts a literature that rarely seems any longer to give off "intimations of the sacred,"[38] not even in the negative and dialectical manner of a Rimbaud or a Kafka or a Camus. To be sure, the classic modern tradition did not itself make any large use of "the finished frames of [theological] doctrine"[39] and was in fact a very radically secular tradition. But it was, nevertheless, a tradition committed to a search for ways of giving a new shape and significance to that "immense panorama" of which Eliot spoke: it was a tradition committed to the search for a new "vision of the whole," and was thus deeply focused on the ultimate issues of human perplexity. So, however radical may have been its abjurations and negations, in being prompted by an extreme metaphysical passion, they could be regarded as but an inverted expression of how persistently the human voyager remains always the *homo religiosus*. But, now, literature is so bent on decontaminating itself of the old *profondeurs* and has moved so deeply into an "anti-teleological" phase that a strange new silence seems to have descended upon it—and not, as some may feel, the rich, fecund silence that theology has occasionally known in its own history (in the great traditions of "negative" and mystical theology) but a silence dry and unpromising and absolute. And the formal, systematic theologian might well, therefore, be expected to con-

---

[38] R. W. B. Lewis, *Trials of the Word: Essays in American Literature and the Humanistic Tradition* (New Haven, 1965), 110.   [39] *Ibid.,* 111.

clude that the "conscience" of this literature is indeed something so
purist, and so ruthless in its exactions, as to have well-nigh annulled
any possibility of further commerce between the two departments
of culture represented by religion and literary art.

Such a termination of the issue would, however, I am persuaded,
be short-sighted and would, in effect, regrettably scuttle a lesson of
still undiminished importance in which, among the great writers of
this century, Franz Kafka and T. S. Eliot are the preeminent
guides.

In his brilliant and bilious little book on Kafka, the German critic
Günther Anders has declared—more emphatically and more pun-
gently than perhaps any of Kafka's other critics have ever done—
that "The meaning of [his] entire work is governed by his awareness of the 'death of God.' "[40] He recalls that remarkable section of
the *Aphorisms* which is devoted to "Reflections on Sin, Pain, Hope,
and the True Way," and he finds Kafka reflected in those royal
couriers whom he imagines in his 45th "Reflection" as hurrying
through the world, and who, "as there are no kings left, shout to
each other their meaningless and obsolete messages."[41] Such a quix-
otic role, says Anders, was precisely that which was enacted by
Kafka himself. For the unexampled art of this tortured Czech
genius forms the prayer of a man who was in fact a "shame-faced
atheist." In his writings the very sense of religious meaning as
irrevocably lost is itself converted into a religious experience: "the
coins of his despair [are changed] into the currency of positive
belief":[42] the sense of ultimate ambiguity is so rendered as to give it
the tonality of some direct awareness of Transcendence. So his
elected role, Anders maintains, was that of "messenger to a king
who does not exist."[43]

Now, quite apart from the valuation which this arch-conservative

[40] Anders, *Franz Kafka*, trans. A. Steer and A. K. Thorlby (London, 1960), 82.
[41] Kafka, "Reflections on Sin, Pain, Hope, and the True Way," No. 45, in *The
Great Wall of China: Stories and Reflections*, trans. Willa and Edwin Muir (New
York, 1946), 289.   [42] Anders, *Franz Kafka*, 83.   [43] *Ibid.*, 82.

places upon Kafka's vision, he does see, I think, with a startling clarity, what it is that makes this remarkable writer so infinitely fascinating in our time. Anders himself, of course, can find nothing but sophistical duplicity and decadence in the example that is presented by an artist who continued to write religiously, despite his having fallen under the spell of "the Muse of Agnosticism." But, though it may be lamented by some, it is, nevertheless, a primary fact of our age, that we are deeply moved only by those religious writers who make us feel that whatever they have won in the way of certitude or hope has been snatched out of abysses of unbelief. For most of us are not certain any longer as to what is the real "shape" of our world, or as to how to take hold of and express the deepest things that are in us, and that man, whether secular or religious, who supposes himself to be outside this quandary is living in a fool's paradise. W. H. Auden said many years ago, in an oft-quoted remark, that "our dominant religious experience [today] . . . is of our distance from God." And this is an experience well-nigh universally known by the men and women of our age, however they may stand in regard to the great received traditions of faith. Paul Tillich told us twenty years ago that now, at the end of the modern period, even the believer, indeed most especially the believer, will find himself mirrored in "the man who longs for God and cannot find Him," in "the man who wants to be acknowledged by God and cannot even believe that He is," and in "the man who is striving for a new and imperishable meaning of his life and cannot [yet] discover it."[44] And thus it is that, in the whole sweep of the biblical narrative, there is perhaps no figure amongst its minor personages who touches deeper chords in us than that father of the possessed child who, when Jesus told him that "all things are possible to him that believeth," is reported in St. Mark's Gospel (9:24) to have cried out: "Lord, I believe; help thou mine unbelief."

Now it was both out of and to such a profound spiritual ambivalence that Kafka was always speaking. And the guiding intention of

[44] Tillich, *The Shaking of the Foundations* (New York, 1948), 139.

his art is beautifully summarized in the "Reflections," most especially in the 104th, where, in talking about the nature of faith, he says, in his typically gnomic and concise manner: "You do not need to leave your room. Remain sitting at your table and listen. Do not even listen, simply wait. Do not even wait, be quite still and solitary. The world will freely offer itself to you to be unmasked, it has no choice, it will roll in ecstasy at your feet."[45] "You do not need to leave your room," not because the immeasurable amplitude of Creation does not extend infinitely beyond one's private chambers, but rather because stillness itself, when intense and concentrated, becomes a profound kind of patience that enables a man to consent, as it were, to what is spoken of in the 66th "Reflection" as "the indestructible element in oneself." Then it is that all striving stops, all attempts to bring reality to heel, all attempts to make the world submit to one's own conceptions of proper design and right order. And, indeed, when the self has been thus silenced, *then* "the world will freely offer itself," or so it may be hoped, in the way of that which comes as a gift of grace. So what is being proposed, always with the subtlest indirection, in *The Castle* and *The Trial* and all the most characteristic instances of Kafka's art is that the cultivation of such a patience may well be our primary human task.

It is the kind of patience—which Keats called "negative capability"—that is explored more profoundly in Eliot's *Quartets* than in any other text of twentieth-century poetry, and most especially in those great passages of "East Coker" where we are told to

> . . . . be still, and wait without hope
> For hope would be hope for the wrong thing; wait without love
> For love would be love of the wrong thing; there is yet faith
> But the faith and the love and the hope are all in the waiting.
> Wait without thought, for you are not ready for thought:
> So the darkness shall be the light, and the stillness the dancing.[46]

[45] Kafka, *Great Wall of China*, 307.
[46] Eliot, "East Coker," *Four Quartets* (New York, 1943), 15.

Indeed, recalling that late story of Kafka's called "A Hunger Artist" in which he bodies forth his whole idea of the artist in terms of this tale about a man dedicated to the art of fasting, we may say that such a waiting, that such a patience, as both he and Eliot were in quite different ways exploring is a kind of Hunger-Art. And Hunger-Art, we may say, is simply the art of abstention, the art of doing without that which human selfhood needs for its felicity and fulfillment—whereby preparation is patiently made for the time when "the world will freely offer itself."

Which brings us back to the immediate scene of our literature today, for is it not the case that, in many of its most characteristic modes now, it seems itself to be a form of Hunger-Art? It seems, it is true, very often to be at a point equi-distant between Antioch and Alexandria, and thus, as I have said, it appears to be neither for Reality nor for the Myth (that is, the Idea, the System, the imposed meaning). But may this not be but a deliberate abstention, a kind of *askésis,* that, whether it is actually intended as such or not, stands to be a most stringent *preparatio?* And if this be so, as I very much suspect it to be, then the new literature, far from having emptied itself of moral and religious profundity, may well be (to borrow a phrase from "East Coker") moving "Into another intensity"—for further explorations, for a deeper acceptance of "the burthen of the mystery."

But the new avant-garde in our literary life is by no means alone today in presenting us with important examples of Hunger-Art. For it is one of the interesting hallmarks of the age that, outside the realms of poesy, it is the theologian who often seems to be incarnating most vividly the image of the Hunger-Artist. And it is partly for this reason that theology, more than any other formal intellectual discipline, may well afford the finest kind of purchase upon the literary imagination in our time. The other humanistic sciences enjoy, of course, small successes in reducing some limited area of experience to manageability, and thus they are often lulled too quickly into a state of being "at ease in Zion." But the essential nature of its endeavor prompts theology to aim for a radically synoptic kind of vision of man's place and prospect, and, from its high vantage point, it cannot easily escape a recognition of the quandaries by which men are beset in this distressed century when they undertake to determine, in any really fundamental way, the true beginning and end of the human adventure. So it begins itself to be a form of Hunger-Art, and, in the realm of systematic thought, it therefore makes a good perspective from which to appropriate those forms of Hunger-Art that are to be found in the imaginative literature of the present time.

The truest exemplars of this new style in the forums of contemporary theology are not, however, I think, to be found amongst that handful of new American theologians who are today agitatedly reiterating Nietzsche's outcry of 1882 (in *The Gay Science*), that "God is dead." The distinguished German thinker, Gerhard Ebeling, is no doubt accurately reading our present situation, when he asserts that "a doctrine of God today . . . is abstract speculation if it does not have the phenomenon of modern atheism before it from the start."[47] But those of Dr. Ebeling's colleagues in recent German theology—and chiefly Heinrich Ott—who, like himself, have been deeply influenced by the late phase of Martin Heidegger reveal perhaps a more authentic contemporaneity than the young Americans (Thomas Altizer, William Hamilton, and their various fellow-travelers) who are espousing what they call "radical theology." The German radicals do, to be sure, accept Heidegger's testimony about ours being a time of profound dislocation in the things of the spirit, a time of failure and privation in which God, having "withdrawn," is absent. But they also accept his further testimony that, *therefore,* in an age which is "the No-more of the gods that have fled and the Not-yet of the god that is coming,"[48] man needs to try

---

[47] Ebeling, *Word and Faith,* trans. James W. Leitch (Philadelphia, 1963), 342.
[48] Heidegger, *Existence and Being,* trans. Douglas Scott *et al.* (Chicago, 1949), 313.

to be a good "shepherd of being"—a course that will involve not any aggressive attempt at *mastery* of the metaphysical situation or at forcing reality to yield up its innermost secrets but that will involve, rather, a "step backwards"[49] into what Heidegger calls "meditative thinking."[50] By "meditative thinking" Heidegger means such a patient openness to the primal realities of human existence as will permit them simply to *be,* and *thus,* finally, to "unveil" themselves before the gaze of the mind. "Primal thinking" is a mode of waiting: it is a form of listening, silently and patiently—to the voiceless Mystery of Being which finds its voice in man himself. The primal thinker, if we may put it so, lets Being be, he consents to be addressed by it, he allows it to find its articulation in his own profoundest acts of prayer, its utterance in his tongue—his discipline, in short, is a type of Hunger-Art.

But those young American theologians who have recently won a certain publicity for the jig that they dance on the grave of God prove how lacking they are in genuine relevance to the religious situation of our period by their quickness to convert perplexity itself into dogma and by the haste with which, as a consequence, they foreclose redintegrative possibilities. That contemporary theology, however, which has spoken to us most movingly is, I believe, deeply touched, all of it, by the attitude of waiting, by the attitude of "meditative thinking," and touched by the modesty and tentativeness which are a part of such an attitude. The grand style—the style of Aquinas and Calvin and Schleiermacher—is not, to be sure, a part of those theologians who have taken the firmest grip on the mind of our generation. It is not the Tillich of the three-volume *Systematic* who moves us most deeply, but the Tillich of *The Protestant Era* and *The Courage To Be* and the sermons. And it is not Karl Barth in his role as system-builder who is felt to speak to us

---

[49] Heidegger, *Essays in Metaphysics: Identity and Difference,* trans. Kurt F. Leidecker (New York, 1960), 65.

[50] Heidegger, *Discourse on Thinking,* trans. John M. Anderson and E. Hans Freund (New York, 1966), 46.

most relevantly, but rather the passionate poet of the human mystery who is speaking, say, in that great section of the *Church Dogmatics* (III/2) which is entitled "Man in His Time." Nor are men like the late Dietrich Bonhoeffer and Rudolf Bultmann and Friedrich Gogarten and Gerhard Ebeling men whose special genius lies in system-building. They are instead men who make us feel that they share with Gabriel Marcel the conviction that "to bear witness is to contribute to the growth or coming of that for which one testifies."[51] And they also make us feel that they would be prepared to agree with Rainer Maria Rilke, when he says: "Be patient towards all that is unsolved in your heart and try to love *the questions themselves* like locked rooms. . . . Do not now seek the answers, that cannot be given you because you would not be able to live them. And the point is," says Rilke, "to live everything. *Live* the questions now. Perhaps you will then gradually, without noticing it, live along some distant day into the answer."[52]

Indeed, it is very much along such a route as this that the most creative theology of our period seems to be moving. It is, to be sure, a theology that often seems to be more at home in the world of doubt than in the world of faith, and whatever it wins in the way of certitude or hope appears to have been just barely snatched out of abysses of unbelief. But this is simply the way things go, in this late and difficult time: theology is not so much seeking answers as it is seeking a way of helping us to live along some distant day *into* the answer: it is a form of Hunger-Art which looks toward a new age, when the Truth "will freely offer itself."

Now it is in their convergence toward this single point that we may discern, I believe, a very remarkable collaboration, as it were, between the theological imagination and the literary imagination of the present time. Both bear the marks of a *post*-modern temper.

[51] Marcel, *Homo Viator: Introduction to a Metaphysic of Hope,* trans. Emma Craufurd (Chicago, 1951), 213.

[52] Rilke, *Letters to a Young Poet,* trans. M. D. Herter Norton (New York, 1934), 33–34.

Neither wants any longer to risk the grand style (whether that of a Yeats or a Mann, or that of a Brunner or a Barth). Neither wants any longer to "compete" with reality, whether in the manner of traditionalist literary modernism or in that of the metaphysical grammar of the *theologia perennis*. Both seem to be guided by a "conscience" that tells the theologian and the artist that the burdened and perplexed people of our age are best served by being invited to be *patient* and to *wait,* at a point somewhere on the road between Antioch and Alexandria, where perhaps the horizons of the two cities, being equally visible, may, together, provide the occasion for that moment which Heidegger's lexicon speaks of by resorting to the Greek term *a-letheia,* which means the "unconcealing" or the "unveiling"—of the Mystery of Being. And it may indeed well be that at this point, midway between the two cities, where one tries, with a great intensity of spirit, to wait and to be patient—it may well be that it is just here that there is to be found the one point of purchase which, just now, we can grasp, with any real confidence and integrity.

Part III

THE CONTEMPORARY SCENE:
TALENTS AND DIRECTIONS

The Unspeakable Peacock:
Apocalypse in Flannery O'Connor

LEONARD CASPER

Anticipation of death, with the possibility of the self's utter annihilation, has always been a primary shaper of man's life-style. For secularized modern man, increasingly acquiescent to discontinuity (the early obsolescence, for example, of industrial products or of international policy), the trauma of physical extinction makes even more frantic the daily search for self-assurance and a satisfactory identity. Frederick J. Hoffman's *The Mortal No: Death and the Modern Imagination* (1964) suggests that the core question of former centuries, "What am I?," has eroded into an alarming "Am I?"

In the growing literature of violence which he documents, endlessly extended battlefields and congested concentration camps function not simply as realistic detail. They symbolize the abstract anonymity to which desacralization threatens to reduce man, as previously he made his own gods impotent; although, in an age of potential nuclear overkill or of wholesale terrorism disguised as popular liberation, these symbols are more dramatic when allowed to represent physical extinction. Confronted with *néantisation,* the solitary self finds tentative consolation in the uniqueness of individual suffering—especially of choice, which is made an exquisite agony by the raw nature of speculation. Under such circumstances, the mission of self-creation can become so intense that, in Richard Ellmann's and Charles Feidelson's metaphrase, "This cultivation of self-consciousness—uneasy, ardent introspection—often amounts to an almost religious enterprise."[1]

If death, both actual and symbolic, is a constant provocation to the religious imagination, one might expect to see its images throughout the work of a "Christ-haunted" writer such as Flannery O'Connor, who had reasonable foreknowledge of her own early doom. In fact, ten of her nineteen collected stories and one of her novels end with the death of key characters. In "A Good Man Is Hard to Find," the Misfit oversees the murder of an entire family. An old man is brutally helped to die on a tenement balustrade in "Judgement Day." Mrs. McIntyre, in "The Displaced Person," becomes an accessory to the deliberate-accidental running over of Guizac by a tractor. Old Man Fortune strangles his granddaughter, in "A View of the Woods"; and young Thomas, in "The Comforts of Home," shoots his mother fatally.

In addition to these homicides, two stories conclude with the suicide of lonely, visionary boys: "The River" and "The Lame Shall Enter First." Julian's mother, in "Everything That Rises Must Converge," dies of a stroke on a crowded street; and Mrs. May is gored to death, in "Greenleaf." The only quiet death occurs in "A Late Encounter with the Enemy," as General Sash, 104 years old, slips into his remembered past forever and so escapes exploitation by his granddaughter on her graduation. More typical is the death of Hazel Motes, in *Wise Blood*, as the result of extreme self-mortification and police brutality.

The nearly obsessive nature of this pattern becomes more apparent if one includes those narratives in which death is the occasion of a major, even if not final, crisis. *The Violent Bear It Away* takes the first third of its structure from the natural death of Tarwater's prophetic greatuncle and the second third from the murder of

---

[1] *The Modern Tradition: Backgrounds of Modern Literature,* ed. Ellmann and Feidelson (New York, 1965), 685.

Bishop. His greatuncle fixes on Tarwater the responsibility of baptizing this defective child. Tarwater prefers to drown him—in order to remove from Bishop, the boy's father, and himself the burden of their uneasy relationship. But Bishop's father intuits that at the last moment Tarwater "had baptized the child even as he drowned him." In "The Enduring Chill" Asbury is prepared to enjoy his last hours of self-pity, as a dying would-be writer; but his whole rationale for accusing his mother and life for his failings crumbles when he learns that he has something like Bang's disease in cows and it is never fatal.

Moreover, there are innumerable examples, in Flannery O'Connor's prose, of images associated with death. Irving Malin has analyzed in some detail the coffin imagery and other boxlike imprisonments in *Wise Blood;*[2] and Stanley Edgar Hyman's comments on the defiant, defiling sexuality of Hazel Motes and others provide a means for relating death, perversion, and mutilations in a variety of symbolic combinations.[3] Nor is it difficult to think of Ruby Hill's fear of pregnancy, in "A Stroke of Good Fortune," as the terror of becoming mummified and unavailable to one's self. The kicking motion of the foetus forces her to identify fearfully with her mother, bearer of eight children: "She felt her face drawn puckered: two born dead one died the first year and one run under like a dried yellow apple no she was only thirty-four years old, she was old." On first presentation, mothers are seen as burdens, in Flannery O'Connor (though not quite so splendid as the Christ-tattoo on Parker's back). So are grandmothers, grandfathers, greatuncles, and most other relatives: as if there were some conspiracy in history to end itself, all the generative power of dynasty betrayed by the pitting of kin against kin, in an epic, retroactive death-wish.

Flannery O'Connor once referred to *A Good Man Is Hard to*

[2] Malin, "Flannery O'Connor and the Grotesque," in *The Added Dimension: The Art and Mind of Flannery O'Connor,* ed. Melvin J. Friedman and Lewis A. Lawson (New York, 1966), 110–11.

[3] Hyman, *Flannery O'Connor* (Minneapolis, 1966), 14, 19, 23.

Find as ten stories on original sin. It would seem more appropriate to speak of this and all her work as variations on the theme of death (from her viewpoint, of course, no contradiction would be involved in doing so, for mortality traditionally has been considered one of the first effects of Adam's corruption). It is understandable, therefore, that even so friendly and thoughtful a commentator as Stanley Edgar Hyman should find this excessive orientation one of her few weaknesses. "Her stories came to rely too often and too mechanically on death to end them. The deaths are ruinous to 'A View of the Woods,' and unnecessary in other stories. Her best stories—'The Artificial Nigger,' 'Good Country People,' 'Parker's Back'—neither end in death nor need to."[4] Hyman uses Miss O'Connor's interview in the June, 1963, issue of *Jubilee* to explain how her theological upbringing led her into the error of "melodramatic endings." On that occasion she had remarked, "I'm a born Catholic and death has always been brother to my imagination. I can't imagine a story that doesn't properly end in it or in its foreshadowings."

Earlier, in 1959, she had made substantially the same statement in the Winter issue of *Esprit:* "In every story there is some minor revelation which, no matter how funny the story may be, gives us a hint of the unknown, of death." But perhaps the most revealing words on the subject were spoken by the Misfit about the grandmother in "A Good Man Is Hard to Find" (first published in 1953): "She would of been a good woman, if it had been somebody there to shoot her every minute of her life."

The work of Flannery O'Connor is remarkably free of morbidity because, like Greek tragedy or Christian myth, her attention is less on catharsis and loss than on transfiguration; less on the fact of death than on its attendant circumstance and aftermath—the apocalyptic vision of possibility. Frank Kermode, in *The Sense of an*

---

[4] *Ibid.,* 45. Peculiarly, Hyman speaks several times of multiple deaths in "A View of the Woods," although it is not at all clear that the grandfather dies. Were the body count more exact, as it is for example in *Hamlet* or *The Duchess of Malfi,* the charge of melodrama might carry more credence. Flannery O'Connor clearly is trying to undercut violence at the end of her story.

Ending: Studies in the Theory of Fiction (1967), records how, historically, expectation of an imminent holocaust and last judgment has provided imperatives for order, potentially redemptive, and not the frantic increase in chaos which one might expect. He speaks of literary plots as tentative "images of the grand temporal consonance," necessarily constructed therefore out of apparent contradictions in search of reconciliation. The thrust of Flannery O'Connor's work too is into the heart of paradox, epitomized by serious consideration that man's mortality might be an act of grace and the occasion of death a prophetic sign.

What actually "dies" in *The Violent Bear It Away* is Tarwater's resistance to his mission, to spread the gospel "of the terrible speed of mercy." When he realizes that his greatuncle whose corpse he tried to burn has been properly buried after all, he capitulates. He has a vision of the fields filled with multitudes as hungry as himself, waiting for the miracle of multiplied loaves and fishes, the universalization of petty particulars. In *Wise Blood,* after Haze has run over Solace Layfield whom he accuses of being a false evangelist because Layfield still believes in Jesus, Haze blinds himself with lime. His explanation is as cryptic as his act: "If there's no bottom in your eyes, they hold more." Eventually Mrs. Flood, who has planned to marry him and then institutionalize him for his money, finds herself looking into his dead face: "She sat staring with her eyes shut, into his eyes, and felt as if she had finally got to the beginning of something she couldn't begin, and she saw him moving farther and farther away, farther and farther into the darkness until he was the pin point of light."

Similarly, the imminence of death converts Grandma, in "A Good Man Is Hard to Find," from a petulant, wool-gathering old lady into a woman of warmth who can identify the Misfit as "one of my own children." The Misfit has been arguing that a disbeliever in Christ ought to "enjoy the few minutes you got left the best way you can—by killing somebody or burning down his house or doing some other meanness to him." But although he personally shoots her, he is as moved as Haze is over the death of Layfield. His final admission that "It's no real pleasure in life" is his own kind of "witnessing." Neither Mr. Paradise in "The River" nor Sheppard in "The Lame Shall Enter First" is ready to admit that the boys in those stories might literally have journeyed into their beatific visions; yet Sheppard at least achieves an insight into the dilemmas of the pastoral figure. The death of Guizac in "The Displaced Person" attacks the conscience of Mrs. McIntyre so thoroughly that "she felt she was in some foreign country." She suffers a debilitating nervous disorder, loses her voice and nearly her eyesight, and listens to an explication of church doctrines weekly by the old priest who comes to feed her peacock. In "A View of the Woods," Mr. Fortune having killed his "disloyal" granddaughter associates his sense of relief with his escape toward "a little opening where the white sky was reflected in the water" of a lake. But he cannot swim and has no boat. The story's imagery becomes transposed: "The place was deserted except for one huge yellow monster which sat on the side, as stationary as he was, gorging itself on clay." He has met himself. Julian, in "Everything That Rises Must Converge," learns how much he depends on his mother only after losing her. The last lines of the story are typical of the rich ambivalence in Flannery O'Connor's characters: "The tide of darkness seemed to sweep him back to her, postponing from moment to moment his entry into the world of guilt and sorrow."

In each of these stories, not death but revelation is the true destination. Usually the vision occurs in a survivor of someone else's death. In three stories, however, whatever pentecostal insight is provided comes through the sensibility of the dying persons themselves. Two are patriarchal figures (in "Judgement Day" and "A Late Encounter with the Enemy") who drift quietly into their dream worlds but claim them, apparently, with at least as much success as the boy-suicides in "The River" and "The Lame Shall Enter First." The risk which Miss O'Connor assumes here is that these stories will be taken sentimentally rather than seriously, or be interpreted as a comic report on senility. An even greater risk, however, is hazarded in "Greenleaf," in which irresistible self-understanding is permitted a dying woman. Although her point of view is sustained, however, direct revelation is avoided by relying on symbolic language rather than on a stream of consciousness. Mrs. May stares with "freezing unbelief" at the trespassing bull which she has ordered shot: "The bull had buried his head in her lap, like a wild tormented lover, before her expression changed. One of his horns sank until it pierced her heart and the other curved around her side and held her in an unbreakable grip. She continued to stare straight ahead, but the entire scene in front of her had changed— the tree line was a dark wound in a world that was nothing but sky —and she had the look of a person whose sight has been suddenly restored but who finds the light unbearable." Finally the author detaches the story altogether from Mrs. May's point of view. Her vision is shared: "She seemed, when Mr. Greenleaf reached her, to be bent over whispering some last discovery into the animal's ear."

Flannery O'Connor undercuts the more sensational or melodramatic aspects of dying, because she is concerned less with documentary realism than with the aura of understanding effected in the agonist himself or in a bystander. Such stories have much in common, therefore, with others in which no death occurs: "A Temple of the Holy Ghost," "The Artificial Nigger," "A Circle in the Fire," "Good Country People," "Parker's Back," and "Revelation" itself. Each of these has its climax in an epiphany of redemption, or of damnation. Not death as such but the travail of salvation, the possibility of resurrection, dominates her fiction. The full implications of the Incarnation are as real for her as for the Misfit who declares, "Jesus thown everything off balance."[5]

The peacock, therefore, traditional symbol of the Second Coming, is the proper private emblem for Flannery O'Connor to have appro-

---

[5] For additional comments on the importance of the Incarnation to modern man's symbolic imagination, see Frederick J. Hoffman, *The Imagination's New Beginning* (Notre Dame, 1967), 8.

priated. In her essay on peacocks in the September, 1961, issue of *Holiday,* she wrote, "I intend to stand firm and let the peacocks multiply, for I am sure that, in the end, the last word will be theirs." That statement is both an appeal to a Last Judgment and submission to the interim mystery. On various occasions, Flannery O'Connor made clear that she was a writer, not a preacher, and that the value of writing comes from its putting abstract doctrine to the test of flesh. In the Winter, 1963, issue of *Fresco,* she wrote that "The more a writer wishes to make the supernatural apparent, the more real he has to be able to make the natural world." But the movement of her interest is cryptomystic. It proceeds from fact to mystery, at "the ultimate reaches of reality." The writer committed to a sacramental view of the universe "will be interested in what we don't understand, rather than what we do." Above all, she has found attractive the mystery of grace. If Flannery O'Connor is essentially a short story writer whose fiction occasionally lengthens into short novels, that fact may be accounted for by her recognition of the "terrible speed of mercy," the traumatic convergence of time and eternity. Her fiction becomes finite testimony to infinity.[6]

Her attendance on the grotesque can be appreciated within the same rubric: the mystery of grace. Sometimes she spoke as if grotesque actions and characters were deliberate exaggerations. For example, in a 1962 interview published in *Critic,* she spoke of knowing that "for the larger percentage of my readers, baptism is a meaningless rite: therefore I have to imbue this action with an awe and terror which will suggest its awful mystery." Later, in her 1963 *Jubilee* interview, she asserted that "We're all grotesque." However, what seems to come closest to her strongest conviction and constant practice is the view expressed in her introduction to *A*

---

[6] By contrast, salvation is earned laboriously and consciously in the fiction of Robert Penn Warren who needs large novels, therefore, to comprehend the stages of the soul's progress. The seemingly gratuitous moment of illumination is as scarce in Warren as it is common in Miss O'Connor.

Memoir of Mary Ann (1961). Good as well as evil has its grotesque aspect, because "in us the good is something under construction."

No man can claim to be the likely instrument of God, no man is worthy. The doctrine of the Incarnation has its irrational side, for why should the image of perfection willingly descend into the flesh of imperfection? What indescribable agony would have to occur for Christ to be born, again and again, in every man? Flannery O'Connor's characters are convulsed in the mystery of that love, as surely as Hazel Motes is "a Christian *malgré lui.*" Should they *not* look grotesque, trying to match God's will as if it originated in themselves? In the Winter, 1963, issue of *Fresco,* Miss O'Connor wrote that although "predictable predetermined actions have a comic interest for me, it is the free act, the acceptance of grace particularly, that I always have an eye on as the thing which will make the story work." Perhaps it is impossible, representationally, to distinguish between human acceptance and divine possession. The problem is one for theologians; but as a writer Flannery O'Connor can leave the final word to the peacocks and meanwhile needs only to render the experience of that impact, to prove its possibility. The principal task of the writer is to make the terms of a vision so intense that, as in Tennessee Williams' *Suddenly Last Summer* or Albee's *Tiny Alice,* the spectator cannot safely deny the invisible presence offstage. The only risk is that the writer may be charged with melodrama and a tendency to travesty—as Miss O'Connor has been charged by Stanley Edgar Hyman—if the vision does not validate itself.

Yet Flannery O'Connor takes that risk at every turn, trying to authenticate mystery rather than resolve it. Critics have already documented her persistent reliance on paradox. Hyman speaks of her use of "Affirmation by Blasphemy" in *Wise Blood* and elaborates on her "Christian dualism," one part of which requires that Protestant fundamentalism be used to dramatize Catholic belief;[7]

[7] Hyman, *Flannery O'Connor,* 15, 37–38, 40.

Hoffman describes the violent coexistence of religious desire and disbelief[8] (whose esthetic counterpart implies that fiction is most humanly persuasive when unprogrammed and doubtridden); Nathan A. Scott, Jr., has traced the strategem of opposites and inversions in *The Violent Bear It Away*.[9] The sacred and the profane are often indistinguishable in her work. They may be parts of the same hyphenated person, the Hulga-Joys; or the self-righteous plaintiff of one moment may be exposed as a Pharisee the next.

Within this elaborate design of mysterious transformations arranged by grace, the apocalyptic vision at death (not of death) has a central place. Part of each man, acknowledged or not, is prophetic; this part searches for signs, yearning after final things. Flannery O'Connor's delight in eschatology, her modest but instinctive habit of prophesy help to shape both the brevity of her work (typified by her discarding half of "The Displaced Person" between magazine and book publication[10]) and its poetic density. Grace is put under pressure, so that its surge can be felt beyond denial and so that vision can be confirmed without reliance on indoctrination. Tarwater speaks in the name of just such an esthetic practice when he declares to Rayber, "All you can do is think what you would have done if you had done it. Not me. I can do it. I can act." The power of Flannery O'Connor's work depends not on external theology, but on the economy of her words, whose very ambivalences and cryptic reprises enact in small ways the plenitude of cosmic design. It depends too on finite discrepancies, and delicate imbalances. In her lecture on the grotesque at Wesleyan College, Macon, Georgia, in 1960, Miss O'Connor said of the new fiction, "The direction of many of us will be toward concentration and the distortion that is

[8] Frederick J. Hoffman, "The Search for Redemption: Flannery O'Connor's Fiction," in *The Added Dimension*, 45–46.

[9] Scott, "Flannery O'Connor's Testimony: The Pressure of Glory," in *The Added Dimension*, 144–50. See also *Flannery O'Connor*, ed. Robert Reiter (St. Louis, 1968), *passim*.

[10] Robert Drake, *Flannery O'Connor* (Grand Rapids, Mich., 1966), 48.

necessary to get our vision across; it will be toward poetry." In her own work, the poetic and religious imaginations coincide.

Not the death but the resurrection of Christ is crucial to the concept of grace made kinetic through love. Similarly, at the core of Flannery O'Connor's value system is what Teilhard de Chardin described as diminishment of self until that "point of annihilation" is reached, after which the "diaphaneity" of God in the veiled world is dispelled. According to Père Teilhard, "The true ego grows in inverse proportion to 'egoism.' Like the Omega which attracts it, the element only becomes personal when it universalizes itself."[11] Of all the "psychic inter-activity animating the noosphere," the energies most necessary to be cultivated are "intercentric." The "hominisation of death itself" is accomplished because of the irreversible convergence of men toward Omega, to be accomplished in perfection at the end of the world.

According to Robert Fitzgerald, in his introduction to Flannery O'Connor's posthumous volume of stories, she had been reading Teilhard since 1961; but she remained true to her experience—to the agony of rising, rather than to the arrival at Omega. Perhaps the supreme example of the "annihilated self," in her fiction, is the hermaphrodite who in "A Temple of the Holy Ghost" declares flatly, "God made me thisaway and I don't dispute hit." At the other extreme are those who at least attempt to take themselves as center and circumference of the world, the know-it-alls: schoolteacher Rayber in *The Violent Bear It Away;* Joy, the doctor of philosophy, in "Good Country People"; or the two students, Julian in "Everything That Rises Must Converge" and Asbury in "The Enduring Chill." Even these, of course, suffer the discomforts of conscience and are not easily damned. If in part they represent the cold pride of intellect so common to the characters of Hawthorne, one of her favorite authors, they seem closer to Hawthorne himself than to Ethan Brand or Chillingworth whose sin of remoteness is

[11] Chardin, *The Phenomenon of Man* (New York, 1959), 263–64.

unpardonable. In her introduction to *A Memoir of Mary Ann,* Miss O'Connor refers to "The ice in the blood which [Hawthorne] feared, and which this very fear preserved him from."

Unquestionably, she would have had no difficulty in agreeing with Teilhard's equation of being with being one.[12] Always the chief object of her criticism is the person who withholds himself from "synthesis," from community. The type includes not only the aloof intellectual but also the supercilious Pharisee (Mrs. Turpin in "Revelation" or the wife in "Parker's Back") and the man who abuses his own kin (Mr. Head in "The Artificial Nigger" or Fortune in "A View of the Woods"). Such individuals lack what the ideal Southerner treasures: a sense of the extended family, a habit of hospitality; and what the ideal Catholic emulates: unrationed charity modeled on the Communion of Saints, living and dead.

The literature of the past hundred years has raged against threats to the survival of self-certitude. It is not only that mass wars have spectacularly demonstrated human mortality. Life itself has become increasingly impersonal, as if it were imitating one of the data-processing novels of Robbe-Grillet which substitute geometrical orders, the remote integrity of things, for man-centered meanings. Other fiction, eschewing the self-destruction inherent in overorganization, invokes disorganization as if it were a creative counterforce, simply because it can be generated spontaneously out of ego-sensitivity. Few of the authors discussed in Hoffman's *The Mortal No* or excerpted in Ellmann's and Feidelson's *The Modern Tradition* are responding to imperatives other than the deep-seated right to exist, preferably on one's own fluid terms. They cling to a neo-Cartesian logic: I doubt, therefore I am.[13]

Flannery O'Connor, on the other hand, has retained respect for and responsibility to history as fable of epic possibility; to social order as ceremony of hope; to place and person as concrete precedent for universals. For her—as for Robert Penn Warren, Katherine Anne Porter, Tennessee Williams, and other Southerners—there

[12] *Ibid.,* 293n.   [13] Hoffman, *The Imagination's New Beginning,* 2.

can never fully be an I unless there is an I-Thou. Much has been made of the existentialist's courage, his limited affirmation in a world that deserves despair. What of the courage to take seriously origin and ends, and so redeem the time between? What of the courage that hazards selfhood, one's last hoard of joy, on a peacock's promise?

We shall undergo; and then—we shall undergo. For Flannery O'Connor, as for Wallace Stevens, change is the agent of permanence.

Mr. Kell and Mr. Burgess:
Inside and Outside Mr. Enderby

CHARLES G. HOFFMANN
AND A. C. HOFFMANN

The recent publication of *Enderby Outside* (1968) by Anthony Burgess completes the portrait of Enderby begun in *Inside Mr Enderby* (1963) but originally published under the pseudonym of Joseph Kell. The dust-jacket blurb of the English edition of *Enderby Outside,* repeated in the one-volume American edition of the two Enderby novels, maintains the fiction that Mr. Kell and Mr. Burgess are two separate authors and that Kell, having died, bequeathed to Burgess "Not merely his copyrights and royalties but also his identity. His dying wish was that Mr. Burgess should conclude the story about Enderby, the poet, already half-told in *Inside Mr Enderby.*"[1] Although Joseph Kell "died" in 1966 when the Penguin edition of *Inside Mr Enderby* was published under the name of Anthony Burgess, the fiction about the identities of Mr. Kell and Mr. Burgess is more than a private joke between publisher and author who know that both names are pseudonyms for John Anthony Burgess Wilson, a retired Colonial Service education officer. It is a recognition of the fact that Wilson has established his

---

[1] Burgess, *Enderby Outside* (London, 1968). Subsequent references are to this edition of the novel.

reputation and come into his own as a novelist under the name of Burgess, a literary identity he never achieved as Joseph Kell.

The significance of the "pseudo-pseudonym" of Joseph Kell lies not in its frankly admitted original intention of hiding over-production[2] (Anthony Burgess, for that is now his public identity, has published seventeen novels since 1956, all but three of them in the past eight years). It lies in the fact that the two strands of Burgess's art, the comic and the tragic, become one vision in the Enderby novels, a black comedy of the contemporary scene. Long before the publication of *Inside Mr Enderby,* Burgess had created a purely comic novel about life in the British army stationed on Gibraltar at the end of the second world war, *A Vision of Battlements,* which although not published until 1965 was written in 1949. And he had already explored the dark side of life in the Malayan trilogy—*Time for a Tiger* (1956), *The Enemy in the Blanket* (1958), *Beds in the East* (1959)—and probed the illnesses of contemporary English civilization in *The Right to an Answer* (1960) and *The Doctor Is Sick* (1960). From the beginning Burgess has possessed as sharp an eye for the ridiculous and ludicrous in human behavior as he has sensitive an ear for the speech rhythms of his characters whether Malayan or English, Cockney or public school. This comic sense of the absurd in human actions tends to overshadow the essentially tragic vision he intended to portray in the life and death of the protagonist of the Malayan trilogy, Victor Crabbe. For example, the farcical situations involving Victor Crabbe's infidelities belie the depth of his guilt feelings toward his second wife, Fenella, compounded by his guilt at having killed his first wife in an automobile accident. In *A Clockwork Orange* (1962) and *The Wanting Seed* (1962) the tragic vision dominates, and although there is comic relief in clever puns and witty slogans, the comedy intensifies the horror of unbridled juvenile violence and unchecked governmental authoritarianism. It was in *One Hand Clapping* (1961), the only

[2] Burgess, *The Novel Now* (London, 1967), 212.

other novel beside *Inside Mr Enderby* published under the name of Joseph Kell, that Burgess attempted to fuse the two sides of his creative vision, and failed.

Taking its title from a play the protagonists, Howard and Janet Shirley, attend—"a play dealing with the decay and decadence in the world about us"[3]—*One Hand Clapping* satirizes the decadent world of supermarkets, television quiz shows, secondary modern schools, council houses, washing machines, vacuum cleaners, all the visible goods that add quantity but not quality to contemporary English life, circa 1960. The phrase "one hand clapping" originates in Zen Buddhism and is, Howard explains, "a way of getting in touch with Reality, you see, proceeding by way of the absurd. . . . It's supposed to be a way of getting to God" (*One Hand Clapping,* 128–29).

Contemporary English life as portrayed in the novel is absurd and materialistic, having substituted Money for God, symbolized by the television quiz show on which Howard wins a large amount of money because he has a photographic memory. With his winnings Howard sets out to prove that Money is a false God, not in the tradition of the biblical prophets but on its own ground, proving that in a mass-produced economy materialism can not give value or quality for its money. Howard comes to the conclusion that death, self-willed and self-inflicted, is the only way to Reality in the modern world. He decides he will commit suicide after first killing his wife, but Janet kills him because she wants to "live," totally accepting the values of the society Howard has rejected.

The novel's failure as a satire is largely that of Burgess's choice of narrator. Janet Shirley is a pleasant but dull British housewife who measures her days and accomplishments throughout most of the novel in terms of material possessions, stacking them up like the tins of baked beans in the Hastings Road supermarket where she works. Her uncomprehending naïveté as she recounts the past is

---

[3] Kell, *One Hand Clapping* (London, 1961), 128. Subsequent references are to this edition of the novel.

equaled by her vapid conclusions when Howard wins the big quiz prize and they can buy anything they desire: the food they eat in fashionable restaurants cannot compare with the tinned delights served by her at home in the Shortshawe Council Estate, and the fast paced life in the big cities of the world is no more exciting to her than a day spent in the supermarket joking with her fellow workers. Such a narrator cannot be selective, must compulsively give endless and seemingly inconsequential information. Lacking sensitivity and articulateness, Janet Shirley's narration clearly reveals the limitations of the Secondary Modern school system where the teachers assume that the students will not be interested in English and history and therefore entertain them rather than teach them; but although the satiric point is clear, it is made at the sacrifice of complexity and subtlety of insight. Her mind is a *tabula rasa*—she does not discriminate between the minutiae and the important fact imbedded within them—yet she must be the narrator, not Howard who attempts to understand and develop beyond the limitations of his environment but who can only solve his dilemma by the desperate remedy of death. Burgess succeeded in creating a viable plot whose ramifications explore the absurdity of contemporary life, but hampered himself with an implausible narrator whose personality changes three-fourths of the way through the novel from a conventional housewife to a *femme fatale* who is unfaithful to her husband, kills him in self-defense, runs away with her lover (the poet Redvars Glass), who then assumes Howard's name and identity. Together Janet and Redvars accompany Howard's body to France, keeping it in a wardrobe and deciding ultimately to dispose of this encumbrance by using it as a scarecrow! However, the bizarre horror of this act and Janet's thinking at the end that she may have to dispose of Redvars in a similar fashion does suggest one thematic direction Burgess develops, the anti-utopian world of violence and inhumanity in *A Clockwork Orange* and *The Wanting Seed,* but in *One Hand Clapping* the reader is unprepared for Janet Shirley's shift in character.

If the failure of *One Hand Clapping* as a satiric portrait of modern society is inherent in the mindlessness of its narrator, its failure to achieve a fusion of the comic and the tragic is implicit in the single-minded despair of its hero. There is no tragic conflict between the absurdity of the human condition Howard Shirley rejects and his will to die. A slave to his photographic memory, he lacks an identity by which the inner reality of his self can be tested against the forces of the outside world. Nor can he reach reality by way of the absurd because he lacks the comic vision to encompass the absurd. It is certain he will die—the only suspense is whether he will take his wife Janet with him—but his death is not at the hands of fate, and Janet who strikes the blow that kills him is no agent of fate. His death is the physical end of a death of the mind that antedates the narrative time of the novel, for he is, except for the quirk of his memory, as much a product of the civilization he has rejected as Janet who accepts it.

Burgess's failure to provide Howard Shirley with an identity by which the comic and the tragic could be combined led him to tackle the problem of identity directly in the Enderby novels. The dust-jacket anecdote about the identities of Mr. Kell and Mr. Burgess reveals, however coyly, the major theme of the Enderby novels, the quest for identity. In *A Clockwork Orange* the problem of identity for the narrator-protagonist, Alex, becomes the focus of the novel's climax. In the Enderby novels the search for self-identity is central to the entire work, and a multiplicity of identities is the means by which Burgess successfully unites the two sides of his art by creating an interaction between the comic and the tragic vision of life.

Whereas the satire on contemporary life is diffuse throughout and dissipated at the end of *One Hand Clapping,* it is sharp and consistent, although more narrowly focused, in *Inside Mr Enderby.* The satiric tone of *Inside Mr Enderby* is set from the beginning in the outer frame which encloses both of the Enderby novels and links them together as a whole. The frame is narrated by a sycophantic teacher-guide whose attempts to pontificate upon the higher meanings of poetry and poets are as far removed from the inner reality of Enderby as his attention to the external details of Enderby's life and surroundings. But the frame narrator's observation that little is known about Enderby because "he was essentially a man who lived inside himself"[4] (speaking in the past tense as a biographer) establishes the theme inherent in the title. Inside, Enderby is the isolated poet completely engrossed by the irrational waxing and waning of his talent that seem to follow the biological rhythms of his viscera. He is the antithesis of the romantic poet inspired by a lofty muse; the process of creation is described in cloacal detail as Enderby, the mid-twentieth-century English poet, sits on a cold toilet seat, an electric fire at his feet, his poems, written on toilet tissue, filling the bathtub. Too much, however, can be made of the scatalogical and visceral details of Enderby's creativity, for Burgess's purpose is not to shock the reader (if indeed the modern reader is shockable) or to deprecate the creative process, but to suggest in the Joycean sense that in the womb the word was made flesh. The privacy of the privy is the only "womb" left for the poet in the modern world with its demand for social identity and social usefulness, the creed represented by the psychiatrists, Drs. Greenslade and Wapenshaw, and given the governmental seal of approval by the National Health Service.

The inward-looking Enderby is no Redvars Glass, although both are poets, for we see Redvars only from the outside as the extrovert, virile, bohemian who betrays Howard Shirley twice, first by cuckolding him and then by violating his role as guest in the Shirley home, turning it over to his indigent friends while the Shirleys are away on their hopeless quest for "all the happiness that money can buy." Nor is Enderby Howard Shirley although he too attempts to commit suicide; Enderby affirms life, if only that of the mind, whereas Shirley, pursued by a self-destructive death-wish, denies life. Enderby inside is happy in the self-imposed limitations of his

---

[4] Burgess, *Inside Mr Enderby* (London, 1966), 13. Subsequent references are to this edition of the novel.

craft, but Enderby outside is an incomplete man, a Huxleyan character, sexually impotent, socially incompetent, emotionally imma-
ture. The dichotomy between the inner reality of his poetic imagination and the outer reality of his social role is too severe,
particularly after he leaves the security of his womb and marries the
vestal virgin of modern womanhood, Vesta Bainbridge; and Enderby breaks down. However, there is more similarity between
Enderby and Howard Shirley than there is between Redvars and
Enderby. Both Shirley and Enderby are driven to their fates by the
inner necessity of a peculiarity in their mental processes over which
they have no control, the one by his photographic memory and the
other by his poetic imagination. The "muse" or inner necessity of
creativity in Enderby is embodied in a will that is as primitive and
natural as his biological functions and is related to them: "The act
of creation. Sex. That was the trouble with art. Urgent sexual desire
aroused with the excitement of a new image or rhythm" (*Inside Mr
Enderby,* p. 27). It is because of his arrested development as a social
and sexual man that Enderby's creative energies are so rawly and
biologically directed in nature. As long as he remains inside the
protective womb of his identity as poet, he is, "taking all things into
consideration, by and large, not to put too fine a point on it,
reasonably well self-sufficient" (*Inside Mr Enderby,* p. 27). But the
poet's search for Beauty, as man's search for Love, if it is to reach
beyond narcissism, is embodied in Woman (even 'Arry the cook
recognizes this when he gets Enderby to write love poetry to
Thelma the barmaid). Creativity is thus related to the ying-yang
motion of the universe, the mysterious forces of life embodied in
women. Enderby's search for Beauty is an alternation between the
ying and yang of the dark and light forces in his life. His physically
repulsive stepmother is the cause of his sexual impotency, yet she is
the Muse who provides him with the financial means to cultivate
his poetry. But Enderby is unable to accept his Muse as an ugly
stepmother who although dead and buried reappears Circe-like in
his life in different guises (the drunken woman in the saloon-bar of

the Neptune; his landlady, Mrs. Meldrum; Thelma the barmaid; Vesta Bainbridge and finally, Miranda Boland) as he journeys forth on his odyssey in the outside world, returning "home" to the womb-like security of the lavatory. Ironically, it is his mother's maiden name, Hogg, which he assumes for his new identity as the scientifically reconstructed man, the non-poet but socially well-adjusted man. Thus Circe who can turn men into swine as well as into lovers literally turns Enderby into a Hogg, at least that part of him which seeks a normal life in modern society by marrying Vesta under the illusion he was creating a new life, a new beginning for himself.

In a scene that anticipates the Orwellian horror of Alex's reclamation in *A Clockwork Orange,* Enderby is cured of his anti-social identity as a poet and rehabilitated into a socially useful person of service to humanity as a bartender. It is at this point that *Inside Mr Enderby* ends and *Enderby Outside* begins. Burgess's intention of making the two novels sequential is obvious not only in the titles chosen and in the repetition of the external narrative frame but also in the thematic development of Enderby's two identities. The change from poet to barman is an incomplete metamorphosis; inside the shell of his new identity as Hogg, Enderby the poet, the word-man, exists in Kafkaesque reality, yearning for recognition and love. As Enderby moves from the inner but safer world of poetry to the outer but frightening world of women's magazines, movie scenarios, hip writers, and pop singers, he loses his original identity; for the poet, Burgess implies, is primarily an anti-social, self-sustaining creature who must remain imprisoned in the cave of his own self if he is to remain free to develop his talents. In *Inside Mr Enderby,* Enderby's attempts to escape the confines of the prison of his art end in disaster—the comic episode of the poets's luncheon in London, the carnival chaos of Rome, the unconsummated marriage to Vesta Bainbridge. But in *Enderby Outside,* Hogg is no more capable of coping with the irrationalities and injustices of life than Enderby was. Accused of murdering Yod Crewsy the modern god (Yahweh) of popular art, Hogg escapes to Tangiers, a fugitive from the wrath of Vesta Bainbridge and the devotees of Yod's Crewsy Fixers whose supposedly martyred leader is resurrected to life as part of a publicity stunt.

Enderby-Hogg can only regain his identity as a poet by assuming a third identity, that of his Nemesis, Rawcliffe, the poet who had borrowed Enderby's poems if not his identity. Enderby's fate is to become a minor poet, for poetry is a minor art in a world that deifies the pop singer Yod Crewsy; that is why Rawcliffe's identity suits Enderby so well, for Rawcliffe has achieved a reputation as a minor poet, mainly on the borrowings from Enderby. In a world where Yod Crewsy is the Son of God the Father, the poet must identify with an earlier mythology; Rawcliffe is Icarus whose dead body is consigned to the sea from an airplane by Enderby, and Enderby, the old artificer Daedalus, Rawcliffe's passport in his pocket, becomes Icarus. Reversing the Joycean motif that the son must displace the father, Burgess suggests that the Creator must become the Son (Logos), the word-man, defying society, rebellious, disobedient, aloof, but yet compassionate and undemanding. Rawcliffe's suffering and death had taught Enderby pity, and he no longer desires revenge against Vesta Bainbridge. He had yet to learn love.

Before Enderby can return to the womb where the word was made flesh, he must trick Circe into giving back his identity as a poet. Circe reappears in *Enderby Outside* in the guise of Miranda Boland, the modern moon goddess, who may not know Greek mythology, failing to recognize the name of Selene, but who knows the science of the moon, being a lecturer in selenography. Enderby is in "disguise" as Enderby, having fled England after the apparent death of Yod Crewsy, dropping the name Hogg and using his Enderby passport to escape. But he is still Hogg the non-poet, poetically impotent, even though he claims to be Enderby the poet. It is at the height of his love-making with Miranda that he regains his poetic gift; "an ejaculation of words" comes. Frustrated and bitter, Miranda penetrates his disguise and recognizes him as Hogg, but it is too late for her; he is in reality Enderby, again poetically potent but still sexually impotent. It is the love of beauty not the love of body that he pursues.

At the end Enderby meets his Muse in the form of a beautiful golden girl, nameless but seductive. Although she offers her body to him, Enderby cannot accept; his sexual impotency is now a recognition that as a poet he must always be seduced by beauty but can never possess beauty for himself. He has learned love, but his love must be a pursuit of ideal beauty not the possession of it. She will inspire him, help him develop a critical judgment for himself, but the beauty he creates will be for others not for himself, just as all his life he has been surrounded by the detritus of other lives, whether it be his stepmother, his landlady, Vesta Bainbridge or Rawcliffe.

Burgess does not disagree with those critics who have found three persistent themes in his novels: "the need to laugh in the face of a desperate future; questions of loyalty; the relationships between countries and between races."[5] In fact, most of his novels deal with all three either directly or indirectly, depending upon the emphasis. In the Malayan trilogy the tragi-comic theme of personal loyalty is tightly bound to the theme of relationship between races in the colonies, as is true of *The Right to an Answer,* in which the lives of the English businessman J. W. Denham and the Ceylonese amateur sociologist Mr. Raj become intertwined. Burgess's most successful novels, however, subordinate these themes to a satiric view of man's folly and the absurd society which exploits the blatant and the bad, places a premium upon notoriety and the creation of public idols. Thus, the violent world of the street gang in *A Clockwork Orange* is rendered through a created language which captures the desperate alienation and hopelessness of youth in a materialistic and disintegrating social order. In *The Wanting Seed* Burgess creates an anti-utopian society in which the problem of overpopulation is solved with scientific detachment through the scholastic logic of a

[5] Burgess, *The Novel Now,* 213.

bureaucracy. The Enderby novels are a further exploration of these themes as Enderby finds himself betrayed on all sides, must exile himself from the womb that is England and make his way in the irrational world of Tangiers, and "laugh in the face of a desperate future." The comic mask that Burgess wears—the Joycean puns, the absurd situations in which his characters find themselves, the ridiculous antics of his characters—is a desperate laughter in the face of the tragic condition of man—the plight of the artist in the modern world, the violence that underlies the veneer of civilized behavior, the Kafkaesque alienation of the sensitive individual, the Orwellian nightmare of governmental controls, the basic conflict of good and evil. But dark laughter, Burgess's recognition of the absurd in life, becomes Enderby's saving grace, the means by which he achieves identity as a poet, using the absurdities of the world outside as the raw material for poetry. Enderby's odyssey is completed, and he can go "home" having returned Lazarus-like from a living death and renewed his gift as a poet.

The Second Major Subwar:
Four Novels by Vance Bourjaily

JOHN M. MUSTE

I

Vance Bourjaily's major achievement so far has been in the four novels which deal with the generation that grew up during the Depression and reached maturity in the Second World War. None of these novels can be called a "combat novel," and only one of the four properly belongs in the broader category of the "war novel."[1] Throughout the series, however, Bourjaily's major concern has been with the relationship of the individual to the violent forces of the modern world whose most explicit manifestation was in the second of this century's major wars. Bourjaily's preoccupation with the war demonstrates not only the importance of the conflict for his life and career but also its significance for a whole generation of writers. Those novelists who came to maturity during the thirties, forties, and fifties have had to try to cope with the special phenomena of modern violence through an art form whose traditions have not

---

[1] The distinction here is between novels which deal primarily and at length with men who are active participants in combat (e.g. *The Red Badge of Courage*, *The Naked and the Dead*, *The Deathmakers*) and novels which center their attention on the war and its consequences for individuals even when they are not directly engaged in fighting (e.g. *Guard of Honor*, *The Gallery*).

always been readily adaptable to altered ways of perceiving reality.[2] Bourjaily is unusual among these novelists. In part, this is because he has displayed a continuing concern with attempting to locate the place of war in modern existence and with trying to trace the complex relationships between aggression as an individual manifestation and the ways in which violence both shapes and is shaped by the special conditions of our civilization.

A fundamental difference between the fiction which developed out of the Second World War and the fiction of earlier wars was the result of a belief shared by many novelists that neither of the traditional explanations of the relationship between war and the individual was by itself adequate to explain their experience. Hemingway's Frederick Henry and Dos Passos' John Andrews were helpless victims of war's violence and dislocation, their war a result of the breakdown of civilization. At the other end of the scale, Crane's Henry Fleming adjusted to violence because it is in part the mirror of, in part the answer to, needs and impulses which are at the roots of the human personality.[3] But for writers like Mailer, Heller, and Bourjaily neither explanation is of itself sufficient. Modern war is clearly more than the simple manifestation of individual aggression; it is too extreme, too widespread, too pervasive to be passed off as some kind of objective correlative of a collective desire to kill one's father. At the same time, it has become difficult to think of war as a departure from civilization; many of the novelists of the Second World War have sought in different ways to deal with the possibility that modern war is natural to our civilization, somehow inherent in our society. The result has been a fiction which has justified the critical assessment that the fiction of the later war, if

[2] See Irving Howe, "Mass Society and Post-Modern Fiction," *Partisan Review,* XXVI (Summer, 1959), 420–36.

[3] Irving Louis Horowitz distinguishes between what he calls political idealism, which sees war's primary causes as "innate propensities to violence, inherent human restlessness, or the spirit of adventurism and heroism fully realized only in combat," and, on the other hand, political realism which emphasizes "external, socially conditioned causes of aggression." *The Idea of War and Peace in Contemporary Philosophy* (New York, 1957), 30–31.

not "better" than its earlier counterpart, has at least been more concerned with the complexity of the problems of violence.[4] In his own fashion, as I hope to show in the following pages, Bourjaily has tried to come to terms with that complexity.

The effort is barely visible in Bourjaily's first novel, *The End of My Life,* very much a young man's book, youthfully romantic in its depiction of love and friendship, youthfully nihilistic in its conclusion.[5] Skinner Galt, the central character, is a conventional figure of war fiction, a knowing young man cynical enough to believe he is immune to the damages which war is capable of inflicting. He fails to realize, however, just how vulnerable he really is, physically and psychologically, until violent death strikes near enough to dislocate him completely. He volunteers in an ambulance unit closely resembling the American Field Service (in which Bourjaily himself served), leaves college, and is shipped first to the Middle East and later to Italy. Along the way he makes several predictable friends (Benny the Communist, Rod the musician, and Freak the All-American boy) and has a predictable love affair with Cindy, an improbably intelligent, tender, and complaisant girl out of the Catherine Barkley mold. Skinner's cynicism, based on the reading of Hemingway and other novelists rather than on any first-hand knowledge of the world, prevents him from committing himself to ideologies, friends, or lovers. This lack of commitment is itself a trap: on the occasions when reality becomes truly ugly, Skinner has no props with which to support himself. Throughout Skinner's adventures the reader has been conscious, as Skinner himself has not been, that beneath the surface toughness which he affects there is a soft core of sentimentality, manifesting itself in his relationship with Cindy, in his taste in music, in his choice of heroes.[6]

[4] Frederick J. Hoffman, *The Mortal No* (Princeton, 1964), 224–26.

[5] *The End of My Life* (New York, 1947). References here are to the Bantam edition of 1962, and will be incorporated in the text.

[6] See especially the juvenile line-ups for a football game (p. 126) in which Marx, Lincoln, Jesus, and Falstaff are listed on the "yea-team" and Eliot, Swift, Hart Crane, and Freud on the "nay-team."

Skinner is least prepared for the very phenomena he had thought himself most immune to: the fact of violence and the physical and psychological dislocations brought by war. While in Syria he is thrown into a deep depression by evidence that his hard shell provides no real defense against the world. His friend Rod, always moody and neurotically wary of women, is made to accept his homosexual inclinations and eventually deserts to live among the Arabs; combined with the other strains of living in a strange place under unfamiliar conditions, Rod's agony and his own inability to help force Skinner into a lethargic withdrawal from life. Eventually he recovers and even finds something worth doing when his unit is sent to Italy and put to work hauling casualties out of the front lines. But Skinner is still too much the dilettante. He forms a loose attachment with a young American nurse and agrees to violate orders and cater to her juvenile curiosity by taking her in his ambulance for a joyride to the front. They are returning from this jaunt when a lone German plane, strafing the road, fires on them. Skinner swerves the vehicle just as the plane makes its pass, and the bullet which would have killed him if he had stayed on course kills the girl instead. Skinner is sent to military prison and withdraws completely from life. When Cindy (improbably) shows up in Italy and visits him, he rejects her because he has rejected his former self:

> "Identity is a funny thing, and I'm losing it. Skinner Galt is on the way out. He had his day, now he's going. When I get out of here, I'll be someone else. Poor Mad Galt, perhaps, Sailor Galt, or Virgil Galt, or even Galt the Ripper. But I'll be Tom Galt. I'm sure of that. I won't be Skinner. I'm sick of Skinner. He's too God damn clever, and he hurt a lot of people." (211)

Skinner's problem is familiar enough in war fiction; it is unusual only in that he seems to have caved in under less pressure than most other fictional heroes. Unlike Frederick Henry, whom in many ways he resembles, Skinner is not physically wounded, he does not have intimate experience with combat, he is not involved in a military disaster like the retreat from Caporetto, and he is not thrust

into a position of having to commit violent acts himself. Nevertheless, Skinner resembles the heroes of World War I fiction in his
rejection of life after experiencing war and in his identification of
the war as the source of his troubles. At the very end of the novel,
Bourjaily represents him as thinking of what he has lost: "There he
could get this all in order: how Freak would not understand, but
must cease to admire, and how Cindy would understand but must
cease to love, and how Benny would have understood, did understand, and how, once the war arrived, it was already over because
people realized that it could not be endless." (212) Even in his
nihilism, Skinner believes that the war is an isolated event which is
responsible for his troubles, and that "it could not be endless," a
point of view which is important because it shows how close Bourjaily was, at this point, to such chroniclers of an earlier war as
Hemingway, Dos Passos, and Boyd; eight years later, when his
second novel appeared, this point of view had been abandoned.

II

"Yet why do I speak of particular wars? Perhaps this depletion is
produced in any people who reach that point of historical sophistication at which they realize that war is not a plural word, that there is
only one war which may be resumed at any time; that this war is,
simultaneously, the chief use to which our human energies are put
and a great eternally sardonic and hopelessly impractical joke of
which we are somehow the helpless self-appointed butts—an awful
joke, this only war, the one fought steadily and with only occasional
exhausted pauses since Cain and Abel, the war between you and me."[7]

The theory advanced in this passage by Al Barker, the central figure
in Bourjaily's second novel, *The Hound of Earth,* places the book at
the opposite end of the spectrum from *The End of My Life.* Barker's commentary on his own actions and on the society of which he
is a somewhat reluctant member seems to place the blame for the

[7] Bourjaily, *The Hound of Earth* (New York, 1955). References here are to Perma
Books edition, 1956, 24–25.

Second World War and for all war on an inherent aggressiveness in man: however remote the destructiveness of modern war may be from the conflicts between individuals, those conflicts are nevertheless seen as the source of the greater violence. Specifically, for Al Barker, the problem has to do with assigning responsibility for the distinctively new element introduced into warfare in 1945—atomic weaponry.

The Hound of Earth is a very different book from *The End of My Life.* The central action takes place sometime in the early fifties, years after the end of the war, and its setting is the pre-Christmas rush in a large San Francisco department store, wholly remote from war-time battlefields. Barker, like Skinner at the end of his story, is a fugitive from the self he had been, but two important differences distinguish him from his earlier counterpart: he knows that his flight is futile because he cannot escape his own humanity, and the cause of his flight is far more specific, serious and distinctively contemporary than Skinner's. Originally a scientist with an ordinary job and an ordinary family, Barker worked unknowingly on one aspect of the development of the atomic bomb. When the news of Hiroshima came he realized that his work was part of the preparation for the holocaust, and his response was to run away, deserting army, job, and family. In the intervening years he has buried himself in a series of menial jobs, eluding the search still being carried on by an F.B.I. agent named Casper Usez, but Barker has not found peace within himself or in any of the social situations of which he has been a part. At the same time, he has refused to flee the country, feeling himself somehow bound to stay in the United States as the only possible location of his salvation and his penance. In the course of the novel an embittered old friend and a beautiful young girl, both of them rich, make separate attempts to induce Barker to escape to Mexico, but he turns them both down, chiefly because his burden of guilt makes him feel that he shares the responsibilities of all his countrymen:

He had tried to run and, weary of running, rested; and resting, been unable to reject forever and ended by accepting them all: his love for Nickie, his pity for Finn, his responsibility to Tom, his fascination and compassion for the horror of Dolly, the impulse to oppose M'nerney—the need to take his stand. These things had held him, involved him, chased and trapped him, deprived him of the freedom to live alone with guilt—the hound of earth had caught him. No man, no matter what his time, his country, his condition, training, heredity or philosophy, forever escapes that hound, his own humanity. (234)

One of the purposes of *The Hound of Earth* is to demonstrate that the conflicts between individuals and the state of society are in fact related to the awesome weapons of destruction, and Bourjaily attempts to do this by examining the behavior of the employees of the toy shop in a department store. Within the central irony of the season dedicated to peace and joy degenerating into anxiety and bitterness there are the peculiarities of the characters. Hub Finn, the buyer, is a degenerate modern version of Mark Twain's hero; born to be carefree, he has been a good salesman but is now unhappy in his more responsible position, venting his frustrations by fighting with those around him and committing a near-rape on one of the salesgirls. Dolly Klamath, the service manager, is in even worse straits; on the verge of a paranoid breakdown, she suspects everyone of having designs on her person or her job, commits her own kind of rape, and eventually tries to revert to babyhood, only to kill herself. Santa Claus is (predictably) an old drunk, the assistant buyer is a vicious seeker for the main chance, one of the temporary salesgirls is earning money to pay for an abortion and another is trying to emasculate her husband by any means possible. Into this jungle comes Al Barker, patient, tolerant, knowing. He is Bourjaily's closest approach to a Christ figure, a role suggested in the early dialogue between Finn and his assistant: "What more do you expect? Jesus Christ with ten years' experience to run the stockroom?" (8) What they get is a slightly soiled Jesus Christ, whose ten years' experience has been in running and hiding. His strength and wisdom gather a few disciples; the novel has its Mary Magdalene, its Judas, and a form of Crucifixion. But Al Barker cannot save himself, has no God to cry out to: before the novel's end we have learned that he will spend years in Leavenworth and probably more years after that in California penitentiaries. If he brings something like grace to a few of those around him, he is to live without hope for himself; his only request of his warders will be that he be transferred from Leavenworth to a West Coast prison, presumably so that he will be one of the first victims of a nuclear attack from across the Pacific.

Barker feels guilty not merely because he has unknowingly helped to create a weapon of unprecedented destructiveness but also because his first reaction to the knowledge of what he had done demonstrated to him the will to destruction that he conceives to be part of all men. Towards the end of *The Hound of Earth* he is pressured by a young disciple into explaining his real motives for fleeing his job and his family, and he admits that the use of the bomb terrified him less than did his own response: " 'For an instant, there, I was glad, before desolation set in; for an instant, I felt myself in exultation, willing the death of the world.' " (233)

The chief weakness of the novel is that Bourjaily never convinces the reader that there is in fact any profound connection between Barker's instant of exultation and the dislocations in the lives of the other characters. There is violence in these lives, but it is almost entirely psychological in nature; although there are two deaths in the novel, the near-rape and other violations, nothing in the actions of the characters is shown to have any real connection with the destruction of modern war. Other societies have lost the true meaning of religious festivals of peace, other societies have fostered frustration and rivalry, other societies have produced mental breakdowns, but only twentieth-century society has produced atomic weapons. The attempt to trace causal connections among these phenomena is doomed to failure, not because such connections may not exist but because we cannot make the leap from the actions of a few characters to the processes by which science and technology are turned to destructive purposes. *The Hound of Earth* is one of the rare attempts to study the psychological consequences of involvement in the production of atomic armaments, but it fails in what was apparently its chief purpose.

III

Bourjaily's first two novels are relatively conventional attempts to deal with problems raised by the war, although they describe different situations and reflect different attitudes. His two subsequent novels, *The Violated* and *Confessions of a Spent Youth*,[8] are in one sense less directly concerned with the war as a phenomenon which needs to be understood as part of "terror's unique enigma." For one thing, the scope of each is broader so that the war itself receives less attention, in proportion to the whole novel, than is the case in *The End of My Life*. *The Violated* traces the lives of its four important characters from their adolescence during the late thirties until their doom in the late fifties; *Confessions of a Spent Youth* covers much of the same ground as did *The End of My Life,* but it too is extended, roughly from 1939 until 1946, and it is a much more thorough study of its narrator, Quincy, than we had earlier of Skinner Galt. In another sense, however, the war is even more significant in these two later novels because it is a symbolic representation of the worlds in which the characters must live their whole lives. Bourjaily has moved, it seems to me, from consideration of the two traditional alternative explanations for man's participation in war to an attitude shared by the most perceptive novelists of World War II. These writers, explicitly or implicitly, reject the idea that war is either the product of man's innate aggressiveness or

[8] Bourjaily, *The Violated* (New York, 1958); Bourjaily, *Confessions of a Spent Youth* (New York, 1960). References to these editions will be incorporated in the text.

of occasional breakdowns in his society; instead, they imply that war is the natural product of society, that war releases but neither creates nor results from individual aggressiveness, that war may stop temporarily but is not otherwise likely to change the direction of individual lives.

This attitude is most clear, I think, in *The Violated*. The suggestion of the title is that the four characters whose lives are detailed in the novel are victims, that they are violated by the inherent savagery of modern life. To a certain extent this is true, in the sense that each of them is somehow shaped during adolescence by forces he cannot control. But the lives of these characters are not that simple. Each is also to some extent a violator, a destroyer, not merely from reaction to stimuli applied during a formative period. Guy Cinturon is violated by the sexual depredations of an older woman, but it is not inevitable that he should react to this by taking as his life's work the seduction of as many girls as possible; he might as easily have taken up painting or baseball or bull-fighting, but he chooses his own pattern of response. Tom Beniger is more acted upon than acting through most of his life, but it is a force within himself that leads him to marry the English girl he cannot love, and he is responsible for the later affair which nearly destroys him. Ellen Beniger is baffled and confused by life, but she is enough of a masochist to invite her own violation.

Tom Beniger and his sister Ellen stand at the center of *The Violated,* representing traditional American WASP culture. Guy Cinturon, scion of an ancient Mexican family, represents the involvement of an essentially European tradition with twentieth-century American culture, fitting in easily enough even while part of him stands outside this culture. The key to the novel, however, is Eddie Bissle, friend of Tom and Guy, lover of Ellen, possibly the father of Ellen's child. He is the son of a recent immigrant family, the raw material of American society, but he is also a kind of walking principle of violence, and to the extent that his life is part of the lives of the other characters, he also represents the potential for violence that is in each of them. As a boy Eddie takes out his frustrations in the violence of football, which he loves for the opportunity it gives him for dealing and accepting punishment. Guy Cinturon is a more famous football player (the three male characters attend the same college, and both Eddie and Guy play on its football team), but he shrinks from the hard contact and gets headlines because of an elusiveness based partly on fear. It is Eddie, however, who loves the cruelty of the game. Later, Eddie is the only one of the characters (in fact, Bourjaily's only character) to see genuine combat action in the war, and this experience helps reinforce his conviction that the world and everyone in it is "crud." He makes a tough, hard infantry officer.

In one combat episode Eddie's humanity comes to the surface. His men capture a German, and Eddie's choice is to kill him at once or send him back for interrogation. His own instinct is to kill the prisoner out of hand, but he has been influenced by the gentle humaneness of Tom Beniger in college and now permits himself to develop a human concern for the German. Given his life, the prisoner attempts to escape, kills one of Eddie's best men, and is obliterated. The episode is confirmation for Eddie of the principle that survival depends on toughness: get them or they'll get you. The episode is crucial to the plot of the novel, which is brought to an end by Eddie's semi-accidental shooting of Tom, long after the war, and by Eddie's subsequent suicide. Disgusted with Tom for engaging in what Eddie mistakenly thinks is a homosexual affair, Eddie reluctantly gives shelter to Tom and his wife and daughter; even after Eddie discovers his mistake about Tom, the need for violence remains, and Tom is killed when he takes a cabbage from one of Eddie's fields:

> Eddie knew it was Tom when he heard it, the old joke of Tom's and Guy's, speaking Spanish to stupid Eddie, and loved the old joke, and forgave Tom everything at last, and forgave himself, and knew it was one of Dio's Puerto Ricans, speaking Spanish, coming at him with a knife, and meant the man no harm, and could see that it was

Guy with a football, Goswith waving Sheila's head, and recognized his grandfather's voice. Knew he held a shotgun, too, but this time he was very careful to get the carbine's safety off before he let the big, blond, German prisoner have it, bang spang and splatter. Right in the cruddy chest. (582–83)

Eddie represents the principle of violence which, Bourjaily says in this novel, is present in all of our lives. It may, and often does, find its fullest expression in war, but it is a delusion to think that war is unusual or in any way foreign to the rest of our experience. War and peace are no longer separate entities, characterized by different kinds of behavior; Eddie Bissle shows this. Further, the war is so deeply a part of our total experience that it does not really change us. Midway through *The Violated,* when the war has ended and the male characters have returned from service, Tom's uncomprehending stepfather remarks that the "war hasn't made . . . a generation of misfits out of your bunch," to which Tom can only reply that "The war may have speeded up our development a little; but I don't think it's changed the various ways we were headed." (265) Tom is headed for various kinds of frustration and eventually for violent death; Ellen's decay has been helped along by Eddie's brutal love-making ("There was real brutality in Eddie, and real response to it in Ellen." [178]), but she still has a long way to go down the road of drunkenness and degradation; Guy's pursuit of women is leading to final frustration, despite all his conquests; Eddie is still on the path of destruction which is also self-destruction. The war has been part of their development in these directions, but it has not changed the directions themselves.

It has been objected that the plot of *The Violated* is sufficiently conventional to contradict the novel's evident argument that life can no longer be controlled by traditional artistic, religious or political forms.[9] This seems to me to be a justifiable criticism only if we look at the skeleton of the novel, not at its texture, and in any case such a judgment ignores the meaning of the sub-plot, which is

[9] See Howe, *Partisan Review,* XXVI.

a specific rejection of the popular modern idea that art can serve where religion and science have failed as a device for ordering chaotic reality. Framing the story of the lives of the four main characters, and occupying an important place in the second half of the novel, is the description of an attempted production of *Hamlet* by a group of children whose guiding genius is Sheila, Ellen's self-sufficient daughter. It is no accident that she chooses a play in which there is so much violence, or that she demonstrates the appeal of the play to somewhat reluctant schoolmates by acting out the scene in which Hamlet stabs Polonius. The children who are involved in the play are sensitive to the fact that the world around them is violent and unpredictable, and their attempt to produce *Hamlet* is an attempt to order that world through the magic and ritual of art; incidentally, it is also an attempt to stab the adults who made that world. The attempt fails because the adult world intervenes. Midway through the performance in an abandoned building firemen and police are called, breaking up the show and scattering its fragments, and incidentally realigning some of the relationships in the adult world. Even in the children's world, art is insufficient to contain or explain the violent and irrational nature of modern existence. It is both necessary and inevitable that the children's experiment should fail.

Violence is not so much at the center of *Confessions of a Spent Youth*. Quincy, this novel's counterpart of Skinner Galt, has a more extensive experience of what it is like to drive an ambulance in combat than was reported in *The End of My Life,* and his other war-related experiences are more varied and more interesting, but Bourjaily's concern in this novel is less with the facts of violence than with what might be called the de-sensitizing of a generation. If the war has a particular effect on the members of his generation, Quincy says, it is the loss of "part of our ability to feel. There seem, and I wish to say this without loaded words, so I shall use doctors' language—to be certain kinds of emotional stimuli to which I am not capable of responding, even now." (318) This inability to feel, to relate to others, is not the product of a guilty conscience nor of exposure to war's brutality. It is rather a product of the whole encounter between the individual, with his own aggressions and reticences, and the violent and violating reality of twentieth-century life.[10]

The importance of *Confessions of a Spent Youth* for this discussion is that once again the experience of war is placed at the center of a generation's development. Quincy is aware of the war, or its preliminaries or after-effects, throughout his life. It is clear from the novel's somewhat unusual structure[11] that the war conditions Quincy's world and his response to it long before he even thinks of joining the ambulance unit, and that war's dislocations and urgencies are not qualitatively different from their equivalents in any other period of our time. Neither Quincy nor the reader feels anything jarring or out of key in the deaths of his friends in the war; they could just as easily have died, in the same ways, in what we call peace. And Quincy's most memorable experience with violent death has a clear point. Driving his ambulance, he sees a soldier hit by a mortar explosion on the road on which Quincy is driving; his impulse is to go to the soldier, to take him in the ambulance if he is wounded or roll him to the roadside if he is dead, but circumstances intervene and by the time Quincy gets back to the man he has been run over by a tank: "He was smashed now, and crushed into the dirt, everything broken, even the skull." (358) On a later trip Quincy sees the corpse again, "flattened like one of those animal bodies that one sees sometimes on a busy highway at night." (358) Dead, the soldier is part of the detritus of our world, a natural by-product of a civilization which has so many ways to kill men.

The description of war's place in our culture to which Bourjaily

---

[10] Harris Dienstfrey takes this loss of feeling as central to all of Bourjaily's work, but it properly describes only the case of Quincy, not that of the earlier characters; see "The Novels of Vance Bourjaily," *Commentary*, XXXI (1961), 360–63.

[11] Although there is a development in time, the basic format of the novel is that of a series of essays, modeled loosely on De Quincey, and dealing with such matters as sex, drugs, vicarious crime, and war in separate places.

moved is not, of course, unique with him: it is to be found as early as *The Naked and the Dead,* as late as *Catch-22* or *The Thousand Hour Day.* But Bourjaily is unique in at least two important ways. For one thing, he has focused his attention on the war as the crucial experience of his generation and of the modern world more extensively than any of his contemporaries, and he has helped to show clearly the various possibilities for viewing that war and its meaning. That the war has so far been his real subject is indirectly suggested by the relative lack of success of his most recent novel, *The Man Who Knew Kennedy,* a much softer and less interesting novel than the two which preceded it. Furthermore, despite the evidence of *The Man Who Knew Kennedy,* Bourjaily is that rarest of phenomena, an American novelist whose fiction shows a clear development in skill and maturity from his first work to his later books. To cite only one of the many pieces of evidence available, there is the difference between the derivative Cindy of *The End of My Life* and the soiled, forlorn beauty of Jeannie Childress in *Confessions of a Spent Youth.* Jeannie is on display far more briefly than her antecedent, but she is one of the few truly memorable women in recent fiction.

Finally, Bourjaily is important because what he has to show us about violence and the modern world is the product of a thoughtful and imaginative mind. His novels are neither sociological tomes nor psychological case studies; they do not propose any cures for our maladies. They nevertheless delineate the state of our society in the last thirty years, and help us to understand what it means to have lived through those years. With increasing force and perceptiveness, Bourjaily has commented on the effects as well as the causes of the violence which appears to be our most distinctive characteristic. Violence is today the most fashionable subject: quarterlies ponder it, symposia debate it, commissions study it, poets lament it, slick magazines deplore it, all the mass media exploit it. We are only beginning to understand, however, how difficult and complex a problem it is. Bourjaily has been writing about this complexity for twenty years, learning that the simple answers are deluding, demonstrating that our society, long before the assassinations or Vietnam, was shot through with violence. The hard lesson of this fiction is that there are no panaceas, that peace and order are not going to be gained by sudden endings to armed conflicts or racial disturbances. The roots of violence are too deeply embedded in our society and in ourselves to be easily reached. There is no easy way out of what Quincy called "humanity's twentieth-century war."

A Bibliography of the Writings
of Frederick J. Hoffman
(1909–1967)

PHILIP R. YANNELLA

1943

"The Little Magazines: Portrait of an Age," *Saturday Review of Literature,* XXVI (December 25, 1943), 3–5.

1944

"Lawrence's 'Quarrel' with Freud," *Quarterly Review of Literature,* I (Summer, 1944), 279–87.
"Infroyce: Joyce and Psychoanalysis," *University of Kansas City Review,* XI (Autumn, 1944), 71–79.

1945

"Research Value of the 'Little Magazine,'" *College and Research Libraries,* VI, 4, pt. 1 (September, 1945), 311–16.
"Psychoanalysis in Modern Poetic Theory," *Contemporary Poetry,* V (Autumn, 1945), 13–15.
Freudianism and the Literary Mind. Baton Rouge: Louisiana State University Press, 1945.

1946

Review of Harry Slochower, *No Voice Is Wholly Lost: Writers and Thinkers in War and Peace. Briarcliff Quarterly,* II (January, 1946), 280–82.

Review of James Laughlin ed., *New Directions 9. Briarcliff Quarterly,* III (July, 1946), 145–48.

"Aldous Huxley and the Novel of Ideas," *College English,* VIII (December, 1946), 129–37.

"Escape from Father," *The Kafka Problem,* ed. Angel Flores. New York: New Directions, 1946, pp. 214–46. Reprint of pp. 181–209 of *Freudianism* (1945).

With Charles Allen and Carolyn F. Ulrich. *The Little Magazine: A History and a Bibliography.* Princeton: Princeton University Press, 1946.

1947

Review of Samuel Putnam, *Paris Was Our Mistress: Memoirs of a Lost and Found Generation. New York Times Book Review,* XCVI (May 18, 1947), 3.

Review of John Lehmann, ed., *New Writing and Daylight. Cronos,* I (Summer, 1947), 39–40.

Review of Leonard Wolf, *Hamadryad Hunted. Western Review,* XI (Summer, 1947), 254.

Review of John Erskine, *The Memory of Certain Persons. Journal of Higher Education,* XVIII (November, 1947), 443–44.

Second edition of *The Little Magazine.* Princeton: Princeton University Press, 1947.

1948

"The Necessity of the Little Magazine. 2. The American Scene," *Meanjin,* VII (Winter, 1948), 117–21.

Review of Paul Rosenfeld, ed., *The Sherwood Anderson Reader. American Literature,* XX (March, 1948), 73–74.

"From Surrealism to 'The Apocalypse': A Development in Twentieth Century Irrationalism," *ELH, A Journal of English Literary History,* XV (June, 1948), 147–65.

Review of E. W. Tedlock, Jr., *The Frieda Lawrence Collection of D. H. Lawrence Manuscripts: A Descriptive Bibliography*. *New Mexico Quarterly*, XVIII (Autumn, 1948), 351–52.

"Aldous Huxley and the Novel of Ideas," *Forms of Modern Fiction: Essays Collected in Honor of Joseph Warren Beach,* ed. William Van O'Connor. Minneapolis: University of Minnesota Press; London: Oxford University Press, 1948, pp. 189–200. Reprint of 1946 article.

"Infroyce," *James Joyce: Two Decades of Criticism,* ed. Seon Givens. New York: Vanguard, 1948, pp. 390–435. Reprint of pp. 116–50 of *Freudianism* (1945).

1949

"The Technological Fallacy in Contemporary Poetry: Hart Crane and MacKnight Black," *American Literature,* XXI (March, 1949), 94–107.

Review of Eric Bentley, *George Bernard Shaw;* and Herbert J. Muller, *Thomas Wolfe. Western Review,* XIII (Spring, 1949), 184–88.

Review of Stanley Edgar Hyman, *The Armed Vision: A Study in the Methods of Modern Literary Criticism. American Literature,* XXI (May, 1949), 255–57.

"The Rhetoric of Evasion: A Study of Resistance to Ideas," *Sewanee Review,* LVII (April–June, 1949), 227–50.

"Philistine and Puritan in the 1920's," *American Quarterly,* I (Fall, 1949), 247–63.

With Milton Ellis, Louise Pound, and George Weida Spohn, eds., *A College Book of American Literature: Briefer Course.* New York: American Book Company, 1949. Second edition.

1950

"Agitato Ma Non Troppo: Ransom's Protective Irony," *Wisconsin Athenaean,* I (Winter, 1950), 17–18.

"Psychoanalysis and Literary Criticism," *American Quarterly,* II (Summer, 1950), 144–54.

"Points of Moral Reference: a Comparative Study of Edith Wharton and F. Scott Fitzgerald," *English Institute Essays, 1949,* ed. Alan S. Downer. New York: Columbia University Press, 1950, pp. 147–76.

1951

"War and the American Novel: The Last Decade," *Wisconsin Athenaean*, II (Spring, 1951), 5–7, 30–31.
The Modern Novel in America, 1900–1950. Chicago: Regnery, 1951.
With Olga W. Vickery, ed., *William Faulkner: Two Decades of Criticism.* East Lansing: Michigan State College Press, 1951.

1952

Review of Van Wyck Brooks, *The Confident Years: 1885–1915. Milwaukee Journal*, January 6, 1952, pt. V, 4.
Review of Clyde Brion Davis, *Thudbury: An American Comedy. Saturday Review*, XXXV (September 20, 1952), 13, 40.
Review of Robie Macauley, *The Disguises of Love. Saturday Review*, XXXV (November 22, 1952), 17–18.

1953

"No Beginning and No End: Hemingway and Death," *Essays in Criticism*, III (January, 1953), 73–84.
Review of Theodore Morrison, *The Stones of the House. Saturday Review*, XXXVI (February 28, 1953), 31–32.
Review of Philip Young, *Ernest Hemingway. Milwaukee Journal*, March 1, 1953, pt. V, 4.
Review of Stanley R. Hopper, ed., *Spiritual Problems in Contemporary Literature: A Series of Addresses and Discussions. Milwaukee Journal*, April 19, 1953, pt. V, 6.
Review of Blake Nevins, *Edith Wharton: A Study of Her Fiction. Nineteenth-Century Fiction*, VIII (December, 1953), 229–32.
"Marianne Moore: Imaginary Gardens and Real Toads," *Poetry*, LXXXIII (December, 1953), 152–57.
Italian translation of *The Modern Novel in America.* Rome: Edizioni di Storia e Letteratura, 1953.
With Harry T. Moore, ed., *The Achievement of D. H. Lawrence.* Norman: University of Oklahoma Press, 1953.
"Lawrence's Quarrel with Freud," pp. 106–27 of *The Achievement of D. H. Lawrence.* Revision of Chapter 6 of *Freudianism and the Literary Mind.*

1954

Review of Philip Young, *Ernest Hemingway*. *American Literature*, XXV (January, 1954), 514–15.

"Un Professeur Américain à Rennes," *Mercure 54, Bulletin de Liaison des Boursiers Américains Fulbright en France*, no. 2 (Février, 1954), 14–16.

Review of Irving Howe, *Sherwood Anderson;* and James Schevill, *Sherwood Anderson: His Life and Work*. *Western Review*, XVIII (Winter, 1954), 159–62.

"Williams and His Muse," *Poetry*, LXXXIV (April, 1954), 23–27.

"The Southern Revival: A Land and Its Interpreters," *Times Literary Supplement* (September 17, 1954), xvi.

Greek translation of *The Modern Novel in America*. Athens: Aetos, 1954.

1955

Review of Lionel Trilling, *The Opposing Self: Nine Essays in Criticism*. *Milwaukee Journal*, March 6, 1955, pt. V, 4.

Review of Grant C. Knight, *The Strenuous Age in American Literature, 1900–1910*. *American Literature*, XXVII (March, 1955), 131–33.

Review of Robert Coughlan, *The Private World of William Faulkner: The Man, The Legend, The Writer*. *Kenyon Review*, XVII (Summer, 1955), 472–76.

Japanese translation of *The Modern Novel in America*. Tokyo: Hyonon-Sha, 1955.

Spanish translation of *The Modern Novel in America*. Barcelona: Editorial Seix Barral, 1955.

The Twenties: American Writing in the Postwar Decade. New York: Viking, 1955.

1956

Review of Louis D. Rubin, Jr., *Thomas Wolfe: The Weather of His Youth*. *American Literature*, XXVII (January, 1956), 602–604.

Review of W. David Sievers, *Freud on Broadway: A History of Psychoanalysis and the American Drama*. *American Literature*, XXVII (January, 1956), 608–11.

"Caroline Gordon: The Special Yield," *Critique,* I (Winter, 1956), 29–35.

Review of F. R. Leavis, *D. H. Lawrence, Novelist. New York Post,* May 13, 1956, Mll.

Review of Frederick W. Dupee, ed., *Henry James: Autobiography. Progressive,* XX (June, 1956), 38–39.

"Katherine Anne Porter's Noon Wine," *CEA Critic,* XVIII (November, 1956), 1, 6–7.

"Psychology and Literature," *Literature and Psychology,* VI (Fall, 1956), 111–15.

Review of Stanley Edgar Hyman, ed., *The Critical Performance. Provincial,* I (December, 1956), 3–5.

Second American edition of *The Modern Novel in America.* Chicago, Los Angeles, New York: Gateway, 1956.

With Edwin Harrison Cady and Roy Harvey Pearce, eds., *The Growth of American Literature: A Critical and Historical Survey.* 2 vols. New York: American Book Company, 1956.

1957

Review of Grace Hegger Lewis, *With Love from Gracie: Sinclair Lewis, 1912–1925. Virginia Quarterly Review,* XXXIII (Winter, 1957), 128–32.

Review of F. R. Leavis, *D. H. Lawrence, Novelist;* and Anthony Beal, ed., *D. H. Lawrence: Selected Literary Criticism. Progressive,* XXI (April, 1957), 35–36.

Review of Walter B. Rideout, *The Radical Novel in the United States, 1900–1954. American Literature,* XXIX (May, 1957), 214–16.

"Criticism and the Usable Past," *Progressive,* XXI (June, 1957), 29–30. [Review-essay on criticism of recent fiction]

Review of William Faulkner, *The Town. Progressive,* XXI (September, 1957), 33–35.

"Psychology and Literature," *Kenyon Review,* XIX (Autumn, 1957), 605–19.

"The Newest Poetry," *Progressive,* XXI (December, 1957), 36–38. [Review-essay on recent poetry]

"The Southern Revival: A Land and Its Interpreters," *American Writing Today: Its Independence and Vigor,* ed. Allan Angoff. New York: New York University Press, 1957, pp. 71–80. Reprint of 1954 article.

Korean translation of *The Modern Novel in America.* Seoul: Soo-Do, 1957.

Italian edition of *William Faulkner: Two Decades of Criticism,* trans. Annina Coppini Levi Della Vida. Rome: Ugo Guanda, 1957.

Second edition of *Freudianism and the Literary Mind.* Baton Rouge: Louisiana State University Press, 1957.

1958

"Letters and Literature," *Progressive,* XXII (February, 1958), 44–45. [Review-essay on collections of letters in modern literature]

Review of Caroline Gordon, *How to Read a Novel. Virginia Quarterly Review,* XXXIV (Spring, 1958), 317–20.

Review of Granville Hicks, ed., *The Living Novel: A Symposium. American Literature,* XXX (May, 1958), 245–46.

Review of Percy Lubbock, *The Craft of Fiction;* and Caroline Gordon, *How to Read a Novel. Progressive,* XXII (June, 1958), 41–42.

"The Knowledge of Literature: Suggestions for American Studies," *American Quarterly,* X (Summer, 1958), 199–205.

"Grace, Violence, and Self: Death and Modern Literature," *Virginia Quarterly Review,* XXXIV (Summer, 1958), 439–54.

"Camus and America," *Symposium,* XII (Spring–Fall, 1958), 36–42.

Review of F. L. Lucas, *Literature and Psychology. Prairie Schooner,* XXXII (Fall, 1958), 160, 233–36.

1959

Review of William K. Wimsatt, Jr., and Cleanth Brooks, *Literary Criticism: A Short History. Western Review,* XXIII (Winter, 1959), 187–92.

Japanese translation of "Grace, Violence, and Self" (1958). *Americana, A Monthly Journal of Humanities, Social Sciences, and Natural Sciences,* V (March, 1959), 78–102.

Review of Horace Gregory, *Amy Lowell: Portrait of the Poet in Her Time. American Literature,* XXXI (May, 1959), 208–209.

Review of Lillian Smith, *One Hour. Progressive,* XXIII (November, 1959), 45–46.

Review of Reginald L. Cook, *The Dimensions of Robert Frost. American Literature,* XXXI (November, 1959), 360–61.

"*Darkness at Noon:* the Consequences of Secular Grace," *Georgia Review,* XIII (Fall, 1959), 331–45.

Review of Norman Mailer, *Advertisements for Myself*. *Milwaukee Journal*, December 20, 1959, pt. V, 4.

"Mortality and Modern Literature," *The Meaning of Death*, ed. Herman Feifel. New York, Toronto, London: McGraw-Hill, 1959, pp. 133–56. Reprint of 1958 article.

"No Beginning and No End: Hemingway and Death," *Interpretations of American Literature*, ed. Charles Feidelson, Jr., and Paul Brodtkorb, Jr. New York: Oxford University Press, 1959, pp. 320–31. Reprint of 1952 article.

Paperback reprint in *Forms of Modern Fiction* (1948). Bloomington: Indiana University Press, 1959.

Paperback reprint of *Freudianism*. New York: Grove; London: Calder, 1959.

1960

Review of Armin Arnold, *D. H. Lawrence and America*. *American Literature*, XXXI (January, 1960), 496–98.

Review of Henry Miller, *The Henry Miller Reader*, ed. Lawrence Durrell. *Milwaukee Journal*, February 21, 1960, pt. V, 4.

Review of William Faulkner, *The Mansion;* and Hyatt H. Waggoner, *William Faulkner: From Jefferson to the World*. *Progressive*, XXIV (March, 1960), 55–57.

Review-essay on Richard Ellmann, *James Joyce*. *Kenyon Review*, XXII (Spring, 1960), 316–23.

"Il Romanzo Americano Dopo il 1950," trans. L. Senatore, *Tempo di Letteratura*, I (Spring, 1960), 104–14.

"Kafka's *The Trial:* The Assailant as Landscape," *Bucknell Review*, IX (May, 1960), 89–105.

Review of Leslie Fiedler, *Love and Death in the American Novel*. *Progressive*, XXIV (June, 1960), 42–44.

"The Scene of Violence: Dostoevsky and Dreiser," *Modern Fiction Studies*, VI (Summer, 1960), 91–105.

"The Moment of Violence: Ernst Jünger and the Literary Problem of Fact," *Essays in Criticism*, X (October, 1960), 405–21.

"The Temper of the Twenties," *Minnesota Review*, I (October, 1960), 36–45.

"Little Magazines and the Avant-Garde," *Arts in Society*, I (Fall, 1960), 32–37.

"Norman Mailer and the Revolt of the Ego: Some Observations on Recent American Literature," *Wisconsin Studies in Contemporary Literature,* I (Fall, 1960), 5–12.

"William Faulkner: A Review of Recent Criticism," *Renascence,* XIII (Autumn, 1960), 3–10.

Review of Hyatt H. Waggoner, *William Faulkner: From Jefferson to the World. Criticism,* II (Fall, 1960), 397–401.

Review of Frederick Bracher, *The Novels of James Gould Cozzens. American Literature,* XXXII (November, 1960), 343–44.

"Freudian Psychology in the Study of American Literature," *Rives,* no. 15 (Décembre, 1960), 11–15.

Review of James Hall, *Arnold Bennett: Primitivism and Taste. Modern Language Quarterly,* XXI (December, 1960), 377–79.

With Olga W. Vickery, ed., *William Faulkner: Three Decades of Criticism.* East Lansing: Michigan State University Press, 1960.

Translation of Jean-Jacques Mayoux, "The Creation of the Real in William Faulkner," pp. 156–73 of *William Faulkner* (1960).

1961

Review of James E. Miller, Jr., Karl Shapiro, and Bernice Slote, *Start With the Sun: Studies in Cosmic Poetry. South Atlantic Quarterly,* LX (Winter, 1961), 95–96.

Review of Louis Fraiberg, *Psychoanalysis and American Literary Criticism. American Literature,* XXXIII (March, 1961), 99–101.

"Freedom and Conscious Form: Henry James and the American Self," *Virginia Quarterly Review,* XXXVII (Spring, 1961), 269–85.

"The Assailant and the Victim: Some Definitions of Modern Violence," *Centennial Review,* V (Spring, 1961), 223–38.

"Form and Circumstance: A Study of the Study of Modern Literature," *Approaches to the Study of Twentieth-Century Literature: Proceedings of the Conference in the Study of Twentieth-Century Literature, first session.* East Lansing: Michigan State University, May 2–4, 1961, pp. 3–16.

"The Wheel of Self: Some Contemporary Examples and Definitions," *Journal of Existential Psychiatry,* II (Summer, 1961), 105–112.

"The Self in Time," *Chicago Review,* XV (Summer, 1961), 59–75.

"*Howards End* and the Bogey of Progress," *Modern Fiction Studies,* VII (Autumn, 1961), 243–57.

Review of Warren Beck, *Man in Motion: Faulkner's Trilogy. Milwaukee Journal,* November 19, 1961, pt. V, 4.

"Gertrude Stein," *Lexikon der Weltliteratur im 20. Jahrhundert,* vol. II. Freiburg, Basel, Wien: Herder, 1961, pp. 1006–1009.

"Marianne Moore," *Lexikon der Weltliteratur im 20. Jahrhundert,* vol. II. Freiburg, Basel, Wien: Herder, 1961, p. 454.

"The Sense of Place," *South: Modern Southern Literature in Its Cultural Setting,* ed. Louis D. Rubin, Jr., and Robert D. Jacobs. Garden City, N.Y.: Doubleday, 1961, pp. 60–75.

"Some Perspectives on the 1920's," *The American Past: Conflicting Interpretations of the Great Issues,* ed. Sidney Fine and Gerald S. Brown. Vol. II. New York: Macmillan, 1961, pp. 389–408. Reprint of pp. 371–91 of *The Twenties.*

Gertrude Stein. Minneapolis: University of Minnesota Press, 1961.

William Faulkner. New York: Twayne, 1961.

Paperback reprint of *William Faulkner.* New Haven: College and University Press, 1961.

1962

Review of Paul Rosenfeld, *Port of New York: Essays on Fourteen Modern Americans. Journal of English and Germanic Philology,* LXI (January, 1962), 199–201.

"William James and the Modern Literary Consciousness," *Criticism,* IV (Winter, 1962), 1–13.

"The Voices of Sherwood Anderson," *Shenandoah,* XIII (Spring, 1962), 5–19.

Review of Robert E. Knoll, ed., *McAlmon and the Lost Generation: A Self Portrait. College English,* XXIV (December, 1962), 252–53.

"Philistine and Puritan in the 1920's," *American History: Recent Interpretations. Book II, Since 1865,* ed. Abraham S. Eisenstadt. New York: Crowell, 1962, pp. 322–36. Reprint of 1949 article.

Arabic translation of *Gertrude Stein.* Beirut: Al-Maktaba Al-Ahlia, 1962.

Spanish translation of *Gertrude Stein.* Madrid: Editorial Gredos, 1962.

Arabic translation of *The Modern Novel in America.* Beirut: Dar As-Sakafa, 1962.

Revised edition of *The Twenties.* New York: Collier, 1962.

Ed., *The Great Gatsby: A Study.* New York: Scribner's, 1962.

Ed., *Marginal Manners: The Variants of Bohemia.* Evanston: Row, Peterson, 1962.

Ed., *Perspectives on Modern Literature.* Evanston: Row, Peterson, 1962.

Conrad Aiken. New York: Twayne, 1962.

Samuel Beckett: The Language of Self, preface Harry T. Moore. Carbondale: Southern Illinois University Press, 1962.

1963

Review-essay on Leon Edel, *Henry James,* vols. II and III. *Virginia Quarterly Review,* XXXIX (Summer, 1963), 518–28.

"Dogmatic Innocence: Self-Assertion in Modern American Literature," *Texas Quarterly,* VI (Summer, 1963), 152–62.

Review-essay on Victor Brombert, *The Intellectual Hero: Studies in the French Novel, 1880–1955;* John Cruickshank, ed., *The Novelist as Philosopher: Studies in French Fiction, 1935–1960;* Frederick Karl, *The Contemporary English Novel;* A. N. Kaul, *The American Vision: Actual and Ideal Society in Nineteenth Century Fiction;* Harry Levin, *The Gates of Horn: A Study of Five French Realists;* D. E. S. Maxwell, *American Fiction: The Intellectual Background;* William Van O'Connor, *The University Wits and the End of Modernism;* and Mark Spilka, *Dickens and Kafka: A Mutual Interpretation. Journal of General Education,* XV (October, 1963), 221–29.

Review of Kenneth Eble, ed., *Howells: A Century of Criticism. Western Humanities Review,* XVII (Autumn, 1963), 374–76.

Review of Thomas Pynchon, *V. Critique,* VI (Winter, 1963–64), 174–77.

"The Booster," *Henry Miller and the Critics,* ed. George Wickes, Preface, Harry T. Moore. Carbondale: Southern Illinois University Press, 1963, pp. 20–22.

Reprint of "Infroyce" (1948). New York: Vanguard, 1963.

Portugese translation of *Gertrude Stein.* São Paulo: Livraria Martins, 1963.

Arabic translation of *William Faulkner.* Cairo: Les Editions Universitaires, 1963.

Paperback reprint of *Conrad Aiken.* New Haven: College and University Press, 1963.

Paperback reprint of *The Modern Novel in America.* Chicago: Regnery, 1963.

Reprint of *William Faulkner: Three Decades of Criticism.* New York and Burlingame: Harcourt, Brace and World, 1963.

Reprint of "The Creation of the Real in William Faulkner" in *William Faulkner: Three Decades* (1963).

1964

Review of Joseph Frank, *The Widening Gyre: Crisis and Mastery in Modern Literature. Choice, Books for College Libraries,* I (March, 1964), 19.

"Iris Murdoch: The Reality of Persons," *Critique,* VII (Spring, 1964), 48–57.

" 'Terror's Unique Enigma'—The American Novelist's Response to World War II," *University, A Princeton Magazine,* no. 20 (Spring, 1964), 23–29.

Review of Howard Nemerov, *Poetry and Fiction: Essays. Choice, Books for College Libraries,* I (May, 1964), 97.

Review of Diana Trilling, *Claremont Essays. Choice, Books for College Libraries,* I (June, 1964), 129.

Review of Theodore Peterson, *Magazines in the Twentieth Century. Library Journal,* LXXXIX (October 15, 1964), 3938.

Review of William Wasserstrom, *The Time of the Dial;* and William Wasserstrom, ed., *A Dial Miscellany. Antioch Review,* XXIV (Fall, 1964), 403–407.

"Faulkner's Concepts of Time," *Bear, Man, & God: Seven Approaches to William Faulkner's* The Bear, ed. Francis Lee Utley, Lynn Z. Bloom, and Arthur F. Kinney. New York: Random House, 1964, pp. 337–42. Reprint of pp. 24–31 of *William Faulkner* (1961).

"The Fool of Experience: Saul Bellow's Fiction," *Contemporary American Novelists,* ed. Harry T. Moore. Carbondale: Southern Illinois University Press, 1964, pp. 80–94.

Korean translation of *William Faulkner.* Seoul: Eul-You, 1964.

Paperback reprint of *Samuel Beckett: The Language of Self,* preface Harry T. Moore. New York: Dutton, 1964.

"L'Insaisissable Moi: Les «M» de Beckett," trans. Paul Rozenberg, *Configuration critique de Samuel Beckett,* ed. Melvin J. Friedman. Paris: Lettres Modernes, 1964, 23–53. Translation of pp. 105–37 of *Samuel Beckett* (1964).

The Mortal No: Death and the Modern Imagination. Princeton: Princeton University Press, 1964.

Paperback reprint of *The Mortal No.* Princeton: Princeton University Press, 1964.

1965

Review of William Faulkner, *Snopes: A Trilogy. Los Angeles Times Calendar,* January 3, 1965, p. 16.

Review of Margaret Duckett, *Mark Twain and Bret Harte. Los Angeles Times Calendar,* February 28, 1965, p. 16.

Review of Harold W. Blodgett and Sculley Bradley, eds., *Leaves of Grass: Comprehensive Reader's Edition. Los Angeles Times Calendar,* March 28, 1965, 21.

Review of Jean Guiguet, *Virginia Woolf et son oeuvre: L'Art et la quête du réel. Etudes Anglaises,* XVIII (Janvier–Mars, 1965), 88–89.

"The Scholar-Critic: Trends in Contemporary British and American Literary Study," *Modern Language Quarterly,* XXVI (March, 1965), 1–15.

Review of Peter Bien, *L. P. Hartley. Journal of General Education,* XVII (April, 1965), 79–82.

Review of James F. Beard, ed., *The Letters and Journals of James Fenimore Cooper. Los Angeles Times Calendar,* April 4, 1965, p. 17.

Review of Robert F. Sayre, *The Examined Self: Benjamin Franklin, Henry Adams, Henry James. Journal of English and Germanic Philology,* LXIV (April, 1965), 337–39.

Review of William Wasserstrom, *The Time of the Dial;* Nicholas Joost, *Scofield Thayer and the Dial: An Illustrated History;* Susan J. Turner, *A History of the Freeman, Literary Landmark of the Early Twenties;* Max Putzel, *The Man in the Mirror;* and Donald Davidson, *The Spyglass—Views and Reviews,* ed. John Tyree Fain. *Southern Review,* I, n.s (April, 1965), 461–72.

Review of Lawrance Thompson, ed., *Selected Letters of Robert Frost. English Language Notes,* II (June, 1965), 315–19.

Review of Bettina Linn, *After the Wedding Anniversary. Kenyon Review,* XXVII (Summer, 1965), 568–69.

Review of Richard Ellmann and Charles Feidelson, Jr., eds., *The Modern Tradition: Backgrounds of Modern Literature. Virginia Quarterly Review,* XLI (Summer, 1965), 460–65.

"The Use of Criticism in the Teaching of Literature," *College English,* XXVII (October, 1965), 13–17.

Review of Conrad Aiken, *A Seizure of Limericks. Satire Newsletter,* III (Fall, 1965), 78–81.

Review of Arthur Koestler, *The Act of Creation. Sewanee Review,* LXXIII (Autumn, 1965), 726–31.

"The Miracle of Contingency: The Novels of Iris Murdoch," *Shenandoah,* XVII (Autumn, 1965), 49–56.

Review of Maurice Beebe, *Ivory Towers and Sacred Founts: The Artist as Hero in Fiction from Goethe to Joyce. Modern Philology,* LXIII (November, 1965), 179–82.

Review of Michael Millgate, *American Social Fiction: James to Cozzens. American Literature,* XXXVII (November, 1965), 344–45.

Review of Lionel Trilling, *Beyond Culture: Essays on Learning and Literature;* and Philip Rahv, *The Myth and the Powerhouse. Nation,* CCI (November 8, 1965), 334–36.

"The Question of Avant-Garde in Modern Fiction," *Arts In Society,* III, (1965), 188–93.

Review of Luis Bunuel, *Viridiana.* Arthur Lennig, ed., *Classics of the Film.* Madison: Wisconsin Film Society, 1965, pp. 194–99.

"Dogmatic Innocence: Self-Assertion in Modern American Literature," *Innocence and Power: Individualism in Twentieth-Century America,* ed. Gordon Mills. Austin: University of Texas Press, 1965, pp. 113–30. Reprint of 1963 article.

"Hemingway and Fitzgerald," *American Literary Scholarship, An Annual: 1963,* ed. James Woodress. Durham: Duke University Press, 1965. pp. 81–91.

"Lawrence's Quarrel with Freud," *D. H. Lawrence and Sons and Lovers: Sources and Criticism,* ed. E. W. Tedlock, Jr. New York: New York University Press, 1965, pp. 101–11. Reprint of 1953 article.

"Theodore Roethke: The Poetic Shape of Death," *Theodore Roethke: Essays on the Poetry,* ed. Arnold Stein. Seattle and London: University of Washington Press, 1965, pp. 94–114.

Second edition of *The American Past* (1961). New York: Macmillan, 1965.

" 'The Seim Anew': Flux and Family in *Finnegans Wake," Twelve and a Tilly: Essays on the Occasion of the 25th Anniversary of Finnegans Wake,* ed. Jack P. Dalton and Clive Hart. Evanston: Northwestern University Press, 1965, pp. 16–25.

Japanese translation of *Gertrude Stein.* Tokyo: Hokuseido Shoten, 1965.

Revised edition of *The Twenties.* New York: The Free Press; London: Collier-Macmillan, 1965.

1966

Third edition of *A College Book of American Literature: Briefer Course.*
New York: American Book Company, 1965.

Review of Sherman Paul, *Edmund Wilson: A Study of Literary Vocation in Our Time. Nation,* CCII (January 17, 1966), 74–75.

Review of Tony Tanner, *The Reign of Wonder: Naivety and Reality in American Literature;* and Martin Green, *Re-Appraisals: Some Commonsense Readings in American Literature. Shenandoah,* XVII (Winter, 1966), 106–10.

Review-essay on Erich Heller, *The Artist's Journey Into the Interior and Other Essays. Kenyon Review,* XXVIII (March, 1966), 282–88.

"The Hardness of Reality: James Joyce's Stephen Dedalus," *Barat Review,* I (June, 1966), 129–37.

Review of R. W. B. Lewis, *Trials of the Word: Essays in American Literature and the Humanistic Tradition. Nineteenth-Century Fiction,* XXI (June, 1966), 103–106.

Review of Sherman Paul, *Edmund Wilson: A Study of Literary Vocation in Our Time. Journal of English and Germanic Philology,* LXV (July, 1966), 632–35.

Review of T. S. Eliot, *To Criticize the Critic and Other Writings. Nation,* CCIII (October 3, 1966), 324–25.

"The Religious Crisis in Modern Literature," *Comparative Literature Studies,* III, no. 3 (1966), 263–72.

"Anderson and Freud," Sherwood Anderson, *Winesburg, Ohio: Text and Criticism,* ed. John H. Ferres. New York: Viking, 1966, pp. 309–20. Reprint of pp. 229–50 of *Freudianism* (second edition, 1957).

"From *Freudianism and the Literary Mind,*" *The Achievement of Sherwood Anderson: Essays in Criticism,* ed. Ray Lewis White. Chapel Hill: University of North Carolina Press, 1966, pp. 174–92. Reprint of pp. 229–50 of *Freudianism* (second edition, 1957).

"Hemingway and Fitzgerald," *American Literary Scholarship, An Annual: 1964,* ed. James Woodress. Durham: Duke University Press, 1966, pp. 82–88.

"The 'Irresistible Lothario': F. Scott Fitzgerald's Romantic Hero," *The Twenties: Poetry and Prose,* ed. Richard E. Langford and William E. Taylor. DeLand, Fla.: Everett Edwards Press, 1966, pp. 59–61.

"Literary Form and Psychic Tension," *Hidden Patterns: Studies in*

Psychoanalytic Literary Criticism, ed. Leonard and Eleanor Manheim. New York: Macmillan; London: Collier-Macmillan, 1966, pp. 50–65.

"The Search for Redemption: Flannery O'Connor's Fiction," *The Added Dimension: The Art and Mind of Flannery O'Connor,* ed. Melvin J. Friedman and Lewis A. Lawson. New York: Fordham University Press, 1966, pp. 32–48.

"The Voices of Sherwood Anderson," *The Achievement of Sherwood Anderson: Essays in Criticism,* ed. Ray Lewis White. Chapel Hill: University of North Carolina Press, 1966, pp. 232–44. Reprint of 1962 article.

English edition of *Twelve and a Tilly* (1965). London: Faber and Faber, 1966.

Paperback reprint of *Theodore Roethke* (1965). Seattle and London: University of Washington Press, 1966.

Portugese translation of *William Faulkner.* Rio de Janeiro: Lidador, 1966.

Second American edition of *William Faulkner.* New York: Twayne, 1966.

1967

Review of Clifton Fadiman, ed., *Fifty Years. Southern Review,* III, n.s. (January, 1967), 229–34.

Review of John Adam Moreau, *Randolph Bourne: Legend and Reality. American Literature,* XXXVIII (January, 1967), 576–78.

Review of Constance Cappel Montgomery, *Hemingway in Michigan. American Literature,* XXXIX (March, 1967), 123–24.

Review of David D. Galloway, *The Absurd Hero in American Fiction: Updike, Styron, Bellow, Salinger. Modern Language Journal,* LI (April, 1967), 223–24.

Review of Leonard Greenbaum, *The Hound and Horn: The History of a Literary Quarterly. American Literature,* XXXIX (May, 1967), 236–37.

Review of Reed Whittemore, et al., *The Little Magazine and Contemporary Literature. Modern Language Journal,* LI (May, 1967), 297–98.

Review of Nathan A. Scott, Jr., *The Broken Center: Studies in the Theological Horizon of Modern Literature. Journal of English and Germanic Philology,* LXVI (July, 1967), 482–85.

Review of S. Gorley Putt, *Henry James: A Reader's Guide. Novel*, I (Fall, 1967), 75–77.

Review of L. S. Dembo, *Conceptions of Reality in Modern American Poetry;* Frederick Will, *Literature Inside Out: Ten Speculative Essays;* Fei-Pai Lu, *T. S. Eliot: The Dialectical Structure of His Theory of Poetry;* and Austin Warren, *The New England Conscience. Poetry*, CXI (December, 1967), 203–205.

"*Symbolisme* and Modern Poetry in the United States," *Comparative Literature Studies*, IV, no. 1 and 2 (1967), 193–99.

"Contemporary American Poetry," *Patterns of Commitment in American Literature*, ed. Marston LaFrance. Toronto: University of Toronto Press with Carleton University, 1967, pp. 193–207.

"Hemingway and Fitzgerald," *American Literary Scholarship, An Annual: 1965*, ed. James Woodress. Durham: Duke University Press, 1967, pp. 90–103.

"Henry Miller: Defender of the Marginal Life," *The Thirties: Fiction, Poetry, Drama*, ed. Warren French. DeLand, Fla.: Everett Edwards Press, 1967, pp. 73–80.

"La Thérapeutique du néant: les romans de William Styron," trans. Jean Dixsaut, *Configuration critique de William Styron*, ed. Melvin J. Friedman and August J. Nigro. Paris: Lettres Modernes, 1967, pp. 33–56.

Paperback reprint of *Freudianism*. Baton Rouge: Louisiana State University Press, 1967.

Reprint of *The Little Magazine*. New York: Kraus, 1967.

The Art of Southern Fiction: A Study of Some Modern Novelists, Preface, Harry T. Moore. Carbondale and Edwardsville: Southern Illinois University Press, 1967.

The Imagination's New Beginning: Theology and Modern Literature. Notre Dame and London: University of Notre Dame Press, 1967.

1968

Review of William A. Gordon, *The Mind and Art of Henry Miller. American Literature*, XXXIX (January, 1968), 580–82.

Review of Kenneth Burke, *Language as Symbolic Action: Essays on Life, Literature, and Method. Poetry*, CXI (March, 1968), 416–19.

Review of Albert Cook, *Prisms: Studies in Modern Literature. Modern Language Journal*, LII (March, 1968), 159.

Review of Stanley Cooperman, *World War I and the American Novel*. *West Coast Review*, III (Spring, 1968), 53–56.

"Aesthetics of the Proletarian Novel," *Proletarian Writers of the Thirties*, ed. David Madden, Preface, Harry T. Moore. Carbondale and Edwardsville: Southern Illinois University Press; London and Amsterdam: Feffer and Simons, 1968, pp. 184–93.

"The Cure of 'Nothing': The Fiction of William Styron," *Frontiers of American Culture*, ed. Ray B. Browne, et al. Purdue University Studies, 1968, pp. 69–87.

"Hemingway and Fitzgerald," *American Literary Scholarship, An Annual: 1966*, ed. James Woodress. Durham: Duke University Press, 1968, pp. 85–94.

"The Knowledge of Literature: Suggestions for American Studies," *American Studies: Essays on Theory and Method*, ed. Robert Merideth. Columbus, Ohio: Merrill, 1968, pp. 40–48. Reprint of 1958 article.

"The Novel of World War I: A Document in the History of Surprise," *The Promise of Greatness: The War of 1914–1918*, ed. George A. Panichas, Foreword, Sir Herbert Read. New York: John Day; Toronto: Longmans, 1968, pp. 517–27.

"Philistine and Puritan in the 1920's: An Example of the Misuse of the American Past," *The American Experience: Approaches to the Study of the United States*, ed. Hennig Cohen. Boston: Houghton Mifflin, 1968, pp. 115–32. Reprint of 1949 article.

"The Problem of Influence of Freudianism on the Literary Mind," *Backgrounds to Modern Literature*, ed. John Oliver Perry. San Francisco: Chandler, 1968, pp. 131–40. Reprint of pp. 106–15 of *Freudianism* (1957).

"The Temper of the Twenties: Secularization and Innocence in the Literary Cosmopolis," *Backgrounds to Modern Literature*, ed. John Oliver Perry. San Francisco: Chandler, 1968, pp. 59–69. Reprint of 1960 article.

"William Faulkner," *American Winners of the Nobel Literary Prize*, ed. Warren G. French and Walter E. Kidd. Norman: University of Oklahoma Press, 1968, pp. 138–57.

Italian translation of *William Faulkner*. Florence: La Nuova Italia, 1968.

"Ernest Hemingway," *Fifteen Modern American Authors: A Survey of Research and Criticism*, ed. Jackson R. Bryer. Durham: Duke University Press, 1969, pp. 275–300.

Waves
form of the
book suggests
isolation, that one
mind cannot relate
to others thought
context refuse idea